MASCULINITY AND THE MAKING
OF AMERICAN JUDAISM

MASCULINITY AND THE MAKING OF AMERICAN JUDAISM

Sarah Imhoff

Indiana University Press

Bloomington and Indianapolis

This book is a publication of

Indiana University Press
Office of Scholarly Publishing
Herman B Wells Library 350
1320 East 10th Street
Bloomington, Indiana 47405 USA

iupress.indiana.edu

Names: Imhoff, Sarah, author.
Title: Masculinity and the making of American Judaism /
    Sarah Imhoff.
Description: Bloomington ; Indianapolis : Indiana University Press,
    [2017] | Includes bibliographical references and index.
Identifiers: LCCN 2016043928 (print) | LCCN 2016045536 (ebook) |
    ISBN 9780253026064 (cl : alk. paper) | ISBN 9780253026217
    (pb : alk. paper) | ISBN 9780253026361 (eb)
Subjects: LCSH: Masculinity—Religious aspects—Judaism. |
    Masculinity—United States. | Jewish men—Religious life—
    United States.
Classification: LCC BM725 .I44 2017 (print) | LCC BM725 (ebook) |
    DDC 296.0811/0973—dc23
LC record available at https://lccn.loc.gov/2016043928

1 2 3 4 5   22 21 20 19 18 17

Contents

Acknowledgments   *vii*

Introduction   *1*

Part I. An American Religion   31

  1 The Reasonableness of Judaism: An American Theology   35

  2 Manly Missions: Jews, Christians, and American
Religious Masculinity   62

Part II. The Healthy Body and the Land   93

  3 Go West, Young Jew: The Galveston Movement, Immigrant Men,
and the Pioneer Spirit   *97*

  4 Indian-Israelite Identification: Claiming a Manly Past for
American Judaism   *128*

  5 Afternoon Calisthenics at Woodbine: Jewish Agriculture,
Religious Ambivalence, and the Male Body   *155*

  6 The Courageous Diaspora: Masculinity and the Development
of American Zionism   *180*

Part III. The Abnormal and the Criminal   *199*

  7 Soft Criminals: Theodore Bingham and the Gender
of Jewish Crime   *205*

  8 Leo Frank and Jewish Sexuality   *225*

  9 Bad Jews: The Leopold and Loeb Hearing   *244*

    Conclusion   *270*

    Bibliography   *277*

    Index   *291*

Acknowledgments

Rabbi nachman of Breslov wrote "gratitude is the experience of heavenly enjoyment and pleasure." This project has brought me immense joy, and I feel it most acutely when I think of the people who have helped me along.

A number of individuals read drafts and humored me by discussing my challenges and queries at length. Ben Berger, Annalise Glauz-Todrank, Kevin Houser, Brandi Hughes, Jenna Joselit, David Koffman, Laura Levitt, Rachel Lindsay, Shaul Magid, and Seth Perry all read and helped improve substantial portions of the manuscript. I couldn't ask for better colleagues, and my conversations with Judah Cohen, Constance Furey, Guadalupe Gonzalez Dieguez, Patrick Michaelson, Mark Roseman, and Jeff Veidlinger have made the book far more interesting. Clark Gilpin has long been quietly instrumental in helping me think through projects, and this one is no exception. Winni Sullivan has been an unparalleled mentor and friend, from reading a complete draft to discussing minutiae.

Institutional support has also been instrumental. I am grateful to the Association for Jewish Studies Women's Caucus, the Southern Jewish Historical Society, and the Borns Jewish Studies Program at Indiana University for supporting the project. The staff of the American Jewish Archives, the American Jewish Historical Society, the Central Zionist Archives, the Dolph Briscoe Center for American History, and the Moody Bible Institute Archives each went out of their way to help with archival materials.

The press reviewers offered generous and constructive feedback and made me think about the project in new ways. This, it seems to me, is the best experience an author can hope for. I also have Dee Mortensen at Indiana University Press to thank for the unambiguously positive experience and encouragement throughout the publication process.

Friends and family have buoyed me during the long days of writing and editing. Eva Mroczek offered unflagging enthusiasm, steadfast friendship, and sharp scholarly insight. My life writing this book would have been far less bright without her. Michael Dodson read and offered his insight on the entire manuscript, encouraged me to write the best book I could, and made me cocktails. For these things and others, he has my undying love. I want to thank my parents for their love and support from a time long before this book was a twinkle in my eye, and so I dedicate it to them.

MASCULINITY AND THE MAKING OF AMERICAN JUDAISM

Introduction

A COUPLE OF years ago, a Jewish men's group invited me to speak at their biennial retreat. They had heard that I was researching American Jewish masculinity, and they wanted me to tell them a little about what I knew. They listened intently to two lectures, and over the next day and a half, they questioned me: Are Jewish men different from their American Christian counterparts when it comes to religious participation? Or to religious leadership? How and why do Jewish men participate in Judaism? Is today's religious landscape different for men than it was in the past? Why are American Jewish men more gentle, family oriented, and less prone to violence than men of other religious groups? I wished I could have answered all of their questions in complete and satisfying ways, but their queries were far too complex for two days of conversations.

I hope these men came away having learned something about American Jewish masculinity from our exchange. I certainly did. I came to realize the durability of some ideas and ideals about Jewish masculinity, many of which appeared as assumptions in their questions. These men assumed that Jews were American and yet also distinctive from their neighbors. They assumed that Jewish men were, in general, more gentle than non-Jewish men. They assumed that violence was uncommon among Jews. I realized that the roots of these men's ideas about Jewish masculinity came from a particular historical moment when different social and religious forces converged. The questions I had been asking in my research were not a faraway set of concerns, even though they focused on an era a century ago. And these questions and ideas about American Jewish masculinity were not merely academic or theoretical, but woven into these men's lives. The social and religious forces of the early twentieth century had left a deep imprint—so deep I could see it in today's ideals about American Jewish masculinity.

The interaction also brought home something more profound, something I had known about gender, but had rarely experienced so directly: Jewish masculinity is opaque even to those people we would imagine would know the most about it. And this was the case, no matter how self-reflective and thoughtful the community in question. The Jewish men I spoke to belonged to Jewish men's clubs. They spent time reflecting specifically on Jewish men's participation in Jewish life. They were actively involved in synagogues, federations, and men's clubs and thought about how to make other men more involved. If anyone in today's religious landscape would understand Jewish masculinity, it seems like it would be these men. And yet, when I explained that scholars do not know all the factors that affect men's experience of Judaism or of their own gender, these men did not tell me that they knew the answers. Instead, they asked me more questions about Jewish men and gender. One man said to me, "Well, you should study *us!*" Others agreed. The offer was tempting, but I am not a sociologist. I did take to heart the impulse behind his request: we need to understand Jewish masculinity better.

This book is the story of how religion shaped American Jewish masculinity in the early twentieth century. It is also the story of how masculinity shaped American Judaism. These two pieces of the narrative—how religion shaped masculinity and how masculinity shaped religion—are not entirely separable. To tell this composite story, then, *Masculinity and the Making of American Judaism* makes two moves. It explores both what American Jewish masculinity looked like, with special attention to religion, and what Judaism in America looked like, with special attention to gender.

Hence the book has a two-part claim: first, in the early twentieth century acculturated American Jews championed a masculinity of self-sufficiency, courage, and physical health, but one that downplayed physical strength, aggression, and domination; and second, they argued that Judaism was an American religion because of its masculine virtues of rationality and universalism. Early twentieth-century American Jewish masculinity was neither the popular Teddy Roosevelt-style strong outdoorsman who dominated nature, nor was it a replica of any of the American Christian ideas of manhood. It did, however, share traits with these versions of masculinity. This book paints this picture by exploring three big themes: the land and the healthy body, the idea of the normal and the abnormal, and the hegemony of Christianity.

The other strand of this story shows the ways masculinity worked as part of the project of making Judaism into an American religion. What would it mean for Judaism to be an American religion? In the early twentieth century, nearly all Americans agreed that Judaism counted as a religion. They might think that Jews were backward or misguided in their beliefs and practices, but they saw Judaism as a religion. Yet Jews felt they had to prove it was American. To argue for its place as an American religion, Jews promoted Judaism's masculine virtues of rationality and universalism. In myriad subtle ways, the acculturated Jews in these pages are staking two claims: that Jews were manly and that Judaism was a good, *American* religion.

Because the processes of constructing gender and religion are often hard to see, I look to the margins, the unexpected places. Despite the fact that most early twentieth-century immigrant Jews came into the country through New York, I focus on a project to bring immigrants through Galveston and settle them in the Midwest and West. Even though most American Jews never worked a day on a farm, I look at Jewish agricultural movements. Most American Jews did not become Zionists, commit crimes, or convert to Christianity. And yet here I tell the stories of those who did. From these margins, we can watch the experiments, the responses, and the rejections and ultimately learn about the making of American Jewish masculinity and an American Judaism.

My research showed me something I did not entirely anticipate: both Jews and non-Jews agreed that Jewish masculinity was somehow different from normative American manhood. In many cases, I found that without the name of the author, it was difficult to predict whether statements about Jewish men were written by Jews or non-Jews. I did an experiment in two undergraduate classes in which I gave students unlabeled primary sources when we studied this time period, and I had them guess whether a Jew or a non-Jew had written them. With the exception of identifying a handful of virulent antisemites, whom they overwhelmingly labeled as non-Jews, barely half of the students' guesses were correct. Furthermore, whether these writers were Jews or non-Jews, immigration restrictionists or liberals, men or women, they also agreed on the general shape of that masculinity. Historians profit from considering ways that Jews and non-Jews interacted, and their ideas about gender were not always so polarized, nor did they often neatly fit into dichotomies such as defamatory versus self-promotional.[1] In the United States, the lines between "Jewish ideas" and "non-Jewish ideas," or even between "Jewish ideas" and "American ideas," were blurry and shifting when they existed at all. The project of shaping a Jewish manhood was not merely an assimilatory project nor was it merely an exclusionary project.

In some ways, the story here runs against the grain of conventional Jewish histories. It does not assume that Jews were forever (or primarily) reacting to non-Jewish norms. Indeed, it rejects such a dichotomy, without denying that there may still be difference. It does not take Jewishness as the marker of the "one true self" or assume that Jewishness is the most essential piece of the selves of people called Jews.[2] It reads the sources for what they say about Jewishness, but does not hold an a priori commitment to Jewish difference. My method began with agnosticism about whether and how Jews were different from one another and from their non-Jewish neighbors when it came to imagining Jewish masculinity. This study is not an investigation into "Jewish identity" or "the Jewish experience," terms I avoid because they imply a unity of the meaning or experience of Jewishness.[3] Put more radically, there is no Jewish experience, or identity, in the singular.[4] Different Jews experienced Jewishness differently. A young male immigrant in New York did not experience his Jewishness in the same way an elderly woman in Galveston experienced hers. Although this book is attentive to power dynamics between acculturated Jews and immigrant Jews, and between Jews and white Protestants, it does not assume that Jews were always disempowered or Protestants were always in power. Instead, it shows local actions of power when Jews told their own stories, as in the missionary memoirs, and when Jews told the stories of other Jews, such as when acculturated Jews sought to "uplift" other Jews by teaching them to be agriculturalists. Nor does it focus on the Jews who seemed to have the most power.

In this sense, the book is not a classic "great man" story. Except for one chapter, little of it takes place in New York City, the capital of American Jewish history. It is not primarily about philanthropy, economics, or politics, though each informs its narrative at times. This is often a story of Jew-meets-Jew, but it does not focus on familiar main characters such as philanthropist Jacob Schiff, lawyer-turned-judge Louis Brandeis, or Rabbi Mordecai Kaplan. A rich literature exists about these elite men and how they influenced others. In contrast, much of this book focuses on "little men," and in doing so, it participates in a development in religious studies that illuminates how everyday people live religiously and how they shape the idea of religion itself.

Yet in another sense, *Masculinity and the Making of American Judaism* does focus on a familiar slice of American Jewry: those people I call acculturated Jews. I use the term "acculturated Jews," rather than "assimilated Jews" or "German Jews," which appear in other scholarly works to designate the upper social strata of the American Jewish landscape at the turn of the century. "German Jews" works as a shorthand for designating those Jews in the United States whose ancestors had emigrated from Western Europe in the early nineteenth century. But by the turn of the twentieth century, many of the English-speaking Jewish cultural elite in the United States had actually emigrated from Eastern Europe in the latter years of the nineteenth century. "Assimilated Jews" misnames the Jews here in a different way. Scholars often use "assimilation" with a negative tone, where it stands for the loss of culture, language, and religion. Sometimes this scholarship suggests that assimilation renders Jews essentially indistinguishable from their non-Jewish neighbors. Although acculturated Jews embraced aspects of American culture, many committed their time and energy to buttressing and improving Judaism and cultural forms of Jewishness. They were not trying to eradicate forms of Jewish difference, but rather to reshape it. "Acculturated," then, refers to Jews who spoke English, discussed American political and cultural issues beyond the Jewish world, and thought of themselves as American. Acculturation was a matter not of birth, but of cultural participation and position. Many Jewish immigrants could and did become acculturated.

Many of these acculturated Jews were Reform, others were a part of the nascent Conservative movement, and a few did not identify with a particular branch of Judaism. Some were born in the United States and some in Europe, but they all participated in American culture. This focus on acculturated Jews does not imply that new Eastern European Jewish immigrants were not real Jews, did not have important stories, or simply replicated acculturated Jewish ideals. Rather, I focus on acculturated Jews because they embodied the norm in the American imagination. Even when it was in the numerical minority, Reform Judaism was the flagship of Judaism in the American imaginary.

Eastern European immigrants, Orthodox Jews, secular Yiddishists, and others did not mimic Reform Jewish ideals at every turn, but their experience was shaped by the specter of Reform Jews as the "good" American Jews. American Jews were "haunted" by Judaism, whether or not or in what way they identified as religious.[5] When the New York Jewish community came together to respond to accusations about crime—a secular affair—they united on the basis of religion, even while they acknowledged that not all Jews were religious. Rabbi Samuel Schulman explained, "There is only one basis of unity and representation and that is the synagogue. . . . We cannot organize New York Jewry on the basis of race or nationality. We exist in the non-Jewish world only as a *Knesset Yisrael*, a congregation of Israel."[6] Schulman did not deny that Jews were a race, only that race was not the logical basis on which to represent Jews to other Americans. Religion was the primary rubric for how Americans thought about Jews, and the dominant ethos primarily figured Jewishness and Jewish difference in terms of religion.[7] Religious Studies scholar Annalise Glauz-Todrank writes, "For Jews to become properly 'American,' Jewish 'difference' had to conform to the category 'religion.'"[8] Even when Jews performed a different Judaism—one that was emotional, embodied, or particularist, perhaps—they were confronted with the norms of Reform as the ideal. We cannot understand Jewishness without understanding religion. In the American ethos, Jewishness was already (over)determined as religion.

By figuring Jewishness in terms of religion, I do not mean to suggest that race or ethnicity is unimportant. "Race," though understood differently from our contemporary notion, was one way of figuring Jewishness in the early twentieth century. Sometimes discourses of race and discourses of religion competed with one another to describe Jews, as Schulman's statement suggests. More often, the two were not competing alternatives at all, but rather worked as shades of meaning in a complex landscape of explaining Jewishness where one could slide into the other. Rich historical works have traced how Jews and non-Jews both imagined that Jews were a distinctive people, in ways that made reference to bodies, geography, and even social traits.[9] But in many of these discussions of Jewishness as race, the implications of religion get lost. This gap occurs not only in the scholarly literature about Jews: scholars who work with the theory of intersectionality have emphasized race, class, gender, and ability as co-constitutive social processes of identification, but rarely include religion. The stories here—most prominently the Galveston Movement, Indian-Israelite comparisons, and the Leo Frank trial, but also the others more subtly—suggest that talk about the Jewish race (or ethnicity) was always, in some way, about religion.

This introduction begins by laying some of the theoretical groundwork for the story to follow. It then discusses the social construction of gender and religion. Next it explores a particular construction of religion: that of the Protestant model of religion in the United States, in general, and in the early twentieth century in particular. It concludes with a discussion of how this story of American Jewish masculinity fits into larger stories of American religious history and broader American history, particularly with respect to masculinity.

The Social Constructions of Gender and Religion

Masculinity and femininity are social ideas—ideas that change, not empirical constants. Although male and female bodies have existed since the beginning of the human species, the social meanings attached to those sexed bodies have developed and changed over time. The category of religion is similar. History shows us that we have not had a single, unchanging idea of what counts as religion. Though "real" or "good" religion has often been pitted against things called magic, superstition, heathenism, and cults, the characteristics that define religion and which things count as religion differ with time and place. Both gender norms and religious norms change with historical, geographical, and cultural contexts—and they change because of what people do and say.

Whether or not we believe that either gender or religion has a fixed essence outside of human culture, we know that humans shape both categories. Scholars of gender studies often refer to this as "construction," a term that implies that gender is made, not given. The idea of construction, which might remind us of a building construction site with its many people and complex assembly of materials, suggests that gender is put together using traits, values, rituals, and ideas already available in the culture. Different people with different skills and motivations contribute to the building of a structure. Building occurs at a specific site, though it draws on the resources and environment around it. So too with gender. Here our "building site" is the early twentieth-century American context. Men and women, lawmakers and laborers, clergy and laypeople, immigrants and the native born all contribute to the construction of gender norms, though they do not all wield equal power or influence in that construction. But unlike the goals of construction, the building of gender will never be finished. Some parts are demolished as new ones are built. It is the continual construction site of a never-finished building. And it is rarely clear who the architect or even the foreman is—or if one exists at all.

Gender is not, in this sense, invented solely as an individual act of will. Nor does it change instantaneously. For instance, I could not wake up one morning, dress myself and comb my hair as usual, declare myself a man, and then expect to be treated as such by everyone I encounter. I am barely five feet tall, I have long hair on my head but no facial hair, and I have a relatively high voice. None of these things means that I am necessarily a woman, but all of them are associated with femininity. Social and historical context also matters for others' impressions about gender. For instance, I also often wear pants, a relatively ungendered clothing item in the United States today, but a masculine one a century ago. There is nothing essentially male or female about an article of clothing that goes around each leg individually rather than wrapping around both together, but there were very strong cultural associations between men and pants at the turn of the twentieth century. Moreover, gender shapes our lives beyond individual or collective identity: social processes and structures, such as the division of labor in a society, are also gendered.

Although gender is constructed and can therefore vary over time, this is not to say its attributes are merely happenstance or easily changed. Gender is a social construct, but it is nevertheless very socially real, durable, and powerful. Gender norms, like many other cultural norms, have two aspects: on one hand, they are ideals or aspirations, and on the other they are what is assumed to be normal. So norms seem to be simultaneously ideals and expectations. To describe masculinity is to describe something that was perhaps only partially realized, yet that was, nevertheless, persistently used as a referent. The ideal and the normal, then, are not easily separated—perhaps it is even impossible to do so.

A word about terminology: By 1900, Americans used both "manly" and "masculine" to talk about traits associated with manhood. "Masculine" had joined "manly" in popular usage in the 1890s as a new way to connote the physical power associated with men. I could have followed suit and used both "manly" and "masculine" as positive terms to describe admirable men, but doing so would have left me without a term to describe things that were generically associated with men, but not necessarily positive. For instance, chapter 7 briefly considers crimes and vices associated with men, such as alcoholism and spousal abuse. These are surely not positive characteristics, but they were (and are) gendered.

Here I use the word "masculine" as the general word for "associated with men" and "manly" to refer to male traits deemed positive by the historical subjects. Thus, "masculinity" is the construction of the male gender whether negative, positive, or something else, while "manliness" denotes strength, health, rationality, and other positive traits associated with men. This usage differs from Anthony Rotundo's classic study, but the sources here offer good reason for this departure.[10] When American Jewish men used the word "manly," they meant "possessing the positive qualities associated with men." It was a compliment. It meant rationality, straightforwardness, physical healthiness, and productivity. American Jewish men very rarely used the word "masculine," except to refer to grammatical gender in foreign languages, where they intended no normative evaluation. When rabbis referred to the word "Gemara" (Talmud) as "masculine," they meant only that the word itself was a masculine noun, not that the Talmud was physically strong or straightforward.[11]

What counts as religion also varies with context. J. Z. Smith has famously articulated why, on encountering the native inhabitants of the Canary Islands, the Spanish explorers insisted that they had no religion.[12] The explorers did not see a church and the native islanders did not refer to a god, and so, the explorers concluded, they had no religion. Without the categories of a religious house of worship and a transcendent god, their beliefs and practices did not look religious to the Spanish. But today we would agree that those natives did have a religion because today our idea of the category is more inclusive of nature-based cosmologies. This anecdote suggests another way that these constructions are not simply acts of will. I have noted that gender is not merely an act of individual will, and here we see how the Spanish understanding of religion was not an act of collective will, in the sense that it was not a project consciously undertaken by one or more people. Like gender, then, religion is also socially constructed, although through different processes and with different consequences.

It is not merely an academic question whether something counts as religion or not. Whether or not one's beliefs and practices are recognized as religion can also have very real political and legal consequences. Mormons reshaped their religion during the late nineteenth century, and when the result aligned more closely with American ideas of proper religion, it helped ease the path for Utah statehood. In the early twentieth century, Native Americans responded to and borrowed from legal and theological discourses to persuade people that their practices should qualify as a religion. In each of these cases, we see how the political situations, norms, and assumptions of the United States are features of the "construction site" of religion.

Early twentieth-century American Judaism gives us a chance to watch construction in action. We might even say it is a chance to watch two such constructions—the shaping of an American Jewish masculinity and the simultaneous shaping of Judaism as an American religion. This book traces the contours of each of these projects and shows how the two intertwined. Creating a kind of masculinity that counted as American helped Jews implicitly validate and promote a particular kind of Judaism that was rational and universal, rather than racial or tribal. This study shows both how religion contributed to the construction of gender and how gender contributed to the construction of a religion.

Masculinity and the Making of American Judaism charts the shaping of the norms of American Jewish masculinity and the related norms of an American Judaism. Both projects can be difficult to see because they are often invisible. Gender norms work so effectively in part because they are naturalized—they seem self-evident. Gender norms can hide in plain sight. For instance, we do not often read in newspapers or hear on television that skirts are associated with women because "everyone knows" it already. So where should we look for gender norms? I take a cue from Michel Foucault and Judith Butler, who each suggest that the way to understand unarticulated norms is to look at the social margins and unexpected places. Foucault looked at prisons, sexual perversion, and madness; Butler has analyzed drag queens and other gender nonconformists. In these locations, social expectations are often violated, and it can be through that violation that we become aware of what those norms were in the first place. Here I look at locations that were slightly more integrated into everyday life, but ones that are marginal nonetheless.

Like gender norms, both individual religions and the category of religion are constructed, but we do not often see the process of construction at work. Recall the example of the Spanish explorers who thought that the natives had no religion. They imagined that their understanding of religion as a category was universal, and so they could not conceive of a different arrangement. This was not a matter of ignorance or backwardness. They had a robust understanding of their idea of religion, and it structured their lives as both subjects and imperial instruments. But they did not see that religion was a constructed category. In part because the construction of the category of religion is not a conscious act of individual will, it can be very difficult to see when, where, and how that process happens.

Just as it is difficult to see the constructed nature of religion as a category, so is it hard to be aware of the constructed nature of individual religions. Leaders and practitioners are often invested in presenting their own religion as timeless and unchanging. If people self-consciously reflect on the contemporary construction of their own religion, it becomes clear that there are elements of it that are contingent rather than timeless or transcendent. In American contexts, concealing the process of religious construction is also of significant value because of the centrality of conscience and sincerity to "good religion." A good religion is a matter of conscience, not coercion, and it is sincerely believed, not merely out of nostalgia, for reasons of personal gain, or even for the benefit of others such as family members. An American religious community would seem insincere if its leaders or practitioners announced that they were constructing their religion such that it would fit culturally appealing parameters. "Oh, we made sure our religion affirmed the Bible because it is already widely recognized as a religious document" or "Our religion has chosen the idea of one transcendent god because it is popular" seem like descriptions of a shallow and insincere religious community. Claims like these, or admissions that people had consciously changed their religion to fit cultural criteria, would negate any claims that belief in this religion was a matter of conscience.

Religion as a matter of conscience and the importance of sincerity are crucial concepts if we want to understand what counts as religion in the United States. Today, for instance, the Supreme Court often uses the criterion of "sincere religious belief" to judge whether a person's religious practices really count as religion. The sincerity of belief is so central to the idea of what counts as religion that it dictates what qualifies as protected religious practice under certain federal laws. If your practice stems from sincere belief, then it might be protected. As many commentators have noted, this belief-drives-practice model of religion is indebted to Protestant Christianity.[13] The category of religion, therefore, might seem natural and unchanging, but it has a very specific context and history. And in the American case, Protestantism plays a major, if often uncredited, role.

Much of the field of Jewish studies operates with dual categories for understanding Jewishness: race/ethnicity and religion. The two most comprehensive recent books about American Jewry have effectively divided this territory: Jonathan Sarna's *American Judaism* largely figures Jewishness as religion, whereas Hasia Diner's *Jews of the United States* figures Jewishness as ethnicity.[14] But this division—which both scholars treat in sophisticated and complex ways—enacts the very Protestantization I describe here. Protestant norms suggest that religion is something primarily personal, interior, and conscience driven and that it is separate—if not always completely—from descent. Oddly enough, then, these rich books about Jewishness are *always* in some way about religion, even when they are not about Judaism or when they figure Jewishness as ethnicity. The very move of using a dual categorization (race/ethnicity versus religion) is one enabled by a Protestantized notion of the self.

In this book, I bring these categories together. By showing how Jews both do and do not fit the Protestant model of religion, the study pushes on the boundaries of how we conceive of religion. Protestant theologies broadly claim that any person can be a Christian, regardless of the body she inhabits. In this ideal, religion's essence is a matter of the heart, mind, and conscience. But Judaism is always also a matter of descent and the body. Discourses about Jewishness include race or ethnicity and religion in ways that are ultimately inextricable. So to talk about Judaism is also to talk about particular bodies. When scholars ask what counts as religion, we attempt to step back from the Protestant legacy we have inherited. And here is what this project offers to a broader scholarly conversation in religious studies: American Judaism adds complications to what religion is. It shows the ways that race, ethnicity, descent, bodies, and community were not merely factors interacting with religion, but in fact *constituted* religion. Because of this, even when acculturated Jews argued for Judaism as an American religion in a Protestantized rubric of religion, they were not always or completely successful. This book shows how they tried—and it also shows the cracks and fissures and ways in which Judaism never quite fit the rubric.

To return to the idea of scholarly assumptions about Jewish difference in light of these observations about social construction, this book implicitly claims that the shaping of this American Jewish masculinity was driven neither by Jewish particularism nor assimilation, but through negotiations between the two. If we take seriously the idea that American Jews did not live lives that were either purely assimilatory or purely particularist, then we should denaturalize categories such as "the Jewish view" and "the non-Jewish view." This is not a book about "how Jews viewed themselves" nor "how non-Jews viewed Jews," but rather about how Jews and non-Jews together constructed Jewish masculinity and Judaism. And in the construction of gender, self-stylization (here: what Jews said and did) always interacts with Althusserian-style interpellation (here: what others said and did) to shape gender norms. For these reasons, each chapter includes Jewish and non-Jewish voices in conversation. Construction is the work of many hands, even of those who do not look like they are working.

The American Construction of Religion

To understand the stakes of this religious masculinity and to see its relationship to the larger American religious landscape (our "construction site"), it is helpful to see how central Christianity was (and is) to ideas about religion. The idea of religion as a category has a particular history, which is closely related to Christianity, as scholars such as Tomoko Masuzawa and J. Z. Smith have argued.[15] We might say that the model of religion used by Americans is an implicitly Protestant model. Like the Spanish explorers, many early twentieth-century Americans assumed that religion entailed certain characteristics that were familiar to their own Christian communities and practices. When they referred to a synagogue as a "Jewish church" or rabbis as "Jewish ministers," they implied that churches and ministers were generic religious terms that ought to show up whenever real religion was under discussion. Religions had churches and ministers, and these ones happened to be Jewish. What this implication does not reveal, however, is that the model for understanding religion in general is a Christian one. Though "Jewish church" might sound strange to our ears, the phrase suggested some assumptions about religion that still exist today. Even now, something is most legible as religion if it appears to have a supernatural god, a house of worship, a central text, and a set of beliefs that form the foundation of practice.

Moreover, this model of religion and its "proper" components permeates American culture in ways that are not always obvious. Janet Jakobsen and Ann Pellegrini call this "stealth Protestantism," that is, the pervasiveness of Protestant Christian traditions in American culture, even when it purports to be religiously neutral or secular.[16] Catherine Albanese has similarly argued that the one religion of the United States is a "public Protestantism."[17] Today, an increasingly visible American religious pluralism challenges this structure, but its influence persists. Even with growing pluralism, this public Protestantism has continued to hold sway, in part because non-Protestants have shared in it and contributed to its maintenance. As Tracy Fessenden argues, even when and where Americans themselves have no personal interest in promoting Christianity, they still use Protestant Christianity as their model for understanding religion. We can see this happening in everyday life, from education to literature to the law. "An avowedly secular United States is broadly accommodating of mainstream and evangelical Protestantism, minimally less so of Catholicism, unevenly so of Judaism, much less so of Islam, perhaps still less so of Native American religious practices."[18] Most Americans think of religion in Protestant terms, whether or not they realize it. Moreover, they implicitly associate Americanness with Christianity: "Religion comes to be defined as Christian by default, and an implicit association between 'American' and 'Christian' is upheld even by those who have, one imagines, very little invested in its maintenance."[19] Even for non-Christians, Protestantism undergirds both the category of religion and American culture.

In the early twentieth century, these assumptions about religion, bequeathed by a Protestant legacy, were even more pronounced than they are today: Stealth Protestantism was then less stealth and more Protestant. The 1916 US Census Bureau's report on "Religious Bodies," for instance, chronicled "separate denominations" and their "history," "doctrine," "polity," "[social] work," and the value of their "church property" and "parsonages."[20] Though the report included Jews, Bahais, and Vedanta societies, it still used these Christian categories to describe and understand these other religious groups. Although these categories might make good sense for the Presbyterian community in a town, to imagine the synagogue as a direct analog of the church would be to misunderstand the role of public communal worship in Judaism.

So what did it mean for Jews and Judaism if Protestant models structured the way Americans thought about religion in general? At the most foundational level, it meant that American ideas about religion did not directly match traditional ideas about Judaism. For instance, the synagogue is not just a Jewish analog of the church. Speaking broadly, synagogues were not the center of religious life for most Jews in most of their history. The practices of Judaism happen in public and private settings far from the "house of worship." Eating kosher food or not working on the Sabbath, for instance, marked Jewish religious life more often and more obviously than synagogue attendance. Especially before the twentieth century, and especially in Europe, women and children often did not even attend synagogue, and when they did, they generally had marginalized roles. Even men's religious practice centered more closely on textual study, which sometimes happened in a synagogue, but also happened elsewhere. If we took the category of "church" then, understood as a religiously special location, and applied it directly to Jews and Judaism, we would have misconceptions about who and how many people belonged to the community, what their levels of commitment to that religious community were, and what was most important to the practice of Judaism.

Early twentieth-century Jews, then, faced a culture in which their religion did not fit neatly into the features of the category of religion. They could have dealt with this in a variety of ways. They could have publicly contended that the model of American religion was deficient or biased. They could have offered alternative models of religion. They could have contested the centrality of the church—and, by parallel, the synagogue—as the primary location of religiosity. They could have even decided to change Judaism so that it did fit neatly into these categories. The former rabbi Felix Adler did something very much like this when, in 1877, he founded the Ethical Culture movement, which borrowed from Reform Judaism but patterned its practices on liberal Protestantism.

But acculturated Jews largely chose a different route: They articulated Judaism by adapting terms, figures, and ideas from the American religious milieu. They compared Judaism and Christianity. They talked about the Jewishness of Jesus. They focused on the Bible at the expense of the Talmud. They wrote about universal ethics as the center of Jewish life. Some of this was a conscious effort to make themselves understandable to their neighbors, but much of it was also a way for them to understand themselves and their own Judaism within their American context. Stealth Protestantism and these Protestant-influenced models of religion, then, played an important role in Jews' construction of an American Judaism for themselves.

Beyond its assumptions about churches, doctrines, and ministers, what did this Protestant-influenced model of religion look like? Religious Studies scholar Robert Orsi makes a distinction between what scholars deem "bad religion" and "good religion." The former describes the emotional, particularistic, ritualistic forms that scholars and students tend to see as lesser or underdeveloped. Good religion, in contrast, is "rational, respectful of persons, noncoercive, mature, nonanthropomorphic . . . unmediated and agreeable to democracy, monotheistic . . . emotionally controlled, a reality of mind and spirit and not body and matter."[21] Orsi's description of scholarly assumptions about what is "good religion" quite closely matches much American religious conversation outside the bounds of the university.

As Orsi intimates, scholars did not invent the idea of the superiority of rational, emotionally controlled religion with universalistic tendencies. It already existed in American culture in the early twentieth century—a time when scholars were trying to articulate what religion is in general, what counts as religion, and how to make sense of religion as they looked at other countries and immigrants coming into the United States. Familiar Protestant denominations such as Lutheranism, Congregationalism, and Methodism were clearly good religion. So was Unitarianism. They all advertised themselves as monotheistic, unmediated, rational, and emotionally controlled. Catholicism, with its many saints, embodied rituals, icons, and festivals, was more suspect. Native

American customs were "bad religion," if and when they qualified as religion at all. "Good religion," then, looked a lot like many forms of Protestant Christianity. If Judaism were going to be a "good" religion, then it would need to highlight these features.

Even more remarkable are the ways that "good religion"—rational, emotionally controlled religion with universalistic tendencies—looked masculine. The history of philosophy, from Plato to the present day, has often aligned reason with masculinity and emotion with femininity. Christian thinkers, too, built on this dichotomy, often asserting this association on multiple levels. On an abstract level, thinkers such as Immanuel Kant suggested that reason itself aligned with masculinity. On a more concrete level, these Christian thinkers also thought that men were more rational and women were more emotional. Although the philosophical level can be hard to connect to people's everyday lives, expressions of this more concrete level abounded in the early twentieth-century United States. Whether they meant it as a compliment or not, many Americans assumed that women had "greater emotional powers," especially in religious matters.[22] Men might not feel religion as acutely, but they understood it through their powers of reason.

Good religion was also universal: its lessons and morals applied to all humans. Ethnic or tribal religion did not qualify as good religion because it was a product neither of one's own individual conscience nor one's own rationality. Membership in it was merely an accident of birth. Ethnic and tribal religions, then, were not "good" religions, nor were they quite American religions. As Tisa Wenger has shown, this was one of the stumbling blocks to making Native American practices legible as religion to white American lawmakers in the early twentieth century.[23] Their beliefs and practices did not make claims to promoting a universal ethic nor to be the product of an internal process of reason, which would be accessible to all people.

In the case of Judaism, few doubted it was a religion. But was it "good" religion? Many Americans, some Christians in particular, saw it as a relic, a premodern religion that had been superseded. Many Christians imagined that Christianity had taken what was good from Judaism and democratized it.[24] Jesus, for many American Christians, had come to universalize the particulars of Judaism. Christianity meant progress, and religious progress meant universalism.

If Judaism were tribal instead of democratic, then it would not really be an American religion. If instead, Jews offered a rational, universalist religion, perhaps it could be a "good" religion, and thus an American one. So arguing for a Judaism that emphasized its rationality and universality—which also meant emphasizing its masculine qualities—meant arguing for an American Judaism.

American Religious Historical Context

I have suggested that Protestant Christianity functioned as the model of religion in the United States. Christianity also permeated American culture in more explicit ways. That is, in addition to providing a template for what counted as a religion, Christian content also appeared commonly as part of American culture. For instance, Jesus was the most popular religious figure in early twentieth-century America, and not just among Christians. Jews also wrote about Jesus, and rabbis spoke about him from the pulpit. Within Christian, mostly Protestant, communities Jesus also took on particularly manly characteristics. A gentle Jesus who turned the other cheek gave way to a physically strong and assertive Jesus who worked as a carpenter and put his enemies in their place. This manly Jesus was not merely an image of a long-dead savior. Many American men, churches, and Christian organizations also affirmed this version of religious manliness.[25]

Jews read about Jesus, wrote about him, and even heard about him from the pulpit,[26] and so they were exposed to this manly Jesus. In a biographical sketch of his fellow rabbi Emil Hirsch, Joseph Leiser compared Hirsch to a manly Jesus: "The courage of the man Jesus, the Galilean carpenter, whose burning zeal fired him with the courage to cleanse the temple of money changers, appeals to the innate manliness of Dr. Hirsch."[27] Leiser was the exception, however, when he compared a muscular Jesus to a fellow Jew. Although acculturated Jews often celebrated Jesus and his ethical teachings, they rarely embraced this muscular Jesus as a model for their own masculinity. They had their own model.

Clifford Putney has defined muscular Christianity as "a Christian commitment to health and manliness."[28] If we likewise decided to call a Jewish commitment to health and manliness "muscular Judaism," then American Jews in the early twentieth century participated too. What is fascinating, however, is that the difference between the two ideas is not merely a difference between Christianity and Judaism. The content of "manliness" also differed markedly. Protestant versions of muscular Christianity, of course, differed from Catholic versions.[29] Protestant versions even differed from one another—how one could become a muscular Christian, whether its primary targets should be the poor or the upper classes, which biblical texts and theologies should be marshaled in its promotion, and what role it played in salvation all differed. But although these and other aspects varied, the characteristics of a muscular Christian had a relatively stable core: physical strength, endurance, athleticism, ruggedness, and dominion over one's environment.

American Jewish commitments to health and manliness, however, did not always or primarily qualify as "muscular." Many Jews were committed to the development of the healthy body and attachment to the American land. They valorized rationality in religion. But American Jews were far less invested in physical strength and ruggedness, spent much less time and energy complaining about women and the "feminization" of religion, and rarely embraced the "barbarian virtues" that Teddy Roosevelt, G. Stanley Hall, and others trumpeted as essential for American men.

In spite of interreligious moves to make American religion in general more manly, Jewish norms of masculinity did not directly mirror their Protestant counterparts. The Men and Religion Forward Movement, for instance, took out ads in the sports sections of all the major New York newspapers in 1911 and 1912, where it targeted "Protestant, Catholic and Hebrew churches."[30] The movement itself, which was largely modeled on Protestant revivals, never gained traction in Jewish communities and soon fizzled out even in Christian ones. But when its promoters advertised to "Hebrew churches," they imagined that the same kind of feminizing problem that they saw in churches also existed in synagogues, and they imagined that the solutions would be the same. Jews, however, did not follow these Christians in championing the same kind of muscular religion.

As the Men and Religion Forward Movement hints, some Christians worried about the "feminization" of the church. Jews could have expressed concern about a Jewish version of this feminization as well, and some historians suggest that they did.[31] Yet the historical sources suggest that this was a very minor concern, and in fact, talk of feminization was more a sign of worry about *men's* participation than about women's. During the late nineteenth and early twentieth centuries in the United States, women became increasingly visible and even assumed some leadership roles in Reform synagogues especially. A few Reform Jews expressed their uneasiness with women's changing roles when they lamented what historians have called the "feminization of the synagogue." By this, they meant in part that Jewish women were attending synagogue and participating in synagogue life. But more often than not, rabbis and leaders lamented the perceived "disappearance" of men from services rather than some kind of invasion of women. In this sense, these laments would be much better characterized as "regret that fewer men attend synagogue," but such a formulation was, apparently, not as catchy for historians. In the end, the sources suggest that Jewish communities expressed very little concern over women's increased synagogue participation.[32]

As this discussion of feminization suggests, rabbis cared about attracting men as men. In this, they were much like American Christian clergy. In 1912 the *New York Times* reported on a Republican Club luncheon panel discussion with three Protestant clergy, one Catholic priest, one Farsi, and the Reform rabbi Rudolph Grossman. All of them agreed that religion was not "declining in the United States," but also that young men would play a critical role in ensuring its continued importance. Grossman was sanguine about the Jewish community: "The young men are more actually loyal to Judaism and things Jewish than formerly.

In hamlets throughout the country as they turn into towns, new congregations are opening, and the message is preached by trained American men."[33] Fewer young men were traditionally observant, but Jews were embracing the core of Judaism: "righteousness above ritual," as he explained his (quintessentially Reform and Protestant-friendly) view. Grossman, like his fellow rabbis, cared that men remain active participants in synagogue life, but he expressed no concern about women's takeover of religious space.

Even if synagogues did not worry about the "woman peril" that churches identified, masculinity nevertheless mattered to Jews, in part because it was connected to their place as Americans. *Masculinity and the Making of American Judaism* argues that in the early twentieth century American Jewish masculinity looked different from American Protestant masculinity and normative American masculinity more broadly. It drew from an American culture of manhood, but also at specific points resisted it. This ideal American Jewish masculinity was a gentler, less aggressive manhood that nevertheless valued a healthy and productive body.

American Historical Context

Why choose this time period and location to examine Jewish masculinity? There are two main reasons: the social dynamics of American Jewry and the cultural visibility of masculinity at the time. By 1900, the arrival of immigrants had already changed the face of American Jewry. About a million Jews immigrated to the United States from Eastern Europe between 1900 and 1924, in addition to the million who had come between 1880 and 1900. The established American Jewish communities, largely made up of Western European Jews and their descendants, reacted to the immigrants with a combination of embarrassment and philanthropic impulse. Dramatic demographic changes and complex interactions between the acculturated and newly arrived immigrants spurred much conversation and communal self-reflection. These dynamics form a significant part of the construction site, both as a motivation for construction and as a feature of the site itself.

This book focuses on the years from 1900 to 1924. The turn of the century was a moment when American Jews were organizing themselves and thinking about what it meant to be both American and Jewish. A cluster of events occurred in 1900 and 1901, including the founding of the Jewish Agricultural and Industrial Aid Society and publication of the first periodical of the Federation of American Zionists and of the first installment of the *Jewish Encyclopedia*. Each event involved both Jews who were American born and immigrants, and each sought to make its mark on American Jewry as a whole. The year 1924 marked the effective closing of the United States to prospective Eastern European Jewish immigrants. The following years saw different social trends, such as increasing nativism, isolationism, and antisemitism.[34] Because there were so few new Jewish immigrants after the mid-1920s, the lines between acculturated Jews and immigrant Jews grew even more blurry. Thus the years from 1900 to 1924 constitute an era during which the norms of American Jewish masculinity had significant continuity. This twenty-five-year period is a critical juncture for American Jewish history.

This is not a history, at least not in the conventional sense of a periodized narrative explaining change over time. It does not trace progress nor declension. The construction of gender is a messy process, and it rarely works in a linear fashion. The study uses archival and other historical materials, but it covers only twenty-five years, just one generation. Focusing on such a short time period allows a rich and detailed snapshot, rather than a feature-length film. As such, this is not a story of major events and how they shifted the historical landscape, but rather an in-depth look at the construction of religion and gender in one moment in time, which allows us to give the complex and contested picture of Jewish masculinity its due. A long history of the changes in American Jewish masculinity remains to be written. This book's claims are not about cause and effect. They show more subtle movements within and across communities. The book also implicitly makes the larger argument that when scholars study religion in any context, they should be attentive to the ways that gender—masculinity, in addition to femininity—and religion are co-constitutive.

This moment offers particularly rich possibilities because historians have identified it as a crucial time for American manhood more generally.[35] A robust scholarly literature on Progressive Era masculinity argues that attention to diverse cultural discourses from imperialism to concerns about "the boy problem" sheds light on what it meant to be an American man. Many historians have explored the pervasiveness—and often the contradictions—of the construction of American manhood during the late nineteenth and early twentieth centuries.[36] These authors have explored how this culture of manliness both produced and was produced by literature, science, medicine, and even armed conflict. The first decades of the twentieth century were the heyday of Teddy Roosevelt and his African safaris, the psychologist G. Stanley Hall and his reclamation of a kind of savage stage of boys' development, and Jewish professional boxers. Some scholars have said that masculinity was "in crisis" during this period. Though there is a joke among gender historians that masculinity is always in crisis, it is true that ideals about manliness played a significant role in politics, culture, and religion in the early twentieth century.

This book not only draws on this rich scholarly literature about American masculinity but it also offers something back to it. The typical story about American masculinity tends toward the dichotomous: there is a culturally approved general American normative masculinity, and then there are varying degrees of deviations, which are less culturally valued. Scholarly literature characterizes this normative American masculinity in the early twentieth century as requiring physical strength, a disciplined body, self-sufficiency, and even aggressiveness at times. For instance, John Kasson's *Houdini, Tarzan, and the Perfect Man* and Gail Bederman's *Manliness and Civilization* both demonstrate how ideal white manhood in this period was civilized but not entirely. This white manhood constituted the American norm, they each argue. My study suggests that we can see the gendered landscape better and more fully if we let go of a strict norm-deviations dichotomy, where the former is culturally valued and the latter is devalued in varying degrees. It shows us an example of a masculinity that was neither the same as this American manhood that these scholars have so richly described nor consistently seen as a denigrated deviation from that manhood.

Considering Jewish men can likewise open a new window into a longer story of American masculinity. In *Manhood in America*, Michael Kimmel suggests that white, American-born men have defined manhood in three ways: by claiming their own self-controlled individualism; by pretending to be men by going West, either at the movies or in real life; and by excluding others from true manhood.[37] Identifying deviations from that norm—a dependent, unproductive weakling Jewish immigrant, perhaps—helped consolidate and reassert this normative manhood. We might assume, because Kimmel offers no analysis of Jews, that Jews primarily played the role of those excluded from true manhood. But this is not the whole story. In fact, non-Jews excluding Jews from American manhood is only one small piece of it. *Masculinity and the Making of American Judaism* shows how Jews themselves embraced some aspects of each of Kimmel's three roles. They claimed self-sufficiency, they valorized settling the West, and acculturated Jews even denigrated the manhood of new immigrants. Jewish manhood was not identical with normative American manhood, but neither was it wholly a denigrated deviation. By showing that Jews embraced these different kinds of masculinity, which were neither the ideal American manly man nor the effeminate sissy, this book shows a history of multiple masculinities.

Though much scholarship on masculinity in the early twentieth century does not deal with it, religion itself was written into the American discourse on manhood. To take one best-selling example, Protestant minister William Forbush, in *The Boy Problem*, worried that boys were growing up sissies because their parents squelched their natural "savage" instincts. Though he disapproved of fighting and aggression in adults, he saw them as essential practices for childhood development: "These savage instincts have no place in mature manhood, but if we commit surgery upon them, instead of using hygiene, we shall never get real manhood."[38] To raise boys into good men, parents and society in general should instead encourage them to embrace their inner savages when they were young. In doing so, they would recapitulate human history, moving from "savage" to "Christian." In perhaps unintentionally gendered language, Forbush wrote,

"Man has been a savage much longer than he has been a Christian," and so it was only natural that if boys were to grow into "Christians" they would have to first go through the stage of being "savages." Christianity was the pinnacle of masculine development.

But if human history was a story of progress from savagery to Christianity, as many Americans thought, where did Jews fit? Forbush did not imagine that Jews were savages, but rather that they were vestiges of bygone eras.[39] Like many other Christians, he saw Jews as a relic that had been superseded. Jewish men were not uncivilized, aggressive brutes prone to violence, as African American men were often caricatured. Quite the opposite: in fact, Jews were gentle, smart, and genial. To support his point, Forbush quoted a Jew who praised Jewish intelligence, pacifism, and agreeableness, but denigrated Jewish men's physical health and strength: "The Jew is the physical inferior of his Gentile brother."[40] For Forbush, manliness was, at its foundation, a religious question, and Jews' masculinity looked different from that of their Christian counterparts.

Forbush's writing also provides us an example of how Jews' masculinity was not merely a function of "ethnic" Jewishness or race, but was also linked to Judaism as a religion. Part of the problem, for Forbush, was that Judaism promoted clannishness, which was likewise backward. He insisted on "the need of teaching a universal sociality," which Christianity offered and Judaism did not.[41] He linked Jews with particularism rather than universality. For Forbush and his sympathetic readers, ideal masculinity was not only strong and assertive but it was also connected to universalist impulses in religion. Religion, then, played an important part in the construction of American manhood in general, and a particularly critical role in American Jewish masculinity.

Jewish History

This book illuminates American Jewish masculinity as a cultural force and ideal. It is not merely the story of men but also of how constructions of gender shaped lives and communities. Moreover, if we want to understand gender and Judaism, it is incumbent on us to understand men. Jewish men are (and have been) the normative Jews.[42] It is men that are the assumed audience of most religious texts, and it is them to whom halakhah is primarily addressed. Literary studies, cultural studies, and other scholarship focused on Jews and Jewishness in contemporary periods have taken up critical study of masculinities, but in much of American Jewish history, "gender" still means "women." In the 2010 edited collection *Gender and Jewish History*, for instance, only one of the twenty-one essays focuses on men or masculinity.[43] Because there is so little precedent, in that essay, Beth Wenger must make the case for the study of masculinity in American Jewish history. Riv Ellen Prell and Paula Hyman each offer rich theoretical understandings of gender as a set of social forces between men and women, but their research is focused largely on women's history. There are a small number of rigorous scholarly books about Jewish men and sports, but these do not focus on gender norms, the perception of Jewish men as men, or on religion.[44]

This gap is not merely a shortcoming of Jewish history. It points to the ways that masculinity has often been invisible. Scholars use the language of "unmarked" to denote the default or the normal, and "marked" to denote difference, otherness, or deviation from the normal. For instance, Protestantism is the unmarked religious category in the United States, whereas Islam and Hinduism represent marked categories in American culture. Philosophers such as Genevieve Lloyd argue that "man" has stood for the universal, and "man" is an unmarked category. We can see how this played out in American Jewish history when, for instance, a Jewish immigration movement's honorary secretary David Bressler complained that Galveston had not received the desired immigrants. "Had they lived up to the agreement with us, they should have sent in the last four consignments 325 persons (excluding women and children), yet they sent altogether 200 persons, including women and children." His letter assumed that "persons" was a category that could exclude women and children. "Persons" meant "men." For Bressler and many others, "persons" and "immigrants" were both categories that were implicitly—even invisibly—masculine. This invisibility suggests that, to see masculinity and its forces more clearly, we may have to look in unexpected places.

This book includes some of these unexpected places, but it cannot explore all of them. If I had chosen different places, there would be stories of different people, but the big picture of masculinity and its interactions with religion would be very similar. For instance, Jewish educational pamphlets and books offered very similar ideas about what Jewish manhood should look like. One article, for instance, criticized Jewish men's physiological shortcomings and suggested they could be remedied by changing the way Jewish mothers raised their boys. Manya Gordon Strunsky, writing for the *American Jewish Chronicle*, claimed that "one singularity that is common to . . . all Jewish mothers was the propensity to push their sons too hard intellectually and neglect physical development."[45] The article, written by one Jewish woman for the benefit of others, went on to explain that mothers' emphasis on books and music at the expense of physical activity was at the root of Jewish boys' physical defects. A traditional emphasis on learning, she implied, was out of touch with American norms of physical culture. In short, the article averred: "The Jewish mother disregards the child's welfare."[46] Strunsky, an immigrant herself, scolded Jewish mothers for creating weak and unhealthy boys by constantly pushing their children to exercise their minds rather than their bodies. Boys should go outside and play. She prioritized physical development over religious development and refined cultural skills. Religious study, in fact, was a detriment: "All that results from his studies in Hebrew and music is his weak physical condition."[47] Ideal Jewish masculinity for Strunsky was healthy and active, and traditional religious learning and observance were marginal to this ideal of Jewish masculinity.

Another place we might have looked for masculinity in American Jewish life is sports. There has been a significant amount of material written about Jews and their involvement in boxing, baseball, and basketball, but much of it is more celebratory than analytical. The few academic studies of American Jews and sports in the early twentieth century do not focus on gender, but if they did, they would have found a similar sort of masculinity to the one illustrated in this book. The Young Men's Hebrew Association (YMHA), modeled on the YMCA, promoted sports as a way to improve Jewish young men. "Jews as a nation have never been actively identified with the manly sports, either in ancient or modern times," a 1907 article from New York's 92nd Street YMHA explained. But in the United States this had begun to change, and the "Y" celebrated that progress: "More attention is being paid by the Jews to the harmonious development of the human form and as a result, we are gradually developing a number of promising Jewish athletes." Creating Jewish men with good "human form" was a central part of the YMHA's mission, and they saw sports as a way to accomplish this goal. "There is something in athletics which appeals to all manly men," the article continued, "and if the Jews will pay more attention to it and through it develop a number of champions, it will do more to raise the status of the race in the eyes of the world than any other single achievement."[48] Promoting Jewish athletics had two goals: first, to make Jewish men more physically healthy and active, and second, to show non-Jews that Jewish men were physically healthy and active.

The YMHA's language of "race" to describe Jews points to a subtle complexity for American Jews: "religion" as a category referred to belief, faith, and conscience as its essential forms, and "race" as a category made reference to geography and to bodies. For Jews, the two categories did more than overlap; they largely co-constituted one another. The YMHA, modeled on a Christian religious organization that characterized its members in terms of religion, instead described Jews as a racial group. Although today the language of "Jewish race" may strike us as odd, perhaps even recalling the Holocaust, in the early twentieth century, it was a common way for both Jews and non-Jews to refer to Jews as a people. Jews were widely—though not universally—considered white. But they were classed as *a* white race, not *the* white race. According to most Americans in the early twentieth century, there were many white races (Nordic, Teutonic, Alpine, Mediterranean, Semitic, and others, depending on who was classifying). Each race had its own characteristics and tendencies, and so some white races were still favored over others. The jury was also still out on how malleable racial traits were: Could a race become taller over the generations? Smarter? Stronger? If immigrant Jews were weak and small, could their offspring be otherwise? As subsequent chapters show, most acculturated Jews were optimistic about racial malleability. They also saw racial changes as inextricably bound up with religion. Acculturated Jews saw backward (what they sometimes called "Oriental") Judaism as both a sign of negative racial traits and a cause of those traits. And those traits, such as weakness and poor health, ran counter to the American Jewish masculinity they championed.

This American Jewish masculinity was distinctive. Comparison with scholarship on earlier varieties of Jewish masculinity shows us that it was not merely a recapitulation of historical rabbinic ideas, nor did it directly mirror its European counterparts. For instance, Daniel Boyarin makes the case for a softer, gentler Jewish masculinity. He uses rabbinic materials to show how this sort of masculinity has deep roots in Jewish textual tradition, and the historical sources in this study suggest a similar, though by no means identical, vision of ideal Jewish men. Yet Boyarin's book has another aim, and that is to rescue and promote this gentler, more bookish masculinity. He explains his goals for his contemporary readers: "I want to use the sissy, the male femme as a location and a critical practice" to "help us precisely today in our efforts to construct an alternative masculine subjectivity."[49] Here I do not set out with the goal of promoting a certain kind of Jewish masculinity, but more modestly seek to show its development in the early twentieth century.

A major challenge to writing about masculinity is that gender seems normal, natural, and given. Masculinity, perhaps even more than femininity, is easy to take for granted. From high school history to news coverage of Muslim-majority nations, American discourses often refer to the changing (or different) roles of women. But we hear less often about the changing roles of men. Masculinity can be invisible, so what can we do to see it? And even when we have trained our eyes to see it, we are left with another challenge: How can we see the processes that construct that masculinity? I hope this book offers a fruitful possibility: to look at the margins, at the unexpected places, at the experimental. In this way, the substance of the book also makes a methodological claim about how we can study gender. Although this book's primary aim is not to expound a methodology, the method of the margins structures my analysis throughout. Here my normative claims are aimed at scholarship about religion and gender, rather than about how today's Jewish communities should see gender. I hope that, by example, this book reminds us that masculinity changes over place and time and that religion shapes cultural constructions of gender in ways that go beyond the familiar tropes of oppression and empowerment. I hope that it helps build bridges between theory and history by bringing together archival work with theoretical literature about the construction of gender and religion.

The Chapters

The first part of the book looks at American understandings of Jewish masculinity in a discussion of what constitutes Judaism, with explicit comparison to Christianity and American religion. The second part examines positive depictions of the masculinity of Jewish men (what the norms included). The third part discusses negative depictions of the masculinity of Jewish men (what the norms excluded). This collection of chapters is not an exhaustive account of American Jewish masculinities, but it allows a view into how American Jews and non-Jews thought about the Jewish past, present, and future in the United States; how it was both similar to and different from other norms of white masculinity; and how it related to Protestant Christianity and broader American ideas about religion.

The first part illustrates a theme that forms the foundation for the other chapters: the creation of Judaism as an American religion. From quotidian manifestations such as blue laws to dominant ideas about what religion is—a matter of individual conscience expressed in practices—conversations about American religion have long taken Protestant Christianity as their model. This part shows that neither American Judaism nor American Jewish masculinity would have come to be what it was in the absence of Protestant Christianity. Though Judaism and Jews are never entirely separable, these chapters concentrate more on how people imagined Judaism than how they imagined Jews.

Chapter 1 shows how Jewish thinkers made Judaism intelligible under the Protestant-structured rubric of American religion. Put more radically, it shows how they made an American Judaism. It begins by examining and establishing what counted as an American religion in the early twentieth century. Protestant forms of Christianity such as Lutheranism, Methodism, and Congregationalism counted. Mormonism did not, nor did Native American customs (ironic in both cases, given their beginnings on American soil). But what characteristics made these groups qualify as American religions or not? An American religion needed to be consonant with reason and universalist or, at the very least, compatible with democracy. These characteristics rested on gendered philosophical foundations: reason, universalism, and democracy are all shot through with Enlightenment assumptions about masculinity. Therefore, when acculturated Jews argued for Judaism in terms of its rationality and universality, it was a gendered construction of Judaism. This Judaism was not merely intelligible under a rubric of conscience, reason, and democracy. Acculturated Jews remade Judaism under that rubric—and thus they constructed an American Judaism.

Chapter 2 explores the world of the religious margins when it analyzes conversion. Jews who converted to Christianity were, quite literally, at the social margins of both Judaism and Christianity. This chapter shows how these converted Jews and missionaries grappled with ways to understand Jewish difference. In the context of American Protestant missions to the Jews, the available social positions were not simply properly manly versus undesirably effeminate: men on the missionary margins associated a physically powerful and intimidating masculinity with Protestants and a gentle, non-violent masculinity with Jews.

The four chapters in the second part analyze Jews' arrival in the United States (immigration through Galveston, Texas) and then Jews' relationship to the American past (historical identification with Indians), present (farming the land through agricultural schools), and future (remaining Americans even if they supported Zionism). Each chapter illuminates the theme of the land and the healthy male body. Overall, the second part shows how this Jewish masculinity mirrored larger discourses of American masculinity in its ideal of the healthy male body and connection to the land. None of the themes of these chapters—the West, Indians, communal agriculture, or Zionism—became the dominant way of imagining Jewish masculinity. Nevertheless, these stories show the ways bodies took on meaning as essential sites for both masculinity and Judaism.

Acculturated Jews knew they wanted immigrants to have healthy bodies, labor productively, espouse a rational religion, and have a relationship with the land. One experimental immigration movement shows how they sought to do this: chapter 3 explores the Galveston Movement, which officially operated from 1907 to 1914, advocating Jewish settlement away from the crowded northeastern cities to the West. There they would reconnect with the land, from which immigrant Jews had—at least in the imagination of more acculturated American Jews—become alienated. For supporters of the Galveston Movement, the immigrants would leave behind the vestiges of a superstitious, law-centered Judaism and the weak bodies it created in favor of an enlightened Judaism consonant with healthy bodies, physical productivity, and Americanism.

Chapter 4 explores Jews' vicarious cultural identification with "Indians." It charts a complex dance of closeness and distance: acculturated Jews appropriated an imagined version of historical Native American cultures, but they simultaneously insisted that they were different from Indians. On one hand, Jewish authors embraced the Indians of the past as courageous, resourceful men who had long inhabited the American land. On the other hand, these authors insisted on the difference between Indian customs and Jewish religion in order to paint Judaism as a civilized religion that was universal rather than tribal. American Jews emphasized the compatibility of Judaism with democracy, and that Jews belonged to a rational religion chosen through reason and conscience. They claimed that Judaism was, in short, an American religion. But Indian practices were not, so identifying too closely with Native Americans would be a liability. This simultaneous push and pull with the figure of the Indian allowed acculturated Jews not only to create a brave, resourceful, and land-centered masculinity but also to reject tribal religion in favor of a rational, American religion.

Chapter 5 deals with Jewish farm schools and planned agricultural communities. These communities allowed Jews to see themselves—and to be seen by others—as productive, healthy workers who were attached to the land and espoused a rational religion. By the early twentieth century, the idea of the farmer-citizen as the paradigmatic American man was a nostalgic artifact, but it still functioned as an idealized path to Americanization and manhood.

Chapter 6 focuses on early twentieth-century Zionism. In European contexts, Zionism valorized the manly pioneer who would cultivate the land and build a society in Palestine, in contrast to the diaspora Jew who was weak, effeminate, alienated from nature, and passive. Very few American Zionists, however, had any intention of immigrating to Palestine, and so the negative idea of diaspora life as emasculating did not resonate with them. The future of American Jews was in America. Even though the Zionist movement did not initially attract the majority of American Jews, some of the gendered aspects of its ideology, such as its physical culture and the romanticization of certain kinds of physical labor, resonated with broader American cultural trends toward the strenuous life of normative American masculinity.

The third part of the book deals with criminality and abnormality. Crime, by its very nature, is abnormal. It is abnormal not in the sense that it is uncommon but rather because defining an action as criminal means locating it outside of social norms. Cultural conversations about crime paint a picture of the undesirable, the sorts of acts and persons to avoid. Exploring this "dark side" offers another perspective on what it meant to be Jewish in America. Conversations about criminals could tell Jews what *not* to be. Whereas the Galveston Movement and Indian-Israelite comparisons illustrate how bodily health and connection to the land became pillars of Jewish masculinity, discussions about criminality show how aggressiveness and violence were considered beyond the bounds of that masculinity. Writing about crime built on the cultural assumption that Jewish men could be on the receiving end of violence, but not the perpetrating end. Despite their markedly different circumstances, each one of the cultural moments analyzed in Part III linked crime with improper masculinity and sexuality; for some observers, the Jewish criminals embodied these abnormal traits, but for others, Jews' different masculinity constituted an argument for their innocence.

These three chapters cover what were arguably the three highest profile moments in American Jewish crime during the era. Chapter 7 explores a moment in the history of Jewish New York. In 1908 New York City Police Chief Commissioner Theodore Bingham announced that more than half the city's criminals were Jews, in large part because they were "men not physically fit for hard labor." He claimed that Jewish criminal activity was of a particular sort: it was nonviolent because Jews rarely "had the courage" or "aggressiveness" to commit other kinds of crime. The Jewish community defended itself against Bingham's "more than half" claim with statistics, but it assented to the characterization of Jewish crime as nonaggressive. Jewish crime *was* different from non-Jewish crime, Jews implicitly argued, and such nonviolent masculinity was a good thing. Some, like Bingham, saw it as a result of cowardliness or weakness, while others saw it as a religious and ethical inclination. But everyone agreed that when Jewish men transgressed the law, they tended to do it in predictable ways. Jewish masculinity, even in its criminal moments, was not an aggressive, physically dominating masculinity.

Chapter 8 explores the media representations of the 1913 Leo Frank trial and its implications for Jewish masculinity and sexuality. When Frank stood trial in Atlanta for the murder of his young employee Mary Phagan, the media—both Jews and non-Jews—paid close attention. Arguing that Frank could not have done it, a former police commissioner said in the *New York Times* that the murderer was "a brute, crude, undeveloped," but Frank was "highly developed, a gentleman, a scholar." Those who thought Leo Frank was guilty called him a soft, weak, pervert and a "libertine Jew," while those who maintained his innocence called attention to his connections to his wife, mother, and rabbi. Both Frank's supporters and detractors imagined that his gender, sexuality, and Jewishness had a close relationship with his guilt or innocence.

Chapter 9 explores what happens when a challenge arises to the shared image of American Jewish masculinity. If Jewish men were seen as nonaggressive and nonviolent, what would the public make of two Jewish men who admitted to committing a violent crime—what was called "the crime of the century"? This chapter analyzes the 1924 Leopold and Loeb hearing in Chicago. Everyone agreed that Nathan Leopold and Richard Loeb were very bad men: they had kidnapped and murdered fourteen-year-old Bobby Franks and left his body in a culvert. Would Americans adjust their views of Jewish masculinity to accommodate this kind of violence, or would they instead find a reason to insist that Leopold and Loeb were an aberration, and therefore that their act did not constitute a reason to revise the existing ideas about Jewish masculinity? Because they had already confessed to the crime before the sentencing hearing, their defense counsel Clarence Darrow used the idea of "abnormality"—which had specific gendered, sexual, and even religious connotations—to argue for their limited culpability. The prosecution, in contrast, insisted that they were fully responsible for the kidnapping and murder because they were not mentally diseased, and they had therefore chosen their religious and sexual deviation.

The norms of American Jewish masculinity, like norms of masculinity more generally, can be invisible, even though they are ubiquitous. But by focusing on these margins, these experiments, and these unexpected places, we see something much more central, diffuse, and widespread. The view from these margins shows American Jewish norms that idealized not only the healthy body, a connection to the American land, productive labor, resourcefulness, and courage but also gentleness and the ability to endure suffering. These masculine norms did not include physical strength, aggression, and domination as essential features. In fact, as the discussions of crime and abnormality demonstrate, it did not even include interpersonal physical violence as a possible pitfall, even though other American masculinities did. While they sought to mold American Jewish men according to these norms, acculturated Jews also sought to construct an American Judaism based on ideas that had been coded masculine since the Enlightenment. They claimed a rational, decorous Judaism consonant with democracy.

Notes

1. For a comparison with Germany, see Benjamin Maria Baader, Sharon Gillerman, and Paul Lerner, eds., *Jewish Masculinities: German Jews, Gender, and History* (Bloomington: Indiana University Press, 2012), 2–3.

2. On cultural identity, see Stuart Hall, "Cultural Identity and Diaspora," in *Identity, Community, and Cultural Difference*, ed. Jonathan Rutherford (London: Lawrence & Wishart, 1990), 223.

3. This is not to suggest that all scholars who use these terms have simplistic understandings of them. See, for instance, the essays in Laurence Silberstein, ed., *Mapping Jewish Identities* (New York: New York University Press, 2000).

4. Jonathan Boyarin, *Thinking in Jewish* (Chicago: University of Chicago Press, 1996), 170; Silberstein, *Mapping Jewish Identities*, 1.

5. Laura Levitt, "Impossible Assimilations, American Liberalism, and Jewish Difference: Revisiting Jewish Secularism," *American Quarterly* 59, no. 3 (2007): 807–832.

6. *American Hebrew*, Oct. 9, 1908, 560. Quoted in Arthur Goren, *New York Jews and the Quest for Community: The Kehilla Experiment, 1908–1922* (New York: Columbia University Press, 1979), 47.

7. Levitt, "Impossible Assimilations."

8. Annalise Glauz-Todrank, "Race, Religion, or Ethnicity? Situating Jews on the American Scene," *Religion Compass* (Oct. 2014): 305.

9. Eric Goldstein, *Price of Whiteness: Jews, Race, and American Identity* (Princeton, NJ: Princeton University Press, 2006).

10. Anthony Rotundo, *American Manhood* (New York: Basic Books, 1993).

11. Harry Friedman, "Gemara," *Hebrew Union College Annual*, ed. Ephraim Frisch (Cincinnati: Hebrew Union College, 1904), 27.

12. Jonathan Z. Smith, *Relating Religion: Essays in the Study of Religion* (Chicago: University of Chicago Press, 2004): 179–196.

13. See, for instance, Donald Lopez, "Belief," in *Critical Terms for Religious Studies*, ed. Mark C. Taylor (Chicago: University of Chicago Press, 1998).

14. Jonathan Sarna, *American Judaism* (New Haven, CT: Yale University Press, 2004). Hasia Diner, *The Jews of the United States, 1654 to 2000* (Berkeley: University of California Press, 2004).

15. Tomoko Masuzawa, *The Invention of World Religions* (Chicago: University of Chicago Press, 2005).

16. Janet Jakobsen and Ann Pelligrini, *Love the Sin: Sexual Regulations and the Limits of Religious Tolerance* (Boston: Beacon, 2004).

17. Catherine Albanese, *America: Religions and Religion* (Boston: Wadsworth, 2013), 276.

18. Tracy Fessenden, *Culture and Redemption: Religion, the Secular, and American Literature* (Princeton, NJ: Princeton University Press, 2006), 3.

19. Ibid.

20. *Religious Bodies 1916: Separate Denominations* (Washington, DC: Government Printing Office, 1919).

21. Robert Orsi, *Between Heaven and Earth: The Religious Worlds People Make and the Scholars Who Study Them* (Princeton, NJ: Princeton University Press, 2005), 188.

22. Kaufmann Kohler, *Jewish Theology, Systematically and Historically Considered* (New York: Macmillan, 1918), 473.

23. Tisa Wenger, *We Have a Religion: The 1920s Pueblo Indian Dance Controversy and American Religious Freedom* (Chapel Hill: University of North Carolina Press, 2009).

24. To take just one example, Peter Ainslie, the founder of the Disciples of Christ, wrote in the *Christian Century* about the Sabbath. Jews, he explained, had continued the ancient assumption that the Sabbath was a day particular to themselves. But in reality, Jesus had come to universalize its meaning: "It was put in the calendar of time for the freedom, the progress and the civilization of mankind. This is what Jesus means when he says, 'The Sabbath was made for man.' And so saying, he lifts it out if its legalism and sets it on broad humanitarian basis. It was not the Jewish Sabbath any more than the Jewish man about which he was speaking. He had in mind this universal day grounded in human nature and all men's right to it." Peter Ainslie, "Revaluation of Sunday," *Christian Century* 8 (Nov. 3, 1921): 10.

25. Gail Bederman, *Manliness and Civilization: A Cultural History of Gender and Race in the United States, 1880–1917* (Chicago: University of Chicago Press, 1995); Clifford Putney, *Muscular Christianity: Manhood and Sports in Protestant America, 1880–1920* (Cambridge, MA: Harvard University Press, 2009).

26. Shaul Magid, *American Post-Judaism* (Bloomington: Indiana University Press, 2013), 133–156; David Novak, "The Quest for the Jewish Jesus," *Modern Judaism* 8 (May 1988): 119–138.

27. Joseph Leiser, "Emil G. Hirsch," in *Famous Living Americans*, eds. Mary Griffin Webb and Edna Lenore Webb (Greencastle, IN: Charles Webb and Co., 1915), 255–256.

28. Putney, *Muscular Christianity*, 2.

29. Patrick Kelly, "The Sacramental Imagination, Culture, and Play" (Licentiate's Thesis, Weston Jesuit School of Theology, 1999); Christa Klein, "The Jesuits and Catholic Boyhood in Nineteenth-Century New York City" (PhD diss., Univ. of Pennsylvania, 1976).

30. "Church Test of Publicity," *New York Times* (Mar. 11, 1912). On the Men and Religion Forward Movement, see Gail Bederman, "The Women Have Had Charge of Church Work Long Enough: The Men and Religion Forward Movement of 1911–1912 and the Masculinization of Middle Class Protestantism," *American Quarterly* 41, no. 3 (Sept. 1989): 432–465.

31. For instance, see Faith Rogow, *Gone to Another Meeting* (Tuscaloosa: University of Alabama Press, 1993).

32. Sarah Imhoff, "The Myth of American Jewish Feminization," *Jewish Social Studies* 21, no. 3 (Spring/Summer 2016): 126–152.

33. "Men of All Creeds Say Faith Will Live," *New York Times* (Mar. 17, 1912).

34. I use "antisemitism" rather than "anti-Semitism" because there is no such entity called "Semitism" to which it can be opposed. Scholars have called attention to the ways the use of "anti-Semitism" reifies and essentializes Jewishness. For a fuller discussion of the political implications of the spelling, see Yehuda Bauer, "In Search of a Definition of Antisemitism," in

Approaches to Antisemitism: Context and Curriculum, ed. Michael Brown (New York: American Jewish Committee, 1994), 22–34.

35. By choosing this particular moment, I do not mean to argue that the early twentieth century is the only important moment—or even the most important moment—for American Jewish masculinity. Indeed, making such arguments about comparative importance proves difficult with little payoff.

36. Gail Bederman, *Manliness and Civilization*; Matthew Frye Jacobson, *Barbarian Virtues: The United States Encounter with Foreign Peoples at Home and Abroad* (New York: Hill and Wang, 2001); John Kasson, *Houdini, Tarzan, and the Perfect Man: The White Male Body and the Challenge of Modernity in America* (New York: Hill and Wang, 2001); and Kristin Hoganson, *Fighting for American Manhood: How Gender Politics Provoked the Spanish-American and Philippine-American Wars* (New Haven, CT: Yale University Press, 1998).

37. Michael Kimmel, *Manhood in America* (Oxford: Oxford University Press, 1998).

38. William Byron Forbush, *The Boy Problem* (Boston: Pilgrim Press, 1907), 12.

39. He explained that twelve years old was the "the Old Testament Era" of male development. Ibid, 15–16.

40. Ibid., 44.

41. Ibid., 45.

42. In making this point, Susannah Heschel asks, provocatively, "Can women be Jews?" Heschel, "Gender and Agency in the Feminist Historiography of Jewish Identity," *Journal of Religion* 84, no. 4 (Oct. 2004): 580.

43. Marion Kaplan and Deborah Dash Moore, eds., *Gender and Jewish History* (Bloomington: Indiana University Press, 2010).

44. David Kaufman's *Shul with a Pool*, for instance, is topically related and well researched, but offers no analysis of gender. David Kaufman, *Shul with a Pool: The "Synagogue-Center" in American Jewish History* (Hanover, NH: Brandeis University Press, 1999). The literature on American Jews and sports, conversely, analyzes masculinity, but says little about religion. See, for instance, Jack Kugelmass, ed. *Jews, Sports and the Rites of Citizenship* (Urbana: University of Illinois Press, 2007) and Steven Riess, ed. *Sports and the American Jew* (Syracuse, NY: SUNY Press, 1998). Although Jeffrey Gurock does not explicitly theorize how gender and masculinity operate in historical context, his work is nevertheless sensitive to both men's experience of manhood and religion. Jeffrey Gurock, *Judaism's Encounter with American Sports* (Bloomington: Indiana University Press, 2005).

45. Manya Gordon Strunsky, "The Jewish Women's Movement: Mothers and Children," *American Jewish Chronicle* 1 (June 23, 1916): 210.

46. Ibid.

47. Ibid.

48. "The Jew as Athlete," [92nd St] *YHMA Bulletin* (April 1907).

49. Daniel Boyarin, *Unheroic Conduct* (Berkeley: University of California Press, 1997), xiv.

PART I

AN AMERICAN RELIGION

Conceptions of religion in American life have long taken Protestant Christianity as their model. Even today we use "church" as shorthand for religion when we talk about "church and state." We talk about "interfaith" efforts when we mean cooperation between religious communities, and we sometimes say "belief systems" or "faiths" when we mean religions. These terms are more than an accident of vocabulary. Using the word "church" self-evidently conjures specters of Christianity. "Faith" and "belief," though less transparently, also gesture toward Protestant Christian models in which the internal modes of faith and belief form the core of religion. Even when it goes unacknowledged, this idea that religion is based on a personal, internal belief is strongly indebted to Protestant models of religiosity. Janet Jakobsen and Ann Pellegrini note the ways that this "stealth Protestantism" structures much of American law and culture, even in spaces that seem to be secular.[1] Protestantism, then, is the unmarked American religious category. In the early twentieth century, these assumptions about religion, bequeathed by a Protestant legacy, were even more pronounced.

Even though Protestantism structured the ways Americans thought about religion in general, Jews rarely contested that model. They might have insisted on the viability of alternative models of religion in which religious practice or ritual played the primary role. They could have challenged the idea that religion was a matter of the head and the heart, in which the body played only a secondary role. But acculturated Jews most often chose to discuss Judaism by adapting terms, figures, and ideas from the American Protestant religious milieu. They compared Judaism and Christianity, talked about the Jewishness of Jesus, focused on the Bible instead of the Talmud, and wrote about "Jewish consciousness" and universal ethics as the center of Jewish life. Engagement with Christianity, sometimes by comparison and sometimes by contrast, became an important way for them to shape Judaism.

Faith and beliefs even appeared as the crucial aspects of religion in governmental documents. When, in 1916, the US Census Bureau issued its report on "Religious Bodies," it called them "separate denominations" and contained sections on each group's "history," "doctrine," "polity," and "[social] work," But although the report included data on Bahais, Buddhists, "communistic societies," Jews, spiritualists, theosophists, and the Vendanta Society, it still used Christian categories to categorize and explain them. The report also omitted some of the categories central to these other religious communities. When American Jewish communities split, for instance, they tended to cleave along lines of practice—the "Orthodox rite," "the Sephardi rite," or Reform liturgy—in which "doctrine" played only a secondary role. Whether or not synagogues would use Hebrew or English, seat women and men together, and use organs or choirs proved much more salient than the precise nature of God's attributes.[2] Yet the Census Bureau still privileged doctrine and assumed denominational organization, even for Judaism and other non-Christian religions.

In contrast to its complete neglect of Native American religions, the Census Bureau report did recognize that these other non-Christian religious groups were, in fact, religious—but it presented them as parallels of Christianity. The report assumed that there were universal religious categories—doctrine, polity, church—that would apply just as well to non-Christian religions. To understand one of these non-Christian groups, it implied, one would need to know its data for each of these categories. In this framework, to say that a religion had no doctrine or that it had no designated worship space would be almost nonsensical. "Doctrine" played an essential role in defining each religion, but rituals went largely neglected in the report. Religion was a matter of belief. When rituals or religious practices did appear, it presented them as an effect of belief, but never as a primary cause of religiosity or religious identity.

Christianity also structured religious constructions of gender. Chapter 1 shows how Jewish thinkers made Judaism intelligible under the Protestant-structured rubric of American religion. First, they articulated a Judaism that highlighted universalism and democracy. Second, they emphasized that Judaism was based on and consonant with reason. Since the Enlightenment, reason had played an important role in garnering respectability for religion, and most philosophers and theologians thought of reason as a (near-) universal human capacity. Of course, this discourse about the reasonableness of Judaism had existed since the eighteenth-century *haskalah*, or Jewish Enlightenment, which had responded to European Protestantism in part. Early twentieth-century American Jewish thinkers put particular emphasis on this discourse in their construction of an American Judaism, especially in contrast to the Judaism of Eastern European immigrants. The characteristics of reason and universalism lay on gendered philosophical foundations. The qualities that made Judaism American also made it masculine (which is not to say manly.) The masculine-feminine binary mapped onto the reason-affect binary, as Genevieve Lloyd has shown in her classic *The Man of Reason: Male and Female in Western Philosophy*.[3] Therefore, arguing for Judaism in terms of its rationality and universality—thereby emphasizing its masculine qualities—meant arguing for an American Judaism. Whether explicit or implicit, these early twentieth-century discussions show how ideas about Protestant Christianity structured American Jewish masculinity and American Judaism.

Other religious Americans also made explicit comparisons between Jewish masculinity and Christian masculinity, as the discourse about Hebrew-Christian missionaries shows in chapter 2. These missionaries painted Christian masculinity with the broad strokes of physical prowess, might, and willingness to fight. They associated Jewish masculinity with gentleness and quietness in the face of suffering, a characterization that neatly aligned both with a Jewish Jesus and the contemporary political realities of pogroms in Eastern Europe. To our portrait of the construction of American Jewish masculinity, this perspective adds an explicitly religious angle. The Jewish masculinity that missionaries—and the Jews responding to those missionaries—saw did not focus on the healthy body or connection to the American land, but neither was it incompatible with these ideas. Bodies were not of pressing theological or social interest to these men. In the context of American Protestant missions to the Jews, the available social positions were not simply properly manly versus undesirably effeminate: both Jews and non-Jews in this missionary context associated a physically powerful and intimidating masculinity with Protestants and a gentle, nonviolent masculinity with Jews.

Notes

1. Janet Jakobsen and Ann Pelligrini, *Love the Sin: Sexual Regulations and the Limits of Religious Tolerance* (Boston: Beacon, 2004).

2. *Religious Bodies 1916: Separate Denominations* (Washington: Government Printing Office, 1919).

3. Genevieve Lloyd, *The Man of Reason: "Male" and "Female" in Western Philosophy* (Minneapolis: Univeresity of Minnesota Press, 1993).

1 The Reasonableness of Judaism

An American Theology

In the years after the turn of the twentieth century, some American Christian men lamented that women had taken over the churches. These men, turned off by "feminized" religion, deserted the pews. Jesus had even begun to look like a sissy because of all this womanly influence. Bruce Barton, American author and advertising executive, wrote about the travesty of the effeminate Jesus in his 1925 best seller, *The Man Who Nobody Knows*. In the storybooks read out loud at Barton's boyhood Sunday School, the pictures of Jesus showed "a pale young man with no muscle" who was "the Lamb of God," which sounded to him "like Mary's little lamb, something for girls—sissified." But when he read about Jesus in the Bible, he thought: "A physical weakling! Where did they get that idea? Jesus pushed a plane and swung an adz; He was a good carpenter. He slept outdoors and spent His days walking around His favorite lake. His muscles were so strong that when he drove the moneychangers out, nobody dared to oppose him!"[1] Men should reclaim Christianity and a manly Jesus, Barton proclaimed.

Early twentieth-century American Jewish men, in contrast, rarely complained of feminine influences on Judaism. They did not create a "muscular Moses," for instance, because they did not worry that Moses had become feminized. Even when Jews talked about Jesus, which they did quite frequently, their Jesus was not the muscular carpenter/businessman of Barton's book: he was a devout Jew with an ethical message for all of humanity. They seldom grumbled about women's presence in the synagogue. Even when some Reform observers claimed that women outnumbered men in the synagogue's family pews, they took it as an indicator of women's commitment and men's shortcomings. When Reform rabbi Emil Hirsch reflected on the growing number and influence of women in his Chicago synagogue, he referred to women as "the mainstay of American Jewish life, of religion and of philanthropy."[2] Yes, Reform leaders sometimes worried about how to attract more young men, but they rarely complained about women's presence or their influence on Judaism. No one protested that increasingly active temple sisterhoods had led to a sissified Moses or Abraham or to an emasculated God.

Even though it never became the brawny brother of muscular Christianity, however, American Judaism did emphasize masculine qualities in the early twentieth century. Acculturated Jewish men did not trumpet physical prowess or domination, but they promoted the less embodied and more abstract qualities of rationality and universality. Acculturated Jews claimed that Judaism was a "good" religion by showing it was a masculine religion—that is, rational and universal. Sometimes they did this by professing Judaism's similarity to Christianity, such as the times when Jews embraced Jesus's universal ethical messages (though not his divinity). And sometimes they did it by claiming Judaism's superiority to Christianity, such as when Reform rabbi and theologian Kaufmann Kohler pitted an "overemotional" Christian church against a rational Judaism.

This chapter uses the writings and speeches of Kaufmann Kohler and several of his acculturated Jewish contemporaries—Hyman Gershon Enelow, Emil Hirsch, Abram Isaacs, Morris Jastrow, and Julia Richman—as a window into American Judaism. It begins by briefly sketching the ideas of their philosophical forebears, widely influential classical and Enlightenment thinkers who laid the foundations for gendering the categories of reason and universality as male. Next it shows how these Enlightenment values of rationality and universalism served as measuring sticks of American religion in the early twentieth century. Then it explores gender's critical role in evaluating American religion in the early twentieth century. In the end, Kohler and his Reform contemporaries argued that Judaism was indeed masculine, but their version of masculinity was not that of a macho Moses. Rather, they argued that Judaism offered a rational, universal, and therefore masculine religion.

Kaufmann Kohler and American Jewish Theology

In one sense, Kaufmann Kohler was anything but marginal. Though he was born in Germany, he became a major presence in the United States. While serving as the rabbi of Temple Beth El in New York, he also played a key role in editing *The Jewish Encyclopedia*, that is, until 1903 when he was whisked off to Cincinnati to become the president of Hebrew Union College, the flagship Reform rabbinical school. Two decades earlier, he had helped found the American Jewish Historical Society and draft the Pittsburgh Platform, the American Reform movement's first unified set of principles. He supported the Jewish Chautauqua Society, which saw shaping young men as its special mission. Though his ideas and ideals rarely went uncontested, Kohler was a leading voice in American Judaism until his death in 1926.

But in another sense, he was an outsider. In 1918, his *Jewish Theology: Systematically and Historically Considered* was published, and yet the very idea of Jewish theology sat at the intellectual margins of Judaism. In his preface, Kohler noted that "a system of Jewish theology was wanting," and he asked why Jews had not yet produced such a theology. Until the modern period, he claimed, rabbinic literature and medieval philosophy were sufficient for Jews. Moreover, he continued, Judaism had never been centered on dogma. "Besides, a real demand for the specific study of Jewish theology was scarcely felt, inasmuch as Judaism never assigned to a creed the prominent position which it holds in the Christian Church. This very fact induced Moses Mendelssohn at the beginning of the new era to declare that Judaism 'contained only truths dictated by reason and no dogmatic beliefs at all.' "[3] Jews had not needed theology because, unlike Christianity, Judaism did not demand faith in things that were counter to reason. Kohler was correct when he suggested that Jewish theology was marginal. When, in 1923 Samuel Cohon inherited Kohler's chair of Jewish theology at Hebrew Union College, vocal members of the school leadership sought to rename the position. Cohon recalled that "proposals were urged to alter its name to something more euphonious" and that they ultimately needed "to justify the place of theology in the curriculum of a rabbinical seminary."[4] It is no accident that Robert Goldy's *The Emergence of Jewish Theology in America* begins its account in the late 1940s.

If theology was marginal to Judaism and few Jews seemed to discuss it, to whom was Kohler talking when he wrote his synthetic Jewish theology? He was addressing American Jews, whether or not they were listening, and offering them a rational, modern theology with universal import. He sought to influence his readers' vision of Judaism, not merely to help them understand some preexisting systematic theology. But he was also talking to American Christians. He explained Jewish understandings of the afterlife, original sin, and forgiveness, all with explicit and lengthy comparisons to Protestant theologies. Throughout his life, Kohler wrote extensively and participated in interreligious events in the hopes that he could influence how American Protestants related to Jews.[5]

Kohler's basic claims about Judaism—that it harmonized with reason and had universalist underpinnings, but that it had not lost sight of the "heart" in spite of these virtues of the "head"—had a long history. In the mid-nineteenth century, American Reform leader Isaac Mayer Wise had envisioned a universal Judaism, predicting that it would become the "common property of the American people" in fifty years.[6] Although his vision did not come to pass, we can imagine why he might have imagined such a scenario. Wise promoted a universalist Judaism, in harmony with human reason and one chosen by the individual based on his or her conscience. All of these aspects reflected broader American ideas about what religion was and what it should be. If Judaism looked like an American religion, perhaps it could become a religion for all Americans.

However, these claims were not the only option for articulating American Judaism, and at the time of Kohler's writings, they were losing ground among American Jews. By the 1920s, Jewish writers' and religious figures' emphasis on universalism had become more muted, though few acculturated Jews would have shied away from claiming Judaism's agreement with human reason. Around the same time as Kohler wrote his *Jewish Theology*, Horace Kallen, for instance, began to promote his idea of cultural pluralism, in which each group has its distinctive contributions to make to the larger society. Kallen and other acculturated proponents of cultural pluralism posited diversity as the essence of democracy, and they saw some measure of particularism as good for the project of Americanization.[7] By the early 1920s, the United States had become increasingly isolationist, and xenophobia was on the rise. The 1924 Johnson-Reed Act effectively closed the gates to new Eastern European immigrants. Given that atmosphere, Jews, as well as other self-identified minority groups, might have thought it wise to circle the wagons, to celebrate their own distinctiveness, and to move toward particularism rather than universalism.[8]

Was Kohler just a conservative old man behind the times? No. Although promoting a rational, universalist Judaism was not foremost on the to-do list of most of American Jewry in the early twentieth century, Kohler was not alone in these claims. Fellow acculturated Jews, such as Rabbis Hyman Gershon Enelow and Emil Hirsch, academics Abram Isaacs and Morris Jastrow, and educational leader Julia Richman, likewise highlighted Judaism's universalism and rationalism. By this, they meant that Judaism's doctrines were compatible with reason and that its texts and ethics offered important lessons to every person, Jewish or not. These authors were all highly educated Jews who were acculturated to American life, though all but Isaacs and Richmond had been born in Europe. Fewer than twenty Jews taught in higher education across the United States from the late nineteenth to the early twentieth centuries, so Jastrow, Isaacs, and Hirsch were part of a small and influential elite.[9] Their writings, as well as those of Kohler, Enelow, and Richmond, covered a large amount of intellectual ground and reached a broad audience: Isaacs wrote an almost purely apologetic text directed at acculturated Jews and non-Jews, Enelow and Hirsch wrote largely for Jews in the (Reform) pews and their own rabbinical colleagues, Kohler wrote a theology aimed at Jews and accessible to educated Christians, Jastrow wrote for an academic audience, and Richmond wrote for acculturated Jewish educators and parents. Even if the average American Jew did not articulate his or her religion in terms of reason, these authors did.

They hung onto ideas of the rationality and universalist goals of Judaism because those concepts helped Jews argue for Judaism as an American religion. They aimed to explain or defend Judaism to relatively uninformed audiences, but they did not assume these audiences were hostile. Even if few non-Jews read these texts, the writings would still shape acculturated Jews' ideas about Judaism and sometimes even provide them with talking points when they encountered their non-Jewish neighbors' ideas about religion. In this sense, these acculturated authors and their texts were strategic. Moreover, when these texts focused on beliefs—and downplayed practice, as they all did—they explained Judaism in a way that fit with other American ideas of what "good" religion was. As the 1916

Census Report suggested, the idea of religion in the United States centered on beliefs or, in a more philosophical register, theology. By writing a book that offered a coherent statement of faith, Kohler could offer an account of Judaism that fit this model. Additionally, by emphasizing the universalist foundations and goals of Judaism, he and others could make claims to the compatibility of Judaism and democracy.

These same characteristics that allowed Kohler to claim Judaism as American also allowed him to portray Judaism as a masculine religion. Judaism was rational, and it had universalist goals. It was not overcome by emotionalism nor blinded by love, as Kohler would characterize Protestant Christianity. Judaism was not manly in the overt ways of promoting strong male bodies, as muscular Christianity was, but it relied on a masculinity indebted to Enlightenment male virtues of reason and universalism.

The Masculinity of Reform Judaism's Philosophical Heritage

Kaufmann Kohler read widely when it came to religious and philosophical literature. In his writings and lectures, he cited the Hebrew Bible, rabbinic texts, medieval philosophers, poets, the Early Church fathers, the New Testament, Plato, Philo of Alexandria, Rene Descartes, Immanuel Kant, Moses Mendelssohn, and others. For the highly learned Kohler, the best moments in Western philosophy could shine through Judaism, and so philosophy became a frequent reference point for understanding and appreciating Jewish theology. Many of these moments in philosophy were also gendered. We have seen some of the ways that Americans argued that masculine religion was "good" religion, or the proper, desirable, civilized religion. Bruce Barton, for instance, celebrated a Protestant Christianity of physical strength. And as subsequent chapters show, the men of the Galveston movement, Zionist movement, and agricultural communities championed a Judaism of healthy male bodies.

But how can we know if a religion is masculine when we are not looking at bodies or embodied characteristics? How do we know when and how theological or philosophical concepts are gendered? Sometimes these thinkers directly identified a trait with one sex and not the other. Physical strength, for instance, was considered a masculine characteristic. At other times, philosophers created clusters of ideas that they labeled masculine and others that they labeled feminine, even in the absence of references to men or women. Even when there was no empirical evidence to associate these particular concepts with men or with women, the concepts themselves became gendered. For instance, Aristotle characterized the concepts of activity, form, reason, and dryness as masculine and passivity, matter, sense perception, and wetness as feminine. A less philosophical example, but one that works similarly, is our gendered assumptions about the colors pink and blue. There is nothing naturally or essentially feminine about pink or masculine about blue, and indeed, these associations have differed over time. In the early twenti-eth century reds and pinks were considered to be more masculine hues.[10] But even in the absence of transhistorical, natural, or essential connections to gender, these colors still send strong cultural signals. Today most Americans assume that babies dressed in pink are girls.

Reason, like the color pink, is not inherently masculine or feminine. But, like the color pink, it has assumed gendered intellectual and cultural meaning. Using Kaufmann Kohler and his philosophical influences, this section first describes how reason has been coded masculine in Western philosophical traditions. Sec-ond, it explains how reason was taken to be universal and how universalism was also coded masculine. Third, it shows how "good" religion was universal. In the end, it demonstrates how a culturally desirable religion in early twentieth-century America would make claims to both rationality and universality, both of which were strongly connected to masculinity. When American Jews like Kohler claimed Judaism was rational and emphasized its universal aspects, they were simulta-neously making implicit claims about its masculinity.

Many of Kohler's philosophical forebears placed high value on the capacity of reason, and many also associated it with masculinity. This intellectual founda-tion fostered a philosophical system in which reason was implicitly gendered masculine, even when a philosopher did not make specific claims to that effect. In her classic philosophical study *The Man of Reason*, Genevieve Lloyd describes what she calls "the maleness of our ideals of Reason."[11] She shows how Western philosophical traditions from the Greeks to the Enlightenment and beyond link the ideas of reason and rationality with masculinity, even when they purport to be gender neutral.

Although Kohler did not systematically articulate the links between mascu-linity and reason, many of his philosophical predecessors did. The Ancient Greek philosophers whom Kohler cited laid the groundwork for seeing reason as masculine. Their conceptions of the world and ways of knowing influenced philosophical and religious thought for both Christians and Jews into modern times. For instance, Kohler cited Philo of Alexandria's creation account, in which Philo explicitly values reason, which he associates with "man," above senses and emotions, which he associates with "woman"[12]: "First He made mind, the man, for mind is most venerable in a human being; then bodily sense, the woman, then after them in third place pleasure."[13] For Philo, the order of creation expressed the order of value: first the man and the faculty of mind, then the woman and the particulars of bodies and senses, and lastly physical pleasure.

Philosophical ideas about the maleness of reason often go hand in hand with the idea that the opposite of reason—usually emotion, sense perception, or some combination of the two—is feminine. As the Philo example suggests, precisely by being disembodied—of the mind, rather than of the flesh—reason could be coded masculine. If, in the Aristotelian sense, matter and flesh are coded feminine, and form and mind are coded masculine, then reason would align with masculinity because it is not a fleshly matter. Lloyd describes the dichotomy: "Rational knowledge has been constructed as a transcending, transformation or control of natural forces; and the feminine has been associated with what rational knowledge transcends, dominates or simply leaves behind."[14] This valuation of masculine over feminine is not simply a surface-level misogyny of philosophers past. Nor is it a purely descriptive account of gender difference. Instead, it expresses hierarchy: reason is superior to emotion, even when the writer gives the latter some value. Kohler and his fellow acculturated Jews assumed the same hierarchy when they held up Judaism as a superior, civilized religion on account of its rationality.

The masculinity of reason was not only an artifact of ancient Greek philosophy. It also permeated much Enlightenment thought, where it often had a close relationship with conceptions of Christianity. John Locke famously argued that the traditions of the Bible agreed with reason. Locke did not argue that every Christian doctrine could be discovered merely through reason, but he did claim that true Christianity did not violate it. When it came to gender, Locke implicitly related reason to men, and especially upper class men, who could exercise their reason as political agents.[15] Immanuel Kant, too, saw Christianity as rational and reason as the human capacity that allowed progress. Indeed, "man's" rational nature was the very end for which he had been created. Furthermore, Kant associated reason with men: people cultivated and demonstrated their reason through "public use" and free public speech—both realms that were coded male and were far more accessible to men than women.[16]

For Kant, moral rules—and therefore good religion—were not only rational but also universal. His vision of morality famously asserts that we can judge an act's morality by the universalizability of the rule or reason for it. That is, a person has acted morally when she based her action on a rule that could apply to everyone everywhere. Ethics, in this picture, are universal, transcending the particulars of individuals and their senses and emotions. Kohler, like many other Reform thinkers, admired Kant, whom he called "the great philosopher."[17] The Kantian assumptions that reason and universalism were connected to ethics and that both should be connected to religion permeated much of Reform thought.

As these close connections between universalism and reason suggest, universalism, too, was coded masculine. By emphasizing reason's non-embodied nature, philosophers could claim its universality. That is, they could argue that reason is not particular; it does not depend on individual differences or experiences. Therefore different bodies do not mean different reason, they could argue, whereas different bodies *do* mean different sense perceptions. Fleshliness requires immersion in particularity—I experience these particular sensory data, my body is different from yours, my body has these kinds of limitations—whereas intellect means not being beholden to the particulars. Kohler himself referred to the "universal laws of human reason."[18] These kinds of assumptions are reflected, for example, in the Cartesian association of the mind with the rational and the body with the nonrational.[19] Across much Western philosophy, (masculine) reason is seen as a "transcending" force because it is universal, and the things and ideas being transcended are feminine. In these philosophical systems, reason is a prerequisite for and the mode of access to the universal.[20] Reason transcends the particulars of bodies, and in doing so, it is both universal and masculine.

Reform Judaism followed in these philosophical footsteps. It celebrated both reason and universalism when it argued for its own superiority to other forms of Judaism, such as Hasidism, kabbalah, and some types of Orthodoxy. Kohler's Kantian ideas came not only from reading Kant but also from his teacher and mentor, the German scholar and rabbi Abraham Geiger, who was a founder of Reform Judaism. Geiger argued that Judaism was a rational religion with a universalist message. With the historical move from the Temple to synagogues, he wrote, Judaism had transcended particularism: "Judaism itself rose by it to a higher plane, offered a high gift to all humanity." Judaism, its texts, and its ethics offered universal messages to humankind. Geiger not only claimed that Judaism was a universal religion but also that it was *the* universal religion.[21] Other religions claiming that mantle—Christianity and Islam—were merely adaptations of Judaism, he insisted.

Geiger also connected religious progress to manliness. Reason and clarity of thought represented ideal religion, whereas emotion or sentiment represented underdeveloped religion. He argued that a religion should have certain characteristics:

> That the clear and definite thought is pronounced and not hovering in general dim sentiment; that the manly, ripe expression takes the place of the childish babble; that man struggles to apprehend with full consciousness his relation to God and to render in definite, clear words, to enter into himself and to securely lay down the resulting contemplations: only then man is truly religious, only then religion has produced ripened fruit.[22]

Geiger claimed that religion itself could and should evolve and that its progress was dependent on its relationship to reason. Geiger equated the "ripe expression" of religion with the adult and the "manly." In its early stages, religion might exist as a form of "dim sentiment," rather than clear and rational discourse. Sentiment, for Geiger, represented an inferior feminine religious stage, whereas clarity and rationality of discourse represented the superior stage of both the religion and the religious man. Geiger's assumptions about the connections among clarity, rationality, and masculinity support Lloyd's insight that "associations between maleness and clear determination or definition" run as a thread from ancient Greek philosophical thought to the present.[23]

These ideas of the rationality and universality of Judaism appealed to many acculturated and educated Jews in Germany and later to American Jews. Kohler— like other Reform Jewish leaders—had an intellectual pedigree that took masculine reason as an essential part of good religion. They thought that a good religion was rational, universal, and manly. Reform Judaism would go on to flourish in both Germany and the United States. These two religious environments may have proved to be fertile soil for the growth of Reform Judaism because they also valued reason and universalism, over tribalism or particularism, as essential aspects of "good religion." And because it was rational and universal, good religion was masculine.

The American Religious Scene

Early twentieth-century elite American Protestants considered their own religion to be rational and universal, and therefore the pinnacle of religion. For example, Douglas Clyde Macintosh, a professor of systematic theology at Yale University and a shaper of modernistic liberalism, compared Judaism and Christianity both historically and in his own time. Christianity came out on top because of its reason and universalism: "As Hellenized Christianity was a new and universal Judaism, rational to the philosophical thought of an earlier day, so the religion which is to convert the world today must be, we may surmise, a new and universal Christianity, rational to the critical thought of a scientific age."[24] Macintosh thought that reason and universalism represented religious progress in past ages and this one. Rational, universal religion was ideal religion.

Here again we see how Christianity formed the model for religion in general. In her work on secularism, religious studies scholar Tracy Fessenden describes how Protestant Christianity structures the very idea of religion in the United States: "Religion comes to be defined as 'Christian' by default, and an implicit association between 'American' and 'Christian' is upheld even by those who have, one imagines, very little invested in its maintenance."[25] She describes how Protestantism-as-American-religion operates even in unexpected places, and her analysis echoes Orsi's characterization of "good religion" as a reflection of Protestant Christianity. It is "rational, word-centered, nonritualistic, middle class, unemotional, compatible with democracy and the liberal state."[26] Conforming to this idea of good religion, with its implicitly masculine philosophical commitments, became a way for Jews to argue that Judaism was an American religion too.

Reason and universality were not hot-button issues for all Christians in the early twentieth century, but there was a general sense of agreement about them. For instance, during the "fundamentalist-modernist" controversies, the two sides disagreed sharply and deeply about many other theological issues—but not reason or universality. The modernists espoused a Christianity that accommodated American culture and critical scientific thought, whereas the fundamentalists (or anti-modernists) saw much contemporary culture and scientific thought as contradicting their principles of Christianity. And yet, for the most part, they both held that Christianity was at once in harmony with human reason and universal in its message to all people. Gresham Machen, a leading voice of anti-modernism, wrote that "rational theism" was "at the very root of Christianity."[27] He also envisioned Christianity as universal in scope: Jesus had died for the sins of everyone, and God was the true god of all people.[28] On the modernist side, Harry Emerson Fosdick wrote in his *Manhood of the Master*: "The universal appeal of Jesus has overleaped the deep divisions of one race to another."[29] In his tract celebrating the manly qualities of Jesus, Fosdick implied that Christianity was also masculine in its universalism and harmony with reason. In their public debates, modernists like Fosdick and anti-modernists like Machen agreed on little. But they did agree that Christianity was universal and rational.

Although most Christians thought that Christianity was both consonant with reason and universal, some Americans did offer different terms to define and evaluate religions, and yet even they retained the same gendered associations. Philosopher William James, for instance, suggested that religion was more about personal experience and individual feeling. To understand religion, we cannot look at doctrine or theology because these, for James, were derivative, diluted religious phenomena: "We must make search rather for the original experiences" of individual people.[30] "If you wish to grasp her [Religion's] essence, you must look to the feelings," he wrote.[31] Of particular note here is James's choice of pronoun. When James defines religion as related to feeling, he also genders religion, making it feminine. The English language, of course, does not typically gender objects as masculine or feminine, so this is a stylistic choice. It seems that James, too, imagined emotion as related to the feminine, though for him this was entirely appropriate and good in religious life. As James shows, when it came to defining what made a religion good or advanced, reason and universalism were not the only game in town.

Kohler and other acculturated Jews, then, could have gone another route if they wanted to describe Judaism in religious terms that would be comprehensible to others. They could have chosen a different vocabulary to describe Judaism in a way that it would be legible to their non-Jewish neighbors. Though Kohler and his fellow Reform Jews rarely denied the elements of emotion and spirit, they privileged reason and universalism. What made these concepts more appealing than other available options, such as cultural pluralism to describe Jewish distinctiveness, or experience and feeling to describe the essence of religion? The implicitly masculine themes of reason and universalism helped these acculturated Jews paint Judaism in a way that made it a good, American religion.

Reason and American Judaism

Kaufmann Kohler was a champion of rational Judaism. But how would he convince his audience that Judaism was rational, as opposed to emotional, sense-driven, superstitious, or woodenly legalistic? One of his strategies to claim Judaism as a rational religion was to compare it favorably with Christianity. As we have seen, many American Christian theologians claimed that their religion did not violate reason. Christianity represented the apex of religious progress because it was rational and universal, especially in contrast to Judaism's arbitrary legalism and particularism. Thus if Kohler could show that Judaism was more rational (and universal) than Christianity, Judaism would be beating Christianity at its own game. As he wrote, "Judaism recognizes only such articles of faith as were adopted by the people voluntarily as expressions of their religious consciousness, both without external compulsion and without doing violence to the dictates of reason." Kohler continued by making an explicit comparison with Christianity: "Judaism does not know salvation by faith in the sense of Paul, the real founder of the Church, who declared the blind acceptance of belief to be in itself meritorious. It denies the existence of any irreconcilable opposition between faith and reason."[32] Kohler, here parting ways with Kant and Locke, claimed that Christianity privileges faith over reason.[33]

Other champions of a rational Judaism also made their point by comparative analysis. Morris Jastrow, professor at the University of Pennsylvania and one of Kohler's fellow editors on the *Jewish Encyclopedia*, claimed Judaism as a rational religion as part of his larger treatise on how to study religion in general. Although Jastrow is largely overlooked in both American Jewish history and American religious histories, the 1901 publication of his *The Study of Religion* was an important moment in the effort to bring *Religionswissenschaft*, or the science of the study of religion, to the United States.[34] Jastrow's central message about American Judaism was that, for analytical, scholarly, and philosophical purposes, it was in the same category of advanced religion as the best of American Protestantism. He likewise argued that Christianity was *not* a religion based on reason. But he saw its development as a historical one: on Jastrow's reading, philosophy and Christian theology had parted ways in the early modern period. Since then, both mainstream Protestantism and Catholicism had fought battles of faith versus reason.

Yet, he went on to explain, not every religious community pits faith against reason or suffers from the separation of religion from philosophy. There is a "persistent," if marginal, influence of philosophy and reason on some religious people, and this could be seen in Reform Judaism, Ethical Culture, and several

"Protestant sects."[35] When he grouped these religious movements together, Jastrow took a different approach from Kohler. He did not argue for Judaism's superiority on the grounds of its rationality, but rather positioned it among the most "advanced" religions of the time. (He would elsewhere suggest that such religions were superior, but fit only for the intellectual few and not the emotional masses.) Jastrow framed his study of religions by thinking about "development"—that is, each religion goes through a process of development, and religions themselves are at different stages of development. Judaism fared well in this scheme: it stemmed from Israelite religion and had progressed over the ages, through lesser stages such as emotional kabbalah, and to higher stages, characterized by reason.[36]

A rational religion, for Jastrow, was a more highly developed religion. This did not mean that all religious truth or value must follow from reason and only reason. Jastrow left space for prophecy and revelation even in developed religions, as long as they did not contradict reason. All religion should take place "within the limits of reason," he wrote, evoking Kant's *Religion within the Limits of Reason Alone*. For Jastrow, a religion of reason meant that it was "in accordance with reason," but like Locke, Jastrow did not mean that religious ideas or tenets could or must be reached by reason alone, but rather that they could not conflict with reason.

Jastrow's colleague and contemporary Abram Isaacs, a Semitics professor at New York University, likewise insisted that Judaism was both rational and universal. Like Kohler, he was born in the mid-nineteenth century (1851), was ordained in Europe (Breslau), and began his career as a pulpit rabbi (in Paterson, New Jersey). Despite his academic position, Isaacs's 1912 *What Is Judaism* tended more toward the apologetic than the writings of Jastrow and even Kohler. Although he insisted that its task was merely to explain Judaism because Americans knew little about it, *What Is Judaism* clearly argues for Judaism as a highly developed tradition that should be seen as a venerated American religion alongside Protestant Christianity. Isaacs made this argument in part by emphasizing Judaism's rationality. He took it for granted that the world needed religion in general, but he questioned what made a particular religion relevant or, as he called it, "necessary." His first answer was reason: "A religion must first be rational—it must appeal to reason and not stultify human intelligence as the fundamental basis of belief."[37] Constructions of American "good" religion, as well as Isaacs's idea of good religion, held the notion of belief to be central and presumed that beliefs should be rational. Though heart and, to a lesser extent, the body, played roles too, the head was the seat of religion. "Judaism is rational," he explained, "for its fundamental doctrines are in accord with human intelligence."[38] That is, its broadest theological and ethical points harmonized with what he saw as common sense: Judaism "has no dogmas that violate reason and strangle common-sense."[39]

Although the philosophical relationship between masculinity and reason was sometimes subtle, when American Jewish leaders wrote for other Jews, they sometimes explicitly connected reason to men. Some Reform Jews suggested the importance of branding Judaism as manly if it wanted to keep young men in the fold. But what would "manly" Judaism look like? The Central Conference of American Rabbis, the national organization of the Reform rabbinate, formed a committee tasked with studying religious work in universities. It concluded that only a decorous and rational religion would attract college men. Here we see a glimpse into the ways that seemingly abstract ideas about the construction of gender structure religious life. The committee asserted: "If the religious appeal is to find a hearty response at his hands, it must be addressed to him in a sane, convincing, virile way. Its message must be a manly message."[40] Sane and virile meant rational and well argued. Such a religion would privilege the "message," not the rituals.

Manly Judaism, then, would mimic Protestant Christianity in some ways, but distance itself in others. Jewish worship would look more like a well-ordered church service with a choir than the traditional Jewish piety of men praying at their own pace, and it would appeal to universalism. These assumptions associated traditional Jewish piety with unmanly images of emotionalism and disorderly sensory data, and Reform Judaism with intellect, reason, and orderliness. But the belief aspect of Judaism would not mirror its Christian counterparts. It would be "sane" and "convincing"—that is, rational. It would not be based on pure faith, and it would surely not promote any faith in opposition to reason. It would be "good" religion. And, if it could do these things, it would succeed in attracting more young men, the committee reasoned.

As the popularity of Bruce Barton's celebration of a manly Jesus suggests, the perceived femininity of white Protestant Christianity became a major engine driving muscular Christianity. But although Jewish women's participation and visibility in religious roles were increasing at this time, there was little complaint of pervasive femininity corroding Judaism. Even to the most pessimistic observers, neither the participation of women nor femininity had hijacked American Judaism. In fact, one Reform rabbi, Rabbi David Goldberg claimed exactly the opposite: what Judaism needed was *more* womanly influence. He claimed that Judaism was both of the head and of the heart. It was both rational and emotional, and he lamented that the rational had nearly eclipsed the emotional. A frequent contributor to the *Jewish Herald*, Rabbi Goldberg was a military man, and in the fall of 1917, he became the first Jewish chaplain in the U.S. Navy. So we might imagine that he, like Barton, would have glorified religious images and practices that emphasized the manly qualities of strength and domination and denigrated religious affect.

Although like Barton, Goldberg saw the dichotomy between reason and affect in the realm of religion, identifying reason with men and affect with women, he valued them quite differently. "It was therefore in accordance with the law of natural selection that the Jewish woman should have chosen for herself to nurture religious sentiment with her whole heart and soul, leaving to man to uphold the rational side of religion through the formulation of creeds and dogmas, statutes and ordinances," he explained. Goldberg's lament indicated assumptions about essential differences between men and women. Men were inclined toward the rational, and women toward the affective. Men were the mind; women were the heart and soul. Women experienced and expressed religious "sentiment," and men emphasized religious reason. In his view, the two should be complementary: "The Jewish religion is both rational and emotional, universal in its idealism and national in its institutions, rites and ceremonies. Nether of these elements of Judaism, the rational and the emotional, may be neglected, without destroying Judaism itself."[41]

The problem, for Goldberg, was that Judaism was too focused on emphasizing the rational and universal. He saw a Judaism that had embraced its rational and universal side and had nearly forgotten its affective side. "Religious decline," as Goldberg put it, was not the result of women taking over the synagogues. Quite the opposite: women had not exercised enough of their feminine religiosity, and Judaism suffered because of it. Heart and soul had gone quiet, he worried, and the rational mind had become the spokesman for American Judaism.

Goldberg was in the minority, and yet his view in instructive. Even though he represents the other side of the debate about the proper gender of American Judaism, his premises were quite similar to those of the other Reform Jews discussed in this chapter. All of them associated reason and universality with masculinity, and emotion and sense perception with femininity. Kohler's voice was not the only voice talking about Judaism philosophically, and his set of assumptions about the gendered aspects of religion were very widely shared, even by those who disagreed with him.

Emotion and American Judaism

Another way of emphasizing Judaism's rationality was to discuss the role of reason's opposite pole: emotion or sense perception. For most Reform Jews, sense and emotion played roles in Judaism, but ones that were subordinate to or complementary to reason. As Kohler would be the first to admit, Judaism, like American Protestantism, had gone through periods of highlighting emotion and periods of highlighting reason. His thinly veiled disdain for the "emotionalism" of kabbalah made clear his preference for the "intellect" of medieval philosophical traditions. He, like Kant, saw moves toward reason and universalism as religious progress and the descent into emotionalism as retrograde. Judaism's ethics and traditions were universally relevant, in Kohler's theology. But he did not champion a purely and exclusively rational religion. "The essence of Judaism," he writes, is "both intellectual and spiritual."[42] Judaism was not wooden rational-ism; it needed the "heart" as well as the head. But Kohler's emphasis remained on the head.

Kohler contrasted Christianity, which he characterized as still emotional (that is, feminine), with Judaism that had progressed into prioritizing the ratio-nal (masculine). In the entry "Christianity in its Relation to Judaism" in *The Jew-ish Encyclopedia*, he highlighted this contrast: "She [the church] did not foster that spirit of true holiness which sanctifies the whole of life—marriage and home, in-dustry and commerce—but in Jewish eyes seemed to cultivate only the feminine virtues, love and humility, not liberty and justice, manhood and independence of thought." Kohler referred to the church with the feminine pronoun, and he asso-ciated it with "feminine" virtues. He continued: "She has done much in refining the emotions, unfolding those faculties of the soul which produce the heavenly strains of music and the beauties of art and poetry; but she also did all in her power to check intellectual progress, scientific research, and the application of knowledge."[43] The Christian church, Kohler argued, had embraced emotion to the detriment of reason. Although Christianity may have produced good art, it had not become a good religion. In its pursuit of (feminine) poetry, it had crowded out (masculine) justice, intellectual progress, and knowledge. Judaism, in con-trast, had privileged reason over emotion without completely silencing the latter, and so it had nurtured "the sanctity of the whole of life."

When he wrote *Jewish Theology* a decade later, Kohler similarly characterized love as the center of Christianity and justice as the center of Judaism. And love, he explained, "feminized" society: "The highest principle of ethics in Judaism, the cardinal point in the government of the world, is not love, but justice. Love has the tendency to undermine the right and to effeminize society." Love, which Kohler associated with Christianity, was an emotion, and it was therefore partial and particular. And emotions and the particular were both coded feminine. Jus-tice, in contrast, was impartial, rational, and universal, each of which was coded masculine. Unlike a love-centered society, one centered on justice would not be effeminate and particularist, but would be universal—treating every person alike and making the same ethical demands of all: "Justice, on the other hand, develops the moral capacity of every man; it aims not merely to avoid wrong, but to pro-mote and develop the right for the sake of the perfect state of morality."[44] Kohler thus promoted Judaism as having a rational (striving for a Kantian "perfect state of morality") and universal ("the moral capacity of every man") goal.

In addition to painting Christianity as emotional, Kohler criticized Chris-tianity for "dragging the Deity into the world of the senses." Christianity was sense oriented and embodied in its practice and its theology. It had an embodied god, one represented as a human.[45] Trying to perceive God through human bod-ies was a mistake: "We know [God] through our minds alone and not at all through our five senses."[46] Christianity had taken the rational monotheism of Judaism and feminized it by privileging the senses as the means to know God. Kohler contrasted manly "Israel" that privileged intellect with the feminine church, with its sensory and emotional approach to God and its embrace of love but neglect of justice.[47]

When he labeled the church feminine, Kohler had a different set of critiques than did Protestants like Barton, who wrote, "The same theology which has painted the son as soft and gentle to the point of weakness has exalted the feminine in the place of worship, and denied any large place for the masculine."[48] A soft and gentle Jesus did not bother Kohler. Nor did women in the pews. Rather, Kohler painted the priorities of Christian theology (love) and the images of the deity (embodied, mired in the sensory world) as feminine. The particular images of a gentle, suffering, pretty, long-haired Jesus that so troubled Barton did not matter to Kohler. He thought that the very idea of having any physical images of a human-bodied god in and of themselves feminized the religion.

Kohler's position on actual women—as opposed to the abstract idea of the femininity of a religion—was progressive, though he espoused the idea of complementarity, rather than the parity of men and women. He was caught between critique and nostalgia in his relationship to Judaism's past treatment of women.[49] On one hand, Kohler celebrated women's "full" participation in Reform services: "With her greater emotional powers she is able to lend a new solemnity and dignity to the religious and educational efforts of the Synagogue, wherever she is admitted as a full participant in the service."[50] In fact, Kohler saw women's participation in the synagogue as an essential piece of the Reform project. On the other hand, Kohler consistently associated "emotional powers" with unsophisticated and underdeveloped religion. Judaism was a religion consonant with reason, not driven by emotion.[51] When he painted Judaism with this brush of rationality but not emotionalism, Kohler privileged a masculine Judaism.

Concern about emotional religion was not the exclusive province of men. Even Jewish women denounced "emotionalism." In her widely used textbook *Teaching Jewish Ethics*, Julia Richman explained how Judaism offered a set of rational, universally applicable ethics. Teaching these ethics was crucial, she warned, because "religion without morals can become mere emotionalism or fanaticism."[52] For Richman, morals formed the content of ethics, and both followed from reason. Without reason, religion would be nothing more than unmoored expressions of emotion. Richman followed Kant's argument that people should refuse to act from "pathological" feeling. When they act from emotion instead of reason, they become caught up in "the mechanism of nature," instead of making rational, moral decisions.[53] For Richman and for Kant, reason and emotion were opposed, and reason should always be privileged in ethics, morals, and religion.

Richman explained where these ethics and morals came from: reason and God. But how could they come from both reason *and* God? She explained: "Because it is moral, therefore God has ordained it." Again echoing Kant, Richman wrote, "Not by divine command does the moral become law, but because its content is moral, it would necessarily, even without an ordinance, become law, therefore is it enjoined by God."[54] Because something is moral, it is law. Moreover, it is law for all people. Jewish morality, then, was a universal morality consonant with reason: "The authority of the Ten Commandments, as of all moral laws, is intrinsic and axiomatic, and independent of any supernatural or miraculous event."[55] It is not merely that Judaism does not *conflict* with reason, she claimed, but that Judaism is the *result* of reason. That is, we do not need revelation to enable us to reach the moral precepts of Judaism. We could get there by reason alone. Richman departed from the claims of Isaacs and Kohler, who still valued revelation as a source of religious knowledge, even though both suggested that Judaism did not conflict with reason. In asserting that Jewish ethics were the result of reason and that humans could come to them in the absence of revelation, Richman created one of the strongest characterizations of Judaism as a rational religion. The fact that reason was coded masculine, then, did not correspond to an ideological divide between the sexes in practice. Far from it: Richman's stance on the rationality of Judaism assigned to reason a more central role than did her male colleagues, at the same time as she celebrated women's participation in Jewish religious life.

Jastrow too saw Judaism as having the potential to be a "good"—that is, rational, non-emotional—religion. He wrote as a scholar of religion and not as a self-styled representative of Judaism. Nevertheless, he echoed many of the arguments of other acculturated Jews. Like Richman and Kohler, Jastrow implicitly connected reason with good religion and emotionalism with underdeveloped religion. "The whole process of the religious development of man may indeed be viewed as a constant struggle between the emotions and the intellect, in which the latter gradually obtains the mastery," he wrote.[56] Progress meant that more intellect and more interpretive weight would be given to reason, and emotion would play only a minor subordinate role. He wrote that "emotionalism," in addition to being a lower form of religion, was also unhealthy: "There are religious communities and religious sects which, whatever else their merits be, the psychologist cannot view in any other light but as diseased manifestations of the religious spirit, produced by overexcitation of the emotions."[57] Jastrow thus compared emotion-driven religious communities to diseased bodies. Emotion might be an acceptable element of religious practice, but when it took the driver's seat, religion became diseased.

Emotion was best when kept in check, he explained. When emotions take over, like in "mysticism, spiritualism, and Christian Science," the religion and its practitioners are "abnormal." But, Jastrow explained, emotionalism was not restricted to these religious movements. All religions needed at least a small element of emotion, but they were susceptible to being carried away by it. Christianity, "in some of its phases, falls victim to exaggerated emotional tendencies, with the result of encouraging morbid views of life, as emphasized in the ascetic orders." Judaism and Islam also had "their 'emotional' periods"—kabbalah and Sufism— "marked by strange teachings and by hysterical cults."[58] Nevertheless, he was careful to situate contemporary Judaism—he assumed a progressive variety of it, such as Reform—as apart from these "emotional" moments. It had outgrown such a particularist, embodied, emotional, and sensory stage in favor of the rational.

Acculturated Jews, both men and women, downplayed the role of emotion to bolster claims of the rationality of Judaism. Too much emotion in religion signaled effeminate religion, a religion mired in sensory life and the particulars of embodiment. Instead, acculturated Jews argued for Judaism's universal aspects. Though universalism would also help Jews craft a masculine Judaism, retaining Jewish distinctiveness while they championed a Judaism with universal meaning would be a challenge.

Universalism

In 1912, Abram Isaacs declared that "the American Jew" practiced a universal religion: "Judaism is to him a broad universalism."[59] By this, he meant that Judaism offered concepts and practices that were applicable to all. This had not always been the case. "As his faith was to be universalized," Isaacs wrote, "so his people were to be scattered from land to land, from East to West—the divine method of preventing any relapse into the Bedouin stage of development, with Judaism, not tribalism, his religion."[60] Like the customs of the imagined "wild tribes" we see in chapter 4, in its past forms perhaps Judaism had been parochial and exclusive— but no longer. Judaism had progressed beyond its tribal stages. Isaacs, Kohler, and other acculturated Jews argued that rational, enlightened Judaism offered universal messages.

The question of universalism has been a recurring and complex one in Jewish history. How could Jews claim a universal religion while holding onto Jewish distinctiveness? In the early twentieth century, most acculturated Jews wanted to have their cake and eat it too: they wanted to be members of a universal religion while maintaining that there was something religiously distinctive about being Jewish. Universalism helped them claim that Judaism was a "good" religion and an American one. Articulating a Judaism of universal ethics helped them argue for Judaism's relevance to all people and to democracy as well. But, as Horace Kallen's move toward "cultural pluralism" suggests, many Jews were not ready to cast off all sense of distinctiveness from their neighbors. Although this desire to hold onto particularism sometimes included ideas about ethnic or cultural traits, as Kallen's argument foregrounded, it also often insisted on religious distinctiveness as well. So how could American Judaism be both universal and particular? And what, precisely, was the content of this religious distinctiveness or particularity?

Navigating claims to universalism and particularism was not easy. Some of these attempts leaned very heavily on the universalist side. Ethical Culture, a movement founded by the former pulpit rabbi Felix Adler and joined by many acculturated Jews, cast the ideal religion as a universal one available to each individual without any particularity. Some Jews even turned to Unitarianism, which posited one god rather than a trinity and thereby removed one of the theological obstacles between Judaism and Christianity. These movements were both populated largely by an urban, educated social elite, which appealed to some acculturated Jews who were themselves urbanized and educated.

If Ethical Culture and Unitarianism offered rational, universalist options for Jews, why would they choose to stay with Judaism? Hyman Gerson Enelow, the rabbi of New York's Temple Emanu-El, wrote *The Adequacy of Judaism*, an impassioned defense of Judaism in 1920.[61] "Should Jews Become Unitarians?" one chapter asked. Absolutely not, Enelow argued, even though he accepted the premise that a universalist religion was best. "We are told it is superior because Unitarianism is a universal religion, embracing people of different kinds, whereas Judaism is merely a racial or national religion." And if Judaism were truly confined to a race or a nation, it would indeed be "a serious indictment." Yet Judaism was not only widely influential in the development of religious civilization but it even had universal aspects: "The very fact that Unitarians admit that they got their ethical and religious ideas from the Jews proves that they contradict themselves when they maintain that Judaism is not universal." If Unitarians belittled Judaism or thought it backward on account of its particularism, they were mistaken. Enelow claimed that "Judaism has been a universal religion in its ideals and teaching from its very beginning." True, only a small percentage of the world was Jewish "in name," but Judaism "has exercised practically a universal influence."[62] Even those who argued that Jews should recognize Unitarianism as the fulfillment of Jewish ideals were actually strongly influenced by Judaism. For Enelow, Judaism formed the religious foundation of Western culture, with the original universal ethics. Jews had the genuine article in Judaism, so choosing to become Unitarian—or even Christian—was to choose a pale imitation of the original.

American Reform Jews embraced universalism, and part of this meant presenting their religion in a way that was recognizable to the Protestants around them. Continuing earlier American Jewish ideals, they put a premium on "decorum," or outward signs of orderliness and rationality, in contrast to more traditional modes of services that might sound or look chaotic to American Protestant observers.[63] A few congregations experimented with Sunday services, many chose English readings of the Torah (sometimes in addition to the Hebrew), most minimized rabbinic texts in favor of emphasizing the Bible, and rabbis frequently delivered sermons about Jesus. As David Novak, Shaul Magid, and others have shown, high-profile Reform rabbis such as Kaufmann Kohler and Stephen Wise spoke at length about the Jewishness of Jesus and held up a dechristologized Jesus as an exemplar. Louis Ginsburg's biographer reported that the famed talmudist went to an American synagogue shortly after his arrival in New York in 1900. "He recognized he was in a synagogue," despite a liturgy with little Jewish content, "for Jesus was no longer a fashionable subject in church."[64] Exaggeration of Jesus's Christian unpopularity aside, Jesus and occasionally even Paul became regular figures in the religious writings of acculturated Jews.

We can see these textual and ritual trends in light of the philosophical ones: when they emphasized universalism, acculturated Jews talked a theological language similar to that of their Protestant neighbors. We might say they were speaking the language of American religion. Reform rabbi Joseph Leiser had his rabbi protagonist in a 1902 serialized story say, "Judaism has been too long a religion for Jews only. It ought to be uplifted by the prophetic spirit, the spirit that does not exclude Jesus or Paul. Our religion belongs to humanity because it is the salvation of humanity."[65] This embrace of Jesus could both make Jews seem more familiar to their Christian neighbors and make a case for Judaism as a universal religion. Jesus might not have been a deity, but he was a superior human being, and a Jewish human being at that. In this theological sense, Reform Judaism could appeal to common ground with very liberal Protestant groups.

In a similar move, acculturated American Jews put much greater emphasis on the Bible and downplayed the Talmud and other rabbinical literature. The Talmud seemed neither universal nor rational in the way they wanted. Rabbinic literature has an epistemology different from the Kantian modes of reason that Kohler and other Reform Jews championed. Rather than employing deductive logic, rabbinic literature uses creative exegesis and associative linguistic moves and embraces the idea of multiple meanings. When Reform Jews wrote about the rationality of Judaism, they could connect with Americans Christians who were more familiar with Enlightenment-influenced modes of thinking than the "legalistic" and strange reasoning of rabbinic literature. Promoting the importance of the Bible was something that Christians and Jews alike could get behind, in large part because of their agreement on its universal import. In his *Adequacy of Judaism*, Enelow called the Bible "the most universal book man possesses" that "is able to appeal to all manner of men and races." Shunning doctrines of Jewish chosenness, Enelow's claim sought to use "universal" in two senses: the Bible was written *for* everyone to read—Christians, of course, could agree to this—and it contained universalistic ethical and theological dicta, which promoted the equality of all "men." The production of this universal document was proof that Judaism was universal, not tribal. "Would this have been possible if Judaism, which produced the Bible, were a mere tribal religion?"[66] Enelow asked. No, he answered, unlike the "bad" religion (or even traditions unrecognizable as religion) of indigenous tribes, Judaism had relevance.

Isaacs likewise insisted the Judaism was universal and not tribal: "Judaism is universal in its scope and influence . . . its tendency is just the reverse of tribal."[67] Moreover, Judaism was even more universal than Christianity with its "sects." The Jew, explained Isaacs, was "peculiarly fitted" to "the uplifting of the people to higher ideals" because "he is happily without sectarian taint."[68] Isaacs made a particular point about Jewish philanthropists—they were superior to generous Christians because they were not mired in sectarian theological bickering and could therefore turn their attentions to the betterment of humanity as a whole— but in doing so, he also made a larger claim about Judaism. "The unsectarian benevolence of Jewish philanthropists" was a sign of religious progress and the distinctive value of Judaism, which was universalism: "Without distinction of creed, are harbingers of the future, faith foregleams of the coming sunshine that shall brighten and strengthen and unify humanity."[69] Judaism did not have sects, nor did it seek converts. (In fact, none of these thinkers proposed that everyone should convert to Judaism or take up its halakhic practices—only that everyone should learn the religious and ethical lessons it offered.) Judaism's only mission was to bring together humanity as one moral people. Isaacs painted Judaism as just like Christianity, only better: it was more universal.

Kohler similarly held up Judaism as universal, though he paid far more attention to the theological questions behind claiming a universalist Judaism. His chapter titled "The Essence of the Religion of Judaism" claimed that Judaism was, at its heart, even more universal than Christianity. Its moral messages were valuable for each individual and community: "When the true object of religion is the hallowing of life rather than the salvation of the soul, there is little room left for sectarian exclusiveness, or for a heaven for believers and a hell for unbelievers." Unlike Christianity with its various stripes of Protestants, Catholics, and Orthodox, Kohler claimed, true Judaism was utterly nonsectarian. Its goal was to make everyday life holy and moral for each person, rather than promoting a goal of a future reward as Christianity did. "With this broad outlook upon life, Judaism lays claim, not to perfection, but to perfectibility; it has supreme capacity for growing toward the highest ideals of mankind, as beheld by the prophets in their Messianic visions."[70] Judaism, for Kohler, was universally applicable: it did not set its sights on an imagined heaven or hell—as Christianity did—but focused on earthly life.

If universalism meant a religious unity, then how could Judaism or Jews be distinctive? To make his Judaism consistent, he would have to reinterpret the traditional ideas of Jews as the chosen people and the biblical covenant between

God and the people of Israel. For Kohler, the divine covenant became "the hope of universal religion." He presented Jews as the chosen people only in the sense that God had assigned to them the task of bringing the universal message to the world: "Progressive Judaism of our own time has the great task of re-emphasizing Israel's world-mission and of reclaiming for Judaism its place as the priesthood of humanity." Kohler framed the covenant not as setting off one group of people from others, but as a pact between God and humanity as a whole: "It is to proclaim anew the prophetic idea of God's covenant with humanity, whose force had been lost, owing to inner and outer obstacles." The task of Jews and Judaism was to overcome these obstacles and retrieve the lost meaning of the covenant—that it included all people, not just Jews. "Israel, as the people of the covenant, aims to unite all nations and classes of men in the divine covenant. It must outlast all other religions in its certainty that ultimately there can be but the one religion, uniting God and man by a single bond."[71] The covenant marked Jews as a particular people with a universal task: to spread monotheism and unity.

Kohler used an interpretation of the Shema, the traditional Jewish prayer, to explain the relationship between universalism and particularism:

> Why do the words, 'the Lord is our God' precede the words, 'the Lord is One'? Does not the particularism of the former conflict with the universalism of the latter sentence? No. The former expresses the idea that the Lord is 'our God' just so far as His name is more intertwined with our history than with that of any other nation, and that we have the greater obligation as His chosen people. Thus JHVH is no longer the national God of Israel."

For Kohler, Jewish particularism came from Jewish history and from the obligation to bring the moral insights of Judaism to others. God had a special relationship with Jews historically and a charge for Jews today, but these did not mean that Judaism was not a universal religion or that Jews had an exclusive claim to God.

Julia Richman's rational Judaism might seem to negate any sense of Jewish difference. One might ask of Richman and her reason-centered Judaism if Judaism and its ethics were universal and rational, was there anything distinctive about Jews? She would have answered in the affirmative by offering the converse of her earlier warning: if religion without morals could degenerate into mere emotionalism, morals without religion could be unstable. "Morals without religion is always a shifty basis for the building of firm character, and an unsafe guide for right conduct."[72] Without the traditions of religion, a person might stray from these morals. They might mistake something for rational when it was not or fail to use their reason to discern what is moral and so act morally. The morals derived from Judaism were universal—everyone could and should learn from them. But Jews needed Judaism and its traditions to make sure that they were using their reason correctly, that is, in accordance with God's will. Tradition was an episte-mological aid, but not a source of the legitimacy of morality. Rational, universal morals and ethics were superior to emotionalism, Richman explained, and Juda-ism was an exemplar of this "good" religion.

According to Richman, Judaism had both universal and particularistic as-pects. Its ethics and moral laws were universal, but Jews had the particular charge to live out these ethics and moral laws as exemplars to others: "It was this Jewish development of the Moral Law which formed the ethical basis first of Christian-ity, and later of Mohammedanism. Thus has Judaism given to mankind and spread through the civilized world the highest ethics by which all humanity is benefitted today."[73] Judaism developed the rational, universal moral law, which Christians and Muslims later adopted. Richman then used this universalism of law as the very reason for Jewish particularism: "Since the Jew can thus prove his claim to having given the world its basis for right living, how clearly must it be shown to every Jewish child that his is the responsibility of living up to the stan-dards his people gave to mankind." Jews were different or special because they had special responsibilities to spread this law. She continued, "He [the Jew] needs to remember that his disregard of ethical duties and his violation of the moral law make him not only unworthy as an individual, but more unworthy as a mem-ber of a religious community still on trial before the world until its mission shall have been fulfilled—the mission of teaching righteousness to all mankind."[74] However, Jewish particularism was only temporary: once all people had em-braced the moral law, there would be no need to continue to emphasize Jewish particularism.

Jastrow argued something quite different when it came to the idea of univer-salism. "There is no such thing as universal religion," he wrote. Although he found the idea of universalism appealing in theory, it remained an ideal, not a reality. Christianity, Buddhism, Islam, Judaism, and Zoroastrianism might strive to be-come "the universal property of mankind," but the fact of the matter was that none had yet attained that goal.[75] Some religions, however, had progressed more than others toward this ideal:

> In our own days we have witnessed in Unitarianism which appears in differ-ent countries under various names and in Reformed Judaism still another at-tempt in the same direction, and the Ethical Culture movement is but one symptom among many, of this constant endeavour among people who have reached higher conceptions of the scope of religion, to realise an ideal which appears indeed to demand an intellectual grasp of the meaning of life, for which the masses never have been, and perhaps never will be, entirely fitted.[76]

Ironically, in Jastrow's account, universalism was only for the elite. It was a "higher" religious form, but average people would have a hard time grasping it.

Nevertheless, universalism remained an ideal for Jastrow. He chastised religious intolerance, at times singling out Christian leaders for fostering it, as a sign of underdeveloped religion. First citing as a negative example Luther's hymn that calls on God to "smite the Moslem and the Pope," Jastrow went on to praise Spinoza for righting the religious path toward reason and the universal: "Turning to the philosophers who revolted from the sway of scholasticism and ecclesiastical authority, it is not until we reach Spinoza that we find an attempt at setting up a system of religious philosophy which is broad and inclusive."[77] Jastrow celebrated Spinoza's turn away from particularism. Even though Spinoza did not reach the universal ideal, at least he moved the development of religion in the right direction. In Jastrow's account, Judaism was not yet universal, but it nevertheless represented religious progress.

Kohler, Richman, Jastrow, Enelow, and Isaacs all mapped the relationship between universalism and particularism differently, but each valued universalism as a marker of religious progress. They each saw Judaism as broadly universalistic in its texts and its ethics. And they each saw this universalism as related to reason. For these thinkers, Judaism espoused these masculine philosophical concepts. This Judaism, with its universalism and rationality, was "good" religion.

Conclusion

Kohler, Richman, Isaacs, Jastrow, Hirsch, and Enelow all explicitly articulated the rational and universal aspects of Judaism. They depicted a Judaism that was a "good religion," an American religion, and even a masculine religion. On the one hand, this Judaism spoke the language of American religion—i.e., Protestantism—when it focused on belief, reason, and universalism and denigrated emotionalism. On the other hand, this masculine Judaism did not mimic its "muscular Christian" contemporaries who championed the strong and healthy bodies of people and Jesus alike.

In the next chapter, the focus on these ideas about the gender of Judaism shifts from the pens of rabbis and academics to the bodies of Americans. It enters the world of "Hebrew-Christian" missionaries, where the construction of religious masculinity begins to show the differences between assumptions about Jewish men and Christian men.

Notes

1. Bruce Barton, *The Man Nobody Knows* (Indianapolis: Bobbs-Merrill Company, 1925), 3.
2. Emil Hirsch, "A Talk with Emil Hirsch," *Reform Advocate* 28, no. 1 (Sept. 10, 1904): 50.
3. Ibid., vii.

4. Quoted in Robert Goldy, *The Emergence of Jewish Theology in America* (Bloomington: Indiana University Press, 1990), 7.

5. Yaakov Ariel, "A German Rabbi and Scholar in America," *European Judaism* 45, no. 2 (Autumn 2012): 61

6. Sarna, *American Judaism*, 124.

7. Daniel Greene, *The Jewish Origins of Cultural Pluralism* (Bloomington: Indiana University Press, 2011).

8. Jonathan Sarna writes of 1920s American Judaism: "Even the community's ideological emphases had changed from the 1870s, tending over time toward greater particularism as opposed to earlier universalism; toward a heightened sense of Jewish peoplehood as opposed to the former stress on Judaism as a faith; toward a new emphasis on the spiritual and emotional aspects of Judaism as opposed to the former emphasis on rationalism." Sarna, *American Judaism*, 206.

9. Paul Ritterband and Harold Wechsler, *Jewish Learning in American Universities* (Bloomington: Indiana University Press, 1994), 237n5.

10. According to a *Ladies' Home Journal* article in June 1918, "The generally accepted rule is pink for the boys, and blue for the girls. The reason is that pink, being a more decided and stronger color, is more suitable for the boy, while blue, which is more delicate and dainty, is prettier for the girl." See Jo Paoletti and C. Kregloh, "The Children's Department," in *Men and Women: Dressing the Part*, eds. C. B. Kidwell and V. Steele (Washington, DC: Smithsonian Institution Press, 1989), 22–41.

11. Genevieve Lloyd, *The Man of Reason: "Male" and "Female" in Western Philosophy* (Minneapolis: Univeresity of Minnesota Press, 1993).

12. Kohler, *Jewish Theology*, 21.

13. Lloyd, *Man of Reason*, 23. Although Kohler did not reproduce Philo's creation account in his own book, he referred to and relied on Philo's exegesis and philosophical claims to support his claims about God and creation in his own Jewish theology.

14. Ibid., 2. For an anthropological perspective on this association, see Sherry Ortner, "Is Female to Male as Nature Is to Culture?," in *Woman, Culture and Society*, eds. M. Z. Rosaldo and L. Lamphere (Stanford, CA: Stanford University Press, 1974), 67–87.

15. Nancy J. Hirschman, "Intersectionality before Intersectionality Was Cool: The Importance of Class to Feminist Interpretations of John Locke," in *Feminist Interpretations of John Locke*, eds. Nancy Hirschman and Kirstie McClure (University Park: Penn State Press, 2007), 155–186.

16. Lloyd, *Man of Reason*, 67–69.

17. Kohler, *Jewish Theology*, 69.

18. Ibid., 8.

19. Lloyd, *Man of Reason*, 47.

20. Ibid., 75.

21. Susannah Heschel, *Abraham Geiger and the Jewish Jesus* (Chicago: University of Chicago Press, 1998), 105.

22. Abraham Geiger, *Judaism and Its History: Vol 2.*, trans. Maurice Mayer (New York: Thalmessinger, 1866), 219. The "clear and definite thought" is likely a reference to Descartes' famous phrase.

23. Lloyd, *Man of Reason*, 3.

24. Douglas Clyde Macintosh, "The New Christianity and World-Conversion," *American Journal of Theology* 18 (Oct. 1914): 343. Macintosh also wrote *Theology as an Empirical Science* (New York: Macmillan, 1919), where he opposed "the Jewish type of thought" with "the modern Christian ideal" (214).

25. Fessenden, *Culture and Redemption*, 3.

26. Orsi, *Between Heaven and Earth*, 1–2.

27. J. Gresham Machen, *Christianity and Liberalism* (Philadelphia: Presbyterian Guardian, 1923), 56.

28. Ibid., 62–63.

29. Harry Emerson Fosdick, *The Manhood of the Master* (New York: Abingdon Press, 1913), 172.

30. William James, *Varieties of Religious Experience* (New York: Modern Library, 1902), 8.

31. Ibid., 494.

32. Kohler, *Jewish Theology*, 5.

33. Kohler never defined precisely what he meant by the "Christianity" to which he compared Judaism. With a few notable Catholic exceptions, Kohler's depictions of Christianity reflected Protestant varieties of theology, even then, they were far too general and uniform to be an accurate description of American Christianity. Still, Kohler's goal was to show how Judaism could outdo Christianity in its rationality, so accuracy and nuance in its depiction were not of foremost importance.

34. Tomoko Masuzawa offers an excellent reading of his relationship to the idea of "world religions" and his skepticism the idea of universal religion. Masuzawa, *Invention of World Religions*, 117–120.

35. Morris Jastrow, *The Study of Religion* (New York: Charles Scribner's Sons, 1902), 238.

36. Jastrow very likely got this idea from Hegel either directly or through the Jewish historian Heinrich Graetz.

37. Isaacs, *What Is Judaism?* (New York: G. P. Putnam's Sons, 1912) 114.

38. Ibid.

39. Ibid., 5.

40. "Report of Committee on Religious Work in Universities," in *Central Conference of American Rabbis: Twenty-Sixth Annual Convention*, ed. Isaac Marcuson (Cincinnati: Bacharach Press, 1915), 107.

41. David Goldberg, "Woman's Part in Religious Decline," *Jewish Forum* 4, no. 4 (May 1921): 872.

42. Kohler, *Jewish Theology*, 15.

43. Kaufmann Kohler, "Christianity in its Relation to Judaism," *Jewish Encyclopedia* (New York: Funk and Wagnalls, n.d.), 4: 49–59.

44. Kohler, *Jewish Theology*, 121.

45. Ibid., 54.

46. Ibid., 69.

47. Ibid., 375.

48. Barton, *The Man Nobody Knows*, 33.

49. Karla Goldman, *Beyond the Synagogue Gallery* (Cambridge, MA: Harvard University Press, 2001), 151–172.

50. Kohler, *Jewish Theology*, 473.

51. For instance, kabbalah, perhaps Kohler's least favorite trend in the history of Judaism, erred when it "overemphasized the emotional element and eliminated much of the rational basis of Judaism." Ibid., 474.

52. Julia Richman, *Methods of Teaching Jewish Ethics* (Philadelphia: Jewish Chautauqua Society, 1914), 11.

53. Immanuel Kant, *Critique of Practical Reason*, 3rd ed. trans. Lewis White Beck (New York: Prentice-Hall 1993), 90.

54. Richman, *Methods of Teaching Jewish Ethics*, 11.

55. Ibid., 12.

56. Jastrow, *The Study of Religion*, 280. See also 63 of this chapter.

57. Ibid., 286.

58. Ibid., 285.

59. Isaacs, *What Is Judaism?* 44.

60. Ibid., 32.

61. Enelow, *The Adequacy of Judaism* (New York: Bloch, 1920).

62. Ibid., 70.

63. Riv Ellen Prell reflected on the ongoing meaning of decorum for American Jews in "A New Key: Decorum and the Study of Jews and Judaism," *American Jewish History* 90 (Mar. 2002): 13–25.

64. Eli Ginzberg, *Keeper of the Law: Louis Ginsberg* (Philadelphia: Jewish Publication Society, 1966), 19.

65. Leiser, "Rabbi Benjamine's Experiment; or From Generation to Generation," *Menorah* (May 1902): 368.

66. Enelow, *Adequacy of Judaism*, 70–71.

67. Isaacs, *What Is Judaism?*, 10.

68. Ibid., 12.

69. Ibid., 61–62.

70. Kohler, *Jewish Theology*, 18.

71. Ibid., 51.

72. Ibid., 11.

73. Richman, *Methods of Teaching Jewish Ethics*, 14.

74. Ibid.

75. Jastrow, *Study of Religion*, 87.

76. Ibid., 115.

77. Ibid., 14.

2 Manly Missions

Jews, Christians, and American Religious Masculinity

A NON-JEWISH WRITER for the New York weekly the *New Outlook* described an Orthodox Jewish service in the winter of 1912. "Black-bearded men, robed in the broad stripes and mellowed ivory hues of venerable prayer shawls" listened to the "quaintly plaintive, at times soul-stirring" voice of the lushly robed cantor, he wrote.[1] In her 1912 memoir *The Promised Land*, the Jewish immigrant Mary Antin described Hasidim at a wedding: "The most pious men in Polotzk danced the night through, their earlocks dangling, the tails of their long coats flying in a pious ecstasy."[2] Observant Jews engaged in "queer" religious "antics," one Christian observed.[3] Even Jews who had grown up in more liberal Jewish environments, such as San Francisco Jewish merchant Harris Weinstock, thought of "long flowing locks and white beard" when they pictured pious Jews.[4]

When early twentieth-century Americans thought of traditional Jewish piety, they often imagined men in flowing cloaks whose bodies swayed gently back and forth in prayer. Whether Jews or Christians imagined observant Jewish men, they rarely pictured strength or physical power. Jews and Christians alike described a Jewish masculinity that was gentle, averse to physical aggression, and even willing to endure suffering. For many Christians, the gentleness and suffering of Jesus resonated with this image of gentle Jewish masculinity. While images of halakhic Judaism sometimes called forth both nostalgia and embarrassment from acculturated Jews, they also inspired comparisons with the gentle masculinity of Jesus.

In this chapter we see that American Christian missionaries to the Jews, many of whom were born Jewish, shared this understanding of masculinity. Their position in the borderlands of American religions offers us a distinctive vantage point from which to view the gendered religious landscape. These men—and they were overwhelmingly men—had experienced life as both Jews and Christians. When they reflected on their lives, they told different tales about what it meant to be a Jewish man and what it meant to be a Christian man. This chapter explores the stories of four such men: Joseph Goldman converted to Christianity and then sought to explain Judaism to American Christians; Leopold Cohn converted to Christianity and built a modest (but quite controversial) New York-based mission; Edward Steiner converted and took up a professorship in "Practical Christianity" and wrote from an academic standpoint; and Samuel Freuder converted to Christianity and back to Judaism and then wrote of his impressions of both communities. They occupied a spectrum of Christian theologies: Presbyterian, Congregationalist, Baptist, Methodist, and without denomination. Despite these differences, each associated Protestant Christianity with one sort of masculinity, and Judaism with another. Both Jews and non-Jews imagined that there was something distinctive about Jewish masculinity, and these men had been on both sides. They, perhaps more than anyone else during those years, experienced the different assumptions, expectations, and norms of religious masculinity. They had to transition from one religious community and set of norms to another, and this transition included not only theological and ritual changes but also gendered changes.

The reflections of these Hebrew-Christian missionaries illuminate one of the ways that Christianity structured American Jewish masculinity. Creating an American Jewish masculinity was not always or solely a comparative project. But Protestant Christianity formed the blueprint for what counted as religion in America, and so it shaped discourses about religious masculinity. In many cases, the Christian influence on these broad cultural conversations was implicit, but here is a place where we see it explicitly. Protestant masculinity, of course, came in many different shades. These Hebrew-Christian missionaries tended to steer away from muscular Christianity, and they embraced a gentle version of Jesus. In addition to shaping how they imagined Christian men and manhood, Christian theological ideas about the suffering and gentleness of Jesus colored how they saw Jews.

Hebrew-Christian missionaries' position in a liminal space allows us a window into American Jewish masculinity. The most familiar historical models we have for Jewish men's gender are the weak, feminized Jew of antisemitic discourse, such as the one that Sander Gilman describes in *The Jew's Body*, and the physically strong Jew of Zionism and *muskeljudentum* or "muscular Jewry" that Todd Presner explores in his *Muscular Judaism*. As these examples demonstrate, there has been sustained scholarly attention to masculinity in the European context, but little in the American scene. These American missionaries show us another instance of how the negotiation of masculinity is not reducible to a contest of the (positive) Jewish vision of the male Jew versus the (negative) non-Jewish vision of the male Jew. The construction of American Jewish masculinity was vastly more complex and multivocal. Between the antisemitic vision of the effeminate Jew and the normative muscular Christian, these American missionaries saw a gentle and sympathetic Jewish man.

This vision of masculinity could fit with the picture of healthy, resourceful, and productive Jewish men that we will see in Part II. And for many acculturated

Jews, it did. Christians, however, sometimes associated Jewishness with disease or disability. Many Christian missionaries used metaphors of illness and blindness to describe the state of being a Jew. Often the conversion tales told by Hebrew-Christian missionaries had underlying motifs of transformation from sickness to health. In missionary contexts, then, Jews and Christians often disagreed and even butted heads. But they nevertheless shared some ideas about the gentleness and noble suffering of Jews.

This chapter begins by exploring the gendered theological assumptions of one Christian missionary, Arno Gaebelein. After providing a brief history of missions to the Jews in the United States, it studies the writings of Goldman, Cohn, Steiner, and Freuder and their ideas about masculinity and religion. Finally, it provides a broader picture of Reform Jewish responses to ideas of missions, religiosity, and manliness. These acculturated Jews responded by claiming that Judaism was already a rational manly religion—or at least their own decorous, modern Judaism was—and that Christian missionaries were the ones being unmanly by inciting conflict and using coercion to add to their flocks. From all this we see a rich picture of American religious masculinity. This portrait of Jewish manhood matched neither the image of normative American manhood nor its negative, effeminate opposite. It offered neither a replica of the ideals of Protestant muscular Christianity nor an antisemitic stereotype of weak and cowardly Jewish men. Rather, these early twentieth-century Jews and Christians on the missionary margins helped construct an alternative: a gentle, nonaggressive manhood.

The Jewish Male Body through Christian Theology

Many strands of Christian theology confronted a problem when considering the Jewish male body. On the one hand, Jesus's human body was a male Jewish body, and therefore the image of the male Jewish body could reflect divinity. But on the other hand, after the coming of Christ, *Jewish* men should have converted and become *Christian* men. Any contemporary Jewish men represented a grave theological error. Male Jews, therefore, at once represented not only a superseded relic but also a reminder and perhaps even a pale reflection of Jesus. What then were Jewish men: reflections of Jesus with admirable qualities of masculinity or errant relics to be pitied and helped?

Much American missionary literature had it both ways. One example from a 1912 missionary journal shows how early twentieth-century science contributed to a distinctive version of this theological interpretation of Jewish masculinity. Progressive Era medical and psychological discourse suggested that hysteria and neurasthenia constituted a significant issue for many Americans and for two groups in particular: women and Jews. In 1912, the Protestant missionary journal *Our Hope* provided an explanation for the origin and meaning of Jewish "nervous disorders." But this journal did not, like others, posit a neo-Freudian conception of repression. Nor did it offer a Lamarckian explanation for the inherited effects of persecution. Instead of pursuing psychological or biological causes, *Our Hope*, the publication of the largest American mission to the Jews, provided theological reasons for the presence of "nervousness" in Jewish bodies. Even though the widespread diagnosis of nervous disorders had only begun after the publication of George Beard's 1881 *American Nervousness*, the journal saw the "divine prediction" of these ailments in Deuteronomy 28:64–67.[5]

According to Arno Gaebelein, longtime editor of *Our Hope* and later contributor to the famed *Fundamentals* pamphlet series, Deuteronomy 28 explained that Jews should expect "a trembling heart, and failing of eyes and sorrow of mind" and "fear day and night."[6] In its Deuteronomic context, the verses outline the terms of agreement of God's covenant with Israel. God promises blessings in exchange for Israel's obedience, but also threatens his wrath if Israel disobeys and breaks the covenant:

> The Lord will scatter you among all the peoples from one end of the earth to the other, and there you shall serve other gods, wood and stone, whom neither you nor your ancestors have experienced. Yet even among those nations you shall find no peace, nor shall your foot find a place to rest. The Lord will give you there an anguished heart and eyes that pine and a despondent spirit. The life you face shall be precarious; you shall be in terror, night and day, and with no assurance of survival. In the morning you shall say, "If only it were evening!" and in the evening you shall say, "If only it were morning!" because of what your heart shall dread and your eyes shall see.

Although Gaebelein knew the original context and, presumably, the historical series of events in which Israelites were scattered into diaspora long before the birth of Jesus, he interpreted the passage as proof that Jews suffered because they had failed to accept Jesus as their messiah. "Despondent spirits" and "anguished hearts" would continue to haunt these scattered present-day Jews.

Gaebelein's pathos-laden interpretation of Jewish diaspora relied on both biblical and scientific texts. "This prediction has found its fulfillment, as well as many others, among the Jews for many generations," Gaebelein explained of the Deuteronomic verses. However, his interpretation of the physical ailments threatened to a disobedient Israel implied something distinctive: as a result of the Jewish people's rejection of Jesus, Jewish men suffered "nervous diseases," which were normally considered afflictions of women. The prediction he read into the text was a medical one, and so he used the findings of medical doctors and anthropologists to buttress his theological interpretation: "A leading Jewish specialist on nervous diseases declares that Jews are more subject to diseases of the nervous system than the other races among whom they dwell. Hysteria and neurasthenia appear to be the most frequent."[7] He went on to cite another scientist's work indicating that Jews were "almost exclusively the inexhaustible source for the supply of hysterical males for the whole [European] Continent. This liability to nervous disorders is the result of the curse which rests upon the race, 'the trembling heart and the sorrow of mind' as mentioned in the above passage of Deuteronomy."[8] Using a complex definition of Jewishness that relied on both religion and medicine, Gaebelein suggested that Jews suffered for both hereditary and theological reasons.

Popular medical discourse had linked these nervous diseases to women or to a failure of proper masculinity in men and often recommended that they be prevented by strenuous physical activity or combated with fresh air. As Sander Gilman and others have demonstrated, early twentieth-century scientific knowledge in Europe and the United States posited strong links among Jewishness, nervous diseases, and femininity.[9] Jews and non-Jews alike participated in the medical discourses that created a constellation of weakness, nervousness, lack of physical activity, and Jewishness. Confounding any essentially biological notion of nervousness, Arno Gaebelein and the readers of *Our Hope* proposed a different treatment for the malaise of these nervous Jews: conversion.

Gaebelein's analysis points to the wider missionary attention to the relationship between Jewishness and masculinity. Other missionaries, in particular Jews who converted and subsequently proselytized among other Jews, grappled with ways to understand Jewish difference in the context of both religion and gender. Their writings were all polemical texts, so it is unsurprising that they highlighted differences between Judaism and Christianity. In fact, their theology hinged on the existence of such a distinction. But two recurring themes underlying this distinction are less expected. First, they depicted Jewish men differently from Christian men, and not merely on the theological grounds that the former had accepted Jesus and the latter had not: they described gendered differences between Jewish and Christian men. There is no reason that making a distinction between Christianity and Judaism would require making a gendered distinction between the two, but these texts did. Second, these texts are remarkable because of the way they value these differences in masculinity. They did not suggest, as we might anticipate, that conversion to Christianity moved Jewish men from an inferior masculinity to a superior one. Although they depicted conversion as a moral and spiritual upgrade, they did not imply it was a gendered one. Jewish masculinity, in these texts, had much to recommend it.

In the context of American Protestant missions to the Jews, the available signifiers were not merely masculine versus feminine. Failure to enact one kind of masculinity did not necessarily imply femininity. Rather different kinds of masculinity could coexist. And in these missionary documents, they did. On the one hand, they painted Christian masculinity with the broad strokes of physical prowess, might, and willingness to fight. On the other, they associated Jewish masculinity with gentleness and quietness in the face of suffering. Sometimes by implicit comparison with Jesus and sometimes by contrast with Christian masculinity, these missionaries show one significant way that ideas about Christianity structured American Jewish masculinity.

Protestant Missions to the Jews

Although conversions from Christianity to Judaism were numerically few, they loomed large in the imagination of both religious communities. For many Christians seeking converts, Jews played a particularly important theological role. And for Jews, the existence and rhetoric of Christian missionaries constituted a major concern by reinforcing ideas of fundamental Jewish difference from other white Americans, especially gendered difference. When missionaries used the language of blind and suffering men, who were perhaps even suffering from neurasthenia as Gaebelein suggested, they implied that Jews were not up to the bodily ideals of American manliness. Such language propagated negative images of Jews, and the Jewish community knew it.

American Protestant missions to American Jews grew in both number and visibility between 1900 and 1924, despite securing few baptisms or permanent converts.[10] This increase resulted from a combination of the rise of premillennialist theology, which emphasized the role of Jews in the end times, and the growing numbers of working-class Jewish immigrants, who were the most responsive to the missions, even if only out of curiosity or a desire for assistance.[11]

Premillennialist theology holds that the human world will deteriorate until Jesus physically returns to earth to usher in the millennium. Many premillennialists also believe that, when Jesus returns to judge the wicked, the faithful will be caught up in a rapture and therefore will avoid the consequent terror and suffering. According to most premillennialist interpretations, 144,000 Jews who knew the Christian gospel but had not yet accepted it would remain on earth during the rapture. Having been taught by Hebrew-Christian missionaries, these surviving Jews would then serve as evangelists to the rest of humankind that had been left on earth. Jews are of additional symbolic importance for premillennialists because any current success in bringing Jews to believe in the Christian gospel was interpreted as a harbinger of the time when the 144,000 Jews would come to believe.

Postmillennialists, in comparison, hold that the kingdom of God will gradually spread over the earth—with the help of humans—and that this gradual improvement will ultimately result in the millennium. Many adherents of the Social Gospel, for instance, held postmillennialist views. Still other American Christians, especially many members of liberal denominations, such as Congregationalists and Episcopalians, were nonmillennialists whose theology remained mainly unconcerned with the end times. Major missionary enterprises to Jews, however, were most heavily concentrated in Christian communities with premillennialist theologies.

Missions to the Jews were urban phenomena. Most openly targeted immigrants, as the predominance of Yiddish in the missionary literature attests. They also tailored their seemingly nonreligious offerings, such as medical care, food, English lessons, and the procurement of employment, to immigrants. Many Jewish immigrants expressed some curiosity—even if it was sometimes mixed with fear—about Christianity, and attending Christian lectures was an occasional practice of acculturated and immigrant Jews alike. Although Eastern European Jews had encountered Christians both before and after immigration, many lacked even a basic understanding of Christianity. Acculturated American Jews, in contrast, were much more familiar with their Christian neighbors' beliefs and practices and also less in need of the basic social services the missions offered. By offering some of the same social services as the settlement houses of the era, missions were able to entice some immigrant Jews to come through their doors. But a soul through the door of an English class did not often translate into a soul won for Christ.

Although these missions had a presence in most major cities with large Jewish populations, they never gained significant numbers of converts. Decades earlier, the *Philadelphia Sunday Dispatch* had wryly noted that the Society for the Promotion of Christianity among the Jews had averaged the conversion of "a sixth of a Jew per annum."[12] The conversion rate had increased only marginally by the 1920s.[13] Despite the larger number of missions, the trend of the fractional Jewish convert continued for many decades. At the 1917 annual convention of the Central Conference of American Rabbis (CCAR), the Reform rabbinical association, Gotthard Deutsch reported that the activities of the mission to the Jews "are very insignificant and [the] results, except in so far as they give employment to a converted Jew, are practically nil."[14] Nevertheless, Jewish communities across the country fought against missionaries and their propaganda.[15] And many Protestants continued to care about these missions because of their theological convictions, in particular the idea that converted Jews could facilitate the fulfillment of prophecy about the millennium.

Though they were least vulnerable to urban settlement-style missions, it was acculturated Jews who objected the most consistently to their activities, as Yaakov Ariel has shown.[16] But why would acculturated Jews continue to expend any effort fighting such unsuccessful conversion projects? They were worried by the continuing presence and message of these missions that emphasized Jews' difference from their mostly Christian neighbors. Acculturated Jews' objections reflected two broad concerns. First, missionary activities suggested that Judaism was not a legitimate religion. Christian missionaries held that Christianity had superseded Judaism, leaving it a religious vestige claiming only benighted souls.

These Christian theological assumptions raised Jewish fears about the public perception of Judaism as unacceptable, premodern, and un-American religion. It was not considered "good" religion because it was stuck in a tribal, particular past that refused the universalizing message of Jesus. Furthermore, missionary literature frequently expressed the content of this theological difference through bodily metaphors, such as blindness and hardheartedness, common biblical tropes associated with nonbelievers.[17] These bodily defects implied that Jews did not meet the standards of a healthy masculinity. If missionaries like Gaebelein were out there painting Jews as people with unhealthy bodies, this talk would directly oppose the image of healthy Jewish men that acculturated Jews were trying to promote.

Their second, and related, concern was that the missionary agenda sometimes conflated Christianity with American citizenship and loyalty. Although American nationalism was always on the radar—and, as Part II will show, connections to the American land were an important part of American Jewish masculinity—nativism became especially visible during the war years. Leo Franklin, in his President's Address to the 1920 annual meeting of the CCAR, complained, "It was perhaps but natural that the Christian churches in their overzeal to gain adherents to their cause, came to identify the terms 'Christianization' and 'Americanization' to such an extent that in many of their public announcements they used the terms interchangeably." These Christian missionary activities conflated normative American manhood and Christian manhood. Both, Franklin was "outraged" to observe, reflected "the implication that Jews are not and as Jews may not be loyal Americans."[18] After noting his success in persuading the Episcopal Church to change the name of its "Bureau of Christian Americanization" to the "Department of Religious Work among Foreign Born Americans," Franklin called for increased public advocacy with the same aim. Christian churches and missionaries "must desist from using such terms as would imply the limited patriotic loyalty of the Jew."[19] Given that such missionary language suggested that Jews were not good American citizens, acculturated Jews sought to curtail or change it.

Acculturated Jews thus sometimes saw missionary activity—whether or not it resulted in conversions to Christianity—as a threat to their civic status in the United States. This civic status, as Matthew Frye Jacobsen, Gail Bederman, and others argue, had close ties to ideas of proper white, middle-class masculinity in the Progressive Era.[20] Some aspects of Jewish masculinity, such as gentleness or nonaggressiveness, would create little friction with images of a good male citizen. But when missionary voices promoted embodied images of Jewish masculinity, such as blindness or moments of weeping, that did not fit neatly with wider American ideas about citizenship, then Jews would want to quiet those voices. Part of the reason that Jews continued to combat these missionary activities, then, was their concern that missionary rhetoric reinforced ideas of Jewish difference, especially gendered difference.

Although the discourses of citizenship and civilization were important for both acculturated Jews and nonmillennialist Protestants, they rarely appeared in the narratives of the millennially inclined Hebrew-Christian missionaries themselves. Eli Lederhendler has argued that the idea of Jewish "regeneration" percolated to the surface during the early twentieth century.[21] He contends that a significant amount of American Jewish rhetoric—from such diverse sources as Judah Magnes and Israel Joseph Zevin, a Yiddish writer known as Tashrak—connected Americanization to the "regeneration" of men in particular. The details of this regeneration and manliness varied from full emancipation and citizenship (Magnes) to self-control and cleanliness (Tashrak).

The missionary literature, however, suggests that, while Lederhendler's thesis about the discourse of "regeneration" and manliness may apply to those specifically interested in Americanization and citizenship, it does not extend to missionary fields. Pamphlets and publications put out by missions to the Jews rarely mentioned the meaning of America, the role of American culture and democracy in the making of manly men, or the value of "one hundred percent Americanism," a popular phrase that emphasized the benefits of complete assimilation. Yet the missionaries cared deeply about masculinity. Instead of making a political argument, they framed their explanations of Jewish masculinity in a theological context. They did not seek to effect "regeneration" or to remedy manliness through secular means such as gymnastics or sports, nor did they think that Jewish gentleness or meekness represented a negative quality.

Because few non-Jews spoke Yiddish or understood all of the cultural idioms and religious practices of Jewish immigrants, Hebrew-Christians urged their Jewish converts to become missionaries themselves.[22] Although there are no definite statistics, a significant proportion of missionaries to the Jews were themselves converts to Christianity, although the raw numbers remained very small. For instance, of the thirty-six American missionaries to the Jews whom Albert Edward Thompson named in his 1902 book *A Century of Jewish Missions*, at least twenty-one were Jewish men who converted to Christianity.[23] (Women occupied only auxiliary roles, typically as helpers to their missionary husbands.) These newly Christian men proved immensely unpopular within Jewish communities—Isaac Mayer Wise once called them "rascals without exception."[24] They wrote mostly for Christian audiences who were curious about Judaism or for potential donors to the cause of Christian missions to the Jews. They did, however, have the experience of living in—although often at the margins of—both Jewish and Christian communities.[25]

Yet Jews who converted, even if they became Christian missionaries, never completely stopped being Jews in the eyes of other Christians. Both theologically and sociologically, they lived perpetually in the liminal category of "Hebrew-Christian." (The converts themselves and the Christian community also used the terms "converted Jew" or "Christian Jew.") These labels themselves emphasized their distinctiveness. Rarely identified simply as "Christians," these individuals gave lectures, wrote reflections, and even identified with communities that made reference to their Jewishness. Missionaries pursued several efforts to create congregations composed solely of Hebrew-Christians. Apart from those congregations, many Hebrew-Christians found it difficult to integrate themselves into gentile Christian communities.

Yet, missions and churches continued to identify Hebrew-Christians by their Jewish roots. It was not solely as a way to mark them as other or lesser. In fact, it served both strategic and theological purposes. In some ways, retaining some Jewish identification was a marketing strategy. Many converts who had had traditional Jewish training, such as Leopold Cohn and Joseph Goldman, even retained the title "rabbi" in their missionary activities. In doing so, they could trade on their intellectual and religious authority as learned men within immigrant Jewish communities. Associating with "rabbis" was also a feather in the cap of these missions, presumably suggesting that they had attracted religiously serious men, not mere hypocrites, ignoramuses, or social climbers. Cohn, Goldman, and many other Hebrew-Christian missionaries continued to refer to themselves as Jewish, and they framed their belief in Jesus as "the real Jewish faith."[26]

Their "real Jewish faith" could even retain elements of Judaism, though the Christian context transformed their meaning. A 1908 conference attended by both gentile Christian and Hebrew-Christian missionaries to the Jews produced "general agreement on the position that Hebrew Christians should be . . . free to observe what Mosaic laws and customs they choose, without depending on them as means of salvation or grace."[27] Continuing the Jewish rituals of their past religious lives was a matter of choice for converts, the missionaries asserted. Yet, salvation could come only through Jesus, and the religious trappings of halakhah became a matter of personal choice rather than divine command. This Christian religion was freely chosen, rather than determined by race or ancestry.

Nevertheless, even absent a distinctive theological meaning in the context of personal salvation, Hebrew-Christians' observance of halakhah served a purpose for the missions. When these converted Jews practiced Jewish ritual, it marked Hebrew-Christians as distinct from gentile Christians. In fact, many missions, such as Gaebelein's Hope of Israel, encouraged Jewish converts to continue Jewish religious practices. Jewish symbols like the Magen David (Star of David) that appeared on the materials of much missionary literature reinforced the continuity of the identity "Jewish" in the eyes of premillennial Protestants. Moreover, identifying Hebrew-Christian missionaries as Jews—and therefore educators of the 144,000—emphasized progress toward the end days anticipated by premillennial Protestants.

Even Jewish communities thought of converts as retaining some sort of Jewishness. When Gotthard Deutsch talked about missions providing employment to the "converted Jew," or when Jews accused other Jews of converting merely for material benefit, they all assumed that the convert was, in some sense, still Jewish. Both Jews and Christians, then, thought of Hebrew-Christians as embodying at least some aspects of Jewishness even after they converted.

Men at the Missionary Margins

The American missionary imagination of gender challenges the scholarly formulation of the "feminization of Jews" in two ways. First, neither Hebrew-Christian missionaries nor their audiences imagined that male Jews were "feminine" in any significant sense of the word. Rather, they perceived Jews as embodying a different kind of masculinity, characterized by gentleness and quietness in the face of suffering. To use the rubric of "feminization" in this case would neglect the complexity present in these multiple constructions of masculinity. Second, the writings of these missionaries confound the idea that a differently gendered Jew is always an idea held by antisemites and self-hating Jews. These Hebrew-Christian missionaries saw themselves as ethnically (or, "racially," to use their term) and physically Jewish, with an identity and religious system that had been fulfilled in Jesus Christ. They did *not* think that they were degenerate or feminine men, and so they did not use the language or concepts of regeneration.[28] Instead, they saw themselves as embodying the gentleness and peacefulness called for by Scripture and epitomized by Jesus, whose Jewishness they often celebrated.[29] Seeing the possibility of multiple coexisting masculinities—rather than seeing any non-normative masculinity as "feminization"—helps us better understand the gendered constructions of American Judaism.

Furthermore, missionary activity and the response to it drew attention from both Jewish and Christian communities and sometimes became the grounds for contest between the two. Many missions heeded Jewish objections to activities that Jews saw as bribery, trickery, and the targeting of children and largely ceased engaging in them.[30] Earlier, nineteenth-century missions, as a stone in the shoe of American Jewry, had impelled Jewish communities to provide needed social, educational, and medical services for working-class Jews.[31] But in the early twentieth century, missionary texts suggest that there were debates not only over social services and theology but also over cultural assumptions (and accusations) about the status of masculinity in Christianity and Judaism.

In these years, Christian missionaries—both men and women—often assumed that men were the "natural" missionaries and that women were best suited to be auxiliaries.[32] Therefore, barring a few exceptions, most American missionaries to the Jews were men.[33] Furthermore, most missions concentrated their efforts on young immigrant Jewish men because they were the ones most likely to convert. Young Jewish men were more likely to immigrate alone, to live apart from parents, and to marry non-Jews than their female counterparts.[34] As immigrants with fewer intimate social and familial ties, some of these young Jewish men seemed to be better targets than women from the missionaries' perspective.

Several of the Jewish men who became missionaries framed part of the difference between Christian and Jewish men in explicitly physical terms. Self-styled "Ex-Rabbi Joseph Goldman" had emigrated to the American West from Russia after his conversion there. He then took up missionary activity, often speaking in Methodist churches.[35] In his speeches and writings Goldman commented on circumcision, the fundamental bodily marker of male Jewishness. In his 1919 *Judaism and Its Traditions: The Conversion of a Hebrew Rabbi*, he wrote, "I could not explain to you the great meaning and benefit to man of circumcision. I may explain to any man privately, or by mail, if required."[36] By declining to discuss circumcision, he shrouded the practice and the Jewish male body in mystery, enhancing its "otherness" for the assumed Christian reader. Despite the fact that the practice was becoming widespread among non-Jews, Goldman framed it as having esoteric meaning.[37] As a Jewish man, he had knowledge of circumcision's sexual "meaning and benefit" that was unsuitable to be shared publicly or with women. The dual characterization of "meaning" and "benefit" indicated that the covenant with God, through removal of the foreskin, was a difference that was at once theological, physical, and essential to Jewish manhood.[38] Goldman's text also reflected the idea that Jewish converts to Christianity could never completely shed their Jewishness in either social or physical contexts.[39] His very discussion of circumcision reinforced this perception: a convert's body would always be marked as Jewish, even if he had proclaimed his belief in Jesus as the messiah. In this sense, the Jewish male body confounded the idea of complete conversion.[40] For Goldman, who remained a Christian for the rest of his life, the Jewish male body also continued to mark Judaism as inherently particularist. The mark of circumcision set Jews apart, a physical marker of the tribal nature of Judaism, in contrast to the universality of Christianity.

Goldman also characterized "the Jewish man" on the Sabbath as a gentle man dressed in flowing garments: "Father comes in looking like a prophet, his long beard combed clean, wearing his silk robe and slippers, a smile on his face. He takes the baby on his arm and the other children [hold] his robe." The picture of robe, slippers, and children suggests a man comfortable and happy with domesticity. The rabbi too, as the leader of the community, fit the same description: "With his long silk robe and white beard, his usual smile on his face and his top hat on his head, he looked like a prophet."[41] In contrast, the Jewish man at work had a "back bent with burden;" he was a "suffering Jew" and "a slave."[42] The Jew was at his happiest on the Sabbath, when he was the learned prophet, benevolent father, and religious practitioner.

Although Goldman portrayed much of Jewish religious practice as superstitious ("The fingernails must be washed because Satan was resting through the night under my fingernails"[43]), he retained a respectful tone for individual Jewish men and women. This was typical of missionaries. Whatever their misgivings about Jews' opinions and behavior, they knew that Jews were essential for the divine plan for the end times.[44] Goldman's picture of the Jewish man was not the feminized Jew of antisemitic literature, but neither was he Max Nordau's muscle-Jew.[45] Instead, he was gentle, learned, physically downtrodden, and suffering.

Goldman titled the pivotal chapter of his book, "My Conversion and Persecution," which detailed the physical abuse he endured as a result of his conversion. He tells tales of congregants pulling him from the pulpit as soon as he uttered Jesus's name, children throwing stones, men spitting in his face, and his "greatest suffering[,] that of a father when he loves his child who is stretching out her little arms for her father to take her," but he could not because his wife had banished him from his home. Christian readers took note of Goldman's autobiography and its message of suffering. A Lutheran review called it "well worth the moderate cost," and the Baptist *Journal and Messenger* expressed its "hope that many of our readers will try to get a hold of the book and read it, to their own profit."[46] William Bryant, a reviewer for the Presbyterian publication *The Herald and Presbyter*, wrote that Goldman's suffering "appeals to our hearts" and that he "must know, as few of us can, how Paul felt under persecution." Suffering borne without retaliation, in Goldman's tale, was associated with Jewishness, Jesus, and Paul.

Goldman's story pulled at the theological heartstrings, but in his review, Bryant also noted the dual importance of Christianity and America: "Ex-Rabbi Goldman was very positive that the only country in the world where a Jew has the right of manhood is America."[47] Yet Goldman had converted to Christianity before coming to America. Either Bryant assumed that Goldman was still, in some important sense, a Jew—such as a "converted Jew"—or he assumed that Goldman had made a statement about the opportunities for his former coreligionists. In either case, both reviewer and author suggested there was something distinctive about America that allowed Jewish "manhood" to flourish in a way that Eastern European countries did not. And this manhood was one that included gentleness and quietly borne physical and emotional suffering, rather than masculine ideals of physical prowess and mastery over the self and environment.

Other Hebrew-Christian missionaries also emphasized the themes of their own physical suffering. Leopold Cohn, who had converted shortly after emigrating from Hungary, received Baptist ordination and opened a mission to the Jews in 1894. Cohn demonstrated a knowledge of rabbinic texts and claimed to have been ordained a rabbi at age eighteen, but Rabbi David Einhorn and other Jewish leaders called that background into question. Instead, they claimed, Cohn's real name was Itsak Leib Joszovics and he had been a saloonkeeper.[48] In 1913, several relatives of Joszovics came forward seeking damages from Cohn, whom they insisted was Itsak Leib. The episode was chronicled in the 1918 *The Strange Story of Dr. Cohn and Mr. Joszovics (with apologies to Dr. Jekyl and Mr. Hyde).*[49]

But whatever the truth of his biography, the author Cohn framed his suffering as an essential part of his story. In his memoir, Cohn relayed stories of Christian children physically abusing his children. After fracturing his son's leg and cutting his lip, these boys said, "This is the way sheenies cry," and "This is the way we have to do with sheenies."[50] The neighborhood boys identified Cohn's children as Jewish, and they suffered as a result. But they never fought back. To comfort them, Cohn's wife, who was also a convert, told the boys "how the Lord Jesus suffered."

In narrating the story, Cohn aligned the Christian theology of the suffering servant—Isaiah 53 was a favorite among Hebrew-Christian missionaries—with the gentleness of Jewish masculinity. His tale also functioned as an inversion of the myth of ignorant Jews persecuting a peaceful and non-retaliating Jesus. Throughout his writings, Cohn most often referred to Jesus as "the Crucified One." The name "the Crucified One" not only emphasized Jesus's suffering but also recalled traditional Jewish references to Jesus: the Hebrew *toleh* and Yiddish *toyleh*, which mean "the hanged one." Both are used in both the Talmud and everyday speech by traditional Jews to refer to Jesus, rather than using his name.

Converted Jews outside of premillenialist communities echoed the assumptions about gender difference, even though their theology excluded the vision of the 144,000 and the end days. Edward Steiner, a Jewish convert who became a Presbyterian minister but never served as a missionary, told the story of his quiet suffering at the hands of the world and his identification with Jesus. As a child in Slovakia, he was punished by both Christians and Jews for habitually peeking into a local chapel. "I felt a premonition that some day I should enter into whatever experiences the cross held for a human soul," he wrote as he reflected on the experience. Steiner also explicitly identified with Jesus because of his Jewishness and his suffering: "I pitied Him, and, oh, I knew just how to pity Him! No Gentile knows the woes of Christ as we who are His kin, and who are not so alien to His spirit as others think. And so I pitied Him because He was a Jew, smitten and cursed, and crucified again, by one for whom He died."[51] Steiner identified with Jesus and his suffering, not in spite of being a Jewish man, but precisely because of it.

Steiner attributed his success to both his Americanization and his Christianity. And both, he indicated, contributed to his ability to become truly manly. "I felt like kneeling down and thanking God for my confidence in my fellow men and for this country; for the opportunity it gives us all to rise from the pit of the mine and from the burning furnaces to the full glory of manhood."[52] Steiner took a particular interest in transforming new immigrants into strong and virtuous young Americans, but he explained that he had "never met more manly men" than his "brother ministers."[53] After completing a PhD at the University of Heidelberg, Steiner arrived in the United States in the 1880s and quickly embraced his new nation. Steiner then converted to Christianity and went on to become a professor of "Applied Christianity" at Grinnell College and a leading voice for the Social Gospel.

Throughout his career, he was a prolific author of texts on immigration and Americanization, and occasionally he tried his hand at fiction. His 1907 novel *The Mediator* told the triumphant story of Samuel, a Jew who becomes a Christian missionary on the Lower East Side. Like the autobiographies of Goldman and Cohn, it "picture[d] the sufferings of the Jews and their noble traits," in the words of *The Missionary Review of the World*.[54] On a literal level, Samuel became the mediator between religions and cultures, but on a literary level, Steiner suggested that Christ was the mediator between Jews and Christians, between immigrants and established Americans. Despite running in different theological, ideological, and social circles from Goldman and Cohn, Steiner associated his pre-Christian— that is to say, Jewish—life with weakness, and subsequent "manly men" with his converted life and Christian brothers.

In a 1925 autobiographical essay, Steiner recalled an episode from his youth. He was having a theological discussion with a Protestant boy and a Catholic boy after they had gone swimming in a pond next to an off-limits orchard. The three argued: If religions were a tree, was Judaism the root? Was Catholicism or Protestantism the leaves, which just died and were good only for mulch? Which was the trunk? After the Catholic boy insisted that the biblical patriarchs were Catholics, the young Steiner piped up:

> "No, they were Jews," I interrupted, nervously fingering my sacred fringes. . . . It took courage to contradict the angered Catholic, whom I feared and envied, and almost worshiped, for he could do all those things I could not do: swim, climb trees, rob birds' nests and ride horses bareback. While I was muscularly weak and physically a coward, I always dreamed of climbing trees and mountains, hunting wild beasts, and fighting in battle, yet I couldn't turn a decent somersault or climb unassisted the wall which led to the forbidden swimming pool and the still more forbidden orchard. This time I was brave, my courage reinforced by kissing the sacred fringes.[55]

Steiner described the Catholic boy with near-religious reverence—a mix of fear, awe, and admiration. This "almost worship" showed the value Steiner placed on a manliness of physical strength and bravery.

Although Steiner dreamt of fighting and conquering, that kind of manliness was not his own. He was "muscularly weak and physically a coward." In this encounter with the Catholic boy, Steiner only managed to screw up his courage on behalf of his religion, not to perform the physical feats of his male peers. His prayer garment brought him the courage to speak up in the beginning when he "nervously fingered his sacred fringes." Then he kissed it, as if it were a talisman, and with that kiss he found some measure of bravery. As the incident continued, however, it became clear that the bravery Steiner required was not the courage to vanquish, but rather the courage to endure suffering.

The theological debate swiftly escalated into a brawl. The Catholic boy held down the Protestant boy and insisted that he would only let him up after the Protestant submitted to his theological metaphor: "Now say this after me . . . The Catholic Church is the root and the trunk, the Jews are nothing at all, and the Protestants are the leaves, out of which cows make manure." Face punching ensued. Steiner characterized himself as a poor fighter but nevertheless duty-bound to defend the Protestant boy and the insult to Judaism: "I did not know how to fight, and when I fought I fought badly—coward fashion—with my fingernails; but, poor fighter that I was, I threw myself on top of the triumphant Catholic."[56] Steiner quickly ended up with the Catholic boy's knee digging into his stomach and the boy's fists flying at his face. "Not a word came from my lips, and I took the repeated blows without crying out," he recalled.

But the pain and the insult became too much when both boys began to beat him. "Finally I burst into tears, for the Protestant joined the Catholic in belaboring the 'Jew-boy.'" The name "Jew-boy" was insulting, but its language recalled another moment in Steiner's autobiographical writings that was not only bitter but also sweet. In a 1910 essay, Steiner clearly remembered the kindness of a woman who fed him and sent him home after a different beating at the hands of Christian children. Steiner was one of three boys who had dressed up as the wise men before Christmas. At one house a boy tussled with Steiner, and the boy's father, learning of Steiner's Jewishness threw him out and down the stairs. But when the boy's older sister came and found Steiner and he blurted out that he was Jewish, she kissed him and told him, "Our Lord was a little Jewish boy, just like you."[57] He recalled the incident with sweetness, remembering her kisses and feeling joy at being compared to Jesus. Likewise, Steiner suffered the abuse of the Catholic and Protestant boys at the orchard but did not recall the incident with shame. The young Steiner, like Jesus, suffered valiantly, displaying the courage to endure rather than attack.

A desire for a certain kind of manliness remained a theme in Steiner's religious life. In "Awakened Judaism," another autobiographical essay, he noted that, had the Zionist movement become influential earlier in his life, he might have embraced it and its visions of Jewishness instead of converting to Christianity. "It is difficult of course to say what would have been my view-point had I met Theodor Herzl twenty or more years ago. I might have returned bravely 'to my people,'" Steiner wrote. "But when one meets Jesus of Nazareth there is no way back; there are new marching orders, and they call 'Forward.'"[58] Once a man met Jesus, Steiner wrote, he could not deny the call of duty. In an alternative timeline, Steiner might have become a brave and manly Zionist, he explained, but in the life he lived, he was a brave and manly soldier for Jesus instead. In his life as a Christian, brave and manly meant identifying with a peaceful and gentle Christ, rather than a strong and muscular Zionist.

Like Goldman, Cohn, and Steiner, Samuel Freuder lived in the marginal space of the Jewish convert to Christianity. But unlike Goldman, who converted to Christianity and then wrote from the perspective of a Hebrew-Christian, Freuder returned to Judaism before writing a book about his experience. His story garnered enough attention that the well-known Zionist and Reform rabbi Stephen Wise wrote the introduction to its second edition.[59] Freuder was born in Hungary, and Jewish religious vocations ran in his family: both his father and grandfather served as *hazanim* (cantors). After a traditional upbringing filled with Talmud study, he set off to Berlin to become a rabbi. Once there, he found the religious innovations of Reform and the historical study of Judaism both alluring and disturbing, and only found relief from his intellectual conundrum when he decided to make a new life for himself in the United States.

Soon after his 1883 immigration, however, Freuder found himself immersed in the intellectual and religious framework he had found so challenging while in Berlin. He went to study at the newly formed Hebrew Union College in Cincinnati and subsequently accepted a series of positions as a pulpit rabbi. These never quite worked out. Then, in 1891, Freuder publicly announced his conversion to Congregationalism. Unlike premillenialist Protestants, Congregationalists espoused a nonmillennialist theology, which does not affirm a literal thousand-year earthly reign of Jesus. The conversion of Freuder, for these theologically liberal Protestants, would not have represented a step toward the end times. But he would still represent an important convert testifying to the universality of Christianity. For seventeen years, first as a Congregationalist and later as an Episcopalian, Freuder pursued religious training and then became a missionary to Jews. Then Freuder dramatically converted back to Judaism. As he told the story (and as it was reported in the *Boston Globe*), he was expected to give a lecture on Jesus in the Talmud. Instead, he stood up, derided American missions, and announced his return to Judaism.[60] Although Freuder's later writing showed a respect for much of Christian theology, he ultimately found the missionary enterprise deceitful and unpleasant.[61] After his "theatrical"[62] return to Judaism, Freuder penned a detailed account of the Hebrew-Christian missionary world and his own experience as a missionary more broadly.

Perhaps in part because the press had printed accounts of Freuder's conversion, other Jews responded in support of his book. Despite concerns about his "grave error" in converting, a geographically and religiously diverse group of Jewish leaders banded together to send letters promoting his *A Missionary's Return to Judaism: The Truth about the Christian Missions to the Jews*.[63] If people were going to talk about Freuder anyway, their response suggests, at least his story could be a cautionary tale about the disappointments and dangers of Jews converting to Christianity. Leading Jewish dignitaries wrote that they were "of the opinion, that Mr. Freuder deserves our generous sympathy and that the book is worthy of a wide distribution."[64] They included Gotthard Deutsch (on the faculty at Hebrew Union College), Max Heller (a New Orleans Reform rabbi and outspoken Zionist), Albert Lucas (the honorary secretary of the national organization of Orthodox congregations and the contact person for ordering the book in bulk), Henry Pereira Mendes (perhaps the most high-profile Sephardic rabbi of the period), Joseph Stolz (a Chicago Reform rabbi), and Martin Meyer (a San Francisco Reform rabbi). Not only did the book present "an interesting document of human psychology," they wrote, but more importantly, "it is a clear presentation of the nefarious practices of the missionaries, and will prove valuable both as an exposure of the methods of Hebrew-Christian Missions and as a warning to our communities of the temptations and dangers to which our young people are constantly subjected."[65] Zionists and anti-Zionists, Reform and Orthodox Jews, such as these men, agreed about the importance of promoting the volume, making it clear that these missions and missionaries concerned a variety of American Jews.

Freuder's book, in addition to exposing "nefarious" practices of missionizing, shed light on perceived differences between the ways in which Jewish men and Christian men enacted their gender, part of what Gotthard Deutsch and his coauthors deemed the book's "interesting human psychology." Freuder disparaged what he saw as the religiously "misguided" gender roles of Hasidic Jews from Eastern Europe: "The Hasidim are fervent in their prayers, . . . which occupy most of the day, while their wives are tending to the shop and other bread-winning occupations."[66] Freuder was dismayed by the plight of Jewish women in Orthodox communities, at least as he imagined them. While their husbands were praying all day, women had to work in shops and other "bread-winning" occupations. These roles of Jewish men and women, which were quite contrary to American norms, struck Freuder as signs of an unwillingness to join modernity.

Freuder portrayed at length one fellow Jew-turned-Christian-missionary. "The missionary *shammos* [attendant or sexton]" as Freuder termed his acquaintance, illustrated assumptions about the differences in masculinity between Christianity and Judaism. Freuder's portrayal of the *shammos* painted a picture of the triumph of the physical over the mental: "His strong arm came to be known and respected by all who brought to the meetings an exuberant spirit of frolic and fun. If any of them showed the slightest inclination to break up the meeting, he would raise his powerful arm, clench his fist, and shout at the top of his voice, 'Say, fellows, if you don't shut up, I'll make you. I'll throw you out of doors, Christianity or no Christianity!'" Freuder identified this missionary by his "strong" and "powerful" arm; unlike the image of the sages of traditional Judaism, this *shammos* was all brawn and few brains. He addressed the other attendees as "fellows" and instructed them to "shut up," and in doing so he commanded respect. Rather than engaging in the respectful debate of traditional Jewish learning, he verbally dominated his opponents. The *shammos* showed his preference for physical strength in the form of forcible removal over any theology when he yelled, "I'll throw you out of doors, Christianity or no Christianity!" Certainly, Freuder had a contentious history with missions, and this is doubtless part of the reason why he implied that the *shammos* knew and cared little about the tenets of his new religion. Nevertheless, it is remarkable that he portrayed the *shammos* as delighting in the physicality of the possible encounter with rabble-rousers.

Freuder explained that the *shammos* also backed up these threats with physical actions: "In case his warning went unheeded he would rush at the offender, lift him out of his seat, and shove him out into the street as if he were a sack of flour. His drastic methods of dealing with refractory hearers of the Gospel were of course openly disavowed by the Christians present, but he did not mind their rebuke, because he felt sure his Christian friends inwardly approved and admired his exhibition of 'muscular Christianity.'"[67] The *shammos*, according to Freuder, used his physical strength and intimidation to control attendees at least in part because he imagined that this kind of display of manliness was an embodiment of the ideals of "muscular Christianity," a contemporary term for the movement that sought to redefine ideal Christian manhood in terms emphasizing physical strength and well-being through competitive sports and physical education.[68] That is, the *shammos* associated Christianity with a masculinity of strong arms and self-assertion. Therefore, he felt certain that other Christians "inwardly approved and admired" his display of these gender ideals.

In Freuder's eyes, unlike the Hasidim who (seemingly ineffectually) sang and danced their prayers while the women did "real" work (which for him should have been the men's responsibility), this *shammos* prayed at a different gendered extreme. "Even while he prayed, he would shake his fist at some disturber,"[69] Freuder recounted. Even Christian prayer, for the *shammos*, was an exercise in exerting one's muscular strength and physical dominance. Proper comportment for a man in prayer, in accordance with middle-class norms of the day, included decorum and reverence; appropriate men would veer neither toward ecstatic dancing and singing nor toward physically dominating others around them. Ultimately, the *shammos*'s career as a missionary came to a fitting end when another missionary made "a slurring remark about the Jews . . . [; the *shammos*] ran up to him, and smote him in the face."[70]

In *A Missionary's Return to Judaism*, Freuder recounted running into him fifteen years later. The *shammos* had left the Christian fold and returned to Judaism, and the two talked about the past and ruminated about the nature of masculinity in religious life. Freuder began his account of the conversation by pointing out the *shammos*'s poor grammar, a sign of his lack of the education so valued in Jewish tradition: "Speaking of his missionary life, he said: 'Christianity has learned me that money is power.'" But if the *shammos* was mostly ignorant and therefore different from the ideal Jewish man, he was nevertheless manly in a different way. Freuder recalled, "On the subject of religion, he delivered himself thus: 'I know very little of religion, but I know as much as most of the religious grafters. I am as good a Jew as anybody, and if any one insults a Jew in my presence I knock him down, no matter how big a man he may be.'" In telling the story, Freuder associated physical intimidation—which the *shammos* discussed in the context of fighting to defend Jewish honor—seamlessly with the *shammos*'s Christian days. In Freuder's account, the *shammos* associated his Christian life with muscularity, physical dominance, and power. "He became suddenly reminiscent, and with pride in his manner and a touch of tenderness in his voice, he exclaimed: 'But didn't I make those fellows at the mission behave?' And involuntarily he raised his arm, still powerful, and rolled his fingers into a fist, just as he used to do nearly a score of years ago when keeping in check the would-be disturbers of the meetings at the mission." Even though he had distanced himself from Christianity, the *shammos* recalled with fondness his ability to "make those fellows" behave.

This association is particularly striking because Freuder's depiction suggests that the *shammos* acted, in fact, violently and aggressively both when he was a Christian and when he was a Jew. But both the *shammos* and Freuder nevertheless linked his Christian experience with physical aggression. Freuder concluded his account by reflecting on how the *shammos* associated physical strength and authority with his Christian days: "How strange, I thought to myself, that the only feature of his Christian life which he considered worthwhile treasuring up in his memory and recalling with a certain pleasure and pride was the brief, little authority which he exercised in his capacity as a missionary *shammos*."[71]

After his experience on the margins of both Christian and Jewish communities, Freuder described a major difference between Jewish masculinity and Christian masculinity, although in the end he suggested that Jewish masculinity would eventually become stronger and more assertive; that is, closer to (what he imagined to be) the American Christian version. Unlike Goldman and Cohn, who remained Christian missionaries, Freuder did not frame the gendered differences in theological terms. Instead, he used the language of modernization and

Americanization, discourses that were more familiar to the Jewish community to which he returned. However, despite his theological differences from other Hebrew-Christian missionaries, his depictions of Christian and Jewish masculinities aligned with theirs. As these Hebrew-Christian missionaries demonstrated, even men who were intimately familiar with both Judaism and Christianity in America saw significant differences between these two masculinities.

Freuder's critique also suggested another important component of Jewish masculinity: not all Judaism was the same when it came to gender. When Freuder disparaged the gender roles of the Hasidim, he complained not only about the "bread-winning" women, but also about the emotionalism and physicality of the men's religious practice, which he saw as unseemly: "The Hasidim are fervent in their prayers, which they recite with a great deal of shouting and even dancing."[72] He compared them to the "shouting Methodists" and the "Holy Jumpers," more familiar ecstatic religious practitioners—and occasional embarrassments to other Christians—on the American scene. Freuder characterized Hasidic Jewish piety as particularly distressing and found the stereotyped image of shouting and dancing men surprising and out of place, especially in prayer. "Decorum" and the idea of orderly, composed worship had become important concepts for nineteenth-century Jews seeking to Americanize. Even when he served in rabbinic posts before his conversion, Freuder approved norms of worship that included orderliness, timeliness, moderated prayer volume, and unified ritual actions rather than individual ones. An article in the *American Israelite* explained that Freuder had discouraged indecorous worship, especially that associated with the popular Spiritualism of the time, in his own synagogue. "Since Dr. Freuder has put his foot down on Spiritualism, its devotees are out of spirits," it cleverly noted.[73] The decorum of acculturated American congregations, which mainly associated with Reform Judaism, was not only more appealing to Freuder but was also seen as more manly because it was less emotional and more measured.

In the conclusion to his volume, Freuder's words reflected some of the discourse about American masculinity. However, he juxtaposed what he saw as enlightened constructions of masculinity with the current state of Jewish men, which he depicted as a consequence of oppressive environments: "In the onward march of progress and enlightenment the Jew will, of course, leave behind him some of the traits of character that have been forced upon him during his weary pilgrimage of centuries." In addition to discarding certain traits, Freuder's future Jew (assumed to be a man) would also become more like a normative American version of the ideal man: "He will grow in physical strength, and will thus be able to take care of himself when a beardless hoodlum feels inclined to pull his beard; he will also give up his patient submission to injustice, and assert and defend his right as a man and citizen under all circumstances; in short, he will give the lie

to the aspersions cast upon the Jewish race by the example of his own life."[74]
Freuder's own millennial Jew (after a sort) would be a physically strong, assertive citizen who could nevertheless stand up for his Jewishness. In Freuder's vision, "progress and enlightenment" would create a Jew who would be both an American man in his body and citizenship and yet still be a Jewish man.

Even though Freuder was on the margins of the Jewish community, his ideas about Jewish gentleness and the value of a decorous, rational, manly religion pervaded discussion about Judaism in America. Despite their different social and religious locations, Freuder, Goldman, Cohn, and Steiner all painted similar portraits of Jewish masculinity: gentle, suffering, and averse to physical aggression. Although Freuder hoped that this version of masculinity would change as Jews became more religiously and culturally "enlightened," he nevertheless saw this gentle Jewish masculinity all around him. Goldman, Cohn, and Steiner saw it too, though they associated it with Christian theological reasons.

Acculturated Jews React to Missionaries

Hebrew-Christian missionaries thought a lot about Christian theology, the body and masculinity of Jesus, and Jews. But less predictably, so did some acculturated Jews. Even though these missionaries converted few Jews to Christianity, their words and organizations garnered attention from acculturated Jewish communities. We can recall CCAR President Leo Franklin's concern about the ways missions conflated the ideas of American citizen and Christian. In many other cases, too, acculturated Jews discussed Christianity and norms of masculinity in the same breath.

Others used the idea of proper masculinity to claim that Jews' religious behavior was appropriately manly, whereas Christian attempts at conversion were not. In his 1906 *A Jewish Reply to Christian Evangelists*, Lewis Hart compared the actions of a Christian missionary to "a litigant to bribe and suborn the witnesses of the opposite party in a lawsuit; or for the rulers of a country or the generals of an army to buy up the statesmen of another country, or to foster treason and rebellion among the soldiers of another state, with which their own might be at variance." Each one of these instances—bribery and intimidation—took place in a traditionally male realm. Courts, politics, war, and nations should be places of manly honor, Hart implied, but these duplicitous men refused to behave in properly manly fashion. He continued, "All work of this kind is held to be treacherous, and disgraceful both to the seducers and the seduced; and honorable men find no excuse for it." Like politics and nations, religion was a forum in which conduct should be properly manly; that is, loyal, forthright, and rational. But when Christians tried to convert Jews, they flaunted these masculine ideals, Hart charged, "And it is this kind of work that Christian ministers are doing when they try to procure the conversion of Jews to Christianity." Hart used norms of masculinity to argue that Christians behaved dishonorably. Because, by and large, Jews did not proselytize, their masculinity was superior.

Ironically, acculturated Jews used Protestant-based assumptions about religion to make the very point that missionary activity was improper and unmanly. They claimed that religion was a matter of individual conscience, and therefore attempts at conversion were manipulative rather than rational and forthright. External coercion was not the way to religion; "reason and conscience" or "conscientious reason," Hart implied, was the correct path.[75] The idea was found in the New Testament, he explained. Thus, by the standards of rational, interior religion, missionary activity fell short.

Jews also used the language of American manliness to privilege the image of gentle Jewishness over an aggressive Christianity. New York rabbi Joel Blau wrote about "a curious paradox." Jews, one might imagine from biblical text, should be ruthless and violent, and yet, they did not act that way: "Theoretically, the Jew is alleged to be an advocate of ruthless revenge. 'An eye for an eye'—a mere legal formula—has been accepted as the literal phrasing of his life-view. Historically, however, the Jews are the most non-resistant people on earth. . . . The Jew lives by the resistless force of his non-resistance." Blau then discussed the Sermon on the Mount and Christians' failure to turn the other cheek in comparison with Jews' gentle acceptance of suffering: "The unfortunate relation, then, between Jews and Christians simmers down to this: peoples that believe in non-resistance, but practice it not, hate a people that believes not in non-resistance, but practices it."[76] Blau's description used a Christian sacred text, the New Testament, to make sense of Jewish traits. Secretary of the Federation of American Zionists (FAZ) Jacob de Haas expressed the same sentiment more bluntly when he said, "At this moment, we Jews are the only Christians. We have not only turned the other cheek to the smiter, but we have repaid blows by love and persecution by loyalty."[77] When Blau and de Haas wrote about Jewish men, they claimed that, in their gentleness and lack of retaliation, they were being more Christian than Christians. They measured this virtue according to a Christian theological value—another example of the hegemony of Christianity in ideas about American religious masculinity.

In his objection to a 1916 Episcopalian resolution encouraging proselytizing among American Jews, Rudolph Grossman, the rabbi of New York's Temple Rodef Shalom, insinuated that Christians had twisted manliness to an extreme. In the process, they had also abandoned American values. "The resolution is not only un-American, an insult to American liberalism," Grossman told the *New York Times*, "but it is petty and trivial, entirely unworthy of a body of earnest churchmen, particularly at the present crisis in the world's history. In a day like the present, when the millions of Christendom are engaged in brutal, f[r]atricidal slaughter of one another . . . would it not seem that a great Church convention would find more important matters to consider than how to lure inoffensive Jews away from their ancestral faith?" Grossman linked Christian civilization with "brutal, fratricidal slaughter," an accusation of muscular Christianity taken to an aggressive extreme. His picture of Christianity hinted at the dark underbelly—its potential for violence—of what seemed to be a manly religion.

Grossman then turned the ideal of manliness from aggression and strength to one of genuine religious persuasion aimed at peace. He continued in explicitly gendered language: "Would it not have been more manly and honorable for that conference of religious leaders to devise methods for converting their own people to the Christian faith, rather than, by such a resolution, to offend and insult their Jewish brethren?"[78] The appropriately "manly" action, he explained, would have been the nonviolent and candid recruitment (not "luring") of "their own people." Grossman also linked proper manliness to Americanism; the ones violating American values were not "inoffensive" Jews, but the overzealous Christians who lured and slaughtered them.

In doing so, Grossman at once contested Christian missionary activity and Christian supersessionist discourse about "civilization," which deemed Christianity to be superior to Judaism. Unlike the premillennialist missionaries (such as Goldman and Cohn) who saw themselves much more as players in an eschatological drama, some Jews and nonmillennialist Christians (such as Freuder and Steiner) situated their ideas about religious masculinity in discourses of historical progress and nationalism.

Scholars of late nineteenth-century gender, such as Karla Goldman and Louise Michelle Newman, have framed womanhood in its relation to the discourse of civilization.[79] The discourse posited that the more "civilized" a society, the larger the differentiation of sex roles, and as a corollary, the more its women were respected. Many Americans of the early twentieth century also saw the differentiation of sex roles in these terms. Many nonmillennialists asserted, for instance, that the downtrodden state of Jewish immigrant life was in part a result of the inferiority of Jewish civilization vis-à-vis Christian civilization. They, like some missionaries, saw immigrant women's work outside the home and peripheral synagogue space as indications of this deficiency. More acculturated Jews countered claims of Jewish inferiority by pronouncing the ways in which Jews had "contributed" to modern civilization.

In contrast, premillennialist missionaries saw themselves much more as players in an eschatological drama, rather than as part of a mundane process of historical progress. Hebrew-Christian missionaries used theological language to link their understanding of Jewish manhood to the gentleness, nonviolence, and willing suffering of Isaiah 53 and as a prefiguration of the suffering to come during the Tribulation.

Most active missionaries to the Jews interpreted both historical and contemporary Jewish life as signs of the unfolding of theological events, not as commentary on the progress of "civilization." They viewed the world around them—from political events and movements such as Zionism to interpersonal interactions between a single missionary and a Jewish child—in the frame of biblical history and prophecy. When they did refer to the wider philosophical and psuedoscientific discourse of civilization, they did so only as a way of supporting their interpretation of the divine schema. In this way, these missionaries placed gender roles in a context that was more theological than sociological. Nevertheless, in their own way, they participated in a broader cultural discourse about religious masculinity.

Conclusion

Freuder, Cohn, Goldman, Steiner, and other Hebrew-Christian missionaries occupied a position at the social margins of both Christian and Jewish groups. Both communities, however, retained a special interest in them. Premillennialist Protestants hoped their own work would help bring about the second coming of Jesus Christ, while Jews reviled their attempts to "steal" young and unwitting Jews. Although they likely never thought of themselves as writing about gender, their observations and ideologies reveal assumptions about what it meant to be a Jewish man or a Christian man. And they show how ideas about Christianity implicitly structured American Judaism and articulations of Jewish masculinity. Although perhaps not for the reasons he expected, Freuder was right when he penned the third edition of his tale: "It cannot but attract the attention of this historian."[80]

Through their writing, these Hebrew-Christian missionaries articulated a distinctive Jewish masculinity. By rejecting the polar opposite images of the weak, feminized Jew and the muscular, brawny Christian, they espoused a different ideal of the Jewish man. Gentle and willing to bear suffering stoically, this image of the Jewish man refracted themes present in Judaism, American Protestantism, and American culture more broadly while refusing to espouse any of them wholesale.

In their reactions to mission activity these Hebrew-Christian missionaries and acculturated Jews imagined an American Jewish masculinity that was thoroughly conditioned by Christianity. Christian missionaries such as Gaebelein emphasized their suffering; Hebrew-Christian missionaries and other Christians painted "converted Jews" in the light of a gentle Jesus; and acculturated Jews insisted that Christians were not being religious in a properly manly way when they attempted to convert Jews. They imagined themselves compared to a gentle Jesus. Although few Jews converted to Christianity, the conversations comparing the two religions occurred widely. And the frequent and deep comparisons to Christian masculinity and Jesus in these conversations begin to demonstrate the hegemony of Christianity in American religious discourse.

Like the acculturated men of the Galveston Movement and the Jews who romanticized Indian-Israelite connections, these Hebrew-Christians imagined a Jewish masculinity that drew on American masculinities, but never mirrored them completely. None of them championed an aggressive masculinity, and all assumed that violence was not a Jewish trait. They all decried traditional Jewish piety as superstitious, backward, and indecorous, although some Reform Jews romanticized parts of Jewish tradition as authentic and therefore thought that maintaining ritual observance in the face of persecution demonstrated aspects of manliness. They all saw bodily weakness and frail health as Jewish traits to be fixed—though they proposed very different prescriptions for how to fix them. On one hand, Hebrew-Christian missionaries imagined that gentleness, weakness, and even suffering were endemic to Jewish masculinity; a healthy, productive, self-sufficient male body was not a Jewish body. For them, Christianity was the rational and universal religion, and it was the religion of manliness. But on the other hand, Zionists, Jewish philanthropists, and acculturated Jews who romanticized Indians all claimed that Jews could and should embrace a masculinity of bodily health, productive work, self-sufficiency, and rational religion.

Notes

1. "The Spectator," *New Outlook* (Dec. 14, 1912): 815. Teddy Roosevelt is listed as a contributing editor.
2. Mary Antin, *The Promised Land* (Boston: Houghton Mifflin, 1912), 40.
3. Georges Kukhi, "Thoughts of Meadville at Pool of Siloam," *Christian Register*, Oct. 7, 1920, 980. For similar gendered images, see also Samuel Freuder, *A Missionary's Return to Judaism: The Truth about the Christian Missions to the Jews* (New York: Sinai Publishing Co., 1915), 132.
4. Harris Weinstock, *Jesus the Jew and Other Addresses* (New York: Funk and Wagnalls, 1902), 12.
5. JPS translation.
6. "Notes on Prophecy and the Jews," *Our Hope* 19 (1912): 509. Thank you to the staff at the Moody Bible Institute's Crowell Library for access to the missionary journals.
7. Gaebelein likely referred to physician and anthropologist Maurice Fishberg's social scientific study, *The Jews*, in which Fishberg associated nervous diseases primarily with environmental, rather than racial or theological factors.
8. "Notes on Prophecy and the Jews," 509–510. The gendered implications of linking Jews and nervousness were particularly striking in this issue of the journal because the "Notes on Prophecy and the Jews" column was directly followed by a column reprinted from the *Maccabaean*, the United States' most important Zionist journal. The *Maccabaean*, with its frequent valorization of Jews in the military, painted quite a different picture of the potential of Jewish masculinity. *Our Hope* tended to reprint the facts rather than the valorization, presumably to be consistent with its overall depiction of the Jew as sad, downtrodden, and blind.

9. Sander Gilman, *Freud, Race, and Gender* (Princeton, NJ: Princeton University Press, 1997), 93–133. Mitchell Hart, *Social Science and the Politics of Modern Jewish Identity* (Stanford, CA: Stanford University Press, 2000), 106–130. Allard E. Dembe, *Occupation and Disease: How Social Factors Affect the Social Conception of Work-Related Disorders* (New Haven, CT: Yale University Press, 1996), 45–54.

10. Yaakov Ariel, *Evangelizing the Chosen People: Missions to Jews in America, 1880–2000* (Chapel Hill: University of North Carolina Press, 2000), 2–4.

11. Also see ibid., 12–15, 38–41.

12. Quoted in Hasia Diner, *A Time for Gathering: The Second Migration, 1820–1880* (Baltimore: Johns Hopkins University Press, 1992), 177.

13. Using the numbers of Louis Meyer, Yaakov Ariel estimates that about 150–200 Jews were converted to Christianity each year. Given that some did not remain Christian, this is a very small proportion when the overall American Jewish population boom is considered. See Louis Meyer, "Protestant Missions to the Jews," *Missionary Review of the World* 25 (Dec. 1902); Ariel, *Evangelizing the Chosen People*, 39.

14. "Report of the Special Committee on Christian Missions to Jews," in *Central Conference of American Rabbis Annual Report* 45 (Cincinnati: Krehbiel, 1917), 105.

15. In addition to many articles and ad hoc community organizations, several more formal efforts coalesced in the early twentieth century. In 1911, after a New York Jewish girl was baptized, a group organized to draft a bill to make the proselytizing of minors illegal. Also, Jeffrey Gurock traces the (brief) work of the Jewish Centers Association in his "Jewish Communal Divisiveness in Response to Christian Influences on the Lower East Side, 1900–1910," in *Jewish Apostasy in the Modern World*, ed. Todd Endelman (New York: Holmes and Meier, 1987), 255–271.

16. Yaakov Ariel, "The Evangelist at Our Door: The American Jewish Response to Christian Missionaries," *American Jewish Archives Journal* (Fall–Winter 1996): 141.

17. *Our Hope* and *The Jewish Era*, for example, describe blindness, crying, and hardened or stone hearts in every issue.

18. Leo Franklin, "Message of the President," in *Central Conference of American Rabbis* 30, ed. Isaac Marcuson (Cincinnati: Krehbeil, 1920), 167.

19. Ibid.

20. Bederman, *Manliness and Civilization*; Julian Carter, *The Heart of Whiteness: Normal Sexuality and Race in America 1880–1940* (Durham, NC: Duke University Press, 2007); Matthew Frye Jacobson, *Whiteness of a Different Color: European Immigrants and the Alchemy of Race* (Cambridge, MA: Harvard University Press, 1998).

21. Eli Lederhendler, *Jewish Responses to Modernity: New Voices in America and Eastern Europe* (New York: New York University Press, 1994), 104–158. This discourse of "regeneration" drew on the French Enlightenment and Jewish emancipation, both of which cast much longer shadows in European contexts than in American ones.

22. By the turn of the century, some—including some Jewish converts themselves—began to question the wisdom of "Hebrew-Christians" as missionaries. Still, knowledge of Judaism and Yiddish was seen as essential for the position, so many missions to the Jews employed a significant percentage of converts.

23. Albert Edward Thompson, *A Century of Jewish Missions* (Chicago: Fleming Revell, 1902), 235–253.

24. Isaac Mayer Wise, *Reminiscences*, ed. David Philipson (Cincinnati: Leo Wise, 1901), 68.

25. If Freuder, Goldman, and Leopold Cohn are any indication, however, many Jewish converts who became Christian missionaries did not always feel that they fit into the larger mis-

sionary community. Leopold Cohn, *The Story of a Modern Missionary to an Ancient People* (New York: American Board of Missions to the Jews, 1908).

26. Leopold Cohn used this phrase frequently. See, for example, ibid., 20, 28.

27. "Signs of the Times," *Missionary Review of the World* 32 (Jan. 1909): 7.

28. Cf. Lederhendler, *Jewish Responses to Modernity*, 104–158.

29. Jesus the Jew was a popular figure in American Jewish pulpits and literature during the early twentieth century. See Stephen Prothero, *American Jesus: How the Son of God Became a National Icon* (New York: Farrar, Straus and Giroux, 2003), 229–266.

30. For instance, see "Stealing Jewish Children," *American Hebrew*, Oct. 16, 1903. See also Abraham Simon, "Conversion," *Emanu-el*, Apr. 24, 1896, 7, quoted in Ariel, "A German Rabbi and Scholar in America," 56, 59–61.

31. Jonathan Sarna, "The American Jewish Response to Nineteenth Century Christian Missions," *Journal of American History* 68 (June 1981): 35–51.

32. Ariel, *Evangelizing the Chosen People*, 35.

33. The best-known exception was Tryphena Rounds, who occupied the position of "temporary" superintendent of the Chicago Hebrew Mission for twenty years. But even for Rounds and the generally woman-friendly Chicago Hebrew Mission, a permanent title of authority was off-limits for women. See Ariel, *Evangelizing the Chosen People*, 26–28.

34. Susan Glenn, *Daughters of the Shtetl: Life and Labor in the Immigrant Generation* (Ithaca, NY: Cornell University Press, 1990); see also Ariel, *Evangelizing the Chosen People*, 38–54.

35. One 1920 lecture, for instance, took place at Portland's Wilbur Methodist Church. "Luther League Convention Held in Portland Closes Today," *Sunday Oregonian*, Oct. 24, 1920.

36. Joseph Goldman, *Judaism and Its Traditions* (Los Angeles: J. F. Rowny Press, 1919), 34. Perhaps he is referring to Maimonides' assertion that circumcision served to curb sexual appetite. See Josef Stern, "Maimonides on the Covenant of Circumcision and the Unity of God," in *The Midrashic Imagination: Jewish Exegesis, Thought, and History*, ed. Michael Fishbane (Albany, NY: SUNY Press, 1993).

37. See David Gollaher, "From Ritual to Science: The Medical Transformation of Circumcision in America," *Journal of Social History* 28 (Fall 1994): 5–36.

38. The idea of Jewish distinctiveness as related to circumcision has a long history. In his *Theological-Political Treatise*, Baruch Spinoza wrote, "The mark of circumcision, too, I consider to be such an important factor in this matter that I am convinced that this by itself will preserve their nation forever. Indeed, were it not that the fundamental principles of their religion discourage manliness, I would not hesitate to believe that one day they will . . . establish once more their independent state and that God will again choose them." *Theological-Political Treatise*, trans. Samuel Shirley (Indianapolis: Hackett, 2001), 46. For a recent scholarly exploration of the meaning of circumcision for the making of Jewish manhood, see Melvin Konner, *The Jewish Body* (New York: Schocken, 2009), 20–47.

39. Paul used circumcision as a central part of his argument against the continuation of Jewish law in general and *mitzvot* in particular. His polemic against physical signs of the covenant and in favor of spiritual signs was rooted in the theological movement from the people of Israel "in the flesh" to a spiritual Israel (i.e., Christians). See Daniel Boyarin, *A Radical Jew: Paul and the Politics of Identity* (Berkeley: University of California Press, 1994), 36–38.

40. Menachot 43b discusses *brit milah* as a fundamental mitzvah. When King David went to the bathhouse and momentarily felt naked of *mitzvot* (no *two tefillin*, *arba kanfot*, or mezuzah), he saw his circumcised penis and felt reassured. Reemerging from the bathhouse, he wrote a specific psalm for circumcision. Even in the event a born [male] Jew became an

apostate, he need only look down and remember his bodily inclusion in the covenant as a Jew. Even for many secular or halakhah-repudiating Reform Jews in Europe and the United States, it was the one (sometimes only) mitzvah they maintained.

41. Goldman, *Judaism and Its Traditions*, 10.

42. Ibid., 14. For one of the most developed instances of this biblical interpretation, in a slightly later period, Hebrew-Christian Max Wertheimer wrote the autobiographical *From Rabbinism to Christ*, where he interpreted Isaiah 53 and dwelled on Christ's suffering at length.

43. This refers to the practice of *nagel wasser* ("finger water"), a kabbalistic custom in which one washes his fingers in the morning before he takes three steps. Ibid., 17.

44. Yaakov Ariel suggests that premillennialist theology thereby created a "new appreciation for the Jews" among missionaries and evangelical Protestants more generally. Ariel, *Evangelizing the Chosen People*, 18.

45. For a thorough analysis of European Zionist masculinity, see Michael Berkowitz, "Mind, Muscle, and Men": The Imagination of a Zionist National Culture for the Jews of Central and Western Europe, 1897–1941" (PhD diss., University of Wisconsin- Madison, 1989).

46. J. A. Singmaster, no title, *Lutheran Quarterly*, July 1920, 408; "Thought and Life in the Kingdom," *Journal and Messenger*, Nov. 13, 1919, 8.

47. William Bryant, "The Jews and Judaism," *Herald and Presbyter*, Mar. 3, 1920, 9.

48. Ariel, *Evangelizing the Chosen People*, 28, 101

49. Alexander Bacon, *The Strange Story of Dr. Cohn and Mr. Joszovics (with apologies to Dr. Jekyl and Mr. Hyde)* (New York: [n.p.], 1918).

50. Cohn, *Story of a Modern Missionary*, 39–40.

51. Quoted in Dennis Haas, "The Conversion of Edward A. Steiner," June 15, 2004, https://www.grinnell.edu/news/conversion-edward-steiner.

52. Edward Steiner, *From Alien to Citizen: The Story of My Life in America* (New York: Fleming Revell, 1914), 121.

53. Ibid., 316, 315.

54. "For the Missionary Library," *Missionary Review of the World* (Jan. 1908): 79.

55. Edward Steiner, *The Eternal Hunger: Vivid Moments in Personal Experience* (New York: Fleming Revell, 1925), 33.

56. Ibid., 36.

57. Edward Steiner, *Against the Current: Simple Chapters from a Complex Life* (New York: Fleming Revell, 1910), 46.

58. Ibid., 222–223.

59. Samuel Freuder, *My Return to Judaism* (New York: Zuckerman and Bros., 1922).

60. Samuel Freuder, *A Missionary's Return to Judaism;* "Apostate Jew Turns from Adopted Faith," *Boston Globe*, June 4, 1908. For a full account of Freuder's life, see Dana Evan Kaplan, "Rabbi Samuel Freuder as a Christian Missionary: American Protestant Premillennialism and an Apostate Returner, 1891–1924," *American Jewish Archives Journal* 40 (1998).

61. Kaplan, "Rabbi Samuel Freuder as a Christian Missionary," 8–12. Freuder never married, and Dana Evan Kaplan raises the possibility that Freuder may have been gay. Ibid., note 71.

62. In its review of the year, the *American Jewish Year Book* called his return to the community "theatrical." Louis Levin, "The Year, 5668," *American Jewish Year Book* (Philadelphia: Jewish Publication Society of America, 1908), 198.

63. Letter from Gotthard Deutsch et al. to Felix Warburg, August 8, 1913. Felix Warburg Collection, box 163, folder 23, American Jewish Archives (henceforth *AJA*), Cincinnati, OH.

64. Ibid.

65. Ibid.

66. Freuder, *A Missionary's Return to Judaism*, 132.

67. Ibid., 139.

68. Putney, *Muscular Christianity*.

69. Ibid., 140.

70. Ibid., 147.

71. Ibid., 148–149.

72. Freuder, *A Missionary's Return to Judaism*, 132.

73. *American Israelite*, Dec. 14, 1888, 7, quoted in Kaplan, "Rabbi Samuel Freuder as a Christian Missionary," 45.

74. Ibid., 185.

75. Lewis Hart, *A Jewish Reply to Christian Evangelists* (New York: Bloch Publishing Co., 1906), 13.

76. Joel Blau, "The Modern Pharisee," *Atlantic* 129, no. 1 (Jan. 1922): 1.

77. Jacob de Haas, *Zionism: Why and Wherefore* (New York: Maccabaean Publishing Co., 1902), 13.

78. "Proselyting Effort Resented by Jews," *New York Times*, Oct. 29, 1916.

79. Louise Newman, *White Women's Rights: The Racial Origin of Feminism in the United States* (New York: Oxford University Press, 1999); Beryl Satter, *Each Mind a Kingdom: American Women, Sexual Purity, and the New Thought Movement* (Berkeley: University of California, 1999) and Karla Goldman, "The Limits of Imagination: White Christian Civilization and the Construction of American Jewish Womanhood in the 1890s," in *Imagining the American Jewish Community*, ed. Jack Wertheimer (Waltham, MA: Brandeis University Press, 2007).

80. Samuel Freuder, *My Return to Judaism*, 3rd ed. (New York: Bloch, 1924), 196.

PART II

THE HEALTHY BODY AND THE LAND

IN 1923, DR. DAVID Perla spoke to a small audience about a big idea: the "health idea." He wanted to put to rest the notion "that in order to refine the mind we must neglect the body." He told his listeners, the advisory committee of New Jersey YMHAs and YWHAs (Young Men's and Young Women's Hebrew Associations), that the "old Lutheran conception" of education by teaching the masses to read scripture alone did not meet the needs of Jews in the modern age. To the contrary, creating ideal Jews required careful attention to cultivating healthy Jewish bodies.

Why would "Lutheranism"—Perla's generic term for Protestantism—be the model for the way Americans thought about their bodies? And why would he assume that his listeners, all Jews, had been operating according to these ideas? When Perla made his point about the importance and improvement of Jewish bodies, he talked about how people learned these values. And these learning processes, he explained, were Protestant in their assumptions and epistemology, even when they were not Protestant in their content. But learning through reading alone, even reading scripture, was not sufficient for American Jews. To make Jews physically healthy, the YMHA and YWHA would offer new ways of learning, such as organized athletic competitions and practical hygiene classes.

The following chapters look at other ways acculturated Jews promoted healthy bodies—particularly male bodies and their relationship with the land, figured through the past, present, and future—and begin to sketch a picture of the norms of American Jewish masculinity.

The influx of Jewish immigrants—about two million in the four decades preceding Perla's speech—had made issues of Jewish health even more significant. Acculturated Jews wanted to be healthy themselves, and at the same time, they wanted to improve new immigrants' health. This latter desire was a combination of altruism and self-regard. They worried about what non-Jews thought about immigrant Jews, assuming that non-Jews sometimes lumped all Jews together in their impressions. They wanted people—Jews and non-Jews alike—to associate Jews with health and wellness, not sickness or weakness.

Though Perla spoke to a small crowd on that day in 1923, his words also reflected the thoughts of many acculturated American Jews. When the *Jewish Center* reprinted his talk, the editor's introduction emphasized the particularly "Jewish aspect" of health: "the truth that Judaism is a way of living in accordance with the fundamental precepts concerning the sanctity of life and the human body."[1] The healthy body had a close relationship to Judaism, Perla said, though he did not explain exactly what that relationship was or how it might work in practice. In all of this, Perla was very much a man of his time. Like other YMHA and YMCA men, he promoted the importance of physical culture. Like American Progressives, he sought to "uplift" immigrants' standards of health, culture, and personal comportment. Like many other religious Americans, he assumed that his religion was a rational one that harmonized with these goals of health and physical wellness.

Nevertheless, in reality, the relationship was a complex one. Acculturated Jews thought that the traditional forms of Judaism practiced by Eastern European immigrants neglected—or worse, debilitated—the body. Real Judaism was a rational religion, they thought, and not only did it make space for healthy bodies but it also actively promoted them.[2] Jewish social projects, such as the Galveston Movement and the agricultural movements, sought to make Jewish men into healthy men, in part by shaping their religion. As Part II shows, healthy bodies and their relationship to the American land formed a vital part of early twentieth-century American Jewish masculinity.

Perla and the Y offer us a glimpse of what Jews thought about masculine ideals and how they sought to mold young Jewish men according to them, but gender norms are often difficult to see. The techniques that people use to produce gender (often unwittingly) can be even harder to see. Sometimes they are almost invisible. These norms and their production are so elusive because they need to appear as natural and given—and not merely conventional—if they are to have such cultural force. A quest to see the production of American Jewish masculinity, then, is no simple task. One such way to do this is to look to the margins. Judith Butler does this when she writes about drag queens to help us see the unspoken norms about gendered bodies. The margins in this book are different ones. Instead of drag queens, there are immigrants, farmers, criminals, converts, and other characters. But looking to unexpected places can still help us see gender norms that are otherwise concealed. None of the themes of the chapters in this part—the West, Indians, communal agriculture, and Zionism—became the culturally dominant image of early twentieth-century Jewish masculinity. And yet each offers an angle from which we can see the contours of its construction—the first about Jews' arrival in the United States, the second about their connection to the American past, the third about the contributions to the American present, and the fourth assurances about their continued investment in the American future.

Part II's four chapters focus on different margins of American Jewry to show the making of American Jewish masculinity. The Jews in these chapters, like Perla, privileged the idea of the healthy male body. They knew that cultivating Jewish men with healthy bodies was a goal, but they did not send a bulk mailer to all Jews in the United States that read, "Now being a good Jewish man means having a healthy body. Please comply." In most cases, these acculturated Jews did not even see themselves as making a change in Jewish masculine ideals. Instead they imagined that they were emphasizing essential and timeless masculine values that some Jews had recently neglected. They did, however, imagine that Jews could change to conform more closely to these masculine ideals, though cultivation of the body could not happen overnight, of course. Perla explained, "Though the Jews are accused of being somewhat backward in their physical development, it must not be forgotten that . . . their highest physical development cannot be achieved in one leap." Most acculturated Jews agreed. Many Jewish men in the United States were not yet healthy, ideal Jewish men, but they could be molded into them.

Jews had plenty of company when they became particularly attentive to the health of bodies. The early twentieth century was a critical moment for American ideas about the body as a site of cultural meanings. For instance, T. J. Jackson Lears's work on advertising shows how the technologies for developing and disciplining the body proliferated in the years after the turn of the century. Even seemingly trivial items like underarm deodorant became important signs of bodily health and hygiene. Bodies mattered, and they sent a strong social message about the person. The result was a new social order where advertising and other cultural forces "redefine[ed] the body as a universe of discourse."[3] As bodies took on new meaning as an essential site for both self-understanding and evaluation of others, they also played a central role in the construction of masculinity and Judaism.

For American Jews, the picture of the healthy male body was closely related to a relationship with the land. This view, however, was not unique to Jews. When Teddy Roosevelt stood over dead large game animals in his safari photos, he was demonstrating his mastery over nature. When Americans waxed nostalgic about the days of pioneering men and the untamed frontier, they were associating an ideal masculinity with subduing the wild lands, from sea to sea of the North American continent. When Americans read Edgar Rice Burrough's *Tarzan* novels and saw the 1918 film with its barrel-chested star, they were admiring Tarzan's ability to live off the land in spite of, or even because of, his untamed ways. The American Jewish masculinity we see here participated in these ties to the land, but it was also distinctly Jewish.

Chapter 3 considers the Galveston Movement, ideas about the land, and the American West. Chapter 4 picks up on an unexpected interest of the Galveston Movement's central rabbi, Henry Cohen: it considers Indians in the imagination of Jews as a way of connecting to the American past. Chapter 5 looks at Jewish farm schools and communal farming settlements as projects to transform the present, and chapter 6 considers American Zionism and its relationship to the future. Each chapter shows acculturated Jews experimenting with ways of shaping Jewish men and their gender, and in each, the health of the male body played an integral role.

Notes

1. *Jewish Center* 2, no. 1 (Dec. 1923): 30.

2. See Mitchell Hart, *The Healthy Jew: The Symbiosis of Judaism and Modern Medicine* (New York: Cambridge University Press, 2007).

3. T. J. Jackson Lears, "American Advertising and the Reconstruction of the Body," in *Fitness in American Culture: Images of Health, Sport, and the Body*, ed. Katherine Grover (Amherst: University of Massachusetts Press, 1989), 49.

3 Go West, Young Jew

The Galveston Movement, Immigrant Men, and the Pioneer Spirit

ONE DAY IN 1912, the Reverend A. E. Patton visited Ellis Island. Each true American, he opined after his visit, should do likewise. On arrival, the "real American" would see "the Jewish hordes, ignorant of all patriotism, filthy, vermin-infested, stealthy and furtive in manner, too lazy to enter into real labor, too cowardly to face frontier life, too lazy to work as every American farmer has to work, too filthy to adopt ideals of cleanliness from the start, too bigoted to surrender any racial traditions or to absorb any true Americanisms." To see these sights would "awaken in his [the real American's] thoughtful mind desires to check and lessen this source of pollution."[1] Patton measured both the "real American" and the "Jewish hordes" by their conformity to the male standards of labor, bravery, and mastery of the land. Patton's "real American" bested these "Jewish hordes" in every category. Where Jews' bodies were dirty and unhealthy, real Americans were clean and healthy. Where Jews were too lazy to farm, real Americans worked the land. Where Jews were too cowardly to move out West, real Americans bravely pioneered the untamed frontier. Where their religion was racially insular and particularist, American religion was democratic. In fact, Patton did not even consider their religion to qualify as religion, instead calling it "racial traditions." This picture of particularist, insular, racial rather than conscience-driven religion placed their Judaism squarely in the category of "bad religion," where it failed to embrace the "good" and masculine religious attributes of rationality and universalism. In other words, these "Jewish hordes," whom Patton assumed to be men, did not fit the picture of proper American manliness.

We might be tempted to chalk up Patton's screed to xenophobia and read it as little more than another instance of early twentieth-century antisemitism. But Patton's characterization also points to a set of ideas about Jewish men that were held far and wide beyond bastions of intolerance. Men as diverse as Teddy Roosevelt, Social Gospel leader Josiah Strong, and psychologist G. Stanley Hall worried about the enervating effects of city living, especially for immigrants and the poor. Patton's complaints exemplified these worries. Even though it is quite unlikely that Patton thought in terms of gender, his words both echoed and contributed to the construction of American Jewish masculinity. In particular, his invective points to the importance of healthy male bodies, labor, land, and religion for forming and conforming to masculine norms. These four themes recurred widely in the writing of non-Jews who thought about immigration. And, as this chapter shows, they also served as central themes for Jews themselves.

Because such a large number of Jews came to the United States in the early years of the twentieth century, and because many acculturated Jews sought to shape those immigrants, immigration became a crucial location for the construction of American Jewish masculinity. Acculturated Jews overwhelmingly, though never uniformly, supported the idea of allowing new Jewish immigrants into the United States. But they also wanted to make sure that these newcomers did not reflect poorly on them, so they created organizations and programs to help (or "help") the immigrants more closely live up to their ideas of what made a good American Jew. For example, some of these programs worked to teach immigrants English, others sought to ensure that young women did not live on their own, and still others taught women how to clean and decorate their living spaces.

One of these programs sought to help immigrants in a different way: by sending them to live in the American West. This chapter focuses on the Galveston Movement, that distinctive immigration plan, which shows how acculturated Jews sought to shape the gendered image of Jewish men. Not every Jewish man was a potential Galveston Movement man. Some guidelines sought to exclude those who were Hasidic (deemed too irrational in their religion) or had "poor physique" (deemed not "healthy" enough to support themselves). But the plan's organizers welcomed able-bodied Jewish men who expressed interest.

The aim of the Galveston Movement organizers was to send immigrants to the American West to cultivate their manliness. The movement, which operated from 1907 until the outbreak of World War I in Europe forced its cessation in 1914, advocated Jewish settlement in areas far from the crowded, large northeastern cities, where acculturated Jews worried that the living conditions and the cultural traditions and practices of the recent East European Jewish immigrants stoked antisemitism. But the movement also encouraged Jews to reconnect with the land, from which they had—at least in the imagination of more acculturated American Jews—become alienated. These Eastern European Jews traveled overland to Bremen, Germany, where they boarded a ship bound for Galveston, Texas. After landing in Galveston instead of Ellis Island the new immigrants were sent to small towns throughout the American West and Southwest, where it was hoped they would settle and acculturate into "productive" American men. During its eight-year existence, the movement facilitated the immigration of about 10,000 Eastern European Jews.

The Galveston Movement reflected not only some of the broad themes in American discussions of immigration in general but also the particularity of

Jewish immigration. Whereas non-Jewish immigrants were also subject to similar critical assumptions—they were dirty, poor, or uneducated—Jewish immigrants faced distinctive evaluations of their bodies, religion, and masculinity, as this chapter's analysis of devout Jewish immigrants, medical evaluations of "poor physique," and discussions of potential male productivity demonstrates.

This chapter begins by briefly situating the Galveston Movement or, more formally, the Jewish Immigrants Information Bureau (JIIB), in the larger cultural landscape. Then it describes the main problem that the Galveston Movement was created to address: the physical and moral corruption of city life. From there it turns to a discussion of the relationship of Jewish piety to the male body and how the movement dealt with observant Jewish men such as Hasidim. It ends by analyzing an issue that haunted the movement: immigrants with "poor physique" and those who were "likely to become a public charge" rather than financially supporting themselves and their families.

Land, Labor, and Religion: The Background to Galveston

Acculturated American Jews might have countered Reverend Patton's assessment of the "Jewish hordes" by insisting that these immigrant Jews were, in fact, properly manly. They might have argued there was nothing wrong with urban living and that cities were an ideal environment in which immigrant Jews could become good, healthy American citizens. Most acculturated Jews, after all, lived in cities, and few yearned to "face frontier life" or do the tasks of "every American farmer." They also might have contended that the immigrants' Judaism was not too particularist, "bigoted," or racially based. They might have claimed that the traditional Orthodox Judaism of many immigrants offered gender roles that were compatible with being American. They could have made all these arguments. But few did.

Instead, most quietly agreed with critiques such as Patton's of the immigrants' masculinity. How could acculturated Jews, who were largely sympathetic to the situations of immigrant Jews, share such a dim view of their coreligionists? They agreed with this perspective because they tended to see the immigrants' masculinity as a temporary malfunction, rather than an inherent defect. Where Patton was concerned *about* the immigrants, many acculturated Jews were concerned *for* them. Both sides agreed that ideal men should have healthy bodies, work productively, connect to the land, contribute positively to the nation, and embrace a rational religion that allowed for physical cultivation. They also agreed that immigrant Jews did not fit that profile when they arrived on American shores. Patton's solution was to keep future immigrant Jews out. But most American Jews wanted to keep the United States' doors open to more Eastern European Jews, and so their solutions aimed to help those immigrants come closer to American ideals of masculinity.

One of the most remarkable things about the Galveston Movement is the similarity between the ideas of the acculturated Jews who organized it and broader American cultural discourses about immigration and masculinity. Indeed, there is little to suggest a Jewish viewpoint that is distinct from a non-Jewish viewpoint. To categorize what Jews said about Jews separately from what non-Jews said about Jews would be to assume that the distinction between Jewish and non-Jewish speakers, or even subjectivities, is crucial. The sources here suggest otherwise. Jews and non-Jews participated in the same cultural conversation about immigration and masculinity. Knowing a speaker's identity is not enough to predict his or her position or rhetoric. Yes, there were non-Jewish nativists like Patton, but there were also non-Jewish voices such as the Kansas City writer who told the story of a "Russian capmaker's Americanization," which he called "one of the fruits of the Galveston Movement." The cap maker, like other male Galveston immigrants, had undergone a "transformation process" in which he went from a "low standard of living" to becoming the model of a self-sufficient working American man.[2] Moreover, gender norms are shaped not only by the people who espouse them—in our case Jewish men. They are also shaped by those who "interpellate" them, or call them out as that gender—in our case, non-Jews and women who commented on Jewish men. So concentrating on Jewish voices alone would give us only a partial picture of the construction of Jewish masculinity, and insisting on the epistemological separation of Jewish and non-Jewish voices would give an artificially tidy picture.

The ideology underlying the Galveston Movement asserted that immigrant Jews had the potential to transform themselves into strong, pioneering, productive men. On the path to doing this, the Galveston Movement's leaders suggested, immigrants would have to shed any attachments to outdated forms of Judaism that focused on study and strict religious observance. Those antiquated and superstitious attachments were not conducive to pioneering lifestyles and strong bodies. The movement deemed pious immigrants and those with a "poor physique" to be undesirable, but it nevertheless operated with a fundamental assumption that Jewish immigrants could be transformed. The movement was undergirded by an anthropology that emphasized the cultural contingency of physical and social traits and the ability of peoples to change. In short, the movement was committed to the idea that, even if these Jews were not yet manly and American, they could become so.

Masculinity mattered for the Galveston Movement because Americans in the early twentieth century, like Americans today, associated the West with rugged, manly pioneers. Just think of the male characters in westerns, a film genre just gaining its audience in the early twentieth century. Western literature and entertainment populated the cultural imaginary with strong, daring, and resourceful men. Owen Wister's best-selling 1902 novel *The Virginian* and its 1914 and 1923 film adaptations, for instance, told the story of a quietly strong, self-sufficient, and resourceful man from Virginia who went to work on a ranch in Wyoming. Galveston organizers associated these same kinds of manly qualities with the West and thought that, if immigrant Jews settled there, they too could become brave, resourceful pioneers.

With the benefit of hindsight, we know that the West never became the dominant image of American Jewish life; today, few Americans associate Jews with the West, especially the romanticized images of the still-untamed "Wild West." But hindsight also illuminates the historical value in the documentary sources of this marginal immigration movement. When they talked about the Galveston Movement with one another and when they promoted it to other Americans, these Jews disclosed their desires about American Jewish masculinity. Even though only a small fraction of Jewish immigrants came through Galveston, the correspondence, published materials, and press about the Galveston Movement paint a distinctive portrait of the ideal goal for Jewish immigrants to America. The Jewish immigrant, almost always assumed to be an adult man, would work productively, develop an able and healthy body, discard premodern religious superstition and piety, have a pioneering spirit, and even help tame the frontier through his settlement of the American West.

More concretely, the Galveston Movement source material shows how the themes of (1) connection with the land, (2) rational religion, and (3) productive labor shaped American Jewish masculinity. A fourth theme—that of the healthy male body—appears again and again as a structuring element of these three themes. More than a thread running through each, the idea of the healthy male body was perhaps part of the pattern itself. As we look at land, labor, and religion, we see ways that each discourse made claims about what counted as a healthy male Jewish body and how one should achieve it.

Connecting to the Land: The Emasculating City and Its Western Solution

If immigrant Jews were going to become properly manly, one of the first steps acculturated Jews proposed was to get them out of the city and into the country. Many Jews and non-Jews alike thought that the city was bad—that it was physically and morally corrupting. Social worker Sidney Teller, for instance, wrote about a Chicago Jewish neighborhood as "an old ghetto, with its mass of unsanitary houses, crowded streets, lack of play space for children, and recreation for adults."[3] In this view, city living impeded Jewish men's paths to a better masculinity because cleanliness, recreation, and play space—all rare in cities— contributed to physical well-being, and physical well-being was central to manliness. Teller touted the transformative nature of one neighborhood gymnasium. It made the immigrant Jews healthier (now they take showers!), better citizens (now they vote! and use the library!), and better men and women: "To the ghetto Jew, held down for centuries, forgetting that physical health helps moral strength, the outdoor gymnasium for the girls and boys . . . means a great deal toward getting back the normal physical standard. . . . With fair play and clean sport the motto for the boys, and healthy and graceful bodies the idea for the girls, the gymnasia are crowded every day."[4] To achieve the "normal physical standard," these urban immigrant Jews had to undertake specifically gendered activities. Although he would not have used this language, Teller saw the gymnasium as a successful project to inculcate gender norms. Boys played competitive sports, and girls cultivated their physical grace, all in an outdoor environment. But this Chicago experiment could intervene in only one neighborhood to make a small "oasis" in the "desert" of the city.[5] Without philanthropic interventions like this Chicago gymnasium, Jewish immigrants in crowded cities would remain unclean and unkempt, unhealthy, and unaffected by American norms of grace for girls and brawn for boys.

If acculturated Jews worried about this "city rot" problem in Chicago, they really wrung their hands about New York. The number of Eastern European Jews in New York grew each year: the population increased from about 62,000 in 1880 to nearly 700,000 in 1905, and the Lower East Side became more crowded by the month, it seemed.[6] The Galveston Movement proposed a solution. By sending new immigrants to settle the West, these men could interact with the real American land, instead of hunching over a sewing machine or Talmud for hours on end.

And so the Galveston Movement is a place where we can see the construction of an American Jewish masculinity in progress. Though historians have studied the Galveston Movement, its story often remains absent from larger narratives of immigration or Americanization, perhaps because of its location far from traditional city centers such as New York and the relatively small numbers of immigrants it settled.[7] But precisely because of its focus beyond the city, the Galveston Movement sources provide a distinctive window into the roles that the male body and the American land played in shaping American Jewish masculinity.

In many ways, the Galveston Movement fit neatly with the gendered goals of other Progressive, Social Gospel, and philanthropic projects.[8] Like their Christian neighbors, acculturated Jews used a variety of social programs—settlement houses, adult educational projects, and newspaper columns—to "uplift" and Americanize immigrants. Jewish settlement house worker Lillian Wald praised the "physical benefit" of the "various Fresh Air agencies throughout the country." She encouraged boys to "elect training in agriculture," a career that she saw as fulfilling, healthy, and appropriately manly.[9] Doctors widely regarded country air to be beneficial for everyone's physical health. It would make men more robust and strong, and give women's cheeks more color. These Progressive activists also encouraged immigrants to adopt Americanized gender norms. Clergy, social workers, and philanthropists helped women learn to set up their kitchens according to norms of "hygiene" and style, how to decorate on a budget, and which forms of entertainment were appropriately ladylike. For some, encouraging immigrants to leave the city meant sponsoring philanthropic efforts to give working girls a weekend in the countryside. But others imagined the project on a much larger scale: "dispersion" movements to relocate immigrants permanently.

While Jewish leaders expressed concern about the immigrants' poor health, hygiene, and lack of manliness as problems for the immigrants themselves, they also worried how perceptions of these immigrants would affect the image of all American Jews. David Bressler, a young lawyer, became a major animating personality of the Galveston Movement. (Bressler spent a lot of time thinking about immigration issues. When he and his wife were expecting a child, he wrote to the Galveston rabbi Henry Cohen expressing his regret that he could not go to a meeting because of "the arrival almost any time now of a little immigrant in the Bressler family."[10]) At an annual Jewish social work conference, Bressler worried that Jews congregating in cities fanned the flames of antisemitism. "Discounting the exaggerations of the muckraking magazines which contrive to find every ill, real and imaginary, in New York's crowded Jewish quarter," Bressler wrote, "the very fact that the peculiar conditions to be found in the quarter make it a fertile field for magazine exploitation and discredit of American Jewry, ought to be of vital concern to those who desire that the settlement of Jews in this country be normal and not involved in any vexing problems."[11] For the settlement of immigrants to be "normal," they should be located outside of densely packed cities. When packed into cities, not only were they involved in "vexing problems" but their vexing problems could also serve as fodder for magazine articles such as the *McClure's* exposés, "The Jewish Invasion of America" and "The Great Jewish Invasion."[12] Jewish leaders worried that this kind of scandal-mongering journalism about urban immigrants made all Jews look bad.

These acculturated Jews' concerns about the effects of city living reflected a wider non-Jewish interpretation of Jewish male bodies. After perusing an article about plants that entrap insects, *Popular Science Monthly* readers could learn about Jewish immigrants and their physical characteristics. In the article, Allan McLaughlin, a US Public Health official, wrote an otherwise sympathetic article arguing that the characteristic Jewish weakness and sickliness were results of long-term persecution and city living. For McLaughlin, Jewish immigrants were not essentially inferior—they were model citizens when it came to education, for instance—but historical and social circumstances had conspired to make Jewish men generally poor physical specimens of manhood:

In physique they rank below all other immigrants, and few seem capable of hard physical labor. They seem to have no muscular development, and are prematurely old at an age when a German or a Scandinavian is still in his prime. This poor physique is due to their living in the crowded quarters of cities and towns and to the occupations in which they have engaged. These were conditions in Europe over which they had no control, as they were not only restricted at to residence, but were prevented by law from engaging in agricultural pursuits. Yet when they are no longer subject to these restrictive laws they cling tenaciously to the life in the slums, and their sweat-shop occupations.[13]

McLaughlin's description shows that the image of the immigrant Jew as weak city dwellers incapable of physical labor was not an idea held only by virulent antisemites. His article praised immigrant Jews in other respects, but when it came to living up to these particular norms of masculinity, they did not clear the bar.

So if urban living kept immigrant men from achieving manliness, what could be done about the problem? One could either move immigrants from cities to the countryside or route new immigrants out West before they had a chance to settle in a crowded and unhealthy urban "ghetto." In 1901, the Jewish Agricultural and Industrial Aid Society (JAIAS) took the former path when it created the Industrial Removal Office (IRO), which relocated immigrant Jews away from New York, Philadelphia, and Boston and into smaller towns and rural settlements.[14] The Galveston Movement took the latter path. In 1904 New York Jewish philanthropist Jacob Schiff, a founder and supporter of the IRO, suggested to the Hilfsverein der deutschen Juden (the most prominent German Jewish relief organization) that together they organize the transportation of immigrants from Europe to other ports.[15] Schiff would later put his money behind his idea and donate generously to the Galveston Movement.

When Jewish communal organizers advocated routing immigrants directly from Europe to points South or West, they participated in widespread national rhetoric. Despite its hardline anti-immigration stance, the National Immigration Conference passed a resolution in 1905 to "improve facilities for handling immigration at the South Atlantic and Gulf ports, in order thereby to promote the distribution of immigration over the undeveloped lands of the South and Southwest."[16] The secretary of the Immigration Restrictionist League agreed that parts of the South and West "demanded" immigrant labor.[17] He railed mightily against Jews, Italians, and Hungarians in particular, and he wanted them kept out of the United States; however, if they were going to come, he insisted that they should be sent out West.[18] Even though most acculturated Jews staunchly opposed immigration restrictions, they agreed about the benefits not only for new immigrants of resettlement in the West but also how the West would benefit from an influx of immigrants. Americans on both sides of the immigration debate insisted that physical health and productivity—two important qualities of manliness—

were desirable, and many suggested that the West could help cultivate these qualities.[19]

The advocates of the Galveston Movement differed ideologically on some major political issues, but they agreed about the value of the American West. For example, the philanthropist Schiff was not a Zionist, and the British playwright Israel Zangwill strongly supported the quest for a Jewish homeland, but the two came together over the Galveston Movement. Zangwill, author of the 1908 play *The Melting Pot* and outspoken Americanization advocate, saw the American West as a safe home for current and future Jewish immigrants: "Every Galveston emigrant therefore will have the mitzvah . . . of opening up new places of refuge to our brethren," he wrote in 1910. In the event of future pogroms, he imagined, this land could be a haven for Jews. He used the religious language of a divinely commanded deed—a "mitzvah"—to describe the act of settling in the American West. Securing the safety of future Jews escaping persecution became a religious act, but rural or small-town settlement was not one of the traditional 613 commandments. (Perhaps he stretched the interpretation of what it means to save a person's life.)

The West was particularly well suited for Jewish settlement, Zangwill argued: "Only a land already half developed like Western America, holds the possibility of receiving and supporting vast numbers of immigrants, and provides by the ever-increasing development of its railway, towns and agriculture, sufficiently profitable opportunities for industry and investment."[20] He saw the American West as part wild and part developed, and therefore ideal for transforming Jews into pioneering men and productive contributors to their new country. When Zangwill suggested that large numbers of immigrants should settle on self-sustaining and independent western ranches and agricultural communes, Schiff vetoed it. But the two agreed on the immigration plan that would become the Galveston Movement. Once they had garnered the support of the Hilfsverein, and the Jewish Territorial Organization (a Jewish territorialist organization cofounded by Zangwill) agreed to supervise recruitment operations in Kiev, the movement had all its high-profile players: a major philanthropist in Jacob Schiff, an international organizer in Israel Zangwill, and the international infrastructure to move immigrants.

Then there were the logistical challenges. The West seemed an ideal place to resettle immigrants, but one reason that people believed that it cultivated manly resourcefulness, productivity, and pioneering attitudes was that it was not easy to get to. In any case, the immigrants would have to disembark at a port city. After dismissing Charleston because of its hospitability only for "Anglo-Saxon" immigrants (they did not elaborate on this judgment), the organizers looked to New Orleans and Galveston.[21] Of the two, New Orleans was more remote from the desirable destinations of the American West, and immigrants might be tempted to stay there, so they chose Galveston.[22] Since 1880, Galveston had been the largest city in Texas, but it did not have the "slums" and "ghettoes" of New York or Boston. Galveston, at a population of fewer than 40,000, was too small to tempt immigrants to stay and create the congested ghettoes that philanthropists and social workers disparaged. The town boasted several Yiddish speakers who could act as interpreters and a significant contingent of established middle- and upper-class Jews, but few opportunities for "sweatshop" or unskilled labor. It would provide warm hospitality, but limited appeal for settlement.

Galveston was also an attractive location because of the seemingly indefatigable Reform rabbi Henry Cohen, who would become an essential organizer and advocate for the immigrants. As Bressler wrote, "Galveston work was synonymous with Rabbi Cohen."[23] Cohen had other ties too; he had been a classmate of Zangwill's in England and the two remained "fast friends."[24] Cohen wrote an account of the Galveston Movement in 1908 that was, perhaps predictably, sanguine and celebratory in tone: "The country need have no fear of this class of alien—and if all signs fail not, the brawn and sinew and for that matter the brain—of the United States will be mightily strengthened by those Jews that pass through its Galveston port!"[25] Cohen's language emphasized the physical capacities of these immigrants—their brawn, their muscles, their strength. As a "class of alien," they could live up to physical standards of manliness. Cohen's description was unusual, in that few other descriptions touted Jewish immigrants' "brawn." Most focused on their potential to be transformed into contributing members of American society, and depicted healthy and productive manly bodies as the goal, rather than the raw material. Cohen's article serves as a reminder that American Jewish masculinity was never singular, even among acculturated Jews, but it nevertheless reinforces the idea that healthy manly bodies played a crucial role in the movement's ideology.

In the paternalistic tone typical of JIIB correspondence, philanthropist and social worker Jacob Billikopf suggested that the American West and Southwest were better formative environments than the cities. Billikopf told the *Galveston News* in 1907, "We don't want to give them a taste even of city life. We want them to be started out in the West and Southwest away from the tenement and shop life."[26] Jacob Schiff touted the "ready employment" and "more attractive surroundings than in the tenement districts of the Eastern city."[27] In a private letter, Bressler told Rabbi Cohen candidly, "I wish to remind you that these immigrants come directly from Europe and therefore have not acquired the evil ways of the New York contingent" of Jewish immigrants.[28] These "evil ways" included the tendency to pack into tenements, "cling" to their backward Old World customs and Yiddish language, and perhaps spend leisure time at questionable dances or theater performances. If they were not exposed to the urban environment, they would not be tempted by such vices.

Acculturated Jews lauded the Galveston Movement on the basis of its bene-fits not only for Jews but also for the United States as a country. Bressler explained that the Galveston Movement "hopes to divert from the Eastern ports a suffi-ciently large number of immigrants to the West and Southwest who will eventu-ally become centers of attraction in themselves, and will make of the Hinterland a reality and rob it of its isolation and uncertainty."[29] Far from being parasitic, weak, and unpatriotic, these Jewish immigrants would improve both the nation and the land itself. A 1912 *Jewish Herald* editorial framed the enterprise as ad-dressing the specific needs of the American land: "the great regions of the South and West [where there] are many communities, and more will spring up, that need the pushful energy of the Jew."[30] The *Herald* editorialist Oscar Leonard, ac-knowledging the "crowding" problem in New York, asked, "What is the rem-edy?" Zionists recommended colonizing Palestine, Leonard explained, but "why not in the large state of Texas where the soil goes a begging for cultivators?"[31] This fantasy of the undeveloped, waiting-to-be-tamed land of Texas mirrored similar rhetoric about Palestine. In some accounts, American land in the Southwest and West bordered on the Zionist image of "a land without people for a people with-out a land."[32] Jewish immigrant presence there would benefit both the Jews and the land.

When it emphasized the strong influence of land and environment, physical potential, and the ability of a people to change, the JIIB reflected a dominant strain of the anthropological discourse of the early twentieth century, especially as it applied to Jews. In his widely cited 1911 *The Jews: A Study of Race and Envi-ronment*, anthropologist Maurice Fishberg argued that rather than being con-fined to expressions of supposedly essential racial traits, Jews and their bodies were products of their social and historical environments. For instance, Fishberg explained the difference between the capacious chest accompanied by "strong, well developed muscles" and the chest "of small capacity, narrow and flat" that was characterized by "weak and flabby muscles." Few of the "Jews of Eastern Europe . . . can boast of a fully developed, capacious chest; most of them have emaciated, flat, and narrow chests." This smallness and weakness were not "a racial trait," but rather a malleable one that could be avoided with "proper sanitary and hygienic measures," such as living away from cities and doing physical outdoor work.[33] If they wanted stronger, better male bodies, Jews need not despair. Smallness and weakness were issues of environment, Fishberg argued.

Smallness and weakness were particularly characteristic of men who spent too much of their time living pious Jewish lives and studying sacred texts, Fish-berg explained. In this way, racial patterns were bound up with religious prac-tice. Smallness of chest was particularly pronounced in Russian and Austrian Jewish pupils who attended religious school, or *cheder*. (Since only boys attended *cheder*, his discussion included only male Jews.) "Games and outdoor exercises are foreign to the Jewish child in Europe," Fishberg wrote. He saw these trends continuing in America where immigrant Jews sent their boys for religious schooling. Such intensive schooling bought "mental and intellectual development" at the "high price" of their physical health and manliness. Boys pursued religious learning "from morning till late in the evening engaged in the study of Hebrew, the Bible, and Talmud," but neglected the cultivation of healthy bodies. Young men who did nothing but study religious texts could not become the kind of young Jewish men that Fishberg and other acculturated American Jews wanted. When they or their parents chose the Talmud over physical exercise, their bodies were disciplined into one kind of masculinity (one of traditional Jewish learning and piety) instead of another (one of physical strength and bodily health). Fishberg suggested this cultural difference: "It has also been observed that the intellectual classes are often deficient in chest capacity unless they engage in outdoor sports and games, as is generally the case with the American college boys."[34] The JIIB leaders shared this anthropological outlook. Jewish immigrants could and should be transformed, and the American West would be just the right environment to promote that transformation.

Acculturated American Jews "knew" that male bodies and habits could be changed by a change in environment. Anthropologists told them so, and so did their own ideals and experiences. They were confident that they could shape immigrants' masculinity, both physically and socially. They sought to mold an American Jewish masculinity with their own discourse, projects, and institutions. So did they think that gender was socially constructed? No, certainly not in the sense that gender theorists today would claim. To the contrary, these acculturated Jews believed that there was something essential and natural about gender. Men were the natural laborers, they assumed, and women were the natural caretakers. Men should be courageous, and women should nurture. They believed that men and women differed essentially and inherently. Still, they thought that men could become more (or differently) manly by changing their habits, practices, and bodies.

In other ways, their assumptions about the biological world allowed for even more change and variation than ours do. They thought that physical structure— for example, the shape of people's skulls—could actually change over generations. They had not incorporated Mendelian genetics into their approaches to understanding human bodies and inheritance, so they had some very expansive ideas about what could change over time and with a change of environment. Without a Mendelian model of inheritance, they often embraced a view that looked much more Lamarckian: if a parent became strong, dexterous, or healthy during his or her lifetime, he or she could pass those traits onto his children. In this way, they had a strong sense of the malleability of the body and some of its gendered traits. In sum, these acculturated Jews believed that they could change both the gender norms of Jewish immigrant men and how well the men conformed to those norms. In the process they would even be changing future generations.

Moreover, they believed that, when they transformed Jewish immigrants, they would be simultaneously changing the way others saw the masculinity of Jews. Bressler explained how to deal with "the" immigrant, whom he consistently assumed was male: put him in the right environment to develop his latent manly qualities. "Let his deficiencies be viewed frankly and tolerantly, bearing in mind that they are neither native nor yet deep-rooted but are rather the effect of persecution," he wrote.[35] Bressler countered antisemitic and anti-immigrant rhetoric of the day by emphasizing that environment, rather than racial determination, had caused the "deficiencies" of the immigrants. The "destiny" of the immigrant was to develop inherent manly virtues that had been suppressed by oppressive circumstances. Settlement in the American West would transform these immigrants into Americans, productive and strong workers, and better Jews.

Many non-Jews agreed. When the first group of immigrants landed in Galveston, the *Los Angeles Times* touted the Movement as "one of the greatest philanthropic events of the century." It celebrated that Jews were being "distributed over that section of the United States where room is allowed for the expansion of character and opportunities are given for the broadening of hope." The movement's noble goal of "upbuilding the race" would transform the immigrants not only into cleaner, healthier people but also from victims of violence to masters of the land. The movement would settle them "inland to the growing towns of the West—scatter them where the air was fresh and the demand for producers was greatest." The journalist C. H. Abbott also assumed that living in the West could and would transform the downtrodden Jews. He even connected the Galveston Movement to messianic or Zionist aspirations: the phrase, "next year in Jerusalem," formed a refrain in his article, and he wrote that "only by the actual elevation of the race," which he assumed the Galveston Movement was doing, "may the Jews of the world ever be assembled again in Palestine."[36] While the Galveston Movement itself did not have explicitly Zionist or messianic goals, Abbott was certain that it was uplifting these Jewish "pioneers" and "pilgrims." Abbott, like the acculturated Jews affiliated with the JIIB and Galveston Movement, saw the West—and not the Eastern cities—as the ideal Americanizing environment to make better Jews.

Piety and the Male Body

Better Jews, however, did not mean more pious Jews. To the contrary, in the eyes of the JIIB men, becoming better Jews meant becoming less wed to traditional forms of Judaism. Getting out of the city would facilitate that change since the Western communities were much smaller and the majority of Jews in the West and Southwest were either not practicing or were Reform in their observance.

Because of the need to work the land, settling out West would keep men from studying all day, hunched over religious texts. It would prevent parents from sending their boys to *cheder* where they would get no physical exercise. It would change their religion from an emotional, superstitious, particularist, and antiquated one to a rational one with universalist impulses. Moving out West would transform these Jews' religion from "bad" to "good," and, more abstractly, some of its feminine aspects (emotion, particularism) for masculine ones (reason, universalism). Acculturated Jews often looked down at the benighted and superstitious practices of the new immigrants, and the Galveston Movement's ideals about the healthy body and masculinity played into those concerns.

Sometimes the JIIB leaders explicitly expressed their concerns about the incongruity of religious piety and healthy, manly bodies. Bressler wrote to the JIIB's general agent Morris Waldman about one immigrant: "Shya Kupferstein should never have been sent. He is a 'Chasid,' and although claiming to be a carpenter he seems absolutely disqualified from taking care of himself."[37] Because he was Hasidic, the immigrant Kupferstein was strictly observant and conversant in traditional texts. But as a worker, he lacked the skills and ability to be a productive laborer or be self-sufficient. Bressler doubted that someone who was a Hasid could also be a carpenter. Because of these failures to live up to masculine norms, Kupferstein could not possibly make a good immigrant.

Why was religious piety a problem? Why couldn't a Hasid be a good candidate for the Galveston Movement? After all, in Eastern Europe, public piety went along with masculinity. Traditional study and visible synagogue participation were the bastion of men and rarely available to women. Though Hasidic forms of male piety never became the American norm, these immigrants also remind us that some Jews resisted the masculinity championed by many acculturated Jews.

Acculturated American Jews knew that this "Old World" public piety was associated with men, but they did not see it as manly. In a pragmatic sense, the problem posed by Jewish piety was the impracticality of halakhic observance: observing the Sabbath, obtaining fresh kosher meat, and even getting a ritual circumcision for infant boys would be challenging in a small western town with few other observant Jews. Even in places without blue laws, little commerce happened on Sundays, and so refusing to work on Saturdays made it quite difficult to earn a living. The original wording of the JIIB guidelines had banned immigrants who were observant or religious functionaries; no "*schochtim* [slaughterers], *melamdim* [religious instructors], or Jews who do not work on the Sabbath" would be permitted. Ultimately, the wording was changed to read: "It is but proper that intending immigrants should understand that economic conditions everywhere in the United States are such that strict Sabbath observance is exceedingly difficult and in most cases impossible," again emphasizing the value of work and self-sufficiency over that of religious observance in the eyes of the JIIB.[38]

But the problem with traditional piety extended beyond the impracticality of halakhic observance in the West. A deeper issue for the JIIB leaders was the imagined incongruity between the kind of masculinity they promoted and the kind of masculinity they associated with Hasidim and other traditional Jews. Not only did the JIIB men see pious Jewish observance as somewhat benighted and backward but they also saw devout ritual observance as a stumbling block to manliness and to enlightened Judaism. Practices such as all-day study would get in the way of economic productivity and of having a strong, healthy, and therefore manly body. The continuous studying of a Hasid like Shya Kupferstein meant that his body was weak, so how could he possibly be a carpenter? His Judaism centered on disciplining his body according to religious norms—of dress, of eating, of sexual activity, of working. If his Judaism shaped his body, and if his Judaism centered on embodied practices, then transforming that body would be difficult without transforming his Judaism too. A body-centered Jewish piety could get in the way of attaining body-centered masculine ideals of strength and working the land. This body-centered piety also placed a barrier between Judaism and "good" religion. Embodiment, particularism, and superstition were not only coded "bad" or underdeveloped religion in the American context but they were also, philosophically and theologically, considered to be feminine qualities. Acculturated Jews did not want their religion to seem mired in outdated superstition and insularity.

But, as Rabbi Cohen's strong presence in the Galveston Movement suggests, it was not a secularist movement. Instead, these acculturated Jews assumed that immigrants could embrace a rational Judaism, no longer beholden to the antiquated body-centered adherence to the letter of halakhah. At its most practical, this implicit endorsement of Reform Judaism meant that immigrants could believe in a monotheistic Jewish god while working on the Sabbath or eating whatever meat was available. Living in the American West, although it might not absolutely demand this flexibility, surely rewarded it.

Moving beyond the disciplined bodily practices of halakhah also meant something broader. If Judaism were centered in the mind or spirit, then Jewish bodies would be less beholden to old ways and old forms. Since this mind- and spirit-centered Judaism centered on reason, belief, and ethics, rather than physically following the ways of the past, the Jewish male body could be transformed into a healthy body without disrupting its Jewishness. By suggesting that immigrants shift from a Judaism they thought centered on bodily practices to a Judaism they thought centered in the head and heart, the acculturated Jews freed up the body as a site to become manly without losing Judaism. The weak, pale scholar need not be the face of Judaism, and the strong, productive worker of the land need not have frittered away his Judaism through assimilation. By leaving behind the disciplined bodily practices of halakhah in favor of the disciplined bodily practices of work, they could become healthy men who embraced "good" religion. A rational, head-centered Judaism left space for embracing embodied manliness.

In this sense, the Judaism promoted by acculturated Jews fit better not only with their vision of masculinity but also as an American religion. Because religion in early twentieth-century America was seen as a matter of individual conscience and belief and indebted to Enlightenment ideas of rationality, then a rational, freely chosen set of Jewish beliefs and practices would look like an American religion. But a Hasid's religion looked more like a body-centered set of practices based on traditional texts, even when they were utterly impractical and seemingly irrational—such as refusing to carry things on the Sabbath or insisting on kosher food in the West.

Even when they were not directly discussing religion, acculturated Jews often hinted at these issues. At the 1902 Conference of Jewish Charities, attended by Bressler and other JIIB associates, social worker and JAIAS manager William Kahn had articulated this ideology: the immigrants came from good "stock," but social circumstances had oppressed them, and so philanthropists should make it their goal "to remove these temporary disadvantages and to help these people cast off their long beards, their soiled clothes, and outlandish habits, and even their moral faults and weaknesses."[39] Kahn's list of immigrant flaws was cast in both gendered and religious terms. When Kahn wrote that "they" should "cast off their long beards," he assumed that the immigrants were men and that those men's bodies conformed to the norms of a pious Jewish masculinity. They did not shave their faces, nor did they conform to American norms of hygiene, as their dirty bodies and clothes indicated. And dirty bodies were not healthy bodies, according to widespread Progressive rhetoric. They also had "outlandish habits," which were religious customs or "superstitions" that acculturated Jews found embarrassing. "Moral faults and weaknesses" too, were vestiges of a particularist and insular religion. Philanthropy, Kahn explained, could help improve these immigrant men's lives in terms of both masculinity and religion.

Living outside of cities would help not only to create manly bodies but also to refine religious practice into a better Judaism. At the same conference, Reform rabbi and secretary of the Jewish Agricultural Aid Society of Chicago Abraham R. Levy explained that piety and superstition served a purpose in Eastern European contexts because there the poor Jews had little else to do with their time. The pious ceremonies and unending study helped distract Jews from their oppression. "However," he wrote, the situation should change now that these men had come to the United States: to continue "such ceremonies where divine and human agencies offer an opportunity for honest and useful toil, would be working against the interest of religion and not for it." If immigrant Jews continued their pious but benighted religious observance, it would preclude them from working and thereby becoming manly Americans. Levy also claimed that this work and manliness actually constituted a higher form of Judaism. Studying all day and sticking to outdated pious practices were actually "against" real religion, while working productively on the American land was "for it."

Levy suggested that old world piety was a crutch and that productive, physical work on the land would cure immigrant Jewish men of their irrational religion: "The Jew, living as a farmer among non-Jews, may miss much which habit and association have made dear to his heart, and which he considers essential to his religion. But the life of usefulness on the farm will wean him off, and bring him away from, many a superfluous ceremony and obsolete observance, the practice of which is more in accord with superstition than religion." Just in case he had not yet made himself clear, Levy explained how his listeners should understand which form of religion was best: "Judging by the facts as they are at hand, one is inclined to the belief that the religious life of the Jewish farmer is an improvement upon the religious life of the average ghetto-dweller." Unlike the urban immigrants, the Jews living in small towns and on farms showed "true religious devotion." This genuine religion was not one of external bodily forms, but was built on the rational cultivation of the mind and heart. "True religious devotion," for Levy, was not studying in a small, cramped room learning from a bearded old man. It was a family hour of reading in the farmhouse—an image that recalled idealized Christian family Bible reading. The Judaism that Levy championed eschewed pious practices of long hours of study, "superfluous ceremony," and "obsolete observance" in favor of productive work and healthy bodies.[40]

Yet the members of the JIIB's hierarchy did not despise old world religion in its entirety. Many were committed Reform Jews, such as Henry Cohen; Morris Waldman, who had been the rabbi at Temple Anshe Emeth in New Brunswick, New Jersey; and Schiff, who was an active member of New York's Temple Emanu-El. "There can be no doubt the Russian Jew is a splendid stock," Schiff wrote, using a common shorthand for all Eastern European Jews, in a letter to Billikopf. "He brings his ideals and a religious background, of which, with our materialistic tendencies, we stand in great need."[41] What was good about their religion was that it could offer a corrective to the materialistic tendencies of American Jews. Acculturated Jews could learn a lesson from an inner religious disposition, but not, he assumed, from ritual observance itself. Ritual observance represented merely an outward form of an inner belief and disposition. Like many Reform Jews of the early twentieth century, Schiff thought that Judaism had an essential spiritual core, a universal ethic anchored in God and the Bible. Schiff suggested that Eastern European immigrants, perhaps unlike American or German-born Jews like himself, were more in touch with these ideals.

These acculturated Jews thought that the right kind of Judaism could play an important role in the immigrants' new pioneering lives. Henry Cohen wrote,

"The pioneers who wooed the West brought their faith with them, and of all the people pioneers need faith! Religion is to them at once a stronghold and an anchorage, and the Jewish people are not an exception to this rule."[42] In Cohen's hands, Judaism became a religion fully compatible with pioneering and the West. As a rational, mind-centered religion, it would support rather than impede frontier life. Cohen also implied that Judaism served the same role as other religions did for American pioneers. Jewish pioneers were just like the brave, manly, and godly Americans who had pioneered the West before them. If Judaism could help men brave the frontier, what better argument could it have for being an American religion?

Somewhat paradoxically, then, the JIIB denigrated religious functionaries such as ritual slaughterers and teachers and then turned around to praise "religion." They had a particular idea of what "religion" should do and what it was good for—and it was not the empty rituals of religious functionaries. The former state to which Bressler, Cohen, Kahn, and others wanted Jews to return was not that of a romanticized traditional religious life. Eastern European Jewish attachment to religion represented degeneration, in their eyes, not the expression of a true Judaism. The Judaism they prized was a rational religion uncorrupted by the superstitions borne of generations of oppression. They hoped that the immigrants would come to discard their superstitious and rigid practices while maintaining religious faith and morals. The immigrants' religious transformation and the transformation to healthy manly bodies would go hand in hand. Perhaps they too would become adherents of an American Judaism.

Productive Labor, "Poor Physique," and the Evaluation of Jewish Immigrant Men

The American West would not magically transform immigrants into the men whom acculturated Jews envisioned. Even if they shook off the irrational bodily practices that prevented them from achieving healthy bodies, they would not become new men overnight. They still needed to take up another core component of American Jewish masculinity: productive labor. William Kahn noted that the Jewish immigrants were "somewhat different from the independent and self-reliant American workingman."[43] But acculturated Jews' philanthropic efforts, such as the JIIB and JAIAS, could help these immigrants erase that difference, Kahn contended.[44] Pushcart peddlers could make a living in New York City by selling other people's wares, but acculturated Jews thought that occupation built neither character nor physique. In small towns and out West, the immigrant men would need to know a trade or be willing to learn one. This kind of labor would produce not only goods and economic value but also the kind of healthy, self-sufficient men acculturated Jews wanted these immigrants to become.

Across the nation, women were much less likely than men to immigrate without accompanying family members, but Galveston attracted an even higher percentage of men. Through 1910, 84 percent of Jews arriving by way of Galveston were men, compared to 57 percent of arrivals in New York.[45] Official standards disseminated in Kiev stated, "The emigrant must not be over 40 years of age. If married, the emigrant, his wife and children must be strong and healthy, and able to satisfy all the requirements of the Immigration Laws of the U.S.A."[46] That "the emigrant" was a man went unquestioned: women and children were not allowed to emigrate alone as part of the Galveston Movement. The receiving communities often explicitly asked for single men and almost always according to the occupation or trade they practiced. In Galveston, disagreement arose about what the correct number of immigrants on each boat should be because when the JIIB requested 100, it meant 100 men. Bressler complained, "The total number of persons . . . fell far short of the agreed number. . . . Had they lived up to the agreement with us, they should have sent in the last four consignments 325 persons (excluding women and children), yet they sent altogether 200 persons, including women and children."[47] Bressler had expected 325 "persons," by which he meant men, but the boats had only brought 200 "persons"—and some of those "persons" were women and children! Leaving aside the fact that Bressler seemed to think that "persons" represents a category that can exclude women and children, this disagreement made plain the idea that the Galveston Movement had the cultivation of men as its object, both practically and ideologically.

Though almost all of the JIIB materials dealt with men, they also suggest something about women. The movement's focus on men helped it quietly avoid two social issues. First, in the early twentieth century, muckrakers, nativists, and even Jews themselves became particularly concerned about Jews' involvement in "white slavery," or the sex trade in women. Jews were accused of a particularly disproportionate rate of involvement—both as slavers and slaves; therefore, despite little evidence of Jewish domination of the white slave trade, Jewish leaders and philanthropists went out of their way to avoid any possible accusations.[48] Discouraging women, especially single women, from immigrating could help avoid the issue. Many of the popular white slavery horror stories involved young immigrant women who had just arrived, which likely influenced the decision by Henry Cohen and his wife to meet each group of new immigrants as they disembarked in Galveston. Second, images of immigrant women working, especially toiling in garment factories, also ran afoul of idealized images of American womanhood. Philanthropists and social workers expressed concern about the physical and spiritual consequences of crowded factory work. Although most immigrant families needed some type of supplement to an adult man's salary,[49] it remained culturally expedient to focus on images of men and labor, rather than women.

Other American writers were also concerned about immigrants' ability to labor productively and to pioneer. In 1914, Edward Alsworth Ross, outspoken nativist and sociology professor, warned Americans about the undesirable characteristics of immigrants. "The Hebrews," he explained, "are the polar opposite of our pioneer breed. Not only are they undersized and weak-muscled, but they shun bodily activity and are exceedingly sensitive to pain." In contrast, Ross praised true Americans by emphasizing their tough physical masculinity and their connections to the indigenous inhabitants of the American continent. "Selection, frontier life, and the example of the red man produced in America a type of great physical self-control, gritty, silent, merciless to the body through fear of becoming 'soft.' To this roaming, hunting, exploring, adventurous breed what greater contrast is there than the denizens of the Ghetto?" Ross suggested that it was no accident that few Jews settled out West. Unlike "Americans"—whom he tied to Native Americans—Jews had neither the taste nor aptitude for frontier life. They could not fend for themselves, show courage, or work the land. The "Hebrews" were not manly men.

Still, Ross grudgingly agreed, the Jews had shown slow progress toward manliness: "The second generation, to be sure, overtop[s] their parents and are going in for athletics." Immigrant Jews, according to Ross, avoided all physical activity, but the American environment had influenced their children for the better. Despite his prejudice, Ross echoed larger assumptions about the mutability of racial types. "Still," he continued, "it will be long before they produce the type who traverses the wilderness, portaging his canoe, poling it against the current, wading in the torrents, living on bacon and beans, and sleeping on the ground, all for 'fun' or 'to keep hard.'"[50] In Ross's eyes, Jewish men would not voluntarily become pioneers. They would not even play at frontier life or mastering nature.

These assumptions about Jews' failure to labor productively, their alienation from the land, and their unwillingness to settle the frontier held sway in circles well beyond the sociological and the academic. Theodore Reyman, the owner of a manufacturing company in New York, wrote to the Department of Commerce and Labor in 1910 to register his complaints about Jewish workers and their effect on the economy: they "are not workers nor pioneer settlers nor do they work on farmland, in the cities they get into trade and begin to ruin prices and drive others out."[51] Ideal economic behavior intersected with ideals about masculinity: for both acculturated Jews and non-Jews, producing goods, especially with one's own hands and strength, was deemed positive for both economics and manliness, whereas buying and selling small goods were inferior modes of employment that did not contribute to manliness.

The "poor physique" problem, one of the most significant challenges the JIIB faced, demonstrates the centrality of the masculine norms of both healthy bodies and productive labor. As at Ellis Island, a physician examined each immigrant to

Galveston to determine his or her fitness to enter the country. Some would be turned away for evidence of disease, while others could be denied entry because of "poor physique," a category that came to preoccupy Schiff, Bressler, and Cohen. The rationale for the decision of immigration authorities to turn away weak, hunched, or sickly bodies was that people with poor physique would not be able to support themselves. At its center, this was a concern about masculinity: without a healthy body, a man could not be expected to perform productive labor, and so he might not be able to provide for himself and his family. Best to keep these unmanly immigrants out of the country altogether, immigration officials thought.

Poor physique and its attendant problem, "likely to become a public charge," cut to the heart of many of the worries about the new immigrants. These evaluations suggested that Jews would be parasitic on the nation, consumers rather than producers, weak, and unable to support themselves. The accusation that Jews—especially Jewish men—were small, weak, and physically inferior, as acculturated Jews knew well, was circulating among European and American antisemites. (Recall Patton's complaint about Jewish immigrants being "too lazy to enter into real labor, too cowardly to face frontier life, too lazy to work as every American farmer has to work.") Medical historians Howard Merkel and A. M. Stern have called "poor physique" in Eastern European immigrant Jews "a favorite 'wastebasket' diagnosis of nativists in the early 1900s."[52] When medical authorities labeled immigrants as unproductive weaklings, it reinforced the specious conclusions of much of the race science of the day, as well as undermined Jewish claims to a masculinity consonant with bodily fitness and good citizenship.[53]

JIIB officials became preoccupied with statistics about the number of immigrants turned away on charges of "poor physique." Not only did these denials decrease the number of immigrants successfully admitted but they also played on these leaders' concerns about Jewish immigrants as weak and unmanly. In Galveston, immigration authorities excluded a significantly larger percentage than in New York, and this served as a topic of much discussion. In general a man committed to the importance of rules and with a relatively low opinion of the mental and physical condition of the arriving immigrants, Bressler had expressed his agreement and sympathy with the denials and deportations early in the movement's operation. But those exclusions for "poor physique" were an exception.[54] He opined, "The 'poor physique' clause is, from my standpoint, entirely overdone."[55]

A 1910 conflict with a Galveston medical examiner demonstrated how important the "poor physique" clause was for establishing the quality of Jewish men as potential Americans. Cohen and Bressler worried that the examiner, Dr. Corput, was exhibiting prejudice against Jewish immigrants by using the "poor physique" clause to exclude them from entry. Bressler wrote to the philanthropist and judge Nathan Bijur, "We are having considerable difficulty with the medical authorities at Galveston in the matter of aliens who are not, so to speak, perfect physical specimens. Mr. Berman [a JIIB agent] writes us that in a number of instances the enforcement of the law with regard to persons liable to become a public charge and 'poor physique' has been unfair and unjust in the extreme." Bressler explained that he had it "on good authority" that Corput had several times expressed particular distaste for Jews.[56] On learning that someone had overheard Corput making anti-Jewish remarks, Max Kohler, immigrant rights activist and son of Kaufman Kohler, suggested filing an official complaint. He decried the expansive category of "'likely to become public charges' on account of medical finding against them because of alleged lack of muscular or physical development." A nebulous and poorly defined medical category allowed examiners to keep Jews out of the United States because of their lack of muscles. In this way, medical knowledge, which we might think of as objective, actually functioned ideologically. Kohler knew that doctors' reports and statistics shaped ideas about Jewish men and how well they conformed to physical norms of masculinity. Not only did he want to make sure future immigrants would be allowed into the country but he also advocated publicly filing charges against Corput.[57] (They chose not to.) Although the next month's passengers made it through the admission process without incident, the percentage of those excluded on the "poor physique" clause remained higher in Galveston than in New York, and the characterization of weak and unproductive Jews remained on the minds of JIIB officials.

Medical examiners and non-Jews, however, were not the only ones to use the categories of musculature and physical fitness to evaluate immigrant men. Bressler, Cohen, and Waldman all described men's physique—though never women's—in their own evaluations of immigrants. Waldman praised a "finely built fellow" as an exemplary immigrant.[58] A 1913 memo noted, in a self-congratulatory tone, "It is a fact that the average type immigrant that has come to Galveston is superior physically and more industrially efficient than those who arrive at the Northeastern seaports."[59] JIIB officials puffed their feathers when they touted the physical superiority and labor efficiency of their immigrants: these categories showed that their immigrant men were better and more manly.

Conversely, when they sought to impugn the character of an immigrant, JIIB agents often used categories of physique and manhood. "Both the rabbi and I thought he was a very poor specimen of physical manhood," Waldman wrote to Bressler about a potential immigrant named Joseph Kohn.[60] Greenberg, another JIIB agent, described another immigrant who had created administrative difficulty as "not a fine specimen of manhood."[61]

The JIIB even used the charge of "poor physique" to discredit an immigrant named Optowski, who criticized the IRO in English and Yiddish newspapers. He claimed that he had tried to find work, but demurred when the IRO offered to procure a job for him. He instead wanted the IRO to pay to send him to Europe because of an ailment he described as being "ruptured." The doctor examined him and reported that he was not, in fact, "ruptured." Instead, the doctor "certified that he was a very weak specimen. . . . He is a runt of a man. . . . Both his physique and inclination bar him from becoming a self-reliant person."[62] When they sought to criticize "our friend Optowski," as Bressler sarcastically referred to him, the JIIB leaders used the same criteria of physical manhood and its relationship to self-reliance. According to these criteria, he failed. Optowski would be no pioneer, no "future citizen," as Bressler called the immigrants.[63] But the order of events reveals another important point. Initially, the IRO thought that Optowski could work and support himself. Only after he failed to gain employment for himself and refused the IRO's offers—and then publicly criticized the organization—did it have him physically evaluated and diagnosed as "a very weak specimen." It was his unwillingness to change, not a physical inability to do so, that barred him from becoming a productive, and perhaps even strong, man. "Our friend Optowski" was not an American man in the making.

Poor physique also sometimes accompanied religious piety in the eyes of JIIB agents. Like the Hasidic immigrant Kupferstein, whom they deemed a poor candidate for immigration, another "yeshiva bucher" [a male yeshiva student] was labeled "unfit for work."[64] According to the JIIB's evaluation, his status as a poor candidate for Americanization because of his religious observance—recall the clause claiming even Sabbath observance would be a hindrance to settlement—was related to his occupation as a yeshiva student and his physical condition of weakness. Acculturated Jews often associated cultural backwardness and physical inferiority with the piety and observance of Eastern European Jews.[65] The ideal immigrant, conversely, would be willing and able to conform to American standards of manliness in his religious customs, work habits, and even body.

Cohen, Bressler, Zangwill, Waldman, and others envisioned these immigrants as pioneers, using rhetoric that tied them to the popular American figure of the rugged and self-sufficient pioneer.[66] Bressler suggested that before the formation of the JIIB, "to take the plunge into the hinterland was left only to the most daring."[67] However, the JIIB made the opportunity to be a pioneer available to any immigrant who was willing and physically able.[68] Brave, daring pioneers, by definition, did something new. They did not buy and resell goods; they needed to be productive and self-sufficient. Schiff wrote to a railway manager in 1909: "They represent the pick of the Trans-Atlantic Jewish migration, and have the pioneer spirit which fits them for pioneer life."[69] On a somewhat self-congratulatory note, in his report to the US congressional committee known as the Dillingham Commission, Bressler wrote, "The effect of the movement has been to infuse something akin to the pioneer spirit into the immigrant."[70]

The efforts of the JIIB also hint at ways that masculinity was never totally uniform. Engaging in philanthropy allowed these acculturated Jewish men to demonstrate their own masculinity. The JIIB men faced a dilemma: How could they insist that the West was best, that it helped immigrants cultivate manliness, Americanness, and a proper Judaism, all the while themselves (mostly) remaining in Eastern cities? Certainly they would not be traveling West with the immigrants. They would not be pioneers in developing the land. None of them made a living as a farmer. Most of them would live the rest of their lives in urban neighborhoods. Nevertheless, they saw themselves as already adequately masculine. They never worried that their own physique, white-collar occupations, or urban lives threatened their manliness. JIIB men solved this dilemma by demonstrating their own masculinity through philanthropy and politics: by organizing and supporting the Galveston Movement, they could idealize healthy male bodies and the American West as properly American without spending their time in the hinterland. They could spend their leisure time and money vacationing outside the city, breathing the fresh air and exercising their bodies. Religiously, they already embraced a rational Judaism, which had moved past ideal male models of all-day religious study that prevented physical cultivation.

Promoting an American manliness of healthy bodies and attachment to the frontier for the immigrants helped acculturated Jews secure their own manliness. As William Kahn said at a 1902 conference of Jewish social workers, removal work "will result in producing self-supporting, industrious and progressive citizens, who will be a benefit to the communities in which they settle, and will reflect credit on the philanthropic gentlemen who have assisted them, in the eyes of both Jews and Gentiles."[71] Acculturated Jews worked for a different kind of "production"— the creation of "self-supporting, industrious" workers and citizens—which would reflect on the philanthropic largesse and effectiveness of the acculturated "gentlemen" behind the projects. Facilitating immigrant manliness would reflect a positive (though more genteel and less focused on physical brawn) masculinity back on the acculturated philanthropists and social workers.

The Galveston Movement leaders saw themselves as instruments in the salvation of immigrant Jews in several senses. First, they sympathized with the plight of Eastern European Jews who suffered at the hands of their countrymen. Reports of pogroms such as the 1903 Kishinev massacre,[72] which resulted in the death of more than forty Jews; the 1905 Kiev pogrom, which left more than one hundred dead; and the even bloodier 1905 Odessa pogrom appeared in American newspapers. Many American Jews donated money, but they also looked for more systematic ways to help their coreligionists. Facilitating immigration to America was one way to do that.

Second, many acculturated American Jews saw Eastern European Jews as physically inferior. Cohen wrote of what he saw as the physical effects of the pogroms and restrictions: "And so with these trials, the very physical likeness of the Jew became changed. An unhealthy mind was coupled with a disturbed body, for the Jew bent his head and could look none in the face."[73] The pogroms, along with laws restricting land ownership and occupation, had transformed Jews both physically and mentally. Persecution and alienation from the land took its toll not only on their culture but also on their bodies. A bent man who could not look another man in the face was not a manly man. Helping immigrants to settle in the American West would allow them to escape persecution and thereby raise their heads again and reclaim some manliness.

The idea that dispersion to the West would transform Jewish immigrants from backward and downtrodden foreigners into American pioneers appealed to those Jews who already saw themselves as American. Instead of reflecting poorly on American Jewry, these immigrants could contribute to the nation through their productive labor and colonization of the West. Acculturated Jews themselves, of course, did not leave their cities in droves to settle the West as they pushed the immigrants to do. But they championed an American Jewish masculinity that was connected to the land, productive labor, rational religion, and healthy bodies, and in the American West they saw the ideal setting to shape immigrants according to these norms.

Conclusion

The Reverend Patton thought that Ellis Island was overrun by weak and unproductive Jewish men, but the JIIB was convinced that settling Jewish immigrants in the American West would change all that. It would change the immigrants themselves into the strong and self-sufficient men that their ancient forebears were, it would change the minds of people like Patton, and it would even change the land itself. The immigrants would leave their superstitious, law-centered Judaism and the weak bodies it created in favor of an enlightened Judaism consonant with physical health and productivity. If immigrant Jews were not yet manly in physical ways, a change of lifestyle, environment, and religion could make them so. Even though this pioneering manliness was not a personal goal for the acculturated Jews who supported the Galveston Movement, they nevertheless upheld it as an ideal for new immigrants.

Judaism mattered to the JIIB, and so we should not see it as just a project of Progressive Era social uplift with the goal of Americanization. While Bressler, Schiff, Cohen, and others sought to transform Jewish religious practice so that it no longer produced the weak, sickly men who studied all day, they nevertheless valued Judaism. The Judaism they offered could harmonize with life on the frontier and healthy, productive male bodies because it did not involve long hours of study, nor did it focus on the particulars of halakhah. The JIIB men assumed the superiority of a rational, belief-centered Judaism located less in the body than in the mind. Without religious norms constantly policing the male body and withering it into weakness, these immigrants could blossom into manly Jews who identified with the American land. Judaism could be centered in the mind and heart, where it would not contribute to "poor physique." This kind of Judaism fit the pioneering immigrant lifestyle they imagined: it was healthy, productive, manly, American, and yet still Jewish.

This project to transform American Jewish masculinity operated on two levels simultaneously. From one angle, acculturated Jews sought to shape the masculinity of immigrant Jews. From another angle, these acculturated Jews sought to change the broader American assumptions about what it meant to be a Jewish man. These two were inextricably linked. Transforming how American Jewish men behaved, how they saw themselves, and what ideals they sought would also change how others saw them. Conversely, changing perceptions and expectations of Jewish men would change how they behaved, how they saw themselves, and for which ideals they strived.

Looking at this complex interplay between bodily actions and the perception of others illuminates how gender is constructed. Gender theorists have used the language of "norms" to describe how assumptions, expectations, experiences, and perceptions of gender happen. The term "norm" has two connotations. It means the normal, the regular, the expected, or the average. But it also means the ideal, the goal, the thing for which we aim. Gender norms, then, seem to be both "normal" and "ideal." For instance, acculturated American Jews expected that men would work to support their families. Male work for pay was a norm because it was common and expected. Most men worked outside the home. But it was also a norm because acculturated Jews thought that work was something men *should* do. Performing some sort of labor, especially if the fruits of that labor supported other family members, was an important part of being a man. A man who did not or could not support his family was less manly than one who did. This story is a story of both sorts of norms. The norms, in the ideal sense, were more consistent than the lived norms, in the normal sense. But gender norms are always contested and a bit messy, and this story is no different. The vast majority of immigrant Jews did not go out West to cultivate manliness, and many found Reform practices alienating or unappealing.

The Galveston Movement, despite its small numbers, tells a bigger story about how the American land, productive labor, rational religion, and healthy bodies came to be norms of American Jewish masculinity. It sought to transform Jewish immigrant men into men with strong, productive bodies, and it saw the American West and Southwest as the ideal locations to do it. This project of manliness was built on the foundation of the idea that Jewish men could change; they might be pale and weak as immigrants, but that was the result of historical oppression, not their essential makeup. In this way, the Galveston Movement depended on an inherent optimism about Jewish male bodies. Provided that immigrants were willing to change their own habits, especially trading any "superstitious" religious piety for a more rational Judaism, they could be molded and shaped. A pioneering lifestyle in the West could help them develop the strong and productive male bodies that Americans venerated.

The Galveston Movement was an acculturated Jewish experiment, one that both disclosed their desires for Jewish masculinity and sought to shape the immigrants according to those desires. The next chapter presents another experiment that also promoted the association of healthy bodies and relationship to the land with Jewish men: imagined connections with "Indians" of the American past. Like the Galveston Movement, it never became the primary way Americans imagined Jewish men, but it likewise helps us see the construction of American Jewish masculinity. Where the Galveston Movement focused on immigrants, the next chapter shows that acculturated Jewish men too wanted to think of themselves as having healthy bodies with attachments to the American land. And to do so, they appealed to an imagined shared past with the original inhabitants of that land: the Indians.

Notes

1. Quoted in Melvin Urofsky, *American Zionism from Herzl to the Holocaust* (Lincoln, NE: Bison Books, 1995), 301–302.

2. M. J. Haskell, "The Galveston Immigration Movement," *Charities and the Commons* 20 (June 13, 1908): 369.

3. Sidney Teller, "Influence of a Recreation Center on a Jewish Community," *Jewish Charities* 4 (Dec. 1912): 4.

4. Ibid., 5–6.

5. Ibid., 4.

6. For statistics, see *The Jewish Communal Register of New York City* (Kehilla: New York, 1918), 89–90.

7. For more details on the Galveston Movement, see Bernard Marinbach, *Galveston: Ellis Island of the West* (Albany, NY: SUNY Press, 1983); Jack Glazier, *Dispersing the Ghetto: The Relocation of Jewish Immigrants across America* (Ithaca, NY: Cornell University Press, 1999); Gur Alroey, "Galveston and Palestine: Immigration and Ideology in the Early Twentieth Century," *American Jewish Archives Journal* 56 (2004): 129–150; Gary Best, "Jacob Schiff's Galveston Movement," *American Jewish Archives Journal* (April 1978): 43–79; and Hollace Ava Weiner, "Removal Approval: The Industrial Removal Office Experience in Fort Worth, Texas," *Southern Jewish History* 4 (2001). Apart from Weiner's work, these studies have focused mainly on Schiff and Israel Zangwill as the major figures of the movement. While both were involved in important ways, this study focuses on how the men (and they were almost entirely men) who administered the movement's day-to-day policies and activities viewed their project.

8. The idea that city living sapped men's vitality was not unique to Jews. Social Gospellers and other Protestants spilled plenty of ink and sweat trying to combat the enfeebling aspects of city living. YMCAs, school sports in religiously affiliated high schools, and church support and participation in athletics all sought to save Christian male bodies from sliding into weak

degeneracy. These Christians worried that not only immigrants but also old stock whites suffered the enervating and embarrassing effects of city living.

9. Lillian Wald, *The House on Henry Street* (New York: Henry Holt, 1915), 95.

10. Bressler to Cohen, April 11, 1912, 3M227, Henry Cohen Papers, Briscoe Center for American History (henceforth Cohen Papers [Briscoe]).

11. David Bressler, "The Removal Work, Including Galveston" (n.p.: n.p., n.d.), 13. A version was presented before the National Council of Jewish Charities on May 17, 1910. AJHS Monographs, American Jewish Historical Society (henceforth *AJHS*).

12. *McClure's*, a monthly magazine, published several articles that dramatized Jewish immigrant life in New York in critical terms. Journalist Burton Hendrick wrote two of the more pointed pieces. Burton Hendrick, "The Great Jewish Invasion," *McClure's*, Jan. 1907, 307–320; and "The Jewish Invasion of America," *McClure's*, Jan. 1913, 125–165.

13. Allan McLaughlin, "Hebrew, Magyar, and Levantine Immigration," *Popular Science Monthly*, Sept. 1904, 435.

14. In 1900, the New York-based Baron de Hirsch Fund and London-based Jewish Colonization Society established JAIAS in the United States. The two philanthropic organizations shared the visions of relocating Jews away from areas of persecution and settling the land, although the Jewish Colonization Society concentrated broadly on facilitating the former and Baron de Hirsch Fund the latter. JAIAS was designed to serve as a lending and granting institution for Jewish agricultural and industrial settlements.

15. Jacob Schiff to Paul Nathan, Dec. 28, 1904, Jacob Schiff Papers, Box 20, *AJA*. As Morris Waldman, an early member of the Galveston Committee, wrote retrospectively of the diminutive but highly dignified Schiff, "He was Jewish philanthropy's statesman. Although we looked to him for gifts, we also looked to him for guidance." Morris Waldman, "The Galveston Movement," *Jewish Social Service Quarterly*, Mar. 1928, 198. Despite the fact that the financier's enormous gifts totaled nearly a half-million dollars, he continued to insist that it "by no means be a Schiff scheme," as he explained in a 1906 letter to the playwright Israel Zangwill. Schiff to Israel Zangwill, Nov 8, 1906, Jacob Schiff Papers, Box 20, *AJA*.

16. Quoted in Prescott Farnsworth Hall, *Immigration and Its Effects upon the United States* (New York: Henry Holt and Co., 1906), 349.

17. Ibid., 122.

18. Galveston Committee treasurer and IRO President Cyrus Sulzberger wrote a scathing review of Hall's book, but he did not dispute the desirability of the West as the best environment for immigrant newcomers. Cyrus Sulzberger, "Immigration Restriction: Its Fallacies," *Menorah* 40, no. 4 (Apr. 1906): 193–202.

19. Restrictionists like Hall were less sanguine about the latter point since they argued that foreign countries kept "at home the strong, healthy, industrious citizens . . . and let go only those who are undesirable." Hall, *Immigration and Its Effects*, 292.

20. Israel Zangwill, "Preface to the Emigration Pamphlet" (1910), Central Zionist Archives, A36, file 95b, 3–4, quoted in Alroey, "Galveston and Palestine," 133.

21. Morris Waldman to David Bressler, Nov. 5, 1906, Galveston Papers, Quoted in Marinbach, *Galveston*, 12.

22. Waldman, "The Galveston Movement," 201.

23. David Bressler to Henry Cohen, Oct. 23, 1914, 3M232, Cohen Papers (Briscoe).

24. The quotation is from folder 3M327, Cohen Papers (Briscoe). The two, both born in England, were classmates at Jews College in London. Hollace Ava Weiner, *Jewish Stars in Texas* (College Station: Texas A&M University Press, 1999), 62. On Zangwill, see Meri-Jane Rochelson, *A Jew in the Public Arena: The Career of Israel Zangwill* (Detroit, MI: Wayne State University

Press, 2008); and Joseph H. Udelson, *Dreamer of the Ghetto: The Life and Works of Israel Zangwill* (Tuscaloosa: University of Alabama Press, 1990).

25. Henry Cohen, "The Galveston Immigration Movement," June 1, 1908. Cohen Papers (Briscoe).

26. "Jewish Immigrants," *Galveston News*, Dec. 7(?), 1907, Galveston Immigration Plan Records, box 2 folder 33, AJHS.

27. Jacob Schiff, "The Galveston Movement," *Jewish Charities* 4 (June 1914): 6.

28. Bressler to Henry Goldstein, Dec. 18, 1907, AHJS Archives, box 2, folder 50.

29. David Bressler, "The Removal Work, Including Galveston," 125–126.

30. "The Galveston Movement," *Jewish Herald*, Jan. 6, 1910, quoted in Bryan Edward Stone, "Edgar Goldberg and the Texas Jewish Herald: Changing Coverage and Blended Identity," *Southern Jewish History* 7 (2004): 91.

31. Oscar Leonard, "Come to Texas," *Jewish Herald*, Jan. 6, 1910, quoted in Stone, "Edgar Goldberg and the Texas Jewish Herald," 90.

32. This slogan traveled in Zionist discourse from the end of the nineteenth century forward. See Anita Shapira, *Land and Power: The Zionist Resort to Force, 1881–1948* (Oxford: Oxford University Press, 1992), 41ff. Both versions of the imagined frontier excluded the land's earlier inhabitants: Native Americans in the Texan case, and Arabs in the Palestinian case.

33. "The rural population is known to have larger girth than the urban population, and the factory worker is at a disadvantage when compared with the outdoor worker in this respect." Maurice Fishberg, *The Jews: A Study of Race and Environment* (New York: Walter Scott Publishing Co., 1911), 86–88.

34. Ibid., 86–87.

35. David Bressler, *The Removal Work, Including Galveston*, (n.p.: n.p., ca. 1910).

36. C. H. Abbott, "Canaan for Persecuted Jews Is Found in the Southwest," *Los Angeles Times*, Aug. 4, 1907.

37. David Bressler to Morris Waldman, Aug. 28, 1907, box 2, folder 41, Galveston Records.

38. Marinbach, *Galveston*, 14.

39. William Kahn, "Jewish Agricultural and Industrial Aid Society, New York," *Second Conference of Jewish Charities* (Cincinnati: Krehbiel, 1902), 94.

40. A. R. Levy, "Agriculture, a Most Effective Means to Aid Jewish Poor," in *Second Conference of Jewish Charities* (Cincinnati: Krehbiel, 1902), 105.

41. Schiff to Jacob Billikopf, May 2, 1910.

42. "Address Delivered by Rabbi Henry Cohen before Congregation B'nai Israel on the Celebration of the Fiftieth Anniversary of the Congregation," May 1921, 3M327, Cohen Papers (Briscoe).

43. Kahn, "Jewish Agricultural and Industrial Aid Society, New York," 87.

44. The type of work also mattered. Kahn wrote about Jewish men who did not receive charity, but still failed to attain "a position of independent and respectable self-support." If they were not receiving charity, these men must have been working, but their occupations did not meet Kahn's standards of respectability for working men. Ibid., 89.

45. For these statistics and other tables about the demography of the Galveston Movement, see Von J. Lestschinsky, "Die Auswanderung der Juden nach Galveston," *Zeitschrift fur Demographie und Statistik der Juden* (Dec. 1910): 177–184. Also see Alroey, "Galveston and Palestine"; and Marinbach, *Galveston*, 114.

46. Jewish Territorial Organization (ITO) papers, A36 file 95b, Central Zionist Archives (henceforth CZA) quoted in Alroey, "Galveston and Palestine," 134.

47. "Immigrants who arrived on SS Frankfurt, January 21, 1908," ITO papers, A36 file 95, quoted in Marinbach, *Galveston*, 54.

48. See Edward Bristow, *Prostitution and Prejudice: The Jewish Fight against White Slavery, 1870–1939* (Oxford: Clarendon Press, 1982).

49. On Jewish women and work in early twentieth-century America, see Glenn, *Daughters of the Shtetl: Life and Labor in the Immigrant Generation* (Ithaca, NY: Cornell University Press, 1990).

50. Edward Alsworth Ross, "Racial Consequences of Immigration," *Century Magazine* 87 (Feb. 1914): 618.

51. Cited in Stuart Rockoff, Galveston Project Symposium keynote address, Sept. 2009. http://www.utexas.edu/cola/depts/history/_files/downloads/news/fall09/galveston-project-talk.pdf.

52. Howard Markel and Alexandra Minna Stern, "Which Face? Whose Nation? Immigration, Public Health, and the Construction of Disease at America's Ports and Borders, 1891–1928," *American Behavioral Scientist* 42, no. 9 (1999): 1313–1330.

53. For the account of this construction of the Jew in its European context, see the now-canonical Sander Gilman, *The Jew's Body* (New York: Routledge, 1991).

54. David Bressler to Henry Cohen, Sept. 11, 1907, box 1, folder 15, Galveston Records.

55. Henry Cohen to David Bressler, Sept. 2, 1907, box 1, folder 15, Galveston Records.

56. David Bressler to Nathan Bijur, Mar. 23, 1910, box 1, folder 2, Galveston Records.

57. Max Kohler to David Bressler, Mar. 28, 1910, box 1, folder 5, Galveston Records.

58. Morris Waldman to David Bressler, July 12, 1907, box 2, folder 36, Galveston Records.

59. "Memo for Mr. [Abram] Elkus," 1913, box 1, folder 4, Galveston Records.

60. Morris Waldman to David Bressler, Dec. 23, 1907, box 3, folder 50, Galveston Records.

61. Greenberg to David Bressler, May 24, 1909, box 1, folder 22, Galveston Records.

62. David Bressler to Morris Waldman, [1907], box 3, folder 48, Galveston Records.

63. David Bressler to Morris Waldman, Aug. 24, 1907, box 2, folder 41, Galveston Records.

64. Goldstein to Morris Waldman, Jan. 21, 1908, box 3, folder 54, Galveston Records.

65. For two examples, see Hart, *Social Science and the Politics of Modern Jewish Identity*, esp. 139–168; and Jack Wertheimer, *Unwelcome Strangers: East European Jews in Imperial Germany* (New York: Oxford University Press, 1987).

66. Waldman explicitly called them "the pioneers." Morris Waldman, June 24, 1907, box 2, folder 37, Galveston Records.

67. Bressler, "Removal Work," in *Senate Documents* (Washington, DC: U.S. Government Printing Office, 1911), 14.

68. Or so they imagined. Single women and older men who were excluded from the Galveston Movement might have disagreed.

69. Schiff to Manager of Trans-Continental Passenger Association, Dec. 22, 1909, Galveston Records.

70. Bressler, "Removal Work," 312. This also appears in Bressler, *Removal Work, Including Galveston*, 16. Schiff likewise touted the "pioneer spirit" of the immigrants. In Schiff's case, however, he suggested that the Galveston-bound immigrants already possessed this pioneering disposition, rather than extolling the immigration and settling project as its cause. Dec. 22, 1909, quoted in Stone, "Edgar Goldberg and the Texas Jewish Herald," 83. Official IRO propaganda advertised that its programs were designed "to serve as a means of educating the Jew of New York on American life and conditions and to create in him a pioneer spirit, to go forth and make his way in a new land." Ibid., 17. This booklet, which Bressler quoted approv-

ingly, sought to promote the IRO and its work not to immigrants who would potentially move westward, but to acculturated Jews who could support the project.

71. Kahn, "Jewish Agricultural and Industrial Aid Society, New York," 94.

72. Close friend to Cohen and involved in B'nai Brith, Leo Levi advised the Roosevelt administration in crafting the American response to the Kishinev massacre. Taylor Stults, "Roosevelt, Russian Persecution of Jews, and American Public Opinion," *Jewish Social Studies* 33 (Jan. 1971): 13–22.

73. "Personal Writings: Essays and Themes, undated," 20, Cohen Papers (Briscoe).

4 Indian-Israelite Identification

Claiming a Manly Past for American Judaism

After the outbreak of war in Europe led to the end of the Galveston Movement in 1914, Rabbi Henry Cohen came across a curious pamphlet. He kept it, carefully preserved, alongside his personal correspondence and family announcements. Its title read, "Comparisons of the Wild Tribes near Galveston a Century Ago to Ancient Semitic Customs." His fellow Galvestonian, the physician and amateur historian Joseph Osterman Dyer, had written the pamphlet in 1916. Its pages detailed the religious customs and social arrangements of the Indians who had lived many generations before Cohen arrived in the United States. In a typical passage, Dyer wrote, "Again the stocky copper-coloured short-haired Coshutta physician, and his confrere, the tall, slim, yellow-faced, long-haired Carancahua [Karankawa] Shaman were worthy successors of the learned Rabbis who dispensed magic, and medicine, and expounded religious and civil law after the Temple."[1] Dyer's pamphlet explained the striking religious similarities of ancient Israelites (or Jews of centuries past) and Galveston's "wild tribes." Cohen and Dyer were not close associates, and so Cohen's interest in the pamphlet cannot be explained away by the fondness of friendship. Why did it capture Rabbi Cohen's attention? Why did Dyer tie the customs of "uncivilized" tribes to his own religion? This chapter shows how Cohen, Dyer, and other acculturated Jews imagined Indians[2] and Israelites as one way to claim an American Jewish masculinity. It charts a complex dance of closeness and distance: acculturated Jews appropriated an imagined version of Native American cultures, but they simultaneously insisted that they were different from Indians.

Cohen was well known and highly respected in Galveston. He led the Jewish community in the official capacity as rabbi at B'nai Israel for many years. Jewish and non-Jewish Galvestonians adored him and turned to him for help and advice. He had provided much practical and emotional aid during the devastating 1900 hurricane and proved a pillar of the community as the city picked itself up from the terrible loss and rebuilt. His involvement in a host of Jewish philanthropic projects led him to think deeply about what American Jews should and could be. His leadership position in the city—and his personal disposition—led him to consider how to represent Jews to non-Jews. Did Cohen think that Jews were like Indians? Or that they should be like Indians? What would be gained, and lost, in suggesting to the larger American culture that Jews and Indians were similar?

When Cohen, Dyer, and others wrote about Indians, especially about Indians and religion, these authors often depicted their bravery, resourcefulness, and attachment to the land. But they shied away from representing savagery or uncivilized traits, even as a developmental stage on the way to manhood. Tribalism was likewise undesirable. They experimented with imagined Indians as a way to represent Jewishness to themselves and to non-Jews.

"Indian-Israelite" comparisons allowed Jews to stake two claims. First, an Indian-Israelite affinity appealed to acculturated Jews like Cohen who promoted a masculinity that was both Jewish and American. Specifically, identification with Indians helped Jews portray themselves as brave, resourceful, and quintessentially tied to the American land. Second, however, this affinity allowed Jews to distinguish themselves from Native Americans when it came to religion. Despite perceived anthropological parallels between Indian religious customs and Judaisms of the past, acculturated Jews stopped short of identifications that would link their religion too closely with Indian customs. If they aligned present-day Judaism and Native American customs completely in their own cultural moment, they ran the risk of painting Judaism as irrational and tribal (aspects of "bad" religion) and Jews as uncivilized and not yet American. Moreover, a "tribal" or ethnic religion fit uneasily with ideals of democracy and universalism (aspects of "good" religion), so it would be difficult to argue that a tribal religion was truly an American religion. Americans in the early twentieth century imagined religion at its core to be a matter of individual conscience, not a matter of descent, as a tribal religion might be.

So acculturated Jews had a dilemma: How could they affiliate themselves with "wild tribes" but not seem tribal? Because tribal religions did not match dominant American models of religion, they would need to downplay any elements of Judaism that might make it appear ethnically particularist. Indian-Israelite comparisons served as a place where Jews negotiated whether and how Judaism was universal or particular. Associating the religious practices of their ancestors—rather than their own—with those of the Indians allowed these Jews to emphasize the distance between contemporary Judaism (universal) and Indian practices and historical Judaism (particular, tribal). In these ways, the Indian-Israelite identification served as a way for Jews to promote the manly qualities of bravery, resourcefulness, and attachment to the American land without sacrificing their claim to having a civilized, rational, and universal religion. With these Indian-Israelite comparisons, they could simultaneously shape an American Jewish masculinity and make Judaism into an American religion.

This chapter shows the subtle tug of war between claims of similarity and maintenance of distance—a phenomenon that social scientists call "social distance." The first section introduces broad American assumptions about Indians and their place in cultural, racial, and religious contexts. The second section has a narrower lens, showing how Jewish authors in particular, including both Dyer and Cohen, embraced Indians when they wrote about the past. The Indians in these histories appeared as courageous, resourceful men who had long inhabited the American land. (Very few Indian women appear in these narratives.) Acculturated Jews' histories downplayed accounts of Indian violence and savagery, though they were common in many other historians' accounts. Where the second section's focus on historical writing highlights the closeness that Jewish authors sought to create, the third section's focus on religion highlights that distance. When these Jewish authors insisted on the difference between Indian "customs" and Jewish religion, it helped them argue for Judaism as a civilized religion that was universal rather than tribal. American Jews emphasized that Judaism was compatible with democracy and that Jews belonged to a rational religion chosen through reason and conscience. They claimed that Judaism was, in short, a "good" religion. This simultaneous push and pull with the figure of the Indian allowed acculturated Jews to create a brave, resourceful, and land-centered masculinity while rejecting tribal religion in favor of a rational, democratic, American religion.

Imagining Indians

There is little indication that Cohen and many of the other historical characters described here interacted extensively with Native Americans, and their depictions often bear little resemblance to what we know of the lived experiences of Native Americans. Yet there is ample evidence that these acculturated Jews spent time imagining how Indians lived. In fact, their relative lack of knowledge about contemporary Native peoples probably helped facilitate their comparisons, insofar as they would not need to worry about seeming *too* similar to the "uncivilized" Indians. Their descriptions were often inaccurate, but the point here is not to list the ways they were wrong or to correct their errors. I ask instead what work these fantasies of Indians could do for them and why, in some cases, these images relied on inaccurately portrayals or neglected the realities of Native American life to do that work. In the end, these Jews imagined the "Indians" of the past as noble savages who were courageous, resourceful, physically fit, and attached to the land—a lot like these authors wanted American Jewish men to be, provided they could disavow the savage part.

It was not just Jews, of course, who mythologized Native Americans: this practice fit with larger patterns of white interpretations of the land. Sacvan Bercovitch has argued that the term "American Indian . . . explained away the otherness of the native inhabitants by translating them all into a symbol (including the bi-polar values inherent in the symbol: savage/innocent, devil/child of nature, etc.)."[3] This transformation of humans into symbols had two effects: First, the symbol could displace representations of real Native Americans, as they grappled with American law, preserved and adapted their culture, and fought for sovereignty, acceptance, or both. Second, the symbol could also help reinscribe the myth of the disappearance of the Indian. When Indians became symbols, they became available for others to use for their own identity claims.

In the early twentieth century, many American men and boys turned to romanticized versions of Indians to get in touch with their own masculinity. As Philip Deloria has shown, Americans have a long history of pretending to be like Indians—but not exactly like them. Richard Slotkin has demonstrated how white heroes made themselves into men by fashioning themselves as Indians—while never giving up their role as subjugators of Indians.[4] Playing Indian became popular at both Christian and Jewish schools and camps as a way to promote manly behavior.[5] The Improved Order of Red Men, a fraternal organization whose white Protestant members performed elaborate rituals impersonating Indians, saw its membership peak in 1921 at about a half-million white men.[6] From the Boston Tea Party to boys playing backyard "cowboys and Indians" games, white men and boys could tap into the "savage" parts of themselves without losing their status as civilized citizens.

As images of "uncivilized" or even "savage" people, Indians became appealing figures for educational and developmental professionals who believed that civilization and culture had made white American men effeminate. Believers in recapitulation theory posited that little boys, like less evolved tribes and races, were savages and should embrace it.[7] Psychologist G. Stanley Hall, a proponent of the idea that boys should enact their savage impulses if they were to grow into properly manly men, wrote that "native indigenous stocks" were "the most precious of all things in the world" because they were constitutionally "natural, vigorous, pure, [and] abounding in health."[8] In 1899, Teddy Roosevelt wrote to Hall, "Over-sentimentality, over-softness, in fact washiness and mushiness are the great dangers of this age and of this [American] people. Unless we keep the barbarian virtues, gaining the civilized ones will be of little avail."[9]

Jews were not, however, identical to their Protestant neighbors in their appropriation of Indian culture. First, Jews did not widely adopt the idea of reclaiming their inner savages to become manly. Some Jews did don "redface" and play Indians in vaudeville performances, and Yiddish journals occasionally printed issues about Indians. But Jews did not latch onto the idea of being savage to reclaim manhood in the way that some of their Protestant neighbors did. They did not widely accept recapitulation theory or Hall's call to cultivate proper manhood by encouraging boys to act uncivilized. Even the Jews who agreed with Hall

Table 4.1

Indians	White people
Children	Adults
Savagery	Civilization (Christian)
Tribalism	Universal religion

when he called for engaging in exercise and competitive sports did not follow him when he championed savage behavior as a path to manhood.

The fact that Hall's message never really caught on in Jewish communities is not terribly surprising. He saw a muscular Protestant Christian religiosity as the ideal developmental (and masculinizing) religious model. He praised the YMCA, exercise as "a form of praise to God," and competitive sports as a means of developing "a spirit of service and devotion . . . to God and the church."[10] Hall's theory allowed white Christians to combine an embrace of primitivism with a sense of their own cultural and religious superiority.[11] In general, recapitulation theories combined the processes of Christianization and civilization, painting civilized Christianity as the height of human social progress. These theories both relied on and further supported ideas about the superiority of Christianity and reinforced Christianity as the norm of American religion.

Second, when Jews experimented with Indian-Israelite identification, they occupied a different cultural space from their Christian neighbors. Using Indians as a way to imagine manhood was actually structured in part by Christianity. The construction relied on a set of parallels. Indians were to white people as children were to adults. Children were to savages as adults were to civilized people. And so on. Imagined as a chart of binaries, the structure would look like table 4.1.

In each case, the former category served as a stepping-stone to the latter. The first was inferior, though it contained important aspects of human development, and the second would supersede it. Children would become adults; in the long view of history, savage peoples would give way to civilized peoples; tribalism would yield to the universal religion of Christianity, which served as the model of both civilization and universal religion.

The binary, supersessionist structure of these cultural ideas looked very similar to a theologically supersessionist picture of Judaism as the precursor to Christianity. In this view, Christianity came along to improve on, perhaps even perfect, Judaism. If a similar chart compared Jews and Christians, Jews would be on the left. They would represent a tribal stage, properly located in the rear-view mirror of religious progress. In this supersessionist view, present-day Jews were relics of history, living reminders of the infancy of Christianity. Judaism was not really savagery, but it also was not a living part of Christian civilization. Although not all American Christians espoused supersessionist theologies, ideas about Judaism as the "root" religion for Christianity ran deep.

Third, claims that Native Americans were descendants of the ten lost tribes of Israel contributed to the distinctiveness of Jews' relationships to Indians. In one way of thinking, Indians metaphorically represented the past of all Europeans because they were a less civilized race. By looking at Indians, then, you could look into the past of the human race. If Indians were the descendants of the ten lost tribes, they were even more biologically and closely—not merely metaphorically—tied to Jews. Even for those who rejected lost tribes theories, both Jews and Indians had customs and religion that were relics of times past. Indians were "savages" and "child-like" because they represented the early stages of the development of the human race, just like children represented the early stages of the human lifespan. Jews represented a prior phase of religious development because Judaism was seen as the foundation of Christianity.

Though they were not identical to their Protestant neighbors, Jews too posited connections to Indians. Attachment to American land was an essential part of manliness, which suggests why Dyer wrote the "Wild Tribes" pamphlet in 1916. Its thesis that some Native American tribes were similar to ancient Israelites was hardly new. Nor were other theories positing Native Americans as the lost tribes of biblical lore, though these theories were widely held to be scientifically inaccurate. Connections between Jews and Indians were compelling for a different reason: they could help guard against xenophobic and antisemitic rhetoric in the United States. A narrative emphasizing Jews' long history on US soil would simultaneously deemphasize Jews as either unproductive immigrants (a stereotype affixed to recent Eastern Europeans) on the one hand or foreigners harboring sympathies for Germany (a concern expressed about largely second- and third-generation German American Jews leading up to and during World War I) on the other. The war and xenophobic cultural currents created an atmosphere in which claiming commitment to the American nation became obligatory for Jews. By tying Jews to Indians, even if only by narrative association or weak anthropological speculation, Dyer could emphasize the Americanness and manliness of Jews and their religion.

Like the Galveston Movement, the Indian-Israelite comparisons crafted an American Jewish masculinity that focused on healthy bodies and attachment to the land, but did not directly reflect a Teddy Roosevelt-style physically strong and aggressive manliness. But these comparisons offer a different vantage point from that of the immigrant-focused Galveston Movement. Comparisons with Indians allowed acculturated Jews to claim bravery and resourcefulness, along with healthy bodies and attachment to the American land, for themselves. In the end, Dyer wrote the "Wild Tribes" pamphlet, Cohen kept it, and other Jews imagined links with Indians because these strategies helped them claim a masculinity that was brave, resourceful, and inherently connected to the American land.

Yet the identification was never total. The comparisons would stop short before they identified Judaism with contemporary Native American religious customs. Although associations between Indians and Israelites could help emphasize the manly qualities of Jews, associations between Judaism and contemporary Native customs would not help in a project of Americanization. Negotiating an affinity between Indians and Israelites brought up thorny issues of religious belonging. In the early twentieth century, white Protestants had branded Native customs irrational, uncivilized, tribal, and benighted. So comparisons to contemporary Judaism might seem ill advised. Acculturated Jews needed to figure out a way to call on Indian-Israelite similarities while still making the case for Judaism as a civilized American religion. Where a religion with only particularist claims aimed at one group might smack of antidemocratic theology and disloyalty or indifference to the nation, one with universal claims could be a freely chosen, rational religion motivated by both the heart and mind. In short, it would be an American religion.

Connecting to a Manly Jewish Present through an Indian Past

When most Americans in the early twentieth century wrote histories of the frontier, Indians often played the part of the violent, savage antagonists. Courageous cowboys and pioneers needed to fight off Indian attacks to make the land safe. These narratives pitted the Americans against the Indians. But when American Jews wrote histories of their states and regions, they often portrayed Indians more sympathetically. In the years before the "Wild Tribes" pamphlet, for instance, both Cohen and Dyer wrote histories that painted Indians as courageous, resourceful, and connected to the land. That is, they depicted Indians as inherently possessing many of the manly traits they valorized. Moreover, some of those histories also posited a connection between ancient Israel and the Indians—usually via the ten lost tribes. One of the appeals of this affinity was that, if Indians possessed desirable masculine qualities, and Jews and Indians shared a history, then by inference, Jews too could possess those qualities.

In its historical moment the "Wild Tribes" pamphlet was not quite the oddity it seems now. White Europeans and Americans had posited an association between Indians and Israelites since the fifteenth century. It offered Europeans an explanation of how these Native peoples could have gotten to the New World: perhaps they were the descendants of the ten lost tribes of Israel. For centuries, some white Americans, both Jewish and not, favored this explanation. William Penn, Roger Williams, Cotton Mather, and Jonathan Edwards all thought that at least some of the Native American tribes were of ancient Israelite origin and descendants of the ten tribes.[12] In the nineteenth century religious leaders including Joseph Smith, Mordecai Manual Noah, and Isaac Leeser espoused similar theories.[13] These American religious figures saw both the Israelites and Native Americans as religious relics, reminders of bygone eras. In other words, Dyer was neither the first nor the last to posit an Indian-Israelite connection.

By the early twentieth century, however, the idea had largely lost favor. In a 1905 *Publications of the American Jewish Historical Society* (*PAJHS*) article, the Reform rabbi David Philipson suggested why: science and history had debunked these specious theories of Indians as the lost tribes. Philipson focused on an earlier archaeological hoax, the 1860 "discovery" of tablets attributed to the indigenous American inhabitants called the Mound Builders. The "Hebrew" lettering on these tablets was soon shown to be, in the words of Abraham Geiger, "religious hocus-pocus."[14] Although he was fascinated by anthropological studies of Native Americans, Philipson denounced other attempts to prove Indians as lost tribes as "equally unsound if not fraudulent." He expressed the dominant interpretation when he wrote that "the unquestionable truth of the matter" was that the lost tribes had simply assimilated into Assyrian culture.[15] As a Reform rabbi, Philipson promoted a rational, even universal Judaism that had transcended any tribalism, and so it sat well with him that science had largely dismissed theories of Native Americans as lost tribes. But not every acculturated Jew agreed. As David Koffman shows in his study of Native American and Jewish interactions, some American Jews held onto a narrative of Indians as members of the lost tribes.[16] And American Jews writing in English, Yiddish, and Hebrew in the early twentieth century often imagined attachments to Indians, even apart from lost tribes theories.[17]

Dyer, too, held onto the lost tribes theory of Indians. While "scientifically" narrating at length the similarities of the customs and physiology of Indians and those of ancient Israelites, Dyer's 1916 pamphlet described the Indians as brave, self-sufficient tribes who had an intimate relationship to the earth. These Indians, he claimed, had a lot in common with ancient Israelites. "Many American ethnologists," Dyer acknowledged, "claim that such ancient Semitic customs in vogue amongst our aboriginal tribes are simply coincident."[18] He nevertheless proffered the possibility that the American continent was originally "populated by hardy explorers."[19] Dyer described the Indians not as savages or inferior human specimens, but as robust. As "explorers," they had been pioneers even before the white men had settled the continent. But from where had these hardy explorers come? Dyer posited that they had traveled over a land bridge from Asia, perhaps because they were one of the lost tribes. Dyer claimed that he left it "up to the reader" to decide how the Indian tribes had come to America, but his pamphlet argued for more than just "coincidence" for the gendered and religious similarities between the Indians of Galveston's past and the Israelites of Jewish history.

In 1916, the year of the "Wild Tribes" pamphlet, Dyer also published a book: *The Early History of Galveston*. Though it never explicitly compared Jews and Indians, Dyer's history painted Indians as brave, resourceful, and attached to the land. Dyer found Galveston's history captivating not only because of his own family's involvement but also because of the appeal of Indian tales: in his preface, he wrote, "The history of Lafitte and the Cannibal Indians presented a 'glamour' to [his] young and active mind."[20] "Young and active" minds would delight in the stories not only of white settlers' battles with uncivilized tribes but also of the ways of the Indians who hunted, fished, and lived off the land. The "glamour" had not entirely disappeared for the adult Dyer. But it had become detached from images of Indian cannibals, whose existence his history largely debunked.

Other Texas histories written in the early twentieth century tended toward the violent and macabre, fixating on cannibalism, bloody battles, and white men's victories over the Indian savages.[21] Dyer's history, in contrast, highlighted Indian resourcefulness and cooperation with white settlers. The "Cokes" and the Karankawa "at no time molested the settlers."[22] French pirate Jean Lafitte, the hero of Dyer's history, fathered children with Indian women, and "treated the Indians with great fairness, and did not fight any battles with them."[23] Dyer called accounts of the "Indian battle" "mostly fictitious," "more sensational than truthful," and "erroneously attributed to Lafitte."[24] Instead, he offered excerpts from letters, in which a general writes that the Indians were "now close by and friendly."[25] Rather than appearing as savage or inherently violent men, the Indians in Dyer's history were cooperative and resourceful, and above all, identified with the land. Even in Dyer's relatively rosy narrative, however, relations between white settlers and Indians deteriorated over time. Still, even when he wrote about violent altercations, the Indians' masculinity remained in a positive light. In 1822 a white treasure-hunting party "fought the Indians on sight." Dyer commented that these battles "made the otherwise peaceable Carancahuas the desperate enemies of future colonists." Although the Indians were not predisposed to violence, according to Dyer, they would defend themselves and their land courageously. Such bravery was precisely the kind of masculinity that many acculturated American Jews sought to cultivate and one they would emphasize when the United States entered World War I the year after Dyer's history and pamphlet appeared: they were not violent or aggressive, but they courageously fought for their country.

When Dyer and Cohen wrote these histories of Jews in their region, they implicitly argued for Jewish historical attachment to the land. Of course, Jews had not lived in Texas as long as Native Americans, but by unearthing and retelling the stories of the earliest Jews who settled there, Jewish historians could demonstrate that Jews too had a close relationship with the American land. Associations with Native Americans, whether speculative and anthropological like Dyer's pamphlet or in narrative form as in the histories Cohen wrote about Texas Jews, allowed Jews an affinity with "wild tribes" and their authentically American history without running the risk of a too-close identification with savagery or racial inferiority. Calling these tribes "wild" implied an inherent lack of civilization and painted a racialized picture of the possibilities of and for Native Americans as Americans. They were not—and could not be—white, so they required "civilization," which was often inseparable from Christianization, even in the rhetoric and policies of the US government.

Cohen had encountered the story of Dyer and his family well before the publication of the "Wild Tribes" pamphlet. Some of Cohen's articles in *PAJHS* even used the experiences of the Dyers and their relatives, the Ostermans, to exemplify his themes. The Dyer family traced its Texas roots back nearly a century, so they were good candidates for a narrative of longevity. And their family narrative also had exemplary moments of male bravery.[26] Joseph's father Leon Dyer had served in the military during the Seminole Wars in Florida, then in Texas during the Mexican War, and later in the war for Texas's independence. In case a long and varied military career was not enough to secure his manliness, the physically imposing elder Dyer once fought a duel in New Orleans. One historian suggests Leon challenged the man—a Mr. Smith from New York—when he insulted his Jewish origins.[27] Joseph Osterman Dyer was clearly proud of this: "A newspaper clipping reporting this affair of honor is in the possession of the writer," he boasted in his history of Galveston.[28] As both part of a southern social order and a gateway to the West, white Texan culture valued the social pedigree, chivalry, and masculinity that such an "affair of honor" would signal.[29] Perhaps, while growing up, Joseph heard his father's stories of combat for honor and country or tales of his hardy pioneer ancestors. His possession of his father's major's commission suggests that he was proud of his family's military record. Apparently it also appealed to a wider Jewish community: the *Jewish Encyclopedia* published an entry on Leon Dyer, complete with details of his military exploits and service to Jewish religious communities in Baltimore and San Francisco. The Dyer and Osterman families' long Texas history and military distinctions made them an appealing subject for Cohen.

In Cohen's eyes, this Texas Jewish experience, like other regional Jewish experiences, was best characterized by highlighting both these families' Jewishness, as expressed through religious observance, and their properly gendered Americanness, as expressed through military and civic participation. Cohen's substantial discussions of Joseph Osterman Dyer's uncle Isidore Dyer and father Leon Dyer suggest that he saw the family as exemplars of Texas Jewry.[30] When the Dyer men served in the military, they were being model men and countrymen. Cohen told the tale of Major Leon Dyer and General Scott's fight against Osceola in the Seminole War, along with Dyer's further military service in Louisiana and

Texas. Cohen's narrative of patriotism, religious practice, and philanthropy painted Jews as brave patriots. The men defended their country with their lives and bodies, and their religious and national affiliations fit comfortably together, all in keeping with early twentieth-century norms.

Although Cohen wrote about Texas Jews living in the nineteenth century, his subject choices, descriptions, and themes tell us more about his own early twentieth-century ideas and context.[31] One of his major recurring themes was the resourcefulness of Jewish pioneer men. In "The Settlement of the Jews in Texas," he dedicated the longest section to the tale of Adolphus Sterne. Sterne had emigrated from Germany when he was sixteen and, after a stay in New Orleans, arrived in Texas in 1824. "He was then," Cohen wrote, "an adventurous, rollicking young fellow, full of fun, and delighting in the dangerous life which then prevailed in this state."[32] Sterne had the constitution of a pioneer, in Cohen's telling. "He spoke French, German, Spanish, and English fluently, and after coming to Texas he learned various Indian dialects. These accomplishments rendered him a useful man to have around in those days,"[33] Cohen explained. Cohen's biographical sketch of Sterne allowed him to paint a picture of an American pioneer, a connection to Indians, and Jewishness, all wrapped up in one character.

As a well-known figure, a friend of Sam Houston, and a veteran "Indian fighter," Sterne appears as the quintessential pioneer statesman: he is manly and adventurous, as well as civilized and educated. "Once while he was serving in the Legislature of the Republic," Cohen wrote, "when the house had been bored with long-winded harangue over some inconsequential matters, he arose and delivered a very solemn address, of a few minutes length, in Choctaw." This episode of Indian speech did not alienate Sterne. Quite the opposite occurred, as Cohen explained: "The effect, as may be imagined, awoke the sleepers and relieved the monotony, bringing the members back to business." In this tale, Sterne's Choctaw spectacle made the statesmen into better Americans: it caused them to go "back to business" and perform their civic duties. Cohen suggested that this episode was connected to Sterne's position as a social hub of mid-nineteenth-century Texas: "He was the life of the lobbies, the wayside taverns and stage-coach parties, and knew all the old-timers, many of whom were frequently guests at his home."[34] Cohen depicted Sterne as a well-connected gentleman who sought out the pioneer life. He was conversant in Indian languages, but always retained his social status as a white settler.

Sterne's connection to Judaism was tenuous, but Cohen could still craft his narrative about a historical, pioneering American Jewishness using Sterne's story. Sterne was born to at least one Jewish parent, but married a Catholic woman and converted.[35] Significant portions of his diary were published in the late 1920s, but they make no reference to his Jewish identity or connection with the Jewish community.[36] Nevertheless, Sterne could still serve the narrative function of resourceful Jewish pioneer, even if the only evidence of any Jewishness was a likely apocryphal anecdote of putting on *teffilin* in the forest. *Teffilin*, phylacteries put on by men during their non-Sabbath morning prayers, would signal traditional male Jewish observance. But Cohen's tale of Sterne and his *teffilin* did not merely serve to claim him as a Jew. The unusual setting of Sterne's ritual behavior hinted at something more. Rather than placing Sterne in a traditional yeshiva, synagogue, or other human-made ritual space associated with traditional Jewish piety, Cohen's anecdote placed Sterne in nature, which recalled the religious rituals of Native Americans. This Jewish man did not hunch his frail and stooped body to study texts. Instead he stood erect among the tall trees. Moreover, the image of Sterne wrapping *teffilin* in the forest hinted at the kind of Judaism that Cohen figured as "good" religion: it was an internally motivated spirituality that found expression in an individual's choice to participate in ritual.

Furthermore, despite Sterne's tenuous connection to Judaism, Cohen could use his story to Americanize Judaism because of the elements of rationality and individually motivated religious practice. As discussed in chapter 1, these two ideas served as key elements in this narrative of Judaism as an American religion in the wider acculturated Jewish world beyond Cohen. Reform rabbi Hyman Gerson Enelow claimed in his 1920 book that "people today require a religion that shall combine two qualities—reasonableness and spirituality. . . . This combination of qualities is just what Judaism possesses. The heart and the mind—reason and spirit—have always played an equally important part."[37] Enelow, Cohen, and other acculturated Jewish leaders sought to position Judaism as rational while nevertheless coming from an internal spiritual space.

Cohen's articles made it clear that he idealized bravery as a marker of manliness, in addition to attachment to the land and resourcefulness. The hero of Cohen's "A Brave Frontiersman" article was a diminutive Jew who proved to be a manly leader nonetheless. He joined a company of fifty men who fought the Indians who stood in the way of the great national project of connecting the coasts by rail. By all appearances, he "seemed to be inferior, and in all respects unfit for the service; a Jew, small, with narrow shoulders, sunken chest, quiet manner and piping voice, but little knowledge of fire-arms or horsemanship; he was indeed unpromising as a son of Mars." The rest of the men in the company were bigger and stronger, and one in particular stood out: "an American, far above the average stature, and who appeared preeminent in knowledge of the Indians, of the country, daring, in short, in all the qualities which constitute leadership upon such occasions." Cohen assumed that all his readers would identify the "American" as the likely hero because of his embodiment of American manliness: he was "far above average in stature," familiar with Indians and the frontier, and daring.

When the hour came to fight the Indians, however, this "large, knowing, and confident man" dug a pit and hid himself, refusing to fight. How could the company defeat the Indian "savages" without him? "The loss of this man's services," Cohen wrote, "was fully made up by the bravery, skill and untiring activity of the despised 'little Jew.' There was no sphere of gallantry or usefulness in which he was not conspicuous."[38] The "little Jew," despite his small stature, turned out to be the bravest, most skilled, most resourceful, and most energetic man. Far from being a helpless coward, he was the best soldier. Both the Indians and the "little Jew" exhibited bravery, skill, and grit on the battlefield. Physical size and strength were thus not necessary traits of true manliness: the biggest, strongest man was a coward, and the smallest, weakest man turned out to be brave and heroic. Cohen closed the historical tale with a poem, which read in part:

> When the foe charged on the breastworks,
> With the madness of despair,
> And the bravest souls were tested,
> The little Jew was there.
> When the weary dozed on duty,
> Or the wounded needed care,
> When another shot was called for,
> The little Jew was there.

The kind of masculinity that Cohen valued did not require physical size and strength. Rather, it valorized bravery, sacrifice, and resourcefulness, the very kinds of qualities associated with Indians. Even when fighting the Indians, Cohen's "little Jew" mirrored the Indians' romanticized manliness.

Cohen's and Dyer's narratives also helped tie Jews directly with the American West, a region long associated with pioneers, hardiness, resourcefulness, and self-sufficiency. At the time, the American West as a region was moving beyond a rough and wild frontier stage to a period of simultaneous urban and rural growth and modernization.[39] As the West itself Americanized, so might the people who populated its land. Jews occupied a place in the racial order that allowed them to do this. Given the presence and the greater racial "otherness" of Native Americans, Latinos, and African Americans in the West and Southwest, Jews and non-Jews alike considered Jews to be Anglos.[40] In their social, philanthropic, and economic habits, acculturated Jews mirrored their Protestant counterparts in Galveston and cities like it.[41] Jews sometimes experienced discrimination, but it was rarely based on assumptions of racial otherness.

Dyer, Cohen, and others invested in the idea of the historical similarities between Jews and Indian tribes in order to claim masculinity and an affinity for the American land, even in the face of social scientists who had dismissed ideas of American indigenous populations as the descendants of the ten lost tribes. But they also embraced an image of Indians that needed to be fantasy for it to function as a masculinizing and Americanizing story for Jews. If Dyer had written accurately about Native American cultures during his time period, he would have had to show peoples who were stripped of their land, accused of being unable to become citizens, and told that they could not govern or care for themselves and were interacting with the land improperly by not adopting individual ownership norms. A complete picture would even have to include the rhetoric that some whites used to feminize Native Americans: they were not fit for self-government because they were emotional and insufficiently rational. All of these traits would have run counter to his purpose of suggesting a Jewish connection to the American land, to manliness, and to good citizenship.[42]

That Dyer, Cohen, and other twentieth-century acculturated Jews engaged little with actual Native Americans makes sense for several reasons. First, and most practically, Indian work and policy were largely Christian affairs. Protestant reformers and missionaries had dominated both early work with Indians and the US government's Bureau of Indian Affairs, although Catholics had gained footing by the early twentieth century.[43] Civilizing Indians was seen as a Christian job. Second, the ideology underpinning agricultural movements differed. American policy makers and reformers saw farming as a step up toward civilization for Native Americans, while Jews imagined farming as a step that would reconnect them with their history and true natural potential. Emphasizing similarities between Jews and contemporary Native Americans might suggest that Jews too were in need of civilization, but agricultural communities and the Galveston Movement sought to prove exactly the opposite: that Jews already had the potential to be productive Americans. Third, an Indian-Israelite affinity provided narrative connections between historical civilizations, not contemporary Jews and Native Americans. The Indians of the past could be imagined as resourceful, masculine, and self-sufficient, but the Native Americans in the early twentieth century constituted a political problem in their failure to assimilate quickly and completely to American life. A Jewish quest to show long attachments to the land would be undone if it entailed a connection to a failure to become American.

Acculturated Jews' broader ideologies about Americanization and immigration suggest that claiming a common ancestry with Indians allowed them to highlight themes of strong ties to the land, bravery, and resourcefulness. In this, they acted much like other whites who "played Indian" in order to identify with and call attention to admirable traits they shared with Native Americans.[44] It is no surprise that Philip Deloria's history of non-Indian Americans appropriating Indian culture includes examples that overwhelmingly feature men and boys. Societies like the Order of the Red Men and even the Boy Scouts identified Indians with mastery of nature and a masculinity that had not been completely tamed by civilization.

Cohen's histories of Texan Jews helped him establish both a brave and resourceful Jewish masculinity and an American Judaism. Adolphus Sterne, the pioneer statesman, at once rational and spiritual, put on *teffilin* in the forest. The "little Jew" demonstrated that manliness required bravery and resourcefulness, but not physical size. Some of the Dyers fought and defeated the Indians, all the while demonstrating a masculinity quite like the Indians themselves. These histories suggested that Jewish masculinity was a brave, resourceful masculinity with ties to the American land. The next section shows examples of more explicit approaches that directly claimed affinities between Israelites and Indians, especially in the realm of religion. While these acculturated Jews pulled the idea of brave and resourceful Indians close with one hand, they pushed away the idea of tribal Indians with the other.

Not Tribal: Claiming Historic Distance from Native Customs

Though identifying with Indians helped Jews claim a masculinity characterized by bravery, resourcefulness, and connection to the land, in other ways they were careful not to identify too closely. Dyer and other acculturated Jews also emphasized distinctions between Judaism and Indian customs. The goal, put broadly, was to convince themselves and others that Judaism was an American religion. But what made a religion count as American or a "good" religion? Two broad themes recurred: first, a religion must be an internally motivated, rational set of religious beliefs and practices, and second, it must be compatible with universalism and democracy. The idea of universality offered a key distinction between the twelve tribes of Israel and the "wild tribes" of the pamphlet. Showing the nontribal nature of the religion of the twelve tribes, they hoped, would allow Judaism to look universal, rational, and Americanized. It would be a "good" religion.

The audience for these claims included both Jews and non-Jews. Cohen's articles in *PAJHS* targeted a small slice of elite, educated American Jews. But Dyer's pamphlet assumed little knowledge of Israelite, Jewish, or Native customs and was addressed to a general regional audience. He also wrote for secular newspapers in a similar vein. In a 1922 *Galveston News* article about Passover, Dyer compared "Indian Customs" in "our own dear Texas" and ancient Israelite customs: Before their corn festival, the Indians "instituted hut cleanings and provided new utensils, and bark garments, and even kindled a new fire in the temple hut to replace the old one." He continued, "Texas also had peoples of the aboriginal types who only used unleavened bread . . . they make a batter of cornmeal and spread it on hot stones, producing so-called paper bread, described by early settlers, thin and white like the Hebrew unleavened bread with a similar taste. The Jewish mazza (plural mazzot) is prepared by special appliances, which not only permit of thin and crisp baking, but perforate the cakes to make them lighter."[45] Baking thin breads was only one of many comparisons that Dyer made. In the "Wild Tribes" pamphlet, Dyer concentrated much of his analysis on descriptions of religious similarities. He detailed prohibitions on eating animal flesh with blood,[46] using oil for ceremonial purposes, ceremonial fasting, an east-facing temple door, women's exclusion from the temple, and women throwing a portion of food into the fire, among others.[47] In doing so, he aligned Native customs with those of ancient Israelites and/or rabbinic Judaism, emphasizing themes of renewal, common food, common rituals, and even common gender roles.

But why would Dyer connect Judaism to the customs of "wild tribes"? In his comparative "Indian-Isralite" article, the ethnographer Garrick Mallery wrote, "Religion, as accurately [understood], embraces only the perficient relations between divinity and man, and the mode in which such relations operate."[48] In other words, religion was properly and essentially a matter between a man and his god. A rational, belief-centered Judaism fit this pattern well, whereas Native American cosmology did not fit neatly into conceptions of a discrete category of "divinity." Before the 1920s, few white Americans used the concept of religion to describe the beliefs and rituals of Native Americans.[49] It was not until the 1920s when a series of public controversies erupted about Pueblo Indian dances that the dominant discourse shifted from indigenous traditions as "savagery" to a legitimate religion that deserved cultural recognition and legal protection. Part of the price of this recognition, however, was the transformation of indigenous practices and institutions into forms that more closely fit American Protestant models of what religion looked like.

Although Native Americans needed to make an argument for why their traditions should be considered "religion" and protected as such, no one doubted that Judaism was a religion. No one tried to prohibit Passover seders as the Bureau of Indian Affairs prohibited some Pueblo Indian dances. Some Americans might deem Jewish ritual backward or see its practitioners as benighted souls, but Judaism and its traditions held a firm place as religious in American culture.

This had not always been the case. When the famed Puritan orator John Cotton opined in his 1642 jeremiad that Protestant Christianity was the only legitimate religion, he lumped Jews and Indians together: "Upon this ground you shall see Indians, and Jews, and Pagans gaping after salvation, when they see by these terrible stormes, and thunders, that all their Religions are but so many refuges of lies."[50] His prediction had clearly not come true, and its way of structuring the American religious landscape no longer dominated religious or national discourse. Although most twentieth-century Americans still counted themselves as Christians, few would have clumped Judaism, Native American culture, and "pagan" practices together in the same category of falsehood. Even those who sought to convert Jews to Christianity saw Judaism as more than merely a "refuge of lies," as Cotton would have it. In contrast, in the early twentieth century, many white Protestants and Catholics, as well as the US government, still considered indigenous traditions not only uncivilized but also heathen. Indians did not have a religion, unless they had adopted some form of Christianity. In the eyes of the American public, however, Judaism was a religion and a legitimate one.

If Dyer wanted to emphasize the Americanness of Jews and Judaism, connecting them to Native American customs that had been deemed "savage" and "superstitions" and were too uncivilized even to count as religion would seem to run counter to his purpose. It would seem more like a step backward to a time where Protestant orators like Cotton painted Judaism and Native American customs with the same brushstrokes as ancient, uncivilized, superstitious, superseded religions. Why make one's own religion out to be similar to that of the savages and heathens, whom both Christian denominations and the US government were desperately trying to "civilize" and assimilate into "real Americans" with limited success? Especially given the concerns about nativist portraits of Jewish immigrants as unassimilable and disloyal, making connections with "unassimilable" indigenous groups seems like a poor strategy.

But Dyer did not intend to align present-day Judaism and Indian customs too closely; rather he detailed ritual similarities while emphasizing historical contrasts. In case the modern reader might scoff at these specious Indian-Israelite comparisons, Dyer warned, "Dear reader, do not smile at the belief of the savage, for it was that of your ancestors." He offered examples from historical Jewish communities: "Hebrews a few centuries ago had their synagogal names in Europe, which were kept secret, while trade and family names were common. Changing the name of a person seriously ill, so as to cheat the angel of death, was an illustration how the name was formerly unified with the body."[51] Dyer discussed the Jewish tradition of adding a new name to a gravely ill person to mislead or thwart the angel of death, because an Indian tribe had a similar practice, he explained. The Comanches, in this case, might be "savage," yet they shared beliefs and customs with Jews from "a few centuries ago"—the naming tradition dated to the Middle Ages and had gained popularity in Kabbalistic circles.[52] These historical comparisons allowed Dyer not only to note the similarities between Indian customs and Israelite religion but also to emphasize the differences between an outdated, superstitious Judaism of "centuries ago" and the rational, civilized Judaism of his day. By referring to Judaism's past commonality with Indian customs, he could demonstrate both a connection and argue for Judaism's comparative advancements.

Dyer also saw communal living as a sign of a shared ancestry among Texas tribes and Jewish sects of antiquity. "The Coshuttas [Coushatta] as well as the Carancahuas lived in communal manner; the former had a common granary, such as existed in the clans of the Essenes on the Dead Sea," he explained.[53] A communal granary hardly represents a rare or distinctive feature of communities, but Dyer presented it as further evidence for Indian-Israelite links. Likewise, he compared tribal fasting with Yom Kippur traditions, however tenuous the actual similarities might be. "The Coshutta tribe had a similar ceremonial lasting one week which included," he explained, "atonement, purification, the harvest feast and offerings of first fruits, all typical Jewish ceremonies of old[,] the day of atonement being kept each year by every Jew at the present time in each and every land of the world."[54] His comparisons of historical Jewish rites ("ceremonies of old") with Indian rituals enabled him to posit historical relationships without forfeiting contemporary Jews' claims to acculturation and participation in modernity. In fact, they hinted at Judaism's advancement over time. No longer did Jews celebrate superstitious rituals like harvest feasts or purification—which could also have been painted as particularist because they related to the Temple—but they still kept a day of atonement, a theological idea that could be seen as individual, internal, and universally applicable.

There is another notable comparison that Dyer did *not* make that others did. In his article comparing Indians and Israelites, the ethnographer Mallery had noted many similarities in religious rituals and beliefs, though he did not subscribe to any theory of biological Indian-Israelite relation. Instead he suggested that the two groups developed in "parallel," with the Israelites becoming more advanced and civilized and the Indians representing a less developed society. Of the similarities between Indian and Israelite practices, one stood out as most common: "The most generally entertained parallel between the Indians and the Israelites," he wrote, "repeated by hundreds of writers, was that they both believed in one overruling God."[55] If this assumption was so widespread and monotheism was a tenet of Judaism that would appeal to American Christians, why would Dyer neglect to make this comparison? Highlighting a theological agreement about monotheism would bridge present-day Judaism and "Indians," which would bring the "wild tribes" and civilized, contemporary Jews too close. As a non-Jew, Mallery had little personal stake in arguing for the civility or Americanness of Judaism. However, Dyer's work made sure not to repeat religious links—even if "hundreds of writers" had already noted them—between present-day Jews and Indians of the past.

The acculturated Jewish writers' emphasis on similar ancestry, rather than modern kinship, sufficiently removed connections to these "wild tribes" from contemporary reality so as to avoid the liabilities of associating with peoples who were often seen as "uncivilized," culturally backward, violent, and superstitious as opposed to religious. Jews could at once share an imagined history with Indians while still claiming a space as pioneers and even fighters against other "wild tribes" during white settlement in the nineteenth century.

Acculturated Jews based an important part of their distinction on "civilization," a perennial keyword in both religious missionary and government attempts to manage Native Americans. Because Judaism was already accepted as a religion, Jews could argue for its contributions, rather than having to struggle for it to achieve recognition as a religion. They could mobilize other cultural discourses, such as "civilization," to build the case for the value and rationality of Judaism. Books and lectures with titles such as *Jewish Contributions to Civilization* and "What Judaism Has Done for Civilization" abounded in the first two decades of the twentieth century.[56] In his 1920 *The Adequacy of Judaism*, Enelow emphasized the religious contribution of Jews and Judaism in a way typical of many accultur-ated American Jews: "No one denies that the Jew has made valuable contributions to civilization. Nevertheless . . . it is by his religious teaching and idealism that the Jew has made his most valuable addition to the civilization of mankind."[57] Jews could argue for the civilized qualities of their religion—that was part of what could make them good pioneers and settlers of the American West or whites in the American South—but they did not need to argue for Judaism's status as a re-ligion, as did the Native Americans who had been branded "uncivilized" and without religion.

The discourse about "civilization" was a two-edged sword, however, so there could also be strategic benefits for Jews to attach themselves to a people who seemed less civilized but more manly. In the early twentieth century there was a widespread worry that modern life emasculated men by overcivilizing them. If men became too refined through distance from physical labor, they would no lon-ger be real men. Once the frontier had closed, men would have no place to prove their manliness through mastery over nature. The pushback against the threats of overcivilizing and feminizing men took many forms, such as the "play" move-ment and popular psychology that encouraged "boys to be boys" and suggested that their early years were properly spent indulging in "savagery."[58] The specter of the overcivilized and therefore unmanly man haunted Jews more than most other men. Linking themselves with a fantasy image of Indians helped Jews seem a little less civilized and therefore more manly. If Jewish men wanted to make a case for themselves as Americans and their religion as good, they would want to show that their Judaism had contributed to civilization without becoming over-civilized themselves.

Conclusion

Henry Cohen saved a quirky pamphlet. Even though many of its facts were more fantasy than reality, the ideas in it exemplify the cultural negotiations of masculin-ity, religion, and American identity. It valorized Indians' courage, resourcefulness, and close identification with the American land. If Jews were like Indians, then Jews too could be brave and resourceful. If Jews and Indians had common an-cestors, then Jews would have inborn—even racial—ties to the American land. Instead of immigrant aliens, Jews would represent the kin of the very earliest

Americans. Comparisons to the "wild tribes" would also allow American Jews to associate themselves with bravery, resourcefulness, and self-sufficiency.

But if they relied too heavily on an Indian-Israelite affinity, the image of Judaism could suffer. American Jews emphasized the distance that their civilized Judaism had come from ancient superstitions like those held by the Indians. As a civilized religion, centered in the head and heart rather than communal rites, Judaism could be rational and compatible with American democracy. Emphasizing similarities with wild tribes could make Jews manly and strengthen identification with the American land, but emphasizing differences from the Indians could make Judaism an American religion.

The idea of Indians never became a controlling cultural metaphor for Jews in understanding their own American Jewishness or explaining it to others. But when Cohen, Dyer, and other acculturated Jews experimented with Indian-Israelite comparisons, they opened a window into their own commitments and desires. Their experiments show what pieces they considered desirable, essential, or undesirable when they crafted an American Jewish masculinity. Because the comparison was an imperfect fit, because Jews wanted to be both like and unlike Indians, they had to tailor their comparisons. And it is in these negotiations that we can see them shaping the norms of American Jewish masculinity.

Not all American Jewish men imagined affinities with Indians, but almost all sought healthy bodies. As the Galveston Movement and Indian-Israelite affiliations show, they wanted others to see that Jewish men had healthy, productive bodies. Both of these experiments to shape Jewish masculinity promoted the association of healthy Jewish bodies with the land, but in indirect ways. The next chapter explores a more direct way in which Jews claimed the association of healthy, productive Jewish male bodies with the land: Jewish agricultural settlements. Where the complex dance of Indian-Israelite identification helped Jews claim an association with an American past, these agricultural schools and settlements helped them stake a claim to their American present.

Notes

1. Joseph Osterman Dyer, "Historical Sketch: Comparisons of Customs of Wild Tribes near Galveston a Century ago with Ancient Semitic Customs," 4, Henry Cohen Papers, American Jewish Archives.

2. I use the term "Indian" rather than "Native American" because it is the term acculturated Jews generally used when they imagined these tribes. I reserve "Native Americans" for discussing Native people themselves and scholarship focusing on them.

3. Sacvan Bercovitch, "The Biblical Basis of the American Myth," in *The Bible in American Arts and Letters*, ed. Giles Gunn (Philadelphia: Fortress Press, 1983), 222.

4. Richard Slotkin, *Regeneration through Violence: The Mythology of the American Frontier, 1600–1860* (Norman: University of Oklahoma Press, 1973), 563–564.

5. Jonathan Krasner, *Benderly Boys and American Jewish Education* (Waltham, MA: Brandeis University Press, 2011), 312–315.

6. See Mark Carnes, *Secret Ritual and Manhood in Victorian America* (New Haven, CT: Yale University Press, 1989), 98–103; Catherine Albanese, "Exchanging Souls, Exchanging Selves," in *Retelling US Religious History*, ed. Thomas Tweed (Berkeley: University of California Press, 1997), 207–208; Alvin J. Schmidt, *Fraternal Organizations* (Westport, CT: Greenwood Press, 1980), 287.

7. Bederman, *Manliness and Civilization*, 92–98.

8. G. Stanley Hall, "White Man's Burden versus Indigenous Development for the Lower Races," *National Education Association* 42 (1903): 1054.

9. Quoted in Jakobsen and Pelligrini, *Barbarian Virtues*, 3.

10. G. Stanley Hall, *Youth: Its Education, Regimen, and Hygiene* (New York: Appleton and Co, 1908), 55; and "The Efficiency of the Religious Work of the Young Men's Christian Association," *Pedagogical Seminary* 12, no. 4 (1905): 478–489.

11. Putney, *Muscular Christianity*, 6.

12. Ronald Sanders details this history in *Lost Tribes and Promised Lands: The Origins of American Racism* (New York: Harper Collins, 1992).

13. On Noah, see Jonathan Sarna, *Jacksonian Jew: The Two Worlds of Mordecai Noah* (New York: Holmes & Meier, 1991). On Joseph Smith, see Fawn Brodie, *No Man Knows My History: The Life of Joseph Smith* (New York: Vintage, 1995), 34–49.

14. David Philipson, "Are There Traces of the Ten Lost Tribes in Ohio?," *Publications of the American Jewish Historical Society* 13 (1905): 44.

15. Ibid., 46.

16. David Koffmann, "The Jews' Indian: Native Americans in the Jewish Imagination and Experience 1850–1950," (PhD diss., New York University, 2011).

17. Rachel Rubinstein, *Members of the Tribe: Native Americans in the Jewish Imagination* (Detroit: Wayne State University Press, 2010). Stephen Katz, *Red, Black, and Jew: New Frontiers in Hebrew Literature* (Austin: University of Texas Press, 2010). Jonathan Boyarin suggests that this relationship has deeper roots in the European imagination of Jews as the primary racial other, which in turn influenced the construction of Christian European identity vis-à-vis indigenous peoples in the New World. Boyarin, *Unconverted Self*. The historical evidence suggests that this imagined kinship with Native Americans did not extend to physical encounters between pioneer Jews and Native Americans. When Jews and Native Americans met, Jews preferred to see themselves in the same terms as the other white settlers: culturally superior and not close kin.

18. Dyer, "Historical Sketch," 4.

19. Ibid., 2.

20. Joseph Osterman Dyer, *The Early History of Galveston* (Galveston, TX: Oscar Springer Print, 1916), 1.

21. See, for example, the recurring portrayal of violent Indians and armed conflict in Frank White Johnson, *A History of Texas and Texans* (New York: American Historical Society, 1916), and Adina de Zavala, *History and Legends of the Alamo and Other Missions in and around San Antonio*, ed. Richard Flores (Houston, TX: Arte Publico Press, 1996 [1917]). Even a high school student's prize-winning essay in *The Texas History Teachers' Bulletin* gave mention to the Caracahuas only to call them a "powerful cannibal tribe." Albert Irving Clark, "The History of Galveston Island, 1518–1900," *Texas History Teachers' Bulletin* 7 (Nov. 1918): 54.

22. Dyer, *Early History*, 7.

23. Ibid., 27, 7.

24. Ibid., 7.

25. Ibid., 10.

26. It seems that there are actually two men named Joseph Osterman Dyer, MD, in the family; they are uncle and nephew. Joseph the elder's brother Leon was Joseph the younger's father. The elder Joseph Osterman Dyer, MD, was born in Galveston to Isadore and Amelia Dyer. *Obituary Records of Yale University* (New Haven, CT: Yale University, 1915). The nephew Joseph Dyer occasionally wrote about Jewish topics for non-Jewish audiences. For instance, "Nuggets of History: The Talmud and Diet" and "The Story of Passover" were printed in the *Galveston News* in the early 1920s. "Newspaper Articles: Galveston News, 1920–1924," J.O. Dyer Papers 2Q501, Briscoe Center for American History, University of Texas at Austin (hereafter cited as Dyer Papers).

27. Jacob Rader Marcus, *United States Jewry 1776–1985* (Detroit, MI: Wayne State University Press, 1989), 274.

28. Dyer, *Early History*, 26.

29. Bertram Wyatt-Brown, *Southern Honor: Ethics and Behavior in the Old South* (Oxford: Oxford University Press, 1982).

30. Again in his 1896 *Publications of American Jewish History* article "The Jews in Texas," Cohen discussed Joseph Osterman and Rosanna Osterman (Dyer) at length. Cohen noted that "the commission attesting Leon Dyer major, signed by the first president of the Republic of Texas—Burnett—is in the hands of Dr. J. O. Dyer, of Galveston." Henry Cohen, "Settlement of Jews in Texas," *Publication of American Jewish Historical Society* (1894); 148. If Cohen personally saw this commission, which, given his interest in regional Jewish history, is plausible, then he likely had a conversation with Dyer. Moreover, the relatively small number of Jews in Galveston and the social prominence and connection of Cohen and Dyer suggest it is highly likely that the two men knew each other.

31. Cohen had been active in the AJHS from its earliest years; he took a special interest in writing about Texas Jewry, which gave him occasion to discuss Indians. "Constitution," *Publication of American Jewish Historical Society* (1894): 203.

32. He presented the "Settlement of the Jews in Texas" at the second annual conference for American Jewish history, he contributed it to the *PAJHS*, and Isaac Mayer Wise's *American Israelite* reprinted it, all in 1894. Both publications were aimed at educated and acculturated American Jewish readers. Cohen, "Settlement of Jews in Texas," 140–141. Reprinted in *American Israelite*, Sept. 13, 1894.

33. Ibid., 141.

34. Ibid.

35. Bryan Stone, "Jews without Judaism," in *Lone Stars of David: The Jews of Texas*, eds. Hollace Ava Weiner and Kenneth Rosenbaum (Waltham, MA: Brandeis University Press, 2007), 23. When the *Southwestern Historical Quarterly* printed selections from Adolphus Sterne's diary, it recorded that "his father was a Jew, his mother a Lutheran." Harriet Smither, ed. "Diary of Adolphus Sterne," *Southwestern Historical Quarterly* 30 (October 1926): 139.

36. *Southwestern Historical Quarterly* published selections from Sterne's diary from 1926 to 1929.

37. Enelow, *Adequacy of Judaism*, 14. This was also reprinted in Emil Hirsch's *Reform Advocate* 61 (Apr. 30, 1921), 294.

38. Henry Cohen, "A Brave Frontiersman," Cohen Papers (Briscoe).

39. See, for instance, Walter Nugent, *Into the West: The Story of Its People* (New York: Alfred A. Knopf, 1999) and Michael P. Malone and Richard W. Etulain, *The American West: A Twentieth Century History* (Lincoln, NE: University of Nebraska Press, 1989).

40. Bryan Edward Stone, *The Chosen Folks: Jews on the Frontiers of Texas* (Austin: University of Texas Press, 2010).

41. See Elizabeth Hayes Turner, *Women, Culture, and Community: Religion and Reform in Galveston, 1880–1920* (Oxford: Oxford University Press, 1997), 6–11.

42. The coexistence of these seemingly contradictory trends was not unusual in American race ideology. See Eric Lott, *Love and Theft: Blackface Minstrelsy and the American Working Class* (Oxford: Oxford University Press, 1993).

43. Francis Paul Prucha, *American Indian Policy in Crisis: Christian Reformers and the Indian, 1865–1900* (Norman: University of Oklahoma Press, 1976); Wenger, *We Have a Religion*, 17–58.

44. For larger discussions of "playing Indian," see Philip Deloria, *Playing Indian* (New Haven, CT: Yale University Press, 1999) and Shari Huhndorf, *Going Native: Indians in the American Cultural Imagination* (Ithaca, NY: Cornell University Press, 2001).

45. "The Story of Passover," printed May 28, 1922, in scrapbook: "Newspaper Articles: Galveston News, 1920–1924," Dyer Papers.

46. Ibid., 5.

47. Ibid., 7–9.

48. Garrick Mallery, "Israelite and Indian: A Parallel in Planes of Culture," *Popular Science Monthly* 36 (Nov. 1889): 57.

49. Wenger, *We Have a Religion*, xiii.

50. John Cotton, *The Powring Out of the Seven Vials, or An Exposition of the 16 Chapter of Revelation, with an Application of it to our Times* (London, 1642), 12–13.

51. "Superstitions and Beliefs of Texas Comanche Indians," p. 89 in scrapbook: "Newspaper Articles: Galveston News, 1920–1924," Dyer Papers.

52. In fact, the custom regained popularity in the early twentieth century with the birth of Jewish Science. Alfred Moses, the intellectual founder of the movement, dedicated a chapter of his foundational text, *Jewish Science: Divine Healing in Judaism, with Special Reference to the Jewish Scriptures and Prayer Book* (Mobile, AL: The Temple, 1916) to "the change of name." Although he indicated that he was at first skeptical, Moses concluded by recommending the rite to "all zealous Jews" (40). On Moses, See Ellen Umansky, *From Christian Science to Jewish Science: Spiritual Healing and American Jews* (Oxford: Oxford University Press, 2004) and "Christian Science, Jewish Science, and Alfred Geiger Moses," *Southern Jewish History* 6 (2003).

53. Ibid., 11

54. Dyer, "Wild Tribes," 8.

55. Mallery himself, however, rejected this interpretation. Mallery, "Israelite and Indian," 58.

56. Joseph Jacobs, *Jewish Contributions to Civilization: An Estimate* (Philadelphia: Jewish Publication Society, 1919). Although he had lived in Australia and England, Jacobs permanently relocated to New York in 1900 to serve as the editor of the *Jewish Encyclopedia*. S. Schulman, "What Judaism Has Done for Civilization," *Menorah* 30 (March 1901): 152–154.

57. Enelow, *Adequacy of Judaism*, 12.

58. See Deloria, *Playing Indian*, 95–127.

FIRST JEWISH IMMIGRANTS UNDER THE AUSPICES

SOME OF THE

NORTH GERMAN LLOYD WHARF, GALVESTON TEX.

Rabbi Henry Cohen (second from left) and JIIB Immigrants in Galveston, 1907, courtesy of the UT Institute of Texan Cultures at San Antonio.

Jewish dairy farmer in Hartford, CT, ca. 1900, courtesy of the American Jewish Archives.

Leo Frank, taken between 1910 and 1913, courtesy of George Grantham Bain Collection. Library of Congress.

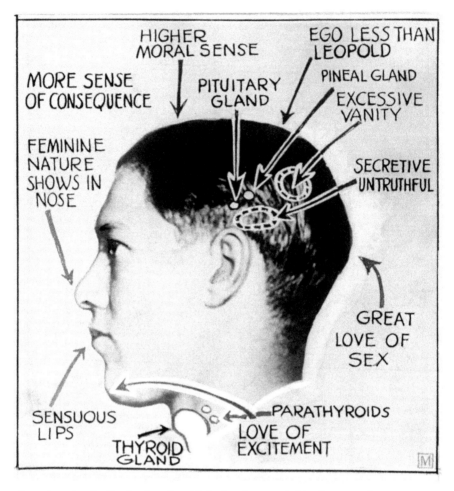

Phrenology sketch of Richard Loeb, published in the *New York Daily News*, July 28, 1924. Getty Images.

5   Afternoon Calisthenics at Woodbine

*Jewish Agriculture, Religious Ambivalence,
and the Male Body*

JOSEPH ROSEN SPOKE to a crowd of students and parents on graduation day at the
Hirsch Agricultural School (HAS) in Woodbine, New Jersey, in 1915. Rosen had immigrated to the United States in 1903 and established himself as a major intellectual
and political figure in both American and Russian agricultural circles.[1] Though he
was not as famous as some of the other commencement speakers at the Jewish agricultural schools—former president William Howard Taft spoke at a ceremony
in 1916—Rosen was a bit of a celebrity to the students, parents, and other audience
members who were committed members of the Jewish agricultural movement.
When Rosen told his listeners, "The foundation strata of a healthy and vigorous
nation are the agricultural elements," he was preaching to the choir.[2] Valorizing
agriculture seemed natural to his listeners, including the young male students
who had enrolled at a school that sought to teach them the most scientific, up-to-
date farming methods. Many had also participated in the wider American back-
to-the-land nostalgia and anti-city rhetoric that had increased since an economic
downturn in 1907 and would hit its peak just before World War I.

But beyond the gates of the Jewish agricultural schools, few people associated Jews with farming. In Eastern Europe shifting and discriminatory laws had
made it very difficult for Jews to work the land, let alone own it. Demographically,
Jews were overrepresented in the urban populations of Russia, especially within
the Pale of Settlement, where most lived. And although almost 20,000 Jews lived
on American farms at the turn of the century, Jews living in Western Europe and
the United States tended to earn their living in urban environments and not in
agriculture. Stereotypes about Jews as consumers instead of producers were particularly prevalent in Europe, but the idea about Jews as unfit to be farmers also
extended to the United States. Rabbi Joseph Krauskopf, founder of the other
Jewish agricultural school, said of his institution, "It is to combat this eternal cry
of 'non-producer' that the National Farm School was started."[3] Krauskopf's
National Farm School (NFS) and the HAS would have to swim against the historical current if they wanted to convince the public that Jews were natural-born
farmers.

Moreover, Jews in the United States had been trying—and failing at—collective agricultural settlements and communes since the early nineteenth century, and these attempts occurred even more frequently in the last decades of the nineteenth century. Of the Jewish agricultural communities started in the United States in the 1880s and 1890s, the majority failed before they reached their second birthday. None lasted as long as ten years without philanthropic help. According to historian Ellen Eisenberg the early movement was plagued by "poor timing and incompatible goals."[4] Moreover, the wider back-to-the-land movement in the United States was fueled at least as much by nostalgia and romantic longing as by economics or health benefits. Most of the people who admired the movement and its writers never quit their jobs to work the land.[5] Like today's readers of *Modern Farmer*, who are far more likely to be lovers of farm-to-table food than farmers, few early twentieth-century back-to-the-land enthusiasts attempted to become career agriculturalists. And overall, fewer and fewer Americans made their livings as farmers.

If the American admiration for the agricultural lifestyle was largely nostalgic, and if the farming communities failed far more often than not, why did some American Jews hold onto the idea of making Jews into agriculturalists? This chapter shows how farm schools and planned Jewish agricultural communities functioned as another experiment in the construction of an American Jewish masculinity. These communities allowed Jews to see themselves—and be seen by others—as productive, healthy workers who were attached to the land and espoused a rational religion. By the early twentieth century, the idea of the farmer-citizen as the paradigmatic American man was a nostalgic artifact, but it still functioned as an idealized path to Americanization and manhood.

This chapter begins by exploring the masculine focus of the farm schools and then illustrates the contours of this masculinity with a story that Rosen told the HAS students as part of his 1915 commencement speech. Next it shows how the relationship with the land played a critical role in the construction of this American Jewish masculinity. Finally it demonstrates that the kind of Judaism championed at these agricultural communities was "good" religion: rational, decorous, and masculine.

American Jewish Producerism

By the turn of the century, there were two major Jewish farm schools in the United States: the HAS, which opened in New Jersey in 1894, and the NFS, which opened in Pennsylvania in 1896. The Baron de Hirsch Fund, the philanthropic founder of the HAS, had chosen to locate the school in Woodbine because of its hybrid agricultural-industrial settlement on land purchased by the Baron de Hirsch fund. By the turn of the century, the community, which was made up largely of Eastern European Jews, numbered about 2,500 people.

Reform Rabbi Joseph Krauskopf was instrumental in creating the NFS in Doylestown, outside of his home in Philadelphia. Though he served as the full-time rabbi at Keneseth Israel, a Philadelphia Reform synagogue, he played a leading role at the NFS until his death in 1923. Each school regularly enrolled between 40 and 150 students. Although the administrative and teaching posts were mainly filled with acculturated Jews and even non-Jews, especially in the early years, well over half of the NFS and HAS students were immigrants.[6] Apart from holiday breaks, the students lived at the schools, which charged no tuition. Though the HAS maintained a curriculum for girls, its mission focused on its male students. The NFS remained a men's-only college until 1969.

These farm schools provide an excellent place to look for gender norms because they were so often explicit about their goals and ideals. When supporters gave fundraising speeches, they articulated a vision of a future where Jewish men would be healthy, productive farmers. Brochures for prospective students and their parents and their interviews with the press explained how the schools would turn boys into productive men. At their well-attended commencement exercises, these supporters celebrated their students' achievements and called on them to go out and make change in the world. The change most frequently called for was the transformation of Jews from unhealthy, weak city dwellers into healthy, productive farmers.

Unlike the Galveston Movement, which generally sought to place men in communities based on their existing vocational skills, the philanthropists, organizers, and immigrants who created Jewish agricultural projects felt that working the land was the best way for Jews to become—and demonstrate to others that they were capable of becoming—healthy, robust, and productive Americans. Though the HAS hired the Russian-born H. L. Sabsovich as its superintendent in its early years, it and the NFS were still very much under the ideological and financial thumb of acculturated Jews and their philanthropy. Smaller Jewish agricultural communities—only a few of which had ties to the NFS or HAS—were located in towns across the United States and were more diverse. Some of these settlements were almost direct outgrowths from Eastern European communities, whereas others were more indebted to American Jewish philanthropy.[7] But despite differences of ideology and perspective, there was a strong consensus that the farming life would improve Jews physically. The relationship among working the land, physical strength, and masculinity saturates the archival materials of both immigrant-led and philanthropically originated communities.

"Producer" quickly became a keyword in American Jewish agricultural circles. Part of the reason was that Jewish agricultural communities and movements functioned in the context of American back-to-the-land movements. Although these movements had some elements of what we might think of as environmentalism, they focused far more on farming's effects on the farmer. In particular, they lauded the healthy and morally upright lifestyle of the farmer because he used the land to produce something for himself and something for society. They thought of farmers as the backbone of the nation. Historians call this ideology "producerism" because of its valorization of production as central to civic life, as well as to human life as a whole.

Producerism struck a chord with many Jews. Both historically and at that time, prevailing stereotypes suggested that Jews were inclined to be consumers and not producers. The agricultural movement struck back at this image. At the 1909 Spring Festival at NFS, Krauskopf said, "In founding and maintaining this Farm School, we are refuting the reproach that the Jew is never a producer."[8] Producerism was gendered male in wider back-to-the-land movements, and it was even more so for Jews. Both Americans and Europeans had a general assumption that men should be producers, so when Jews were accused of failing or refusing to produce, it was also a critique of their masculinity. They should provide for their families, be able to make things with their hands, and be able to grow things. We can see similar assumptions even in contemporary American gender norms, wherein building homes and furniture is seen as a male task. Even today, every man should be able to "milk a cow" and "build a fence," according to *Esquire* men's magazine.[9]

These farm schools sought to train boys into "men capable of rightly locating and properly starting agricultural communities."[10] They wanted their graduates not only to be farmers but to lead other Jews in communal farming.[11] They would learn the latest techniques—"scientific" was a favorite word to describe them— and run farms and farming communities accordingly. Agricultural schools would train the leading lights of the American Jewish future, their founders and supporters hoped. The picture of the ideal Jewish farmer man was no "clod-hopper," as Krauskopf described the stereotype of the strong but dim-witted rural worker.[12] He did not dominate the land with his might alone. Rather, he was a physically healthy, smart, and productive man who knew how to work *with* the land.

One of the crucial elements of future leadership and production was having a healthy, agile body, or "physical vigor," as spokesmen like Krauskopf often called it. These farm schools sought to produce "morally and physically vigorous bread-winners as well as bread-producers."[13] This ideology of the healthy body as the active body harmonized with the larger American interest in physical culture, and the farm schools embraced this fit. The students learned the latest farming methods in classrooms, but they also spent much of their time outside learning in the fields. The fields also hosted a different kind of class. The young men of the Woodbine Colony, for instance, also did calisthenics there.

The NFS and the HAS both sponsored athletic teams for their male students, and they were both fond of printing photos and stories of these young men. In its first years, the NFS student publication the *Gleaner* printed a triumphant story of young Jews becoming athletic men through their experience at the farm school. "The majority comprising our team had never seen a football game let alone been in one," wrote the student journalist. The NFS football team lost the first game, but they won four of their next five contests because, as the journalist wrote, "they had the endurance of farm horses, and their strength, skill and agility were unexcelled in the field."[14] Of course, the school's newspaper would likely exaggerate the ability and athletic prowess of its own students. But it is clear that the young men at the school cared about having healthy, agile bodies even if they had not previously played organized sports.

Where did girls and women fit in this picture of production and physical vigor? The HAS's "Circular of Information," aimed at potential students and donors, began with its mission: "The purpose of the Baron de Hirsch Agricultural School is to prepare Jewish young men to become intelligent farm helpers, with the aim of eventually having farms of their own."[15] The sisters of many of the Woodbine boys were students at the same time, but the circular said nothing about making girls into women. It was clear that the emphasis lay on boys, which made sense given the gendered critique of Jews as nonproducers: women farmers would not help alleviate the image problem of Jewish men as insufficiently manly.

Yet this emphasis on boys and men did not indicate complete neglect of girls and women. Both the men and women involved in the agricultural movement imagined a role for women—one that was different from but complementary to the role of men. The HAS catalog described its female curriculum as "practical work for girls":

> The girls throughout the entire course will have practical work in sewing, cooking, caring for the poultry, dairy, etc. They will also be employed in doing the household work of the dormitory, and will be given such instruction in practical housekeeping as to enable them after graduation to make useful housewives, or to earn a living as housekeepers or in domestic service.[16]

Women, then, could and should participate in farm life. But they were there as "helpmates," as a popular adaptation of a biblical reference would have it. Their tasks included caring for cows and chickens, which aimed at the goal of training them in "housekeeping," as "useful housewives" for potential farmers.

In the middle of the 1910s, the NFS decided it also would like to enroll female students, and both the men and women involved assumed that meant they would need a different curriculum. If they wanted to train girls, they would need to develop a "domestic department" concentrating on canning, preserving, pickling, jellying, and floriculture.[17] Krauskopf said at the 1918 graduation, "We need to train our girls for agriculture just as we need to train our boys. In the hearts of our girls we must implant the love for rural surroundings, and in their minds the skill to be real helpmates."[18] Jewish women could and should live on farms, which would make them healthier and happier. But they would not live lives nor do work that was identical to their farming brothers or husbands. Girls needed to be trained to "love" the "rural surroundings" and support their husbands, Krauskopf said. Women needed the affective development of learning to love and support, in addition to the knowledge of cows, chickens, fruits, and jellies. Men needed the physical knowledge and development that came from tilling the soil.

Even ideologically, women played only a secondary role to men in the agricultural movement. When Robert Watchorn, the commissioner of immigration at Ellis Island, visited the NFS in 1907, he praised it for its vision of "those ideal conditions for which women have prayed and men have toiled, lo! these many centuries."[19] Watchorn imagined that men's role had been toil, and women's role had been "praying." Whether he imagined this prayer as a literal religious practice or a metaphorical reference to providing hope and support, it was clear that women were the emotional adjuncts to the men performing the physical task of farming in these ideologies.

Of course, as a practical matter, women farmers often engaged in quite strenuous physical labor. But that fact ran counter to American domestic ideals, and so women working plows rarely played a significant role in the promotion of agricultural life. The NFS's 1912 annual report included a photo taken at the Clarion, Utah, agricultural colony, which was run by four NFS graduates. It showed children sitting in the foreground while women worked the fields. The accompanying caption explained, "The women [in Clarion] have a two-fold happiness—one, helping their husbands garner the result of their labor in the fields, the other, the knowledge that their babes, weeds of the Ghettoes, are now strictly American growths, safe from the moral and physical dangers of the tenements and city streets."[20] The caption and the photo told two different stories. The photo showed women working in the fields, performing productive labor, but the caption implied that their happiness in the farming life was vicarious and that they lived through their husbands and children. Neither the caption nor the article mentioned anything about agriculture's benefits for the women themselves. The rhetoric of the agricultural movement was overwhelmingly the rhetoric of men.

Krauskopf and the wider Jewish farming movement believed that agriculture could redeem Jewish men's masculinity. But what, specifically, did that masculinity look like? When Joseph Rosen told a story to the crowd gathered for the HAS's commencement speech in 1915, he sought to impress on the graduates the importance of their choice to become farmers. The story he told the graduates, though it was neither historically accurate nor American in origin, illustrates the masculine ideals of the Jewish agriculture movement.

Rosen began, "Once upon a time a score of heroes were traveling along the road to Kieff-town. Among them were ten mightiest defenders of the nation, sons of warriors, preachers, merchants, and noblemen. They have returned home after a great victory, and felt hungry and thirsty." Along the roadside, one of the heroes noticed a plow with the inscription: "Turn a furrow, and Mother Earth will open up her bosom and everybody will have enough to eat, and drink to his heart's desire."[21] Each of the hungry heroes tried his hardest, and they even teamed up, but they could not even manage to move the plow. These seemingly manly men, these heroes, had just won a great battle, but they could not manage to feed themselves. They might be strong, and rich, but they were not self-sufficient, and they could not manage to produce anything.

Rosen continued: "At that time there happened to pass along the road, Mikula, the peasant's son. He noticed the heroes' trouble, and with his bright smile, he offered to help them out. The strong men scoffed at the peasant's son and ridiculed him, but Mikula merely touched the plow with the little finger of his left hand, and the plow moved along and made a deep furrow." Unlike the heroes, Mikula the farmer did not seem physically strong. And indeed, he was not. He used only his left pinky to make the earth yield her produce. No sooner had he done it than "Mother Earth opened her bosom, and everybody had enough to eat, and drink to his heart's desire." The farmer did not need to overpower the feminine figure of the land. This ideal-type of a farmer man touched the earth, gently putting his plow into it, and she "opened her bosom" to him. He inserted his plow, and she gave forth life. We need not be Freudians to see how the gendered imagery works here. The farmer-man puts his plow into the earth-woman, and then out of the woman comes his fruit. The fact that the farmer is a man, then, is not incidental. His identity as male is part of what makes the heterosexual, reproductive image work. Rosen did not reflect on this gendered interpretation, and it is likely that the images and ideas of farmers as men and the agricultural movement as male were so engrained that he rarely thought of gender at all.

Rosen then explained the moral of the story for his listeners: what the farmer in the story did "is what the farmers, as a social group, do for a nation: therein is their own and the nation's strength."[22] The strength of the farmers is not one of muscle-bound bodies but one of self-sufficiency, of productivity, and of finesse, rather than aggression. Here Rosen subtly refuted the accusation that Jews were not productive members of society. As Rosen suggested, this valorization of the male farmer also fit in with the ideology of the larger American (and even international) back-to-the-land movements and producerism.

Just in case it was not already clear that the ideal man was the farmer—and not the warriors, priests, or noblemen—Rosen's story had a coda. In it, the farmer also became a hero, though not of the same kind as the others. "Shortly after, the peasant's son himself became a hero, and has been victorious in fights with the strongest of men. Often in the midst of a great battle, Mikula would feel exhausted and worn out, but as soon as he would lie down on the ground and press his heart to Mother Earth, he would regain all his might." The farmer became a "hero," but not an overpowering one. In fact, he would become tired during fights and lie down! He won fights not because of his innate physical strength but because of his natural connection with the land and ability to make things come out of her.

Rosen then used what looked like a Zionist idea—the idea that Jews became unhealthy because they lived in exile away from the land of Palestine—and instead made its center the land in general, rather than the particular land of Palestine. "Nations have to be rooted in the soil to make a healthy growth. We Jews, as a nation, are uprooted. It is not so much the loss of our country, as the severing of our nation from the soil, that brought us centuries of misery."[23] Jews had suffered from their alienation from the soil, Rosen explained, and the solution to that alienation, its unhealthiness, and its stagnancy was reconnection to land in general, which included farming in the United States.

Rosen's imagery also placed masculinity as a central theme of this "national movement." Although he never said that he meant to address men exclusively, the image of the Jew in relation to the earth is the image of a man's relation to a woman. "If we are ever to regain our might and vigor as a nation, we must press our heart to Mother Earth. In this national movement, the Hirsch Agricultural School can, and must play an important part."[24] If men wanted "might and vigor," they should "press" themselves to the earth, which he portrayed as a woman. If Jewish men wanted to be more manly, they needed to enter into a metaphorically heterosexual embrace with the land.

Rosen's story depicted a masculinity of productivity, self-reliance, and physical health. But dominating the land did not require or especially promote muscular bodies. The ideal was a smart, healthy man who knew how to make the land work. The real heroes of the nation were not the fighters, but the farmers.

"Maker of Sturdy Men": The Charm of Agricultural Life and the Evils of the City

The idea of settling Jews on the land had widespread appeal. Like some other Americans who supported back-to-the-land movements, a few acculturated Jews took up the farming life—or at least tried for a while. And, like other Americans, many Jews found the *idea* of Jews farming immensely appealing. But although some probably sat in their city apartments and fantasized about what it might be like to raise chickens or grow corn, most American Jews never seriously entertained the thought of becoming farmers. What many did advocate, however, was for other Jews to farm. This way Jews and non-Jews would know that Jews were producers, that they were healthy, and that they were good male citizens of the nation.

The list of agricultural supporters had some unexpected bedfellows. The *Maccabaean* journal, published by the Federation of American Zionists, praised the NFS and the HAS and their methods in several articles in the early years of the twentieth century. These laudatory articles are even more remarkable given that a high profile anti-Zionist organization—the official body of Reform rabbis, the Central Conference of American Rabbis (CCAR)—also gave the agricultural movement its public support. Krauskopf himself, as well as the majority of Reform rabbis, had earlier lent their support to the 1885 Pittsburgh Platform, which denounced the Zionist project. In 1901, the CCAR passed an official resolution praising the NFS and calling on rabbis to speak about it from the pulpit on Sukkot: "Resolved: That in our annual Succoth Sermons we endeavor to interest our respective congregations in the national character of this institution [the NFS], and plead for the more generous cooperation and larger support it so richly deserves from every Jewish community in the land."[25] That year the CCAR even opened its annual conference and had "devotional exercises" on the grounds of the NFS.[26] That both Zionist and largely non-Zionist organizations endorsed the agricultural movement make it clear that the movement and its ideas had wide-reaching appeal: both signed onto this agricultural vision of the Jewish man.

These ideas about the healthy, productive Jewish male farmer also transcended roles at the farm schools. The largely acculturated Jewish leaders trumpeted their ideals most loudly, but many of the farm school students also promoted the picture of the transformed Jewish man. Soon after Rosen's address, one student echoed this version of masculinity in his article in the *HAS Record* student publication. The student, a young man named Samuel Richert, contextualized the story of improved masculinity through agriculture as an American story: "In the past decade or two the United States has witnessed a great 'back to the soil' movement," made more compelling by the "unsanitary conditions in our large, congested cities." Recognizing the enervating nature of city life, people began to realize that farmers were not merely dim-witted yet strong country bumpkins. Farming "is a business and a science [and] the man with the brains is superseding the muscular individual of the past."[27] Richert explained that the "muscular" man of agricultural history whose life was consumed by repetitive physical labor had been replaced by the man who made the land productive, not by force but by intelligence and efficiency. Jewish men who became farmers, then, were not choosing brawn over brains. They were pursuing a healthy, productive manhood. Students at the NFS also used this masculine rhetoric. In his valedictorian's address, Louis Hirschowitz told his fellow NFS graduates, "By contact with nature alone do men become stronger and resourceful, and herein, members of the graduating class, lies our destiny: to fulfill the object of the school, to go forth as sturdy warriors and proclaim its noble cause, and strive of its destined purpose."[28] This image of the Jewish man, then, was not merely the fantasy of a handful of men who ran these agricultural schools. The students too participated in the talk of healthy, productive masculinity and the idea that it would come from a life spent working the land.

Supporters who were neither teachers nor alumni of the farm schools likewise affirmed this vision of the agricultural movement as a means of improving Jewish men's bodies. Philadelphia philanthropist Ralph Blum, who had been involved with fundraising for the NFS since its inception, proclaimed to the graduating class in 1904, "To [the naysayers who refused to donate] we said that we were going to take young men from the disease-breeding sweat-shop; from the ghetto where the germ of tuberculosis was eating up young lives inch by inch; and from the streets of our busy business markets, and bring them out into the country to make sturdy, muscular and healthy men of them."[29]

Though the agricultural movement and its ideology focused on men, women also participated in the discussion about men and masculinity. When they did, they similarly emphasized students' physical transformation from weak and unhealthy city boys to healthy, able men. The 1911 "Matron's Report" at the NFS crowed over the students' "increase in weight soon after entering."[30] The group of women who canned, jellied, and sewed clothes for the students each year likewise discussed the benefits of farm school in terms of increased health and vigor. These women also expressed their worries about the urban environments from which these students came. Farm life was good in and of itself, but it was also good because it would get boys and men out of the enfeebling environment of the city.

One of the ideological cornerstones of the agricultural movement was the critique of city life. A rural agricultural life brought health, strength, and productivity—in short, it helped cultivate manhood. City life was emasculating, these agricultural boosters claimed. In 1902 Krauskopf explained in the pages of the American Zionist journal *Maccabaean* that his Pennsylvania farm school had two goals: to alleviate the health and "social problems" inherent in city living and to "restore the Jew . . . to the place which his natural agricultural instinct entitles him." The appeal of this vision of Jewish bodily health and productivity would be evident to all who encountered it, Krauskopf wrote. What was more, it fit with American ideas. Krauskopf quoted both Washington and Jefferson in his celebration of the masculine, productive agricultural life: "Gradually it is beginning to dawn on the laboring people that it was a profound truth which Washington uttered, when he pronounced agriculture to be the most 'healthful, the most useful, the most noble employment of man.'"

Krauskopf's discussion of gainful employment suggested that his focus was on men. He also gendered the land female and spoke of the earth as a woman to be "embraced." City dwellers suffered because of their estrangement from the land: "They are beginning to tire of narrowing, stifling, stunting city-life, and, like penitents, long to return to mother earth, whose fond embraces they have spurned and fled. They are beginning to feel that the large cities are huge furnaces, in which their best mental and physical vigor is being consumed." By spurning "mother earth" in favor of stifling city life, these men had lost some of their manhood and both "mental and physical vigor" in their exile from the land.[31] Agricultural life could restore their manhood.

Krauskopf sang the same tune all the way until his death in 1923. In 1912, he warned that city life harmed people, but that farm life could repair that damage. "The teaching of farming to the youth of our land will also mean a greater sanity of body and mind, among the people. Our population that threatens to become citybred, is in danger of onesided development: brilliant and clever, but not well rounded and well balanced. No society can long be divorced from immediate contact with earth and growing things, and remain normal."[32] A "normal" society promoted producerism, healthy bodies, and clear minds, while cities produced unhealthy, cerebral men who were unbalanced. In 1920, he wrote, "Congestion of cities brings with it not only a famine of food, but also a decline in moral and mental and physical health among large numbers of the congested." Immigrants crowded into cities could not flourish because of the unhealthy urban environment. He continued with a description that sounded very much like the critiques of other American Progressives, who warned their readers of the ills and evils of city life: "The crowding into the tenement districts of more families than they can decently accommodate, results in wresting them from a sane, wholesome and normal life, and produces the defective, the dependent, the deficient. In this class crawl the defeated, the despairing, the despondent, the rebellious."[33] City life sucked away sanity, physical health, and strength. It made Jewish men less manly. And it was not "normal," a category that Part III of this book shows played an important role in categorizing Jewish men.

Bernard Palitz, the superintendent of the Woodbine Colony and HAS, agreed with Krauskopf's critique of the enervating nature of city living. Palitz wrote in 1907 that the agricultural colonies had two messages:

> They are sufficient to convince the anti-Semite that the Jewish conception of life is not commerce, that he loves the beautiful, the quiet and the natural life of man and lives it when equal opportunities are offered to him. To the Jew who wastes away his life and the lives of his children in the death-traps of the sweat shop, in the immoral and unhealthy surroundings—they cry out: come back to your natural calling, to the healthy life-prolonging occupation, to more light and purer air; harden your muscles and broaden your mind for the struggle that Israel is yet to meet before his mission is accomplished and his prophecies fulfilled.[34]

For Palitz, agricultural communities not only would show critics that Jews could be productive citizens but they also provided an example for other Jews of the benefits of leaving unhealthy cities and developing their bodies and minds. He also hinted that this physical and mental development had a religious value, but did not elaborate on its particulars.

These concerns about city life's weakening effects, especially on immigrants, appeared in both Jewish and non-Jewish texts. In response to the anti-immigrant declarations of Sen. Henry Cabot Lodge and Immigration Commissioner Frank Sargent, Krauskopf asked, "What is their alarm but an echo of our own?"[35] Both sides expressed concern about the physically unhealthy and morally questionable Jewish immigrants in cities. Unlike immigration restrictionists, however, Krauskopf thought the problem of weak, unhealthy immigrants could be solved by means other than keeping them out of the country. Teaching them farming would help combat the "evils of the ghetto" and answer the Jewish question.

The self-presentation that Krauskopf, Palitz, and others in the agricultural movement promoted did not go unheard. Non-Jews also saw the agricultural movement as a way to improve Jewish men. Former president William Howard Taft and Progressive journalist Jacob Riis praised the movement for its noble goals of creating Jewish farmers and a Jewish farming culture. Robert Watchorn, the Ellis Island commissioner, congratulated the National Farm School on "transforming [immigrants] from the cowering, hunted, persecuted subjects of an ignorant and cowardly dynasty into the manly, upright citizens of a glorious Republic."[36] Watchorn, like many of the non-Jewish visitors and speakers at the NFS and HAS, reported seeing healthy men pursuing productive means of living. They praised the ability of these farm schools to transform weak, unhealthy, ignorant immigrant boys and men into manly Americans.

Articles about the farm schools and agricultural communities garnered positive coverage in the newspapers. Photos of the students working in the fields, young men doing calisthenics, and a meeting taking place in Woodbine room with American flag and a portrait of George Washington all appeared in a 1908 *New-York Tribune* photo essay. The accompanying story featured the colony as an exemplar—not just of Jewish agricultural work, but of the work of the upcoming spring season for all farmers.[37] Two years earlier, a non-Jewish *New-York Tribune* reporter wrote a lengthy article titled "Getting the Jews out of the Ghetto and on to the Farm." Its first sentence revealed his skepticism: "'Can the Jew become a successful farmer?' is a question which seems in the minds of most people almost as difficult to answer in the affirmative as was the query." But his examination of the Baron de Hirsch Fund's activities and the Woodbine agricultural community convinced the reporter that Jews could indeed become productive and healthy farmers. After praising the industriousness and health of Jewish farmers, he concluded his article: "The Gentile [the journalist] left the exhibition convinced that the question could be answered in the affirmative."[38]

After a visit to the Woodbine Colony, a Boston reporter exclaimed that the babies are "fairly bursting with health" and "the boys of the farm school [Woodbine] shown stripped for the plunge [swimming] display a development superb for any race and truly amazing for the fragile Jew."[39] She praised the colony for its self-sufficiency, its producer ethic, and especially the healthy bodies of its male inhabitants, which she saw as a vast improvement over weak Jewish men.

The famed lawyer and future Supreme Court Justice Louis Brandeis visited the NFS in 1914, and his remarks about the Jewish men who had become farmers neatly encapsulated a general consensus among Jewish and non-Jewish observers: "The Jew, a city dweller for many generations—weak, frail and nervous as the result of congested conditions under which he has lived, has developed in the Massachusetts and Connecticut farms, as fine a physical development as any of his neighbors."[40] The weak, unhealthy, and inadequately manly city Jew had been transformed into a fine physical specimen of a man, and he had farming life to thank for that.

This rhetoric of a Jewish healthy, productive masculinity changed little from the turn of the century until after World War I. Although the war itself changed life at the farm school, it did little to change the picture of the ideal farmer. The school's ideal of masculinity picked up martial metaphors, but its focus remained the same: "Our salvation lies in training and fostering, to the fullest extent possible, a great army of food-producers, a real Army of Peace."[41] Despite the farm school's support of the American war effort (the NFS donated thousands of pounds of food to the war effort), it still did not promote a masculinity of aggression, violence, combativeness, or even physical fighting. Its army was one of the scientific production of food. It was an army of peace. Jewish men, to be good men, would be producers.

When a veteran enrolled in the NFS after his discharge from the army, he was called "the hero of the lost battalion," and the school celebrated his service in terms that reiterated this ideal of peaceful, productive masculinity. Its 1919 Annual Report described the new student as "now applying the same earnestness, which he brought to the grim business of war, to the work of the great Agricultural Army of Peace, whose slogan is: 'They shall beat their spears into pruning hooks, and their swords into plowshares,'" a reference to Isaiah 2:4.[42] The NFS annual publication promoted his heroism not as leading to martial victory, but as a form of biblical producerism.

"The Gospel of the Farm"

Krauskopf used religious language when he referred to his students: they were the chosen people. His foreword to the 1911 NFS Annual Report described them as "physically and morally healthy" and said they had become well suited to "country life on the farm." He continued, "These are the chosen of God to found a few colonies in different parts of our continents. These are the chosen of God, to make, after a few years, a signal success of their undertakings. These are the chosen of God, to demonstrate by their successes, that a splendid living can be made on the farm, to invite large numbers of people to follow their example, and to settle on farms under their leadership."[43] God had chosen these young men, Krauskopf explained, to bring farming to other Jews. They would be leaders, spreading "the gospel of the farm," as Krauskopf had called it several years earlier.[44]

But what, exactly was the content of this gospel of the farm? Who was this God who had chosen these young men? What did religion look like for these Jews at the farm schools? Their Judaism was a rational religion, in harmony with science, and a universal religion, where laws of nature and divine laws were sometimes inseparable. It was a "good" religion, and it was manly.

Its text was the Bible, not the Talmud or Midrash or Hasidic tales. Biblical texts were an authoritative source to promote the value of farming to Jewish and Christian audiences alike. Although there are a multitude of talmudic texts about farming, the Jews involved in the agricultural movement almost never referred to them. Instead, like most acculturated American Jews in the early twentieth century, they preferred the Bible and displayed it as the central text of Judaism. In fact, the most oft-quoted text in farm school publications was the Bible, followed closely by the writings of George Washington. Appeals to the Bible worked in two ways. One emphasized a Jewish (or, more properly, Israelite) agricultural past, while the other held up the Bible as a resource for contemporary farming theories and methods.

Jews who were involved in the agricultural movement, as well as those who supported it financially, often used the Bible to support their claim to a Jewish agricultural past. For example, Oscar Strauss, who served on the board of directors of the Baron de Hirsch Fund and was a vocal advocate for both farm schools, used the biblical text to argue for their value. He told the students at the NFS that farming was not only a sacred activity but it was also a historically Jewish one. It was part of their heritage, as one could see from the Bible. In a 1903 speech at a school ceremony, he said,

> No vocation of life is entwined with such sacred and hallowed memories as that of the farmer, because "the people of the Book" were an agricultural people, and some of the most beautiful celebrations that our religion enshrines commemorate agricultural festivals, the changing of the seasons, the first fruits and the harvesting of crops. The ideals of happiness are pictured in the Biblical words: "Shall sit every man under his vine and under his fig tree; and none shall make him afraid." The Puritans who settled in New England drew their inspiration from Israel's history in the Bible, and

that history made doubtless a deeper impression upon them because they, too, were an agricultural people, and because they were an agricultural people and, like Israel, cultivated the soil as well as their souls, they have left such a precious heritage of sterling manhood to the generations that followed them.[45]

In this speech, Strauss, who would soon become the Secretary of Commerce and Labor under Teddy Roosevelt, tied together biblical history and American history. The "people of the Book," the Israelites, were agricultural, and their religion reflected the farming life. Strauss identified this agricultural religion and people as Jewish, but their story had also inspired the non-Jews who had built America. Puritans "drew their inspiration" from this biblical history, the story of the Jews. Both the Puritans and the Israelites instilled in their descendants "sterling manhood" because of this agricultural and religious lifestyle.

Non-Jews too used the Bible to appeal to the idea of a Jewish agricultural past and its present revival. In Secretary of Agriculture James Wilson's address at the NFS's first commencement in 1901, he anticipated Strauss's veneration of biblical history and its assertion of a Jewish agricultural past. His oration connected this biblical history with the improvement of Jewish male bodies: "The Jew is a thoroughbred, with a history running back to the time when Abraham dwelt in Ur of the Chaldees. . . . He desires to restore the physical vigor of the race where it requires it, by returning to the early vocation of its founders. It is wisely resolved that young men be educated in the sciences and arts relating to agriculture."[46] Wilson's reference to the Bible was another instance of the inextricability of race and religion for Jews: Abraham was both a religious forefather and a racial one, and Wilson suggested no difference between the two. Appeals to the Bible allowed Jews—and non-Jews, such as Wilson—to frame Jewish farming as a return to the land, bodily health, and "physical vigor" of an imagined Jewish past, rather than a brand-new activity for Jews.

This relationship of the Bible to agriculture suggests the second way that appeals to the text worked: participants and supporters alike agreed that biblical accounts were compatible with science. At his commencement speech in 1901, Wilson also told the NFS audience, "There is no book . . . that gives so many hints to the farmer about his business as the Bible. Every student of agriculture should be entirely familiar with it."[47] Two years Wilson wrote in a letter to Krauskopf, "The whole Bible story is full of valuable suggestions regarding the atmosphere, the soil, the plants and the animals; and no fact along these lines mentioned in the bible has ever been controverted by science."[48]

Wilson and others who thought about religion in relationship to the movement characterized the Bible as universal (for farmers everywhere, not just the Middle East) and rational and even scientific, helping these men be productive manly men. That is, when they suggested the universally applicable, scientific uses of the Bible, they claimed that it was a document of and for "good" religion.

This rhetoric accorded with the emphasis in both the NFS and the HAS schools on the importance of science in making good farmers. The schools promoted their classes by advertising that they incorporated the latest in scientific knowledge. The majority of the NFS annual reports included photographs of young men in chemistry classes, showcasing the importance of science in its teaching methods.

The Judaism of these farm schools looked a lot like Reform Judaism. Halakhah was not a priority. For instance, both farm schools and many of the agricultural settlements kept pigs. When the student publication *HAS Record* quoted the director of "Dairy and Swine Husbandry" as saying, "What you young men need is an injection of a big dose of Judaism," it was being only a little tongue in cheek. Some Jews in the agricultural movement connected bodily improvement to religious enlightenment; their idea of civilized religion closely aligned with Reform Judaism and denigrated the benighted ways of "superstitious" Hasidim or Orthodox Jews. Many immigrant Jews themselves, especially those involved in agricultural movements, harbored antipathy toward traditional piety and religious institutions such as the *cheder*, or Jewish religious school, in favor of a rational, post-*haskalah* (Jewish enlightenment) Judaism and Jewish culture.

Jettisoning halakhah did not mean that these schools were secular, however: Judaism mattered at these farm schools. The NFS opened each day, each school-wide exercise, and even each meeting with prayer. Every morning at 6:30 a.m. students reported for "breakfast and devotion." "Divine services" happened each weekday, as well as on Saturday and Sunday. Students had to choose to "keep Saturday holy" or "keep Sunday holy" and to do indoor work on the other weekend day.[49] HAS had "Sabbath School instruction" every Saturday. Both HAS and NFS calendars included Jewish holidays, but not Christian ones. Rabbi Krauskopf opened each retreat and meeting with a prayer, except when he had a guest clergy member do it.[50] One graduate identified himself as "me, as a Christian," indicating that his experience was unusual. The NFS did admit non-Jewish students, but only a few.

Yet the Judaism at the farm schools was not a simple mimicry of the Reform Judaism happening beyond its gates. The schools elevated the fall holiday of Sukkot, because of its agricultural character, to a major and meaningful Jewish holiday. The NFS held a leaders' retreat and celebration each year on Sukkot. "The annual Succoth pilgrimage is of a religious character, and it is fitting" that it takes place at the farm school, Krauskopf insisted.[51]

The agricultural communities varied more in their religious observance, but they too tended toward a rational Judaism that did not require ritual observance. Tevye Goldhaft, who lived at the Alliance farming community near Vineland,

New Jersey, "wasn't particularly pious, although he would go to the synagogue as a fairly regular thing," his son recalled. "Mostly he would go there for a good argument, taking the side that religion was superstition."[52] Many agricultural colonies had synagogues, unlike secular kibbutzim in Palestine, which were their ideological brethren when it came to ideas about agriculture, production, communalism, and physical labor, but which generally avoided religious observance. While Saturday was the day of rest for most American Jewish agricultural communities and some farmers kept kosher or observed the Sabbath, many others did not. In the early years, ardent secularists dominated Am Olam colonies; they saw traditional religion as superstitious, and their ideals focused on brotherhood, production, health, and labor. Yet even in Am Olam colonies, many men and women maintained some Jewish ritual practices that they felt fit with their agricultural lifestyle.

Some Yiddish materials advertised the value of the "religious freedom" afforded by the American agricultural lifestyle. "And in the country the Jew finds an advantage of peace and happiness that are impossible in the city," the 1912 *Guide to the United States for the Jewish Immigrant* announced, "because in the city it is difficult for him to observe the Sabbath as his conscience dictates; but in the country he has complete religious freedom, and in peace can worship God according to the custom of his fathers."[53] The *Guide* was written by acculturated Jews, but it aimed to shape immigrant Jews. Farming while strictly observing Jewish law would make for a difficult life, but the pamphlet sought to convince immigrant Jews to take up agricultural lifestyles anyway. Most acculturated Jews who supported the agricultural movement assumed that rural life itself would inspire religious lives, but that those religious lives would be rational Jewish ones. Perhaps they hoped that the farming life would nudge pious immigrants away from "superstition" and toward rational, masculine Judaism.

The leaders, supporters, and students involved in the agricultural movement often drew connections between natural law and God's law. Their Judaism was not only rational and compatible with science but it was also intimately related to nature, natural law, and the natural world. The NFS student newspaper *The Gleaner* printed an article in which a student journalist referred to "the Law of God" as "natural law."[54] He meant it not in a Hobbesian sense, but rather in the sense that divine laws were one and the same with the laws governing the natural world and the earth in particular. In this view, natural law and divine law were both universal.

Because of what they saw as intimate connections between God and the earth, many supporters, both Jewish and non-Jewish, assumed that farming would make people more religious. During the formal installation of its 1909 freshman class, Krauskopf celebrated the NFS students' entrance into a career that "placed them in actual partnership with God."[55] Perhaps he imagined this "partnership" as one of creation. As God created, the farmers too would create. God, in this sense, was the ultimate producer. As farmers, these young Jewish men would also become producers, working in close and continual contact with God's production.

This connection between nature, God, and the farmer also entailed a gendered portrait of the farmer. Reform Rabbi Joseph Leiser wrote a poem titled, appropriately, "To the National Farm School":

> Strong arms have they who turn the turf,
> Whose plough-share cuts the grass-webbed sod;
> Self-poised and firm they walk the earth,
> The splendid instruments of God.
> The work they do is a daily need,
> Whereby the teeming millions feed.
> No weaklings they![56]

These farmers had "strong arms," and they were not "weaklings." In Leiser's portrait, the Jewish farmer was "an instrument of God," but he was also self-sufficient. Even better than self-sufficient, his work produced food for the "teeming millions." These farmers were healthy and productive men, and they were also men of God.

The particularly Jewish back-to-the-soil narrative inflected by theology was not one espoused by Jews alone. In his 1901 NFS commencement address, James Wilson also said, "I am delighted to see the children of Israel doing this work. . . . You educate along these lines because it brings your people back into contact with the soil, the plant and the animal; to contact with Nature and the God of Nature— relations so intimate and so prominent in the history of your race."[57]

Although some, like Wilson and many Jews, tied farming to the history of ancient Israel and assumed there was therefore something distinctively Jewish about it, others suggested there was something generically religious about agriculture: if men became farmers, they would come back to religion. In 1904, Reform Rabbi William Rosenau gave a speech to the NFS graduates in which he connected the agricultural pursuits of the present to the biblical past of the Israelites. To the students, he said, "This day is one wrought with holiness for you. . . . I am led back in thought to that Book, sacred to the entire world." He told the story of the messengers going into the land of Israel from the encampment in the desert. Only Joshua and Caleb came back optimistic, but their assessment was correct. These students, too, would have a hard row to hoe, but Rosenau was encouraging: "You, like the children of Israel of old, will win the day, though the path be hard."[58]

Rosenau suggested that the students, and the agricultural movement more generally, could solve the historical problems of Jewry: "You are aware of the fact that the Jew has been a problem to the world ever since he has been a member of society. From olden times to the present day Israel has ever presented this problem. There are a thousand solutions offered. Among these is nationalism (Zionism), or the purchase of Palestine and assimilation. Neither of these has solved the problem." Rosenau, like most American Reform Jews of his day, was not a Zionist. But he recognized the problems that Zionism identified, such as its critique of the urban, male Jewish body, and he proposed to solve them by other methods:

> The most healthy, the most practical solution, however, is to bring the Jews back to the soil to which they belong, and to endow them once more with the agricultural ability that belonged to their ancestors. You will thus show that the solution lies in colonizing the Jews and taking them away from our over-crowded cities. Be Joshuas and Calebs.

He concluded with an injunction for the students to embrace both God and agricultural work: "Let confidence in God and confidence in yourself encourage you in your work, proving that the Jew can once more become a farmer and help to solve the problem of the centuries."[59] For Rosenau, the biblical story was part and parcel of the story of the Jews. And the biblical agricultural episodes served as inspirations for solving the problems of modern Jews, who had become emasculated by city life.

Other rabbis also connected the agricultural life to wholesome religious life. New York Reform Rabbi Maurice Harris argued that Christianity retained its adherents because, when Christians moved from rural atmospheres to the city, they brought their faith with them. His article in the *Menorah* journal claimed that the rural atmosphere and agricultural lifestyle were more conducive to religion: "The strength of the Church lies in the fact that every year there come from the country to the town reinforcements of young people bringing their fresh and simple faith acquired in the fields and vineyards of the land." Although Jews had once been models of religious life, they had lost some of that connection when Eastern European governments pushed them to live in more urban, nonfarming environments. "Therefore, perhaps the cruelest persecution of Russia against the Jews is the driving them from the country places and forcing them into the towns." Harris lamented that "Jews, who were once the patterns of believers and whose mission was to be the witnesses of God, contribut[ed] more than their proportion of skepticism to the unbelievers of the modern world."[60] A move back to agricultural pursuits would not only make Jews more healthy and productive but would also facilitate their return to religion.

Taking a similar idea and universalizing it from the Jews to everyone, Oscar Strauss touted, in his 1903 speech, "the marked religious benefit to be derived from agriculture." Rural agricultural life brought people to religion—whether that religion be Judaism or Christianity. The real concern was that city dwellers were abandoning religion entirely. "We hear a great deal to-day about the unchurched. There is no one who questions that in the cities this unchurched condition of the people is more marked than in the country. Religious indifference is a disease afflicting Jew and Christian alike, and because a prevalent ailment it has no special causes in the Jew as its sufferer."

Strauss thus posed the problem as an urban one, not a particularly Jewish one. Jews and Christians alike were more likely to neglect their religious lives if they moved into the city, he explained. The most significant cause of "the lack of the proper religious spirit among people dwelling in cities as the peculiar constitution and environment of city life." City men came into contact with brilliant inventions such as the telephone, the telegraph, and the skyscraper. By bringing them to "worship the genius of man," these marvels would turn them away from the proper object of worship: God. If, instead, the city man lived a life that put him in contact with the natural world, he would see God more clearly: "What does man see in the city of Nature, who speaks a various language, to him who communes with her? It is a fact that in the rural districts religion plays a greater part than in the city." The difference between the city man and the country man, Strauss explained, was related neither to temperament nor sociology: "In the country man comes face to face with the genius of the universe instead of the genius of man. He finds tongues in trees, books in the running brooks, sermons in stones." Urban men were confronted with marvels of human making, but farmers were confronted with marvels of divine creation.

Though both Jews and Christians suffered from a turn away from religion when they became city dwellers, Strauss explained, Jews had a historical resource that Christians did not. Biblical history showed that the Israelites were farmers, and it was this very occupation that gave them their genius for religion:

> Why is it that Israel was in the past a people with a pronounced religious talent? Because Israel was an agricultural people. Because it was in everlasting contact with Nature. Because it saw the finger of God in everything that met its gaze. Why is it that the Psalmist sang hymns which are still the inspiration of millions? Why is it that the author of the so-called Song of Solomon sang of Spring? Because they and all others in Israel's temple of literary fame heard the voice of God in the babbling of the brook, the chirping of the birds, and the music of the spheres. Had Israel been other than an agricultural people it might have become a people with a special talent for law and art. We need to bring religion back again into the soul, with its rich flower morality, into daily life. Agriculture will help us to do it, for it is sure to give to man the stimulus for the cultivation of faith and of hope. Israel needs to develop its traditional character—the talent for the religious. Herein lies the justification of its existence. If the significance of agriculture to the Jew we would know, let us bear

in mind that it is of the same nature as that for the non-Jew. Let agriculture be pursued more extensively among us than it is at present and we shall witness a regeneration, social, economic, hygienic, professional, religious and moral.[61]

Agricultural life, Strauss argued, would improve Jews' bodies and also their religion. Jews and Jewish history were religious exemplars because of their agricultural lives. If they could reconnect with the land, they would be healthier, fitter, and more properly religious. For Strauss, being properly religious meant worshiping God and appreciating God's creation. But it did not mean following halakhah; rather, being religious meant expressing a profound appreciation for the earth and the laws of nature.

Rabbis Krauskopf, Rosenau, and Harris sounded very much like the Jewish politician Strauss and the non-Jewish politician Wilson when they connected good religion with agriculture, and both with the healthy bodies of farmers. When Krauskopf told the NFS 1904 graduating class and their supporters that they were descended from agriculturalists, he used biblical language to do it. Their work, he said, would "vindicate their claim as descendants of those who in ancient days kept the Promised Land 'flowing with milk and honey.'"[62] His religious rhetoric signaled far more than a cliché about living a good life. The biblical citation was no idle catchphrase—Krauskopf was a rabbi, after all. Krauskopf, the NFS, and the larger Jewish agricultural movement saw working the land as a route to good religion. Farmers would not only be manly, healthy producers but they would also embrace a rational religion compatible with natural law and science.

Conclusion

Most of the agricultural communities had failed by the time the United States closed its doors to Eastern European immigrants in 1924. The Woodbine settlement largely closed in 1919, shuttering the HAS when it did. In 1922, the *Nation* referred to "this Jewish settlement in Cape May County" as "nothing more than a bare monument to a gigantic but futile effort."[63] The NFS lived on, though it began to shed some of its specifically Jewish character, especially after Krauskopf's death. If only a tiny percentage of American Jews ever farmed and if most of these efforts were failures, why should we pay any attention to the Jewish back-to-the-land movement?

These farm schools and agricultural communities, in spite of their marginality, give us a picture of an aspirational American Jewish identity. Even though few American Jews farmed, many others supported the enterprise because it would help Jews become productive, healthy, self-sufficient, and good citizens. The agricultural life even encouraged "good" religion—a religion that was rational, universal, and compatible with being a good American. Closeness to the land could do all these things. This ideal of a productive, healthy, good citizen was part of the picture of the ideal American Jewish man, and the idea of a rational, universal religion, as Part I showed, was a masculine religion.

Krauskopf summed up the hopes of the American Jewish agricultural movement when he wrote in the 1904 NFS Annual Report that people were heeding the call to go back to the soil: "The debilitating and demoralizing congestion of city ghettos and slums is destined to be relieved by a return to mother earth of those sorely in need of its invigorating and ennobling influences." He praised both the philanthropists and the immigrants themselves for their roles in this transformation from unhealthy, enervating city life to uplifting farm life: "The thought of the true philanthropist is turning from merely remedial to preventive work and a prophecy that not forever shall people suffer poverty and disease to intrench [sic] themselves in the overcrowded districts of cities and breed physical and moral wreckage." There was an alternative to this weak, diseased city life that sucked away men's physical health and natural connection with the land. Instead, these men and their families should disperse "over God's broad acres where the fountains of food and health and morals flow unceasingly, they might become independent and vigorous and prosperous bread-winners and bread producers, and as such be welcomed everywhere as desirable colonists or immigrants."[64] They would connect with God through nature, they would be producers, they would be strong and healthy, and they would become good citizens. In short, farming would make these Jews manly.

As we see in the next chapter, the broader connection of the land, healthy bodies, and Jewish masculinity resonated in circles beyond the agriculturalists. For some Jews, the location of the soil was not incidental. Famous Zionists Louis Brandeis and Henrietta Szold praised the Jewish agricultural settlements, but their hopes extended beyond New Jersey and California: They hoped that Jews could one day work the land in Palestine. If Indian-Israelite affinities helped create a narrative of a manly American Jewish past, and agricultural schools and settlements promoted an image of a manly Jewish present, Zionism would gesture toward Jews' future Americanness and manliness.

Notes

1. Jonathan Dekel-Chen, *Farming the Red Land* (New Haven, CT: Yale University Press, 2005).

2. Joseph A Rosen, "The HAS and the Jew in Agriculture," *Commencement Number of the HAS Record* (Woodbine, NJ: Hirsch Agricultural School, 1915), 18.

3. Joseph Krauskopf, "President's Annual Message," *Sixth Annual Report of the National Farm School* (n.p.: n.p., 1903), 13.

4. Ellen Eisenberg, *Jewish Agricultural Communities in New Jersey* (Syracuse, NY: Syracuse University Press, 1995), xxiii.

5. Dona Brown, *Back to the Land: The Enduring Dream of Self-Sufficiency in Modern America* (Madison: University of Wisconsin Press, 2011), 21–51.

6. In 1902, twenty-eight of forty students had been born in Eastern Europe. Krauskopf proclaimed, "Rich and poor alike [cried] 'back to the soil!'" Joseph Krauskopf, "President's Annual Message," *Fifth Annual Report of the National Farm School* (n.p.: n.p., Oct. 1902), 13–14. For NFS statistics, see Joseph Brandes, *Immigrants to Freedom: Jews as Yankee Farmers! (1880's–1960's)* (Bloomington, IN: Xlibris, 2009), 126.

7. Eisenberg, *Jewish Agricultural Communities in New Jersey*, 1–60.

8. Joseph Krauskopf, "Spring Festival," *Twelfth Annual Report of the National Farm School* (n.p.: n.p., 1909), 8–9.

9. Tom Chiarella, "The 75 Things Every Man Should Do," *Esquire*, Apr. 22, 2015, www.esquire.com/features/75-things-0808#slide-26.

10. *Catalogue of the National Farm School* (Philadelphia: National Farm School, 1898), 3.

11. *Fourth Annual Report of the National Farm School* (n.p.: n.p., Oct. 1901), 13.

12. Joseph Krauskopf, "A Statement of the National Farm School by Its President," *Twelfth Annual Report of the National Farm School* (n.p.: n.p., Nov. 1909), 18.

13. Joseph Krauskopf's speech, "Commencement Day," *Fifth Annual Report of the National Farm School* (n.p.: n.p., Oct. 1902), 32.

14. "Athletics," *Gleaner* 1, no. 1 (Feb 1901): 9.

15. "Circular of Information," Baron de Hirsch Papers, AJHS.

16. Baron de Hirsch Papers, *Catalogue of the Baron de Hirsch Agricultural and Industrial School* (New York: De Leeuw and Oppenheimer, 1898), 14.

17. Hetty Abraham, "Domestic Department Report," *Sixteenth Annual Report of the National Farm School* (n.p.: n.p., 1913), 39.

18. Joseph Krauskopf, "An Ounce of Prevention or a Pound of Cure," *Nineteenth Annual Report of the National Farm School* (n.p.: n.p., 1916), 14.

19. Robert Watchorn, "The Bearing of Agriculture on Immigration," *Tenth Annual Report of the National Farm School* (n.p.: n.p., 1907), 32.

20. Photo caption, *Fifteenth Annual Report of the National Farm School* (n.p.: n.p., 1912), 35.

21. Rosen, "The HAS and the Jew in Agriculture," 18–19.

22. Ibid.

23. Ibid.

24. Ibid.

25. "Central Conference of American Rabbis," *Fourth Annual Report of the National Farm School* 11 (n.p.: n.p., 1901), 22.

26. "Resolution Commending National Farm School," *Yearbook of the Central Conference of American Rabbis* (n.p.: n.p., 1901), 85.

27. Samuel Richert, "Agricultural Progress," *Commencement Number of the HAS Record* (Woodbine, NJ: Students of the Hirsch Agricultural School, [between 1915 and 1917]): 9

28. Louis Hirschowitz, "Valedictory Address" *Gleaner* (June 1903): 13.

29. "Ralph Blum's Address," *Seventh Annual Report of the National Farm School* (n.p.: n.p., 1904), 39.

30. Hetty Abraham, "Matron's Report," *Fourteenth Annual Report of the National Farm School* (n.p.: n.p., 1911), 49.

31. Harry Hochstadter, "The National Farm School at Doylestown, Pa," *Maccabaean* 2 (Feb. 1902): 89–91.

32. Joseph Krauskopf, "Go Forth and Possess the Land," *Fifteenth Annual Report of the National Farm School* (n.p.: n.p., Oct. 1912), 7.

33. Krauskopf, "Solving the Food Problem," *Twenty-Third Annual Report of the National Farm School* (n.p.: n.p., 1920), 9.

34. Bernard Palitz, "The Borough of Woodbine," 1907, box 2112, AJA .

35. Joseph Krauskopf, "President's Message," *Seventh Annual Report of the National Farm School* (n.p.: n.p., 1904), 26.

36. Watchorn, "The Bearing of Agriculture on Immigration," 35.

37. Photographs show a Woodbine meeting where eight men sit under a large American flag and photo of George Washington (the forty-five-star flag indicates it was likely taken between July 1896 and July 1908): "Men in Meeting, Woodbine, NJ"; men doing calisthenics in a Woodbine field ("Pupils Drilling [Calisthenics] at the Woodbine Agricultural School, New Jersey"). Baron de Hirsch Fund Records, 1870–1991, I–80, Center for Jewish History. An April 5, 1908, *New-York Tribune* photo essay also highlighted the "Woodbine Agriculturalists" as their example of agricultural work in the beginning of spring.

38. "Getting the Jews out of the Ghetto and on to the Farm," *New York Tribune*, Oct. 14, 1906.

39. Mary Bronson Hartt, "The Growing Jews: Vivid Illustration of Their Progress," *Boston Evening Transcript*, Nov. 17, 1906, 40.

40. "Eighteenth Annual Meeting and Succoth Pilgrimage," *Eighteenth Annual Report of the National Farm School* (n.p.: n.p., 1914), 24.

41. Krauskopf, "Solving the Food Problem," 17.

42. "Abraham Krotoshinsky," *Twenty-Second Annual Report of the National Farm School* (n.p.: n.p., 1919), 24. There is also a photo of him.

43. Joseph Krauskopf, "Forward to the Soil," *Fourteenth Annual Report of the National Farm School* (n.p.: n.p., Oct. 1911), 11.

44. Joseph Krauskopf, "The President's Message," *Tenth Annual Report of the National Farm School* (n.p.: n.p., 1907), 11.

45. Oscar Straus, "Baccalaureate Oration," *Gleaner* 3, no. 5 (June 1903): 16.

46. "Oration of Hon. James Wilson," *Fourth Annual Report of the National Farm School* (n.p.: n.p., Jan 1901): 25.

47. Ibid., 24.

48. Letter James Wilson to Joseph Krauskopf, printed in *Sixth Annual Report of the National Farm School* (n.p.: n.p., 1903): 26.

49. *Twelfth Annual Report of the National Farm School*, 13.

50. "Fifth Annual Meeting and Succoth Pilgrimage," *Fifth Annual Report of the National Farm School* (n.p.: n.p., Oct. 1902), 11. A Unitarian minister led the 1902 opening prayer at Commencement. "Commencement Day," *Fifth Annual Report of the National Farm School* (n.p.: n.p., Oct. 1902), 28.

51. "Ninth Annual Pilgrimage to the National Farm School," *Ninth Annual Report of the National Farm School* (n.p.: n.p., 1906), 11.

52. See, for instance, Ellen Eisenberg's discussion of the relationship that Am Olam members had with Judaism: Eisenberg, *Jewish Agricultural Colonies*, 96.

53. John Foster Carr, *Guide to the United States for the Jewish Immigrant: A Nearly Literal Translation* (n.p.: n.p., Connecticut Daughters of the American Revolution, 1912), 22.

54. "Self-Preservation a Duty," *Gleaner* 1, no. 10 (Jan. 1902): 5.

55. Krauskopf, "Spring Festival at the National Farm School," 9.

56. Joseph Leiser, "To the National Farm School," *Tenth Annual Report of the National Farm School* (n.p.: n.p., 1907), 2.

57. "Oration of Hon. James Wilson," 23.

58. "Rev. Dr. Rosenau's Baccalaureate Sermon," *Seventh Annual Report of the National Farm School* (n.p.: n.p., 1904): 42.

59. Ibid., 42–43.

60. Maurice Harris, "Israel's Calling," *Menorah* 38, no. 6 (June 1906): 344.

61. Straus, "Baccalaureate Oration," 16.

62. Krauskopf, "President's Message," *Seventh Annual Report*, 24.

63. BC Vladeck, "Professor Sabsovich," *Nation* 114, no. 2967 (May 17, 1922): 602.

64. Krauskopf, "Introduction of Dr. Edward Lauterbach," *Seventh Annual Report of the National Farm School* (n.p.: n.p., 1904), 50.

6   The Courageous Diaspora

Masculinity and the Development of American Zionism

Masculinity plays a starring role in the traditional story of European Zionism: the diaspora made Jews weak, hunched over, and passive, but Zionism would bring reconnection with the land and the regeneration of the strong male body. Even European Zionism's most famous visual images, such as the Galician Zionist E. M. Lilien's iconic paintings, promoted these themes. Strong male bodies and phallic images populate Zionist landscapes, whereas old, weak, frail religious scholars symbolize diaspora life. German Zionist Max Nordau famously called for a "Muscle Jewry," and claimed that diasporic Jewry was effeminate and degenerate.[1] Indeed, diaspora life had sapped Jewish manliness: "In the narrow Jewish street our poor limbs soon forgot their gay movement; in the dimness of sunless houses our eyes began to blink shyly; the fear of constant persecution turned our powerful voices into freighted whispers, which rose in a crescendo only when our martyrs on the stakes cried out their dying prayers . . . at last we are allowed space for our bodies to live again." For Nordau and others like him, Zionism and the land of Palestine would restore a manliness that the diaspora had robbed. He exhorted his audience, "Let us take up our oldest traditions; let us once more become deep-chested, sturdy, sharp-eyed men."

If Palestine symbolized strength and manliness, and the diaspora symbolized weak passivity, where could American Zionists fit in the story? How would American Zionists deal with this masculinity question? Many American Zionists were outspoken in their commitment to the United States, and only a minority had any intention of immigrating to Palestine. The negative image of emasculating diaspora life did not resonate with Americans, and so they would have to tell the Zionist story differently.

Despite the marginal nature of American Zionism, the movement and its participants provide a window into American Jewish masculinity. Scholars have noted *that* American Zionism was masculine, but they have not analyzed the features or implications of that masculinity. Mary McCune, for instance, writes in her article about American Zionist women that the "male leaders of the Zionist movement used explicitly masculine imagery."[2] She and other scholars are surely correct in suggesting that pervasive masculine imagery marginalized both femininity and women themselves from Zionism and the Zionist narrative; they offer a sorely needed corrective to any purely "great man" histories of Zionism by providing the important stories of women in the Zionist movement. Though the focus here is on men, the point is not to turn back to that kind of great man history. Rather it is to explore American Zionist discourse in light of its construction of masculinity, to see the contours of that constructed masculinity, and to learn about what it meant to be an American Jewish man in particular.

Many histories of American Zionism assume that men are the default humans and that women are the special case. Philosophers use the term "unmarked" to describe the assumed, default position, whereas "marked" means the particular, different case. Men, in Zionist histories and many others in Western culture, are the unmarked sex, and women are the marked sex. We can see the scholarship on American Zionism in this light: it assumes that women and their gender roles are the special case and that men's gender is neither particular nor worth analyzing in depth. There are several excellent studies on women and Zionism, and there are plenty of studies, especially older histories, that are almost entirely about men.[3] But the latter scholarship never identifies that it is about "men and Zionism." In fact, it rarely interrogates what it means or why it matters that its characters are men. It rarely even acknowledges the fact that its story is dominated by men. But what if we took seriously the idea that men's gender is every bit as historically contingent as women's gender? Beyond stating that the Zionist movement was masculine, we would then ask what this masculinity looked like. What images did it use, and how did they reflect or differ from other non-American Zionist images?

When I started this project, I expected to find that images and descriptions of strong, muscular male bodies were ubiquitous in American Zionism. Not only did these images appear in European Zionist circles but also the image of the muscular, self-determined man grew immensely in the United States as a widespread ideal of masculinity in the early twentieth century.[4] Teddy Roosevelt proudly and iconically stood over a rhinoceros he had killed, Tarzan captivated American audiences, and some American Protestant Christians emphasized a strong, manly, business-like Jesus.[5] If the European Zionist movement and much of white, American culture at large both embraced strong, muscular male bodies that dominated nature, we should expect to see similar images throughout American Zionism. But American Zionist materials mentioned male bodies rarely and depicted them even less. Unlike European writers, American Zionists spent little time in the early years of the twentieth century promoting muscular or strong bodies, and they rarely paired these characteristics with Palestine.

Instead they allegorized manly strength and bravery to be political and philanthropic and reshaped the geography of *galut* (exile, or diaspora) so America was not a place of exile. The American Zionist image of the ideal American Jewish man had two distinctive features: first, it transcended geographical boundaries and second, it centered on nonphysical traits, such as courage. American Zionist writings cast this courage not as a physical capacity, but as a political willingness to embark on statecraft for the benefit of Jews from other lands. The two aspects of the American image bolstered each other ideologically—courage need not be located in the body, and manly bodies need not be located in Palestine. Instead, they abstracted courage and manliness into the political realm, where they focused on forming political bodies more than fleshy ones. Building and securing a society for the vulnerable was the central task of American Zionist masculinity—not bodybuilding, but society-building.

This version of Jewish masculinity that deemphasized the particularities of geography and bodies fit well philosophically with the argument for Judaism as an American religion. And American Zionism also had a close—though not simple—relationship with Judaism. There is general agreement in scholarly circles that Zionism was, at its core, a secular movement. This narrative sometimes pits Zionism against Reform Judaism, in a battle of what Naomi Cohen has characterized as "secular nationalism vs. universalist religion."[6] But a close look at American Zionism suggests this story of opposition is too simple. Most American Zionists promoted enlightened religious practice, and although they sometimes criticized the Reform movement for its naiveté, the movement included Reform leaders among its leading lights. Conversely, the Reform movement accepted outspoken Zionists as leaders, such as Rabbis Bernard Felsenthal, Gustav Gottheil, and Max Heller, the last of whom served as president of the Reform rabbinical body, the CCAR, from 1909–1911.[7] All of these men were acculturated Jews who turned to Zionism long after they settled in the United States. Though Zionists were the minority within Reform circles, then, they were not outcasts.

Reform Jews and Zionists were not locked in a culture war of secularism versus religion. In fact, even when they argued with one another, Zionists and Reform Jews each claimed that they were the ones promoting real Judaism. Louis Lipsky, for instance, positioned himself as a true expositor of the real Judaism when he criticized Reform rabbis for conforming to "religion in the Christian sense, as a creed, which the Jewish religion never was."[8] Even when they did not say so explicitly, American Zionists often sought to make their movement compatible with ideas about American religion. Zionists wanted a movement that was both good for the Jews and "good" religion.

This chapter highlights the distinctiveness of American Zionism and its relationship to masculinity and religion. Although the Zionist movement, leadership, and supporters changed significantly from the turn of the century until the early 1920s, the American Zionist images of American Jewish masculinity displayed remarkable continuity. The first section shows the contours of this masculinity by highlighting the differences between American and European Zionism. The second section focuses on the *Maccabaean*, the United States' most widely read Zionist periodical, and shows how its authors and editors used ideas about religion and the land to construct a vision of American Jewish masculinity that valued courage and political work on behalf of others.

European and American Zionisms

European Zionists focused on state-building, and they thought that the state would be for all Jews, including themselves. Through an embrace of physical culture and a discourse of political self-determination, Herzl, Nordau, and others linked a Jewish state to the physical and political regeneration of all Jews.[9] Jews had degenerated physically over the centuries, this ideology claimed, and Zionism would help redeem and reform the weakened Jewish body. European Zionists built gymnasiums and promoted gymnastics. They published images of strong Jewish male bodies. Perhaps this is why the historiography of European Zionism does not suffer from failure to analyze masculinity nearly as acutely as does the American scholarship. For instance, Todd Presner, Daniel Boyarin, Mikhal Dekel, and others all attend carefully to the cultural constructions of masculinity in the context of the European Zionist project.[10] But while these scholars offer us subtle and theoretically rich accounts of the ways masculinity shaped these political movements, their narratives cannot simply be transposed onto the American context.

American Zionism differed politically from its European counterparts, which also meant that it was different with respect to gender and religion. This section begins by briefly sketching American Zionism's political context, then discusses how the American Zionist movement's ideals about Palestine fit with its construction of masculinity, and finally considers the relationship of religion, masculinity, and Zionist political ideals. Each element has continuity with European Zionist ideas, but each also tells a story of a Zionist masculinity that was distinctly American.

In many ways, American Zionism began the twentieth century as the little brother of European Zionism. It was numerically much smaller, had to fight to be taken seriously intellectually, and largely relied on European thought as a model for its identity. Americans were largely excluded from the leadership positions at international Zionist conferences. Especially before World War I, the Zionist movement claimed only a small percentage of American Jews. Though Arthur Hertzberg's characterization of American Zionism overstates its irrelevance and narrowness when he calls it a "moribund affair, totally shunned by the wealthy, assimilated Jewish community,"[11] it is nevertheless true that the Federation of American Zionists (FAZ) was a small and relatively marginal organization. Two years after its founding on the symbolic day of July 4, 1898, it had about 3,800 dues-paying members.[12] Despite the immigration of well over half-million Jews, it grew slowly, reaching about 15,000 members in 1914.[13] The 1917 Balfour Declaration, in which Britain's foreign secretary Arthur Balfour wrote that "His Majesty's government view with favor the establishment in Palestine of a national home for the Jewish people," buoyed Zionists when it gave state recognition to their goals. The declaration invigorated the American Zionist movement, but its number of adherents remained small.

When Louis Brandeis famously said, "to be good Americans, we must be better Jews, and to be better Jews, we must become Zionists," he was in the minority among acculturated American Jews.[14] The anti-Zionist Jewish education expert Julia Richman expressed a more commonly held interpretation: "A Jew cannot be both a Jewish citizen and an American citizen. He cannot be a good Jew and a bad citizen. He ought to be and often is a true American citizen of the Jewish faith."[15] Like Brandeis, she identified American values with Jewish values, but she rejected the connection with Zionism. For Richman, Jewishness was not about an imagined polity; it was about Judaism as a religion—a religion compatible with reason, universalism, and democracy. In short, she argued that Judaism qualified as "good" religion, which harmonized with the values of American citizenship.

As Richman's assertion suggests, a wholehearted embrace of political Zionism would come with significant liabilities on the American scene. Accusations of "dual loyalty" were not confined to antisemites and nativists. If American Jews worked for an independent Jewish state, how could they be good Americans? Settlement in Palestine was a noble goal, especially given the persecution of Eastern European Jews, but the Herzlian idea of a single Jewish state ran counter to the Judaism and the Americanism with which most American Jews identified. In "The Dangers, the Fallacies and the Falsehoods of Zionism III," outspoken anti-Zionist Reform rabbi Kaufmann Kohler wrote, "Zionism is nothing more or less than land hunger such as all the nations of the world manifest today, a desire quite natural and justifiable in the fugitive, homeless Jew of Russia and Romania."[16] Zionism was an understandable nationalist project, insofar as its goal was aiding Eastern European Jews. But, as yet another iteration of modern nationalism, Kohler argued it was too particularistic and ran counter to the values of American Judaism. He summarized, "It cannot be *our* homeland of the American Jew."[17] Kohler saw Judaism as a universal religion, and embracing political Zionism would render its commitments tribal and parochial. Many acculturated Jews worried about how non-Jewish Americans would perceive Zionism, and their worries were not entirely without cause.

Unlike the dominant trends in European Zionism, American Zionism focused far less on creating a new Jewish state that would become *the* homeland for *all* Jews. Instead they envisioned projects in Palestine as a philanthropic effort primarily on behalf of other Jews. These projects would have the added benefit of promoting and consolidating Jewish culture, arts, and knowledge for all Jews. Even the anti-Zionist Kohler was sympathetic to Zionism's practical project of saving Eastern European Jews. Reform Rabbi Gustav Gottheil spoke for most American Zionists when he wrote that Zionism was about "securing a home for the homeless."[18]

But America's Jews were not "homeless," even according to the outspoken Zionist Gottheil. For him, as for most American Zionists, the United States was the exception. And this American exceptionalism was not only political: it was also religious. Jews elsewhere were subject to the church of the state and to state-sanctioned oppression, and Zionism was intended to help those Jews. Gustav's son Richard followed in his ideological steps. Richard Gottheil was a professor of Semitics at Columbia University in New York and became the first president of the FAZ. His interest in shaping Jewish men through Zionism extended beyond the FAZ and its official hierarchy. He also founded the first American Jewish collegiate fraternity, ZBT, as a Zionist youth organization. ZBT, which now identifies itself as the three-letter Greek "Zeta Beta Tau," originally stood for Zion BeMishpat Tipadeh.[19] Gottheil thought that young Jewish men were quite at home in the United States and Canada and that creating young men's Zionist organizations would help shape these young adults into ideal Jewish men.

Richard Gottheil, who had moved from England to New York when he was eleven years old, claimed that the American political context was exceptional because of its constitutional tradition of disestablishment and its social and political inclusion of Jews. In contrast, the political situation in post-Enlightenment Europe had led to Jewish exclusion: "Church and Society joined hands, and once more there was no place for Jews, who held with tenacity to their separate existence and refused to lose their existence."[20] Gottheil's subtext was not so subtle. The political arrangements of European states precluded Jews from remaining distinctively Jewish and fully participating in "Society" because of the marriage of "Church" and "Society." The United States, with its avowed separation of church and state, was exceptional, and it fostered "good" religion—religion based on individual conscience and compatible with democracy—whereas European systems brought with them religious coercion and discrimination. America's political arrangement was good for the Jews, while Europe's marginalized them.

Gottheil also expressed his advocacy of Zionism because it would provide a haven for Jews seeking refuge from Eastern Europe. The United States had already provided a fertile land for the flourishing of Jewish immigrant life, but he was skeptical about its capacity to accommodate all the needy and oppressed would-be immigrants. He wrote in 1914, "But such immigration cannot continue indefinitely, and the continued depression of the masses in Eastern Europe is having its effect in making the material with which the reconstructive process in the West is being carried on less worthy of its purpose and less effective in carrying it out."[21] For Gottheil, a "reconstructive process" transformed oppressed Jews back into productive, self-sufficient, and proud Jews. But Palestine was not the only option that could remedy the ills Gottheil identified as "active antisemitism on the one hand and passive social oppression on the other."[22] He began by noting that the United States had already been performing this function. Zionism, in his view, could continue and expand it.

Gottheil and other American Zionists' advocacy also hints at how acculturated Jews thought that Eastern European Jews lacked particular aspects of manliness. Similar to European Zionists' claims about diaspora Jews in general, some American Zionists claimed that Eastern European Jews were weak and alienated from the land. The "physical want and suffering" of Eastern European Jews ended in "physical and moral demoralization, a trampling of men's bodies and women's souls," FAZ secretary Jacob de Haas told a crowd gathered at New York's Temple Emanu-El.[23] Acculturated American Jews also often saw "downtrodden" Eastern European immigrants in similar terms. Those Jews with their unhealthy bodies and underdeveloped religion needed help, they thought. Like the Zionists, but unlike most antisemites, acculturated American Jews largely thought that weakness and physical inferiority were but a matter of environment, and therefore within a generation or two of living in the American land of opportunity, these Jews would become uplifted.

Very few American Zionists had any intention of immigrating to Palestine (sometimes called "making *aliyah*"). Even the *Maccabaean*, the publication of the FAZ, did not promote *aliyah* for American Jews. Apart from one article about an eighteenth-century rabbi, titled, lukewarmly, "Why Not Live in Palestine?" it presented American Zionism as a project of Jewish renewal that its supporters would, it assumed, conduct from the United States. By putting the idea of moving to Palestine in the mouth of a rabbi who lived long ago and far away, the magazine indicated the remoteness of that possibility for most of its readers. The *Maccabaean* and the FAZ emphasized the compatibility between being good Americans and being good Zionists: American Zionists were Americans. The negative narratives painting all Jewish life outside of Palestine as emasculating, therefore, held little allure for them.

The description of diaspora Jewry as effeminate, American Zionists thought, only applied to those poor diaspora Jews in Eastern Europe who had suffered the ill effects of persecution. And they were effeminate not because of living in the diaspora per se, but as a result of political and social oppression. In 1902, rabbi of New York's Shearith Israel Henry Pereira Mendes wrote an article that clearly revealed his assumptions about the different masculinities of American Jews, other diaspora Jews, and Zionists. As a proponent of Zionism, Mendes advocated the settlement of Palestine, but not for the purpose of bettering his own readers. American Jews, he assumed, would not be the primary inhabitants of Palestine, but Mendes called on his own readers to "help" the "thousands of Hebrews [who] will flock there and will need to be helped, settled, and absorbed. Every Jew whom we can rescue from a Russia or a Roumania will be a deed well done, and never must effort be relaxed to turn the pallid, narrow-chested victim of persecution into the stalwart son of the soil."[24] Working the soil in Palestine would help transform weak Jewish men into men with healthy bodies. What had caused these Eastern European Jews to become weak and unhealthy was not living in the diaspora. It was persecution. American Jews, in his view, were not weak and unhealthy, but they should support settlement in Palestine because it contributed to the "rescue" of the victims of persecution.[25]

Religion also played an essential part in these philanthropic, health-minded American Zionist ideals. In 1906 Solomon Schechter, the architect of Conservative Judaism, identified Zionism as a source of strength for all Jews, even while denying that all Jews needed to move to one homeland. This strength was not limited to a physical location in Palestine—its effects were profoundly religious. Zionism was "a true and healthy life . . . invigorated by sacred memories and sacred environments, and proving a tower of strength and of unity not only for the remnant gathered within the borders of the Holy Land, but also for those who shall, by choice or by necessity, prefer what now constitutes Galut."[26] Schechter explained that participating in the Zionist project, in whatever location, created the "true and healthy life." In America, Zionism could mean strength and manliness, but those characteristics took on metaphorical more than embodied meanings, and they did not often have an explicit connection to Palestine. Here Schechter offered a stark distinction from some of the most prominent European Zionists. Hebrew poet Chaim Nachman Bialik's 1898 poem "HaMatmid" starkly depicted memories of the past through a physically weak, if nevertheless romantic, figure of the Talmud student. Where Lilien and Bialik depicted hunched, weak, and old observant Jews studying, Schechter saw traditional texts as invigorating, not enervating. Zionism would "invigorate sacred memories and sacred environments" with its reference to the land of Palestine. These sacred communal "memories," a reference to a biblical past, would prove a "tower of strength." Far from aligning textual study with bodily weakness, as Lilien or Bialik had, Schechter saw these textual memories as the very source of the strength of the Zionist project. He did not celebrate the particular figure of the Eastern European Talmud student, but he did embrace the texts themselves as a source of Jewish emotional and communal strength and bravery.

Others made even more explicit connections between Zionism and religion. Mendes's 1902 article "Spiritual Zionism" insisted on the centrality of religion to the Zionist enterprise. "Spirituality," he began, "that is the keynote of Judaism and all Zionism that is not in harmony therewith is unreal Zionism."[27] For Mendes, there was no conflict between secular nationalism and universalistic religion. Far from seeing the universalist impulses of Reform Judaism and the national goal of building a Jewish society in Palestine as inimical, he saw them as fundamentally intertwined: "I will never be content with the realization of my dream, my hope, my belief, unless 'Palestine for the Jews' means not simply the erection of a Jewish state, but the creation of a spiritual centre for all mankind, a source of spiritual inspiration for Jewish communities throughout the world, so that Palestine shall be for all men a gateway to God." Mendes framed the familiar Reform understandings of Judaism's universal message and a Jewish religious mission to all humanity as central to the Zionist enterprise.

Mendes provides an example of what historian Alon Gal has called the "mission motif."[28] This "mission" idea, consonant with universalist religious impulses and most popular in Reform circles, asserted that Jews in exile would become an example "for men of all nations," as Mendes wrote.[29] Though scholars generally imagine the idea of a universal mission as an anti-Zionist motif, here Mendes shows how it existed within Zionist circles. He wrote, "I can conceive of no *raison d'etre* for the Jew on the stage of history except to exercise spiritual influence, to lead men to God, that their thoughts shall be Himward, their characters patterned after the pattern God sets us in the Holy Book, that our lives shall be consecrated by a consciousness of the Fatherhood of God, of nearness to Him, and of His nearness to us! 'Bring God into human life'—that is Zionism." Mendes's version of American Zionism was anything but secularizing. It was both universalistic and religious in its commitments. This commitment to universalism also recalls the philosophical idea of universalism as masculine, as we saw in chapter 1.

Although European and American Zionism shared many texts and ideals, they developed in different political, religious, and gendered contexts. Most European Zionists subscribed to the idea of *shlilat hagalut*, or the negation of the diaspora. In this formulation, diaspora life is inherently negative, and the only salvation of the Jewish people can come from a Jewish return to Palestine. As we have seen, however, very few American Zionists, however, thought in these terms, and *shlilat hagalut* never caught on in the United States. Furthermore, most American Zionists did not even think of the United States as *galut*. In part because of this refusal to classify American Jewish life as exilic (and therefore negative), as the next section suggests, American Zionism never painted American Jews as effeminate. Instead, American Jews were masculine in their philanthropic and political effort to support the cultivation of the land on behalf of other Jews.

Galut, the Land, and the Maccabaean

In 1901, the emerging American Zionist movement began to publish its own journal. In its first issue, the *Maccabaean*, the print organ of the FAZ, declared its purpose: "to reconstruct the Jewish people, to lead them to an organized national existence, to make Jewish religious life possible, to foster the study of Jewish literature and history, to provide a stable home for the oppressed and downtrodden of our race."[30] This five-part agenda predictably included a sense of Jewish peoplehood, Jewish culture, and Jewish history alongside an "organized national existence." But it also framed that national existence as a means to an end: a "stable home for the oppressed and downtrodden." Zionism, in this sense, was a benevolent political movement aimed at helping other Jews. Even its word choice suggested this goal when it referred to the Jewish people as "them." It did not seek to "foster *our* knowledge," or "develop *our* national existence" or "create a stable home for *ourselves*," even while it referred to "our race." The reference to "our race" indicates that American Zionists had a sense of the Jewish collective, but they nevertheless did not associate the whole of the Jewish collective with future life in Palestine. The *Maccabaean*'s mission statement did not suggest that Zionism would help transform its own readers into more physically healthy or strong men, but it did suggest that they could participate in a project to uplift their fellow Jews in faraway lands. As its declaration of purpose suggested, the *Maccabaean* also promoted Judaism. Creating a home for downtrodden Jews would be one part of making "Jewish religious life possible," and its pages would also promote religious knowledge among its readers.

The *Maccabaean*'s audience was largely acculturated Jews. Although in its initial layout, each issue concluded with a Yiddish section, these pages were phased out less than a year from the journal's inception. In an article on "the immigrant," the journal made clear who its audience was (and was not). "The so-called East Side is taking care of itself to a very large extent. Considering their numbers, we may expect that in the next decade responsibility for the improvement of Jewish conditions will be transferred to them."[31] The *Maccabaean* referred to immigrant Jews on the Lower East Side as "them," and "they" needed care, though it seemed that they were beginning to be able to provide it themselves. This paternalistic attitude—a combination of responsibility for other Jews and condescension—also informed the readers' attitude toward Eastern European Jews who remained in Eastern Europe and faced antisemitism, lack of economic opportunity, and other undesirable situations. The *Maccabaean* styled itself as a periodical for cultured, educated American Jews.

In its early years, the American Zionist movement did borrow from the European Zionist movement, including some of its ideals of masculinity. The early issues of the *Maccabaean* occasionally reflected European ideas of the masculine Zionist body, sometimes almost literally: it reprinted Herzl's writings at length—*Altneuland* appeared in serialized form, for instance—and Max Nordau's writings, letters, and speeches appeared at length in about half of the issues published in its first eight or nine years.[32] Yet, especially in the years after Herzl's death in 1904, the *Maccabaean*'s pages featured more American Jewish writers, and a distinctly American perspective began to emerge. Although it still deified Herzl, it printed fewer and fewer of Lilien's sketches and openly criticized Nordau.[33] American Zionist writers took their places, and their ideological dependence on European Zionism faded.

Reporter Louis Lipsky was the first editor of the *Maccabaean*, and he passed the reins to the British-born and newly arrived immigrant Jacob de Haas in 1902. In 1914, Lipsky would leave his position as editor of *The American Hebrew* and return to edit the *Maccabaean* when he became secretary (and later president) of the FAZ. Even during his time away from editing, Lipsky contributed to the journal often. In December 1907, he wrote "The Festival of Chanuka: A Talk with Jewish Boys and Girls," in which he called Zionists "the modern Maccabaeans."[34] Though it at first appeared to be an educational discussion for children, the article was actually a didactic piece that sought to reorient and reinvigorate the American Jewish community around the ideas of land, soil, and healthy bodies. Ultimately, the article suggested that Jewish manliness was actually about politics, not about physical transformation. Lipsky's ideal Jewish community did not center on building stronger bodies, but rather on creating a safe haven for all Jews. To do this, Jews had to reconnect with their peoplehood and history.

Lipsky began his December article by asking his readers: "Why was the Festival of Chanuka so endeared to you, and why did you as boy or as girl, feel, as if, of all Jewish holidays, that holiday was the dearest, the best, the most enjoyable?" Despite the title and opening question, however, girls quickly dropped out of his audience. Hanukkah was the best holiday, he explained, not because it was the Jewish answer to Christmas but "because it was the holiday appreciative of the spirit of resistance! How often had your boyish soul been pained by the tales of the submissiveness of the Jewish people." He told his boy readers that they held images of Jews as an oppressed and downtrodden people, but that Hanukkah made them feel good about being Jewish. "Because Chanuka noted an event telling of resistance, you, as a boy, felt that you could celebrate it." Boys rightly eschewed political submissiveness and identified with political resistance, in Lipsky's formulation.

Hanukkah provided a chance for Jewish boys to connect with the Jewish people, Lipsky assumed, because it connected their own Jewish history to their admiration of men who defended the American land: "You admired the heroes of the Civil War, when you thrilled as the veterans of that war passed before you on Decoration Day; so too when you heard of Judas Maccabeus, of his brave brothers, of that heroic old man who struck the first blow, your youthful soul expanded, and you felt yourself at home among the Jewish people." Lipsky's imagined boy audience already admired American soldiers because of their brave feats (though, notably, there was nothing about their physical bodies or appearance). And when they learned about the story of Hanukkah, they could admire historical Jews too.

This move—arguing for the value of Zionism by showing its similarities to American wartime or pioneering conquests—relied on the value of a masculinity of bravery and willingness to do political work on behalf of others. Later Lipsky compared the "Pilgrim fathers" to the Zionists and argued that Zionism was "compatible with American tradition, with democratic principles, [and] with present American citizenship."[35] More than just compatible, Lipsky's conceptions of Zionism and American citizenship were quite similar in both their political and gendered ideals.

Throughout these writings, Lipsky took for granted that his readers both knew American stories of courageous, martial, and pioneering masculinity and were enchanted by them. His imagined audience, the "boy," however, did not know about the parallel Jewish ideas and history until he was taught. Only when the boy "heard" about Hanukkah could he have the same feeling of pride in manliness about Jewishness. Learning of this model of the spirit of political resistance, Jewish boys could feel "at home among the Jewish people." They could feel "at home" because the Jewish men in this history behaved bravely and embraced a masculinity of which they would be proud:

> They were not a Jewish people holding its breath for fear of the wicked opinion of the world, but a daring people. They were guerrillas, at first, and how fine it was to think that Jews, too, laid in ambush awaiting their foe, that they, too, experienced the midnight prowling in the forests, the cautious peering through the thickets, the thrilling daring of the midnight attack. And when you read how they fought in the open, having won their right to their soil, what a relief to know that you could celebrate the anniversary of their bravery in spite of their subsequent defeat.

The thrill, the bravery, the daring—these were the things that made Jewish history relatable and a source of pride. The courageous masculinity of the Hanukkah story ensured it would resonate with American Jewish men.

"In brief," Lipsky wrote, "Chanuka gave you a satisfactory explanation of the Jewish Goluth [*galut*]. The Jewish people, you thought, were a strong, not a suffering people; a virile, not a supplicating people." The story of Hanukkah assured Jewish boys that Jewish masculinity was admirable masculinity and that living in the diaspora was nothing to be ashamed of. Those Maccabean diasporic Jews were manly, not effeminate, and the Hanukkah story was splendid despite "their subsequent defeat." Lipsky's version did not, however, focus on strong or muscular bodies but rather celebrated courage, demonstrated in a martial action toward a political end.

Lipsky, however, admitted that a triumphalist narrative of Jewish history was not warranted from a contemporary global perspective. "The majority of our people are the victims of persecution," he wrote, and other Jews have assimilated so thoroughly that they are no longer Jewish. But Zionism, with its celebration of Jewish bravery and political assertiveness, was the solution to this historical downturn. "Our celebration of Chanuka, our Zionist celebration, is a protest and a jubilant song. We who are Zionists offer you once more the youthful dream." Readers, whom he now addressed as adults who could "once more" experience youthful ideas, should claim Judas Maccabaeus as their hero because he was "the warrior Jew, who fought the battles of his people."

Even if Judas Maccabaeus was a hero because of his battles and not because of the miracle of the oil, Lipsky insisted that the "manly life" Zionism offered was not separable from Judaism. "The Jewish law, the ineradicable basis of the Jewish religion, was given to a nation. That law grew out of the life of a people living on its own soil. Every particle of Jewish religious thought received its coloring from the life and history of a nation." Nationalism and religion were two sides of the same coin. Lipsky closed with a call to American Jews to become Zionists: "Who would not be in the ranks of such a cause, fighting, as they did two thousand years ago, for the preservation of our national integrity? . . . who would not strive for the revival of a sturdy, self-reliant, wholesome Jewish nation upon its own soil?" There was no separation between secular nationalism and religion—though here Lipsky had less interest in universalist ideals than many other American Jews. For Lipsky, Hanukkah inspired boys because it provided historical examples of ideal Jewish masculinity: men who bravely embarked on a political quest on behalf of the safety and religious freedom of the Jewish people.

A political episode seven years later—what became known as *milhemet hasafot*, "the war of the languages"—helps us see how American Zionists imagined their own situation to be different from that in other *galut* countries and what the implications of those differences were for masculinity. In its "Review of the Month" in February 1914, the *Maccabaean* complained that the German Jewish philanthropic organization called the Hilfsverein advocated German-language use at the newly formed Technicum, Palestine's first university and forerunner to today's Technion. American Zionists objected, and the *Maccabaean* characterized German Zionists as "unmanly." The piece reported that "the American directors have spoken with a unanimous vote" for Hebrew and against German. Then its author, editor Israel Goldberg, upbraided these German Jews for their "unmanly golus attitude." American Jews did not suffer from this unmanly diasporic affliction, he implied, but some Germans did: "Against those who do not belong to our camp we prefer not to raise the banner of revolt against our brethren, poisoned with the virus of an undignified and unmanly *golus* spirit." To combat this undignified, unmanly, and contagious attitude, he urged American Zionists to "take up arms, and declare that Palestine is beyond their jurisdiction, that Palestine belongs to our national future, and across its threshold no Jew may cross who does not leave behind him all thought of any other nationality but that which is being created in Palestine."[36] It was American Zionists' job to combat an "unmanly golus" attitude in German Jews, but here is also a remarkable moment: Goldberg positions Palestine as "our national future" to the exception of "any other nationality," and yet he put American Jews together with Palestine's Jews. "Their fight is ours," he wrote. He sought to protect Palestine's Jews from the interests of German Jews because of the latter's diasporic interests, and he portrayed Americans and Palestinians together opposing this "unmanly" project.[37] Goldberg placed German Jews and their interests on the side of unmanliness and implicitly placed American and Palestinian Jews together on the side of manliness. This German-language proposal, then, failed one of the two key elements in American Zionist manliness: a universal benevolence to Jews escaping the diaspora.

The next segment of the "Review of the Month" expressed concern about the proposed Burnett bill, an act to restrict immigration. In this case Goldberg's concerns were not about Jews in America, but Eastern European Jews—"large numbers of our brethren"—who would want to "emerge out of their sad condition." Goldberg spoke out against the immigration restriction, and simultaneously positioned Zionism as an important fallback measure: if the United States were not open as a safe haven, then settling Palestine became all the more important. Unlike the German Jews who sought to project their own interests onto other Jews, a "manly" attitude meant helping one's suffering brethren.

American Zionists also fashioned the category of *galut* into a novel shape: Palestine was Zion and Eastern Europe (or Europe more generally) was *galut*. But they rarely suggested that the United States was exile. In March 1914, for example, the *Maccabaean* section, "News and Views, in the lands of Goluth" included news briefs with the following headlines: "Ministers Change: Antisemites Remain," "Echoes of the Beilis Trial," "Persecution of Jewish Artisans," "Jews Flee from Lodz," " 'Enlightened' Germany, Antisemitism Rampant," " 'Brave' Austria, Antisemitism among Austrian Officers," " 'Liberal' France, French Catholic Press Attack Jews," "And Roumania, the Struggle for Jewish Rights." These "lands of Goluth" never included the United States. This list of Jewish troubles abroad implied an especially Zionist form of American exceptionalism—that is, that exile was elsewhere.[38]

Beyond the pages of the *Maccabaean*, this classification—other lands as *galut*, America as different—also took on gendered meaning. When David de Sola Pool wrote about a Jewish cultural celebration for the journal *Jewish Charities*, he lauded both the immigrants and the United States itself, which he did not mark as *galut*. By celebrating his (or her, presumably, because there were women in attendance) Jewish culture, "the immigrant was making a manly assertion of his own individuality." This manly assertion of individuality also served as one element of the connection between the immigrant and the United States: "The Jewish evening marked a clearly defined step upward in its conception of mutual responsibilities between the immigrant Jew and his adopted land . . . and gave some measure of guarantee of a future Jewish development of the Jew in America."[39] Far from being *galut*, then, the United States would serve as a place for the *Jewish* development of the Jew. For Goldberg, the *Maccabaean*, de Sola Pool, and other American Zionists the United States did not—and should not—demand complete assimilation, nor did it allow the kind of Jewish oppression as did the "golus tragedies of Eastern Europe." "Golus tragedies," it seems, were not the sort that occurred in America.

On the rare occasion that the *Maccabaean* mentioned that American Jews might move to Palestine, it posed this immigration as an altruistic decision that benefited the cause much more than the individual. When Helena Cohn wrote about "Palestine and the Jewish Colonists," she was insistent that Palestine needed "strong and sturdy" men and women "filled with the pioneer spirit." And although she vigorously promoted settlement in Palestine, when it came to discussing potential American "pioneers," she emphasized sacrifice, altruism, and utility to the Zionist cause: "The American Jew will have to give up much that has made his life pleasant in America, but owing to his economic situation and his mental qualities he will be able to do useful work in Palestine and to lead a life which, although full of hard work, will afford him leisure to indulge in intellectual and aesthetic pleasures."[40] Her description suggested that American Jews would be "useful" to the project, more than the project would be useful to them. As already courageous, pioneering, and self-sufficient, American Jews would bring their manly virtues to support Palestine and the Zionist movement, rather than Palestine Zionism instilling those manly virtues in them.

The *Maccabaean* even celebrated Jews as exemplars of masculinity. When, in May 1914, the United States sent troops to Veracruz to intervene in the Mexican Revolution, the *Maccabaean*'s first page began by extolling the manly virtues of Jews as American soldiers. Three of the seventeen marines who died during the skirmish were Jewish, and Goldberg tied this to a history of Jews as brave volunteers for the American nation: "This is in keeping with American tradition. The Jews of this country have always offered their lives in excess of their numbers."[41] Jews had always expressed their courage in support of the United States.

This Veracruz military action, along with later wartime discussions, was one of the few times that the *Maccabaean* focused on physical acts of bravery. Yet even here Goldberg emphasized the psychological motivation—the "subconscious feeling," he called it—behind the act of enlistment. "When they were admitted into the army anywhere, they seemed imbued with superhuman powers of endurance, as if they were determined to show the incredulous world that the calumny against their people was not deserved." Goldberg set these particular acts of Jewish bravery in the broader framework of convincing others of the value of Jews as manly members of nations. This bodily sacrifice was a means to the end of quashing non-Jewish stereotypes of Jews as disloyal citizens. He did not value "superhuman powers of endurance" as essentially Jewish—or even as a desideratum—but he saw Jewish veterans' actions as a way to promote positive images of Jewish men as citizens.

Moreover, this bravery held an inverse relationship to the usual Zionist geography. Rather than linking it with the land of Palestine, Goldberg valorized the diaspora as the location of bravery. "This is no new Jewish trait, the valor," he continued. "It is as old as the golus." Exile, not Zion, was the breeding ground of manly Jewish valor. He then urged that this American Jewish brave masculinity serve as a model for Zionist masculinity, and Jewish masculinity in general: "He fights as an American soldier to show the world that Jews have the fighting spirit. May this fighting spirit animate all Jews in doing battle for their own country, as well as for their adopted countries." Goldberg held up American Jewish men, in volunteering and fighting for the US Armed Forces, as the exemplars of masculinity.

Conclusion

The American Zionist movement, then, did not simply mirror its European counterparts, or celebrate *muskeljudentum*, gymnasium fitness, and physical culture in a full-throated or unambiguous voice. The conjunction of Zionism and American exceptionalism produced a different discourse about gender. American Zionist manliness largely took the form of the nonphysical traits of courage and benevolence, while redefining the geographic boundaries of *galut* and any attendant effeminacy so as not to include the United States. Acculturated American Zionist men saw this manliness as something they were uniquely poised to have: in their eyes, as Americans and Zionists, they were already doing an excellent job of Jewish manliness.

Although most acculturated Jews denounced political Zionism, its rationale and rhetoric bore many resemblances to the physical culture and the ideology of simultaneous self-sufficiency and communal responsibility of the broader Zionist movement.[42] Like Zionists, many acculturated Jews saw settlement of the land as a way to revitalize Jews and Jewish culture. Part of this regeneration explicitly aimed to make men more physically fit and healthy, and they also saw cultivation of the land as a way to create better Jewish citizens.

Even though the Zionist movement did not initially include the majority of American Jews, some of the gendered aspects of its ideology, such as the embrace of the rural and agricultural, physical culture, and the romanticization of certain kinds of physical labor, resonated with broader American cultural trends toward the "strenuous life" and critiques of the unhealthiness of cities. Like the imagined

Indian culture, Zionist rhetoric drew on the language of closeness to the land, masculinity, health through physical labor, and self-sufficiency.[43] The Galveston Movement, agricultural communities, and Indian-Israelite connections offered ways for Jews to embrace this vision of Jewish manhood, strength, and productivity without the liability of appearing disloyal or uncommitted to the United States as a nation.

Part II of the book considered the ways Jews rendered the arrival of Jews in the United States (the Galveston Movement), their American Jewish past (via affinity with Indians), their present (via agricultural movements), and their future (via Zionism). These movements all had strong aspirational elements. That is, they sought to "uplift" immigrants and portray Jews and Jewish masculinity in a positive light to both themselves and their neighbors. The next section looks at another side of Jewish masculinity, namely the vices and negative aspects associated with it.

Notes

1. Max Nordau is probably the best-known Zionist thinker to articulate this view, and his ideas gained widespread support and development in Zionist circles. He espoused the idea of muskeljudentum, which would use physical exercise such as gymnastics and other competitive sports to reverse the physical effects of persecution. For Nordau's narrative of the historical suppression of Jewish physical prowess, see Max Nordau, Degeneration (Berkeley: University of California Press, 1898). On *muskeljudentum*, see Max Nordau, "Muskeljudentum," in Zionistische Schriften (Cologne; Juedisher Verlag, 1909), 379–381. A translation is printed in Paul Mendes Flohr and Jehuda Reinharz, *The Jew in the Modern World* (New York: Oxford University Press, 2010).

2. Mary McCune, "Social Workers in the Muskeljudentum: 'Hadassah Ladies,' 'Manly Men,' and the Significance of Gender in the American Zionist Movement," *American Jewish History* 86, no. 2 (June 1998): 134.

3. For instance, though these volumes mention Hadassah and Henrietta Szold, they are all histories focused on men. Arthur Hertzberg, *The Zionist Idea: A Historical Analysis and Reader* (Philadelphia: Jewish Publication Society, 1979); Walter Laqueur, *A History of Zionism: From the French Revolution to the Establishment of Israel* (New York: Schocken, 2003); Melvin Urofsky, *American Zionism from Herzl to the Holocaust* (New York: Bison Books, 1995).

4. These broad questions are taken up in Kimmel, *Manhood in America*, and Rotundo, *American Manhood*.

5. See Kasson, *Houdini, Tarzan, and the Perfect Man*; and Bederman, *Manliness and Civilization*.

6. Naomi Cohen, "The Maccabaean's Message: A Study in American Zionism until World War I," *Jewish Social Studies* 18, no. 3 (July 1956): 166.

7. See Jonathan Sarna, "Converts to Zionism in the American Reform Movement," in *Zionism and Religion*, eds. S. Almog, Jehuda Reinharz, and Anita Shapira (Waltham, MA: University Press of New England, 1998), 188–203.

8. Louis Lipsky, "The Duty of American Jews," *Maccabaean* (Feb. 1909): 41–46.

9. Todd Samuel Presner, *Muscular Judaism: The Jewish Body and the Politics of Regeneration* (New York: Routledge, 2007). See also Lederhendler, *Jewish Responses to Modernity*.

10. Boyarin, *Unheroic Conduct*; Presner, *Muscular Judaism*; and Mikhal Dekel, *The Universal Jew: Masculinity, Modernity, and the Zionist Movement* (Evanston, IL: Northwestern University Press, 2011).

11. Hertzberg, *American Zionism*, 2.

12. Cohen, "Maccabaean's Message," 163.

13. Naomi Cohen, *American Jews and the Zionist Idea* (New York: Ktav, 1975), 9. It had also hovered there for a decade. Hertzberg, *American Zionism*, 106.

14. Quoted in Jacob de Haas, *Louis Dembitz Brandeis: A Biographical Sketch with Special Reference to His Contributions to Jewish and Zionist History* (New York: Bloch, 1929), 163.

15. Richman, *Methods of Teaching Jewish Ethics*, 75.

16. Kaufmann Kohler, "The Dangers, the Fallacies and the Falsehoods of Zionism III," *Reform Advocate* 33 (1907): 350, quoted in Yaakov Ariel, "Kaufmann Kohler and His Attitude toward Zionism: A Reexamination," *American Jewish Archives Journal* 43 (1991): 212.

17. Kaufmann Kohler, *Palestine and Israel's World Mission* (Pittsburgh, PA: Rodef Shalom Congregation, 1918), 4, quoted in Ariel, "Kaufmann Kohler," 213.

18. Gustav Gottheil, "The Mystery of Our Mission," *Maccabaean* (May 1902): 243–244.

19. *American Jewish Year Book 1900–1901* (New York: American Jewish Committee, 1901), 182. For the history of ZBT, see Marianne Sanua, *Going Greek: Jewish College Fraternities in the United States* (Detroit, MI: Wayne State University Press, 2003)

20. Richard Gottheil, *Zionism* (Philadelphia: Jewish Publication Society, 1914), 26.

21. Ibid., 206–207.

22. Ibid., 205.

23. Jacob de Haas, *Zionism: Why and Wherefore* (New York: Maccabaean Publishing Co., 1902), 10.

24. Henry Pereira Mendes, "Spiritual Zionism," *Maccabaean* 2 (Jan. 1902): 16.

25. Ibid.

26. Quoted in Cohen, *American Jews*, 10

27. Mendes, "Spiritual Zionism," 15.

28. Sarna, "Converts to Zionism," 196–197; Alon Gal, "The Mission Motif in American Zionism, 1898–1948," *American Jewish History* 75 (June 1986): 363–385.

29. Mendes, "Spiritual Zionism," 15.

30. *Maccabaean* 1 (1901): 3–4.

31. "Review of the Month," *Maccabaean* 22, no. 6 (Dec. 1912): 182. Cf. Cohen, who suggests that the audience was immigrants ("Maccabaean's Message," 164).

32. In 1907, for example, the *Maccabaean* included "The Decadence of French Jewry," (Feb. 1907); "Dr. Nordau to English Zionists" (Feb. 1907); "Dr. Nordau on the Program" (Apr. 1907); letter sent to American Jewish Congress (Aug. 1907); speech at 8th Zionist Congress; and "Dr. Nordau on Political Zionism" (Dec. 1907).

33. In 1914, for instance, several issues criticize Nordau at length.

34. Louis Lipsky, "The Festival of Chanuka: A Talk with Jewish Boys and Girls," *Maccabaean* 6 (Dec. 1907): 246–248.

35. Lipsky, "The Duty of American Jews."

36. "Review of the Month," *Maccabaean* 24 (Feb. 1914): 36. Goldberg held American Jewry as distinctively valuable throughout his life. He later—and most famously—wrote *The Jews in America*.

37. This had also happened before 1914. HUC professor Caspar Levias had also harshly criticized "honest Jews" who opposed Zionism. He diagnosed them with the "German Ghetto" mentality that was "unable to rise to the manly, self-respecting and only true conception, that one's right to existence is the mere fact of his already existing; but they clutched at the servile and degrading claim of a Jew's usefulness. Such a claim, it can safely be said, would not enter the head of a Hottentot. Why should the Jew, of all peoples, have to apologize for their existence? If they suffer persecution, it is not for want of right, but for lack of might." But he blamed it on "German Jews," gave German examples, and never suggested that American Jews might be similarly implicated. "The Nostrum of the German Assimilators," *Maccabaean* 5 (May 1907): 177–179.

38. "News and Views in the Lands of Goluth," *Maccabaean* 24, no. 3 (Mar. 1914): 89–90.

39. David de Sola Pool, "A Jewish Evening," *Jewish Charities* (1906): 7.

40. Helena Cohn, "Palestine and the Jewish Colonists," *Maccabaean* 25, no. 2 (Aug. 1914): 70.

41. "Review of the Month," *Maccabaean* 24, no. 5 (May 1914): 131.

42. I do not mean to suggest that the Zionist movement had a monopoly on these ideas. The labor movement, for instance, shared in a similar attitude of promoting physical labor and communal responsibility.

43. For analysis of the gendered aspects of Zionism, see Dekel, *Universal Jew*; Michael Berkovitz, *Zionist Culture and West European Jewry before the First World War* (Chapel Hill: University of North Carolina Press, 1996); and Michael Stanislawski, *Zionism and Fin-de-Siecle: Cosmopolitanism and Nationalism from Nordau to Jabotinsky* (Los Angeles: University of California Press, 2001).

PART III

The Abnormal and the Criminal

In 1908, NEW York City police commissioner Theodore Bingham announced in the *North American Review* that half of the city's criminals were Jews. Adding insult to injury, he insinuated that Jews committed cowardly crimes: "The crimes committed by the Russian Hebrews are generally crimes against property. They are burglars, firebugs, pickpockets and highway robbers—when they have the courage."[1] In 1913, the inflammatory politician Tom Watson described Atlanta businessman Leo Frank, who was standing trial for murder as "the typical young libertine Jew . . . who has an utter contempt for the law, and a ravenous appetite for the forbidden fruit—a lustful eagerness enhanced by the racial novelty of the girls of the uncircumcised."[2] In 1924, Nathan Leopold and Dickie Loeb confessed to kidnapping and killing a fourteen-year-old boy. During the nationally covered sentencing hearing, one phrenologist pronounced Loeb to be a "boy of a feminine type of mind, eager for applause and easily led,"[3] and a journalist discussed his "delicate hands."[4] Leopold was notable for "his lack of physical prowess in athletics," opined another, and rumors of a sexual "pact" between the two circulated throughout the case.[5]

These events are central to the next three chapters. At first the three—one public relations blunder (and a statistical error), one the trial and lynching of a man innocent of murder, and one the sentencing hearing of two young murderers—seem to be only distantly related. The 1908 Bingham affair highlighted both tensions and attempts to create a unified community inclusive of immigrant Jews and the acculturated Jews of New York City. The Leo Frank trial brought the highly complex relations between whites and blacks, native Southerners and "Yankees," and workers and capitalists in Atlanta to the attention of the nation. The Leopold and Loeb hearing became an occasion for phrenologists, progressive social activists, and even fundamentalists and modernists to debate the nature of crime and punishment and the reasons these young Chicago Jews had gone wrong.

What can these seemingly isolated events show us about the lives of American Jews more generally? Crime, by its very nature, is abnormal—not in the sense that it is uncommon, but rather in the sense that defining something as a crime means locating it outside of social norms. And here lies the value of studying cultural conversations about crime: they paint a picture of the undesirable, the sorts of acts and persons to be avoided. Exploring this dark side of American Jewish life offers another perspective on ideas and ideals about what it meant to be Jewish in America. If religious educational pamphlets or philanthropic efforts to mold immigrants told listeners how to be good Jewish boys and men, conversations about criminals told them what *not* to be. Where the Galveston Movement and Indian-Israelite comparisons illustrate how American Jews included bodily health and connection to the land as pillars of masculinity, these discussions about criminality show how using that strength aggressively or violently was beyond the bounds of that Jewish masculinity.

Part III of the book argues that, first, despite their markedly different circumstances, each of these three cultural moments painted a similar picture of Jewish men as lacking physical courage, having a distaste for violence, and preferring manipulation over brawn when committing criminal acts. Furthermore, each linked crime with improper masculinity and sexuality. For some observers, the Jewish criminals embodied these abnormal traits and were therefore guilty. But for others, Jews' different—softer, gentler—masculinity constituted an argument for their innocence. In the first interpretation, these embodied traits were read as abnormal and even were sometimes linked to a perverse masculinity. In the second interpretation, these very same traits were read as virtuous and as indicators of a gentle masculinity. Thus, these gendered constructions were not uniformly negative. Sometimes they could elicit condemnation, such as Tom Watson's indictment of Leo Frank and his deviant effeminacy, but others could elicit sympathy, as when the *New York Times* portrayed Frank as a gentle, soft-spoken husband and son. Each of these three cases—the Bingham affair, the Frank case, and the Leopold and Loeb case—illustrates cultural ideals and assumptions about Jewish masculinity in America.

Second, these chapters show how, in each of these three moments, the cultural conversation aligned proper religion with normative gender and sexuality, and it associated the lack of religion with abnormal gender and sexuality and crime. This idea of proper religion, as Part III shows, centered on an internal, rational, and universalizable set of beliefs. For some like Tom Watson, white Protestant Christianity was the only religion to qualify as proper. But for most other Americans, doctrinal particulars were relatively inconsequential for preventing criminal behavior. Any good religion—including Judaism—would do. Although Leopold and Loeb claimed that their atheistic Nietzschean ideas were rational, the press, the witnesses, and Christian and Jewish religious communities all agreed that their religious ideas were not proper: they were perverse.

Each moment also occurred in front of the backdrop of a wider American cultural anxiety about how to manage difference in an era of immigration. Identifying, classifying, and scientizing crime and criminals could make them seem more predictable and understandable, and it could also fortify social boundaries between immigrants and acculturated Americans. Social reform efforts such as the settlement houses and concerns about "city rot," as well as social-scientific discussions of immigrants and crime, often attempted to manage and regulate peoples who seemed culturally different from white, American-born citizens.

Public conversation about crime provided an opportunity for Americans to reify their own sense of the boundaries of the normal. If certain Jewish men represented non-normative gender and also criminal activity, people could reassure themselves that those men and their sexuality were different, perhaps even dangerous. The Jews who stood accused of these crimes also stood accused of social and gendered deficiencies: cowardice, weakness, lack of patriotism, excessive education at the expense of the body, and other abnormal physiological and psychological traits. For those who were concerned about Jewish criminality, these crimes showed that criminality and deviation from normative masculinity went hand in hand. For those who defended Jewish men, certain elements of a different masculinity—aversion to physical altercation, mildness, and privileging brains over brawn—were all evidence of how Jewish difference contraindicated criminality. These defenders, who included Jews and non-Jews, also argued that Jews were quite inside the boundaries of the normal. As good citizens who worked, supported their wives and children, practiced an enlightened religion, and loved their country, Jewish men lived up to American norms of masculinity. In the unfortunate cases that suggested otherwise, these defenders of Jewish men claimed, the failure was not their Jewishness, but rather their lack of or deviation from Judaism. But rarely did any of these voices try to argue that these potentially criminal men were not really Jewish.

Both sides seemed to recognize the cultural power of the nexus of gendered or sexual difference, abnormality, and criminality. If Jewish gendered difference was abnormal, Jewish criminality could make sense. People who violated one set of social norms—norms of masculinity—could violate others, such as legal norms. On the other side of the discourse, showing that Jewish sexuality was a normal (heterosexual, family-oriented) sexuality would aid the case that there was nothing particularly criminal about Jews. As Michel Foucault suggests, the social construction of the criminal has become intimately related to the social construction of abnormal sexuality. The criminal who violates both the law of the land and the law of nature is, for Foucault, "the major model for every little deviation." The model of abnormal sexuality/criminality becomes the paradigm and "the principle of intelligibility" for understanding all cases of abnormality and criminality.[6] "Sexual abnormality . . . emerges as the root, foundation, and general etiological principle of most other forms of abnormality"[7] and, most notably for our purposes, the criminal. By something like the transitive property, therefore, criminality and non-normative sexuality became culturally entwined discourses. American historians have also offered accounts of criminality that support Foucault's more theoretical claims. Regina Kunzel likewise asserts the relationship of criminality and non-normative sexuality in wider American cultural discourse: "Criminality and sexual perversion had long been understood to exist in a tautological relationship, such that attention to one naturally and inevitably invited attention to the other."[8] In early twentieth-century America, the presence of racial and ethnic minorities and immigrants proved fertile ground for the multiplication of simultaneously criminalizing and sexualizing discourse.

Analysis of these cases, then, allows us to see more clearly the construction of Jewish masculinity because we can see its edges. The Bingham affair emphasizes the cultural consensus about a Jewish male aversion to interpersonal violence and physical aggression. The Leo Frank case demonstrates the stakes involved in the construction of Jewish masculinity: his defenders insisted he was normal with respect to gender and sexuality, and his detractors (and murderers) insisted he was abnormal. The Leopold and Loeb hearing shows us what counted as normal (healthy male bodies, heterosexuality, proper religion) and what counted as abnormal (diseased male bodies, homosexuality, perverted religion).

These three chapters work together to show what lay beyond the norms of American Jewish masculinity. Chapter 7 analyzes the 1908 Bingham affair and shows how both Jews and non-Jews assumed that Jewish crime was nonviolent. The next chapter builds on this idea of a Jewish avoidance of interpersonal violence to discuss the gendered assumptions in the 1913 Leo Frank case. The final chapter explores the connections between sexuality and crime in the 1924 Leopold and Loeb hearing. Even though the three events spanned sixteen years and three cities, they pictures they present of Jewish masculinity have a remarkable amount in common. Analysis of the Bingham affair, the Leo Frank case, the Leopold and Loeb hearing, and the extended conversation they spurred provides more than just a series of illustrations in a narrative of American antisemitism. It shows us how Jews and non-Jews shaped the conversation about American Jewish masculinity. We can see the assumptions, the contested ideas, and the expectations of what Jewish men were, what they were not, and what they should not be.

In the early twentieth-century United States, abnormal gender was not purely a function of criminality, nor was criminality a function of abnormal gender. But the two were related. In the case of Jewish men, this meant both bodies that deviated from dominant American masculine norms and tendencies in crime that also differed from those commonly expected of men. The Jewish community and many non-Jews defended Jewish men against claims of widespread crime and abnormal sexuality, but they assented to the characterization of Jewish crime as nonaggressive. Jewish crime *was* different from non-Jewish crime, Jewish defenders implicitly argued, and such nonviolent masculinity was a good thing.

Notes

1. Theodore Bingham, "Foreign Criminals in New York," *North American Review* 188 (Sept. 1908): 383.

2. Tom Watson, *Jeffersonian*, Apr. 14, 1924.

3. "Another Study of Slayers," *Chicago Daily Tribune*, June 5, 1924; "Loeb Followed Leopold Whims, Expert Asserts," *Chicago Daily Tribune*, June 5, 1924, quoted in Paul B. Franklin, "Jew Boys, Queer Boys," in *Queer Theory and the Jewish Question*, ed. Daniel Boyarin, Daniel Itzkovitz, and Ann Pellegrini (New York: Columbia University Press, 2002).

4. "Elite of the Jail Think Leopold Aint So Much," *Chicago Daily Tribune*, June 4, 1924.

5. "Loeb Followed Leopold Whims"; "Slayers King and Slave: Loeb 'Master' of Leopold under Solemn Pact Made; Sex Inferiority is Factor," *Chicago Daily Tribune*, Jul. 28, 1924.

6. Michel Foucault, *Abnormal: Lectures at the College de France 1974–1975*, trans. Graham Burchell (New York: Picador, 1999), 56.

7. Ibid., 168.

8. Regina Kunzel, *Criminal Intimacies: Prison and the Uneven History of American Sexuality* (Chicago: University of Chicago Press, 2008), 7.

7 Soft Criminals

Theodore Bingham and the Gender of Jewish Crime

"It is not astonishing that with a million Hebrews, mostly Russian, in the city (one quarter of the population), perhaps half the criminals should be of that race," New York City's police commissioner Theodore Bingham announced in a 1908 *North American Review* article. And thus the firestorm began. Although Bingham would soon retract his statistics—it turned out that Jews were statistically slightly underrepresented among criminals—the accusation and rebuttals stirred discussion among both Jews and non-Jews about the nature of Jews and criminality. Some responded with thinly disguised antisemitism, and others defended Jews as lawful citizens. However, almost all Jews and non-Jews alike agreed that when Jewish men committed crimes, they were of a certain sort. Murder, assault, drunkenness, and abuse were decidedly un-Jewish. Jews were not inclined to these masculine vices. Instead they tended toward theft, arson for money, and deceit, rather than bodily violence.

This chapter argues, perhaps unexpectedly, that Jews and non-Jews shared strikingly similar ideas about Jewish masculinity when it came to crime. It begins by analyzing and contextualizing Bingham's rhetoric and shows how he was one of many Americans, both Jewish and non-Jewish, to paint this "soft" picture of Jewish criminality. It continues with Jewish responses to Bingham's article and to his subsequent retraction. Finally it considers how both Jews and non-Jews proposed religion as an antidote to Jewish crime. If these criminals would just embrace a proper religion, they argued, it would solve the problem of Jewish crime.

Bingham and the Classification of Jewish Criminals

In his article, Commissioner Bingham argued that there were two reasons that so many Jews committed crimes: they were immigrants who did not assimilate, and they lacked healthy bodies needed to work productively. He explained that the large number of criminals who were Russian Jews—widely used shorthand for all Eastern European Jews—should come as no surprise "when the circumstance is taken into consideration." Bingham's description of New York City's "circumstance" began with a statistic about immigration: no single police precinct in Manhattan contained a majority of "native-born heads of family," and the one with the lowest percentage of native-born household heads, at 3.12 percent, was the "densely congested East Side quarter, largely peopled by Russian Hebrews." But what did this statistic mean? What did it say about crime? This "circumstance" was the biggest city in the United States, packed with first- and second-generation immigrants, resulting in a crowded urban environment that fostered weak bodies and poor morals. For acculturated Jews, Progressive philanthropists, and public figures such as Bingham, these statistics suggested that the Lower East Side was ripe for the growth of unseemly lives and habits.

Statistics were not the whole story. Data gave way to narratives and anecdotes on the second page of Bingham's article. These narratives show that, for Bingham, "the circumstance" extended well beyond statistics about immigrants and neighborhoods. It also included the history, culture, and, although he would never have used this term, the gender of New York Jews. Bingham understood the (imagined) high crime rate among Jews to be part of a cultural, situational, and dispositional condition. Immigrant Jews' lack of assimilation, he explained, "particularly among men not physically fit for hard labor, is conducive to crime; nor is it strange that in the precinct where there are not four native-born heads of families in every hundred families, the percentage of criminals is high."[1] Bingham's logic showed a veritable knot of associations between criminality and masculinity. Proper men, especially immigrants, should be physically fit and work for a living. Those who could not, in Bingham's eyes, failed to meet not only the expectations of manliness but also sometimes the expectations of the law. He linked assimilation to American culture with "labor," productivity, and proper family leadership, but indicated that immigrant Jewish men had not achieved these norms.

Bingham painted Jewish men as physically weak, unassimilated, and unable to make money to support their families: either by historical circumstance or by essence, Jewish men were weak and therefore ill equipped for productive labor. In this sense, Bingham's depictions of Jewish men echoed some of the concerns of the acculturated Jews leading the Galveston Movement. But Bingham's assumptions about Jewish immigrant masculinity differed from those of the acculturated Jews in an important way: where acculturated Jews thought that any failure to live up to norms of masculinity was a temporary state of being, Bingham thought it was much more ingrained, perhaps even essential, and where acculturated Jews pushed immigrants to pursue healthy living because it would transform them into better men, Bingham thought they were unable or unwilling to adapt to American culture at all. He emphasized immigrant Jews' failures to emulate American masculinity. They did not support their families as proper "heads of household," and they failed to labor productively.

Bingham linked immigrant Jews' physical weakness, inability to be productive laborers, and failure to assimilate with certain kinds of crime. But how could these weaklings be criminals? When he described the "foreign criminals of New York," Bingham claimed a pattern of nonviolent crimes and freely added his own interpretation: "The crimes committed by the Russian Hebrews are generally crimes against property. They are burglars, firebugs, pickpockets and highway robbers—when they have the courage." The New York City police commissioner implied that certain criminal acts entailed courage! He also implied that Jews tended not to commit courageous crimes, but rather chose crimes where they did not have to confront their victims directly. Highway robbery required courage, implied the commissioner, but burglary and pickpocketing did not. Though they were all forms of stealing, they demanded different dispositions of their committers. Bingham offered a psychological account of these imagined patterns: lack of courage, according to the commissioner, prevented Jewish men from committing daring crimes.

Accordingly, Bingham chose pickpocketing as the paradigmatic example of Jewish crime, explaining, "Though all crime is their province, pocket-picking is the one to which they seem to take the most naturally." He noted "the superiority of the Russian Hebrew in that gentle art."[2] Far from requiring strength, prowess, or courage, picking pockets—as practiced by Jewish men—was "gentle" because the deed relied on manipulation rather than intimidation of its victims. Because of their weak bodies, Jewish men were neither physically equipped for productive labor nor emotionally equipped for dangerous crime. Almost as if to emphasize the lack of physical strength and manliness required, Bingham singled out Jewish boys—not even men—as the paragons of the pocket-picking art. "Among the most expert of all the street thieves are Hebrew boys under sixteen, who are being brought up to lives of crime. Many of them are old offenders at the age of ten."[3] If the crime of choice of Jews were pocket picking, and some of the most skilled pickpockets were mere children, it could not be a dangerous, violent, or manly crime. Bingham also described a con in which "a Hebrew, an Italian, and a Greek" were arrested together for picking pockets. The Hebrew, he explained, was "always selected for the 'tool,' as the professionals term that one who does the actual reaching into the victim's pocket." The others, meanwhile, would create a distraction or "start a fight." Even when the Jewish criminal worked with other immigrants, he would be the one to do the gentle task that required finesse, while the others fought.

Bingham's characterization of Jews as soft criminals—and the Jewish community's agreement—is all the more remarkable given the reality: New York City had a number of violent Jewish criminals, some of whom were growing quite famous. Although the heyday of Jewish gangsters would not occur until a generation later, Jews in the early twentieth century were hurting, intimidating, and even murdering within the city limits. On May 18, 1908, just five months before Bingham's article appeared, two Jewish mobsters were shot to death at Coney

Island by a member of a rival gang. In that incident, Louis "The Lump" Pioggi ambushed and gunned down Max "Kid Twist" Zweifach, who ran the Eastman Gang, and his associate Samuel "Cyclone Louie" Tietch, a former wrestler and Coney Island sideshow strongman who was famous for twisting iron bars around his arms and neck. Two more stereotypically violent men would be hard to come by. Earlier that year, they had forced Pioggi to jump out a second-story window at gunpoint, motivated merely by *schadenfreude* and their own amusement.[4] Despite these colorfully violent Jewish criminals, Bingham never mentioned Jewish gangsters, murderers, or those committing crimes of intimidation. They did not fit his characterization of the kind of criminals Jewish men might become.

Whether or not he knew the history of stereotypes of Jews, Bingham's assumptions recalled European tropes, in particular the idea that Jews were physically weak and its corollary that they were consumers rather than producers. In his 1781 *On the Civil Improvement of the Jews*, Christian philosopher Wilhelm Frederick von Dohm had influentially argued that Jews' economic habits and structures focused on commerce rather than production.[5] If the state wanted productive citizens, Dohm claimed, the Jews should leave their occupations and become farmers and artisans. As a friend of Moses Mendelssohn and an Enlightenment thinker in his own right, Dohm firmly believed in the potential for the betterment of the Jewish people, but improvement in their civic status depended on improvement of their occupations and physical bodies. Dohm's Enlightenment ideas about improving the civic status of the Jews echoed not only in the thought of antisemites in the subsequent centuries—such as Houston Stewart Chamberlain and Otto Weininger, both of whom claimed that Jews were inherently parasitic and degenerate rather than productive—but also in the words of Jews. More than a century later, the Zionist and physician Max Nordau would also connect national advancement and productivity to physical and occupational signs of strength, masculinity, and sexuality. Nordau's vision of the Zionist "muscle Jew" called for civic improvement through physical strength and productivity.

Historical constructions of Jews as physically degenerate and unproductive bolstered Bingham's point about Jewish difference. But he did not simply mimic European antisemitism in the manner of Chamberlain, nor did he indiscriminately spout anti-Jewish vitriol. Despite the actual presence of Jewish organized crime, Bingham did not suggest that Jews were responsible for murder, assault, or intimidation. He neither claimed nor suggested that Jews were inherently and indiscriminately predisposed to criminality. Rather, he claimed that a certain kind of Jewish degeneracy—physical weakness, lack of productive labor, and lack of assimilation—was linked to criminal activity that required no physical strength or bravery.

Although Bingham thought all immigrant groups had criminal elements, he did not paint all groups with identical brushstrokes. The American press, like Bingham, at times depicted Irish, Italians, and African Americans as particularly prone to criminal behavior, but it depicted Jews alone among them as simultaneously criminal, unaggressive, physically weak, and cowardly. After announcing his Jewish crime statistics, Bingham fumed about the "audacity" of Italian "cold-blooded, premeditated" murders and kidnappings, and he retold at length the story of an Italian who "had the courage to stand up against a gang of blackmailers." The "gentle art" of Jewish crime and lack of "aggressiveness" and "courage" of Jewish criminals stood in sharp contrast to the "audacity" and "courage" of Italian criminals.[6] Bingham's explicit comparison shows that his assumptions about Jews were not merely reducible to their status as immigrants, working-class men, or non-native English speakers. Bingham was no big fan of Italian criminals, but he did not suggest that they were weak or cowardly. Jewish criminality alone took the hue of cowardice, weakness, gentleness, and failure of manliness.

Bingham hardly invented these stereotypes from whole cloth. Had he sought academic support for his arguments, he would not have needed to look far. In a 1903 study including an examination of "crime along racial lines" in Boston, sociologist Frederick Bushee depicted the "moral degeneration among Irish families on account of drink," anger that led to violence like "assaults" among Italians,[7] a propensity for gambling among Chinese immigrants,[8] and in general a "very much greater criminality" both violent and nonviolent among African Americans,[9] as well as other stereotypes of immigrants. Bushee assumed that racial and ethnic groups had particular tendencies, as many anthropologists and sociologists of the time did; not all immigrants or racial groups were criminal in the same fashion. "Serious assaults" were characteristic of Italians and African Americans, but he explained, "the Jews do not commit serious assaults."[10]

Life magazine, which was not above printing antisemitic articles in the early twentieth century, published a short article that discussed Bingham's characterization of Jewish criminals. It quoted David Blaustein, a well-known Jewish leader involved in philanthropic social work, who objected to Bingham's erroneous statistics, but also implied a reason for Jewish crime: Jewish men's bodies. "In speaking of the physical unfitness of the Jews, Dr. Blaustein says: 'Of the older Jews this is to a certain extent true. For reasons that I cannot go into now they were compelled to work with their minds to the neglect of their bodies.'"[11] Blaustein likely had in mind Eastern European occupational restrictions on Jews and their physical consequences, but the *Life* writer took Blaustein's words and their shared assumptions about Jewish men's bodies as an occasion to recycle stereotypes about Jewish men's lack of productive physical labor. The writer announced, "And they are still doing it. They find more profit in trading on the results of other people's labor than in using their own muscles." A story about Blaustein's refutation of Bingham's statistics thus became a story about Jewish men's unwillingness or inability to use "their own muscles." Both the criminal tendency toward committing nonviolent offenses and the stereotypes about employment choices suggested that American Jewish men differed from other American men. Like Bingham, who argued that immigrant Jewish men's bodies were ill suited to productive labor, the *Life* article claimed that Jews were not producers. Productive labor was an important part of American norms of masculinity, as the men of the Galveston Movement and Jewish agricultural movements knew. These portrayals of Jewish men not only propped up accusations of criminality but they also impugned Jewish manliness when they presented them as unfit for physical labor and thereby dependent on the strength of others.

Another *Life* article responded directly to Bingham's statements and suggested in a tongue-in-cheek, nevertheless antisemitic, tone that once Jews discovered they make up only 16.4 percent of New York criminals, they would attempt to increase their criminal market share: "They are spirited and aspiring people, and when they learn from the statistics furnished by their blood brethren that, far from showing special talent as firebugs, fraudulent bankrupts, burglars, forgers, and pickpockets, they are not even getting their fair share of the emoluments of these professions, one is loath to conjecture what the effect will be."[12] *Life* again listed the crimes considered typically Jewish—those not requiring strength or "courage" and focused on acquisition rather than, say, revenge or heat-of-the-moment anger.

An accompanying cartoon added a sexualized element to this unmanly Jewish criminality. A Jewish man, dressed as a firefighter, watches a building burn. As he looks at the smoke billowing out of the building, he sees it take the shape of a dollar sign. The Jewish man does not point the fire hose at the building, however. He holds the nozzle in a sexually suggestive way near the front of his pants, and it spurts liquid. He gazes up at the building with a contented look and a small smile. The overall effect of the image recalls stereotypes of arson as a Jewish crime and suggests that the Jewish man has become sexually aroused and gratified by the monetary gain from a fire insurance scam. Jews as profit-driven arsonists appeared as objects of humor frequently in *Life* and *Puck*, which printed cartoons showing arsonists with names such as "Flameski," "Burnopski," and "Cohen."[13]

The cartoon creates the impression that arson causes sexual excitement in the Jewish man, even though the crime of arson depicted in this image was not, in and of itself, a sexual crime. The *Life* illustration shows a Jewish man's nonnormative sexuality: he becomes excited by committing monetary crimes. Unlike the stereotype of the sexually aggressive black man, Jewish men were rarely portrayed as violent sexual predators.[14] Although the American media rarely printed stories about Jewish men accused of physical violence, Jews were frequently accused of participating in "white slavery," or the prostitution of white women, wherein men with money manipulated vulnerable women.[15] Leo Frank is a rare and dramatic example of a Jewish man accused of rape, but even then his purported victim was a girl, not a woman. Jewish men might be sexually deviant, but they were rarely represented as sexually powerful. Rather, the *Life* cartoon can be read to suggest a Jewish man expressing his sexuality in an inappropriate way, at an inappropriate time, and with an inappropriate object. In this sense, Jewish men's sexuality was imagined to be at once excessive and deficient, akin to what David Biale has called the "sexual schlemiel" in a literary context.[16] Although the criminal cases of Leo Frank and Leopold and Loeb illustrate these points in a much more dramatic way, a general discussion of Jewish criminal proclivities also reveals the extent to which Jewish men were seen as sexually abnormal. As the *Life* cartoon suggests, the Jewish man was not driven by aggression, rage, and power, but instead by his misguided sexual instinct and desire to profit. The non-Jewish media claimed that the Jewish man did not act in a properly masculine way, but neither did he *act out* in the normal masculine way.

Others also claimed a Jewish aversion to violent crime, but looked on the trait as an asset rather than a liability. What some decried as lacking in courage, others touted as a praiseworthy asset, at least when it came to criminal accusations. An article in the *Christian Observer* weighed in on the Bingham debate and came down in favor of defending the Jews, but the same essential ideas about Jewish gender underwrote its logic. "There are certain crimes and misdemeanors, to which the Jews are far less inclined than others," it explained. "For instance resistance to the law, criminal assault, malicious destruction of property, assault and murder, in short all crimes which demand aggressiveness and initiative are relatively unknown among them."[17] Where Bingham had insisted on the widespread occurrence of Jewish crime but noted its tendency toward revealing Jews' lack of courage, the *Christian Observer* emphasized the ways that Jewish aversion to crimes of "aggressiveness" was a credit to the Jewish people. Where Bingham had suggested that Jews were insufficiently manly because of their lack of courage and aggressiveness, the *Christian Observer* saw a Jewish aversion to stereotypically masculine vices.

The New York Jewish community responded quickly to Bingham's statement about "Hebrew criminals." Immigrant Jews held protest rallies in the Lower East Side. The Jewish press, along with a nascent communal organization called the Kehilla (Hebrew for "community") began by fighting statistics with statistics. They cited and disseminated the results of a 1907 study in which a Federation of Jewish Organizations employee named Mark Katz had counted the numbers of Jews and non-Jews charged with felonies.[18] Although the Federation never functioned as the unifying organization its name optimistically suggested, it did attempt to take a panoramic view of New York Jewish life. In so doing, it had commissioned its own study of New York Jews, crime, and delinquency, and several articles in the *Federation Review* published the survey's findings in 1907.[19] Its results, Katz wrote, showed that Jews should be proud of their low levels of criminality as measured by both the number of criminal felony charges and the size of the incarcerated population. Katz's study proved a useful tool for Jews in refuting Bingham's erroneous data.

Most Jewish responses implicitly agreed with Bingham's characterization of the nature of Jewish crimes, even though they vehemently disputed the statistics. No, "perhaps half" was entirely too large an estimate, they contended. But Bingham's characterization of the types of crime—pickpocketing and insurance schemes, but not assault or murder—was a different story. Yes, many New York Jews implied with their silent assent, Bingham was right on that account. Jewish newspapers vociferously objected to Bingham's statistics. Every newspaper, including the socialist *Forverts*, its rival the *Warheit*, the more conservative *Morgen Zhurnal*, and the Orthodox *Tageblatt*, printed columns, letters, and editorials.[20] "He exaggerates facts; he exaggerates figures," the *Forverts* remarked; the *American Hebrew* doubted that the data counted legitimate crimes only but rather tabulated such horrific offenses as leaving banana peels on the sidewalk together with theft; a letter to the *Forverts* from "a thief from the Tombs" contended that Jews of the criminal world were arrested more frequently than their non-Jewish counterparts because they were unable or unwilling to shoot police officers. Even the *Independent*, a non-Jewish weekly magazine published in New York, printed a lengthy article on "Jewish Criminality," which spent much of its space refuting Bingham's statistics.[21] These responses all objected to the statistics, but none disputed the characterization of Jewish criminals as tending toward certain kinds of nonviolent crime.

Although Bingham's comments served as the occasion for spirited conversation about the gendered traits of Jewish criminality, this line of thinking extended from well before the incident to long after it. William McAdoo, who had preceded Bingham as police commissioner, espoused similar ideas about Jews during his days in office. In 1906 he had written in his memoir, "The East Side Jew rarely commits a crime such as assault and murder. Among themselves disputes are mostly confined to wordy arguments."[22] The commissioner's characterization of Jewish "wordy arguments" instead of crimes of physical strength may have also been related to the public perception of the religious practice of discussion of texts. Many of those religious texts were structured as a series of opinions of learned sages, and young men brought up with traditional Judaism would learn to value good argumentation. In the same month as the Bingham affair, the *Atlantic Monthly* printed an article about antisemitism in which Edwin Kuh lamented that Jews are "lacking in physical courage,"[23] but nevertheless praised other Jewish social traits.

In 1899 Mark Twain wrote an essay, "Concerning the Jews," for *Harper's*. Earlier that year, he had written about riots in Austria that had taken on an anti-Jewish character. Why, American letter writers had asked Twain, were people prejudiced against the Jews? They should not be, Twain argued. "The Jew," he noted, "is not a brawler or a rioter." Interpersonal physical altercation was not on the list of Jewish pastimes, in Twain's mind. He continued, "With murder and other crimes of violence he has but little to do. He is a stranger to the hangman. In the police court's daily long roll of 'assaults' and 'drunk and disorderlies' his name seldom appears. That the Jewish home is a home in the truest sense is a fact that no one will dispute. The family is knitted together with strongest affections." Twain claimed that Jews were prone neither to violence nor alcoholism and immediately followed with a characterization of the charm of Jewish homes, which he characterized positively. Jews might be weak or unmanly—Twain did not say—but they also did not commit stereotypically masculine crimes of violence. Twain wrote that the Jewish man "has a reputation for various small forms of cheating, practicing oppressive usury, and for burning himself out to get the insurance," but he portrayed these as small faults spurred by contest with "vexatious Christian competition." When he connected the idea that the male Jew "seldom transgresses the laws against crimes of violence" seamlessly with the idea of harmonious home life, he also that law-abiding behavior was linked to the proper functioning of gender and domesticity.[24]

The tendencies toward nonviolent crime stemmed not from Jewish dispositions or Jewish history but also from Jewish bodies. As the appeals made by the missionaries in chapter 2 demonstrated, Jews held ideas about Jewish men's gentleness and disinclination to retaliate. In 1912, the *American Hebrew* explained, "That Jews are less addicted to crimes of violence may be put down to their slighter physique and general tendency to suffer ills without retaliation."[25] However, what seemed like liabilities—physical smallness and an aversion to fighting back—were, in a way, assets. Yes, Jews are smaller, the *American Hebrew* agreed, but that physiological fact discouraged them from committing violent crimes. Combined with the social and perhaps even religious propensity to turn the other cheek, Jewish smallness meant that vices of aggression rarely afflicted Jews.

Two years later, an anti-immigrant sociologist offered an account that resonated with that of the *American Hebrew*. Edward Alsworth Ross, who was known for his nativist stand, took the same image of the nonaggressive, nonviolent Jew, but inverted its normative value. In *The Old World in the New* Ross explained that because Jews were "too cowardly to engage in violent crimes, they count on shrewdness." Like Bingham, Ross suggested that some crimes required bravery, but Jews did not commit such crimes. Thus, both those accusing Jews of criminality and those defending Jewish men from these charges agreed on a single line of reasoning: Jewish men were physically small and constitutionally disinclined toward violence, so when they committed crimes, they were unlikely to be physically aggressive and more likely to be crafty.

Jews faced similar assumptions about their penchant for certain legal but socially frowned-upon vices. They might have immoral habits, but those habits were not characteristically manly or aggressive. For instance, social improvement movement advocates explained that Jewish men were rarely guilty of alcoholism, a vice generally associated with men in the Progressive Era, or of spousal abuse, a "vice" of exerting physical power also associated with men and the misuse of strong bodies. After noting that Jews did not assault others and that "the appropriations which they make of their neighbor's property ordinarily come within the limits of the law," Frederick Bushee granted that, "although they drink, they are not drunken."[26] New York Baptist minister Madison Peters credited Judaism with instilling Jews with restraint when it came to alcohol: "The normal Jew, the Jew who holds dear his patrimony as one of the chosen race, never drinks to excess, and it is to be doubted if a police blotter in the world has ever had to record the crime of public drunkenness against one who rigidly adhered to the faith of Abraham."[27] The lack of association between Jews and alcoholism is especially interesting because anti-immigrant sentiment and nativism were widespread in the temperance movement.[28] So it would have seemed natural, even expected, that Jews would have been painted with the same brush as other immigrants when it came to alcohol. Yet, even though Jews were targets of anti-immigrant rhetoric and political action, they were rarely accused of being alcoholics. Jews were, however, often accused of selling booze, charges that were sometimes well-founded, given the realities of the liquor trade.[29] These accusations likewise reinforced ideas about Jewish criminal craftiness or moral deficiency, but not masculine vices. Many Jews assumed that members of their communities did not participate in "Christian vices," and when they did, it must have been a direct result of the ill effects of non-Jewish groups and environments.[30] Jews and non-Jews alike agreed, despite evidence to the contrary, that Jewish criminals were not strong, aggressive, and violent.

After the public refutation of his data, Bingham soon retracted his statistics. He had made an error, he admitted. But in his retraction he stood by his reasoning and his methodology, and he affirmed the essence of his criticism. "A special knowledge of racial customs and manners is essential to the attainment of the best results by the police in the investigation of crimes committed by and against those of foreign origin,"[31] he wrote in the *New York Times*. Thus, even as he distanced himself from his original incorrect statistics, he held fast to the methodology of racial typing. Race, for Bingham as well as many other early twentieth-century Americans, signified a combination of inborn traits and traits developed or emphasized by social circumstance through a process that we might think of as social Lamarckism. Perhaps he had been wrong about the statistics, Bingham implied, but he had been studying both crime and immigrant populations in the way that would produce the "best results."

The Jewish community was glad to hear the "retraction," and many responded by praising Bingham. The language of their praise is striking. After reading Bingham's response, Jewish communal leader Louis Marshall praised the "manliness" of both Bingham and the Jewish community. Printed in both the *Warheit* and the *New York Times*, Marshall's response read, "Commissioner Bingham is entitled to credit for the manly and courageous manner in which he has acknowledge his error. . . . His frank recognition that he had unwittingly wronged the Jewish people will be accepted by them in the same frank and manly spirit."[32] Manliness, which here took the form of taking responsibility and granting forgiveness, would save the day and close the matter. The New York rabbi Judah Magnes also praised Bingham's manliness at the same time that he emphasized the honor of the Jewish community: "The Jewish people is not thirsting for revenge. It knows how to value a manly admission of error."[33] Magnes claimed that Jews knew manliness and how to value it, but he also held onto the idea that Jews were not vengeful, violent, or aggressive people. These reactions are all the more remarkable in light of the fact that, when it printed Bingham's initial comments, the *New York American* editorialized that he had acted "with the recklessness of a man in a bar-room altercation."[34] When Bingham mischaracterized Jews, it claimed, he acted rashly and aggressively, as if he were fighting in a bar—exhibiting exactly the negative masculine traits that Jews did not. But when he retracted his statistics, they praised him as manly. Manliness, for Magnes and Marshall, was demonstrated in taking responsibility and not seeking revenge. Their responses suggested that Jewish masculinity, while not aggressive or physical, valued courage in a different context. Contrary to Bingham's and Ross's ideas about Jewish criminality, courage could be intellectual and not physical.

Bingham's statistics painted Jews as criminals. The Jewish community loudly and publicly disputed those statistics and stories. But even as the two sides disagreed about how many Jews committed crimes, they agreed about something fundamental: Jewish men did not commit violent crimes. From any of these points of view, American Jewish masculinity excluded aggression and violence. Even when Jewish men went wrong, they went wrong in distinctive ways that were not stereotypically masculine.

Judaism as Criminal Antidote

Pronouncements of Jewish manliness, however, did not erase the concerns that the Bingham incident had raised, and preventing a future Bingham affair quickly became a communal goal. But how could they achieve it? They could refute statistics, but that was like putting out fires, when what they wanted to do was prevent the fires in the first place. Jewish leaders focused on two responses: ameliorating overcrowding in cities and promoting good religion. Sociologist and settlement worker Charles Bernheimer had explicitly blamed crime on city living: "There is probably no nationality less prone to serious crime than the Jewish. It is true, we see evidences of juvenile delinquency among the immigrant portion of this nationality," he admitted. But those problems were a result of "the city environment of the children," with its "absence of sufficient play space" and "lack of playgrounds and breathing spots."[35] Americans could not expect Jewish boys to grow to be good Jewish men without space to exercise their bodies. Like the acculturated Jews of the Galveston Movement and agricultural schools, Bernheimer saw the cultivation of a healthy body as essential to developing boys into proper American Jewish men.

Bernheimer also claimed that religion played a critical role in making law-abiding citizens: "The Russian Jew brings with him the quaint customs of a religion full of poetry and of the sources of good citizenship." Although Bernheimer did not endorse all the aspects of the "quaint customs," he saw religion as a safeguard against crime.[36] The particulars of that religion were far less important than its role in shaping the man: Religion "in its essence it is neither Jewish nor Christian."[37] It was religion as such, not one form of Judaism in particular, that helped reduce crime.

Other Jewish leaders who responded to Bingham claimed that religion would help remedy the crime problem in two specific ways: first, Judaism would help form young Jews who would grow up to be upstanding members of the community instead of criminals, and second, communal leaders would unite New York Jewry under the banner of Judaism. Spurred by Bingham's statements, Jewish leaders met with the goal of establishing a united voice for the Jewish community of New York. As Arthur Goren has shown in his study of the Kehilla, the idea—and the challenge—was to create an organization to represent the entire Jewish community: immigrant and native, "Russian" and "German," Orthodox and Reform, Ashkenazi and Sephardi. Without such an organization, when antisemitic criticisms or claims by future Binghams flooded the news, there would be no unified Jewish voice to respond. Yet creating that organization was no small challenge. The diversity of language, culture, income, occupation, education, geography, and religious practice was vast. How could one organization represent all of these people? Were the Jews of New York, in fact, a unified people in any way other than the fantasies of antisemites, and what could serve as the foundation for that unity?

New York Jewish leaders decided that religion, not race or nationalism, was that foundation. The Kehilla's mission statement issued in 1909 announced that its purpose "shall be to further the cause of Judaism in New York City, and to represent the Jews."[38] Rabbi Samuel Schulman had earlier proposed the change in wording from "represent the Jews of New York City with respect to all matters of local interest" to "further the cause of Judaism." As Schulman had explained in his 1908 Yom Kippur sermon, "there is only one basis of unity and representation and that is the synagogue. . . . We cannot organize New York Jewry on the basis of race or nationality. We exist in the non-Jewish world only as a *Knesset Yisrael*, a congregation of Israel."[39] Rabbi David de Sola Pool, of the Spanish and Portuguese Synagogue, agreed. Jacob Schiff, the noted philanthropist and highly visible Jewish leader, suggested barring all "political organizations" from membership and prohibiting the Kehilla from creating any "propaganda of a partisan political character."[40] Instead it should be based solely on religion. Even the Zionist Judah Magnes agreed, although he offered a picture of a community united in a religiosity that was already nationalistic in his view. All agreed that the antidote to crime, or at least the charge of crime, was religion.

In addition to positing Judaism as the focal point of communal identity, these leaders thought that it was the answer to Bingham's charges in another sense: religion could combat juvenile delinquency and thereby future crime. The conversations about delinquency began before the Bingham affair, but they intensified in its wake. As Jenna Weissman Joselit and Irving Howe have shown, the Jewish community, like Bingham, did not call attention to violent Jewish criminals. Howe claims this communal quietness came from a Jewish "cultural style encouraging prudishness and self-censorship."[41] Joselit writes that the Jewish community attempted to keep "social and psychological distance" from criminality because it disrupted their ability to see themselves—and project an image of themselves—as a more moral community. When Bingham publicized his statistics, the Jewish community was obligated to respond, she explains. Although these are compelling explanations, they do not account for the explosion of public discussion in the Jewish community about Jewish juvenile delinquency. Bringing juvenile delinquency to light was surely neither flattering, nor helpful for Jewish leaders who wanted to cultivate the image of a moral community and fend off non-Jewish criticism. Moreover, the Jewish community had discussed juvenile delinquency publicly before the Bingham affair, when there was no major precipitating event to force discussion.

Part of the reason that Jews confronted juvenile delinquency head-on while pushing Jewish gangsters into the communal closet concerns their conceptions of gender: Jewish juvenile delinquents fit with their assumptions about Jewish men, whereas the gangsters did not. The juvenile delinquents committed petty theft and ran pickpocket scams. These were hardly Jewish values, but it made sense to the Jewish community that when Jewish boys went astray, they might do such things. The acculturated Jewish community saw these boys' criminal activity as a Jewish communal problem, and they sought to remedy it with practical measures such as establishing settlement houses and care institutions and through ideological projects such as promoting religion. The violent Jewish criminals were another story. It was not that Jews denied the existence of Jewish gangsters. But they imagined them as individual criminals, as anomalies, rather than as a Jewish problem. Jewish men were not violent, they assumed. They did not do things like murder. So when individual Jews did such things, it was easy for other Jews to see them as outliers. And it was much easier for Jews to see gangsters as outliers than it was to change their view of Jewish masculinity. Thus the acculturated Jewish conversation about juvenile delinquency, when paired with the silence about Jewish gangsters, shows some of the power and durability of masculinity as a cultural force.

If Jews committed crimes, many Jews and non-Jews argued, the fault lay not in their nature, but in the bad influences of cities. The Baptist minister Madison Peters suggested that urban environments could make property-based crimes profitable and attractive to Jews: "The poor Jew was too weak, too human to resist the temptation to get a part of the swag, and so he was drawn into the maelstrom of vice." Only then did the Lower East Side become a "hotbed" of crime. Peters's solution to this Jewish criminality was religion. He suggested, "As long as the Jews remain true to the traditions of their race and the faith of their fathers, they are able to rise above all environment, overcome all temptation, resist all vices, and become good and loyal citizens of the countries of their adoption."[42] Not unlike the Kehilla, Peters suggested that religious identification was the path to ideal manliness, one that produced "good and loyal citizens."

Peters offered American Indians as a comparison to explain how Jewish masculinity had been corrupted: "Once the American Indian was among the finest specimens of physical manhood on God's footstool, conscious of his strength, noble in his courage, immovable in his purpose, determined in his convictions. Today he is weak both physically and mentally, vacillating, wavering, unsteady, even cowardly. What brought about the degeneration?" In the American Indian case, interacting with white men "brought them down from their high pedestal of manhood to a level with their exemplars in vice. So it was the coming to the cities that made the Jews criminals. They were not criminals by instinct, but they became criminal by example."[43] By creating a parallel with Indians, Peters sought to explain how and why some Jews committed crimes. His comparison implied that Jews too had been strong, noble, and determined, but that close contact with others had introduced criminal examples. Peters subscribed to a theory of gender and race that saw masculinity not only as malleable over generations but also based on descent. This idea about degeneration also had a positive flip side: It meant that groups like Jews and Native Americans could potentially become more manly. They could become (or again become) strong and brave. A change in environment and attention to religion could stamp the race with gendered characteristics for either better or for worse.

An ongoing conversation about the need for a Jewish "protectory," or facility for Jewish juvenile delinquents, exemplifies both the assumed evils of the city and also the redeeming properties of religion. Children's court Judge Julius Mayer explained that from 1902 to 1903, only about 25 percent of the children arraigned before the court were Jewish and, of those, only 7 percent were being "disorderly."[44] Although Jewish children did become involved in crime, Mayer used statistics to show that these crimes were nonviolent and often economically and circumstantially motivated. "A large percentage were charged with theft, and this was undoubtedly due, not to the example of the parents, who were in most cases respectable, law abiding people, but rather to the lack of parental control, due to economic conditions. The parents, foreigners, fail to discipline their children, who are Americans and become quite independent in manner." Mayer's comments suggested that in the process of becoming Americanized, the children evaded the discipline of their parents and even sometimes the law. City life, not bad pedigree, was to blame: "The children are also frequently influenced by the bad condition of the city life which they lead, and the parents, owing to their poverty and distress are frequently unable to modify it." Because of the growing Jewish population and the growing number of Jewish juvenile offenders, a Jewish protectory, a specifically Jewish-run organization for delinquent children, had become "a necessity." Mayer insisted that the protectory, like the Kehilla, would be based on Judaism, that is to say religion, and not on Jewishness alone: "A Jewish child subjected to discipline in an institution presided over by persons of its own faith ordinarily would be much more amenable to such discipline. The Jewish feature of such a protectory should, however, be solely religious, and not racial." The children must interact with an authority figure who is someone of the "Jewish faith," not merely Jewish by lineage. Despite insisting on the importance of Judaism, Mayer seemed to care little about the content of that Judaism. Its important facet was a universally applicable set of ethics. Whatever its particular form, Judaism was an essential element in creating proper law-abiding Jews.

The protectory would use religion to shape errant Jewish boys into proper Jewish men. *New Era Illustrated Magazine*, formerly the *New Era Jewish Magazine*, ran an article about the value of establishing a Jewish-run protectory. "Saving Citizens: The Children's Court Is Doing—A Jewish Protectory in Sight"[45] began with the story of an observant woman concerned that her son was made to pray to "graven images" in Christian worship at a home for juvenile delinquents. Many of these homes were religiously affiliated, and when the children of Jewish immigrants were sent there, they were often exposed to Protestant beliefs and practices. To reform Jewish children without this Christian influence, the Jewish community would set up its own protectory.

The article reflected a broad cultural agreement that religion served as an antidote to criminality, and author Judith Herz called for Jews to follow suit. Whether or not the observant woman's "religious distrust" was well founded, Jews needed to pay attention to juvenile criminality. She praised the Sisterhood at New York's Temple Emanu-El for "leading the way" in establishing a program to correct wayward Jewish youth.[46] Herz noted that the Catholic Church had been quite successful in combating the pickpocket problem among Italian immigrants, and if religion had worked for the Catholic Church, it would work for the Jewish community. (The protectory was, in fact, established later in 1904 and "managed on lines similar to the Catholic protectory."[47]) The fact that Catholicism and Judaism had different beliefs and practices played no part in her analysis. Each was a religion, and religion was the antidote to juvenile delinquency. Like Mayer, Herz claimed that Judaism and religious communities would help solve the Jewish juvenile crime problem, but did not articulate any particular content of that Judaism.

As part of its goal to prevent future crime, the protectory also attempted to instill a Jewish masculinity that looked quite similar to that promoted by the acculturated Jews in Part II. The protectory, located outside the city, was "essentially a home for the boys, where they the lead healthy, normal life of a boy in a country village," the magazine *Architecture* explained. There, the boys "attend school, work on the farm, receive training in technical work and have their share in the usual athletic sports of boys."[48] *Architecture* had no particular stakes in the image of American Jewish masculinity, and yet it praised the protectory's activities designed to create healthy male bodies. Charles Bernheimer explained the work training process in more detail. By the time a boy was discharged from the protectory, he would "be proficient in a trade which he has learned and able to support himself in a respectable manner." Through the Industrial Removal Office, Bernheimer explained, "he may be sent to other parts of the country to work at his trade, to support himself and others, and bequeath to the next generation a fair type of American manhood."[49] The protectory's goal was to turn juvenile delinquent boys into ideal American Jewish men—productive laborers, providers for themselves and their families, and perhaps even pioneers. It also had a synagogue and required regular attendance at services to expose the boys to religion.

The idea that religion prevented, cured, or otherwise reduced crime circulated in Protestant and Catholic circles too. In 1906, the Episcopal Diocese of New York considered passing a resolution targeting Jews for conversion. The incident caused a small ruckus, both within the diocese and between the diocese and New York Jewish leaders. The focal point of the disagreement was crime. W. R. Huntington, the rector of Grace Church, defended the resolution: "It is not a question of the conversion of the Jews, but of the large numbers of them that have gone into agnosticism. An examination of the criminal records of New York City for the last few years is all that is necessary to convince any mind that an alarming condition exists. Religion is in great part lost among the Jews."[50] Huntington argued that Jews had become agnostics, and all the evidence one needed to see this trend was a quick look at the names in New York City's criminal records. His defense of the resolution relied on a Protestant notion of religion: when Christians sought to target agnostic Jews, it was not really "a question of the conversion of the Jews" because in becoming agnostic the Jews had already given up their belief. And, to his mind, religion was a matter of belief, so they were no longer really Jews.

Others disagreed with his stance on targeted conversion, but they agreed about the close connection between Judaism and law-abiding Jews. Frederick de Sola Mendes, rabbi and co-founder of the *American Hebrew*, replied to Huntington that if he and his fellow Episcopalians "wanted to improve conditions in congested quarters, let them contribute toward the establishment of Jewish places of worship, . . . subsidize generously Jewish religious schools." The answer to Jewish crime was less crowded city living and more Judaism, which the Episcopalians were welcome to help subsidize. In his reply to Mendes, Huntington backed off his call for Jewish "Gentilization" and instead emphasized the need for adherence to theistic religion in general. It was not a particular variety of Protestant Christianity that would help reduce crime rates, he implied. "In tracing the connection between agnosticism and crime, I did only what I supposed all consistent theists, whether Jewish or Christian, would agree in doing."[51] Both Mendes and Huntington advocated a generic theism as the primary solution to crime. They assumed that the rational nature and universal ethical impulses of either religion would have the same effect of decreasing criminal behavior.

Baptist minister Madison Peters agreed that religion was the way to decrease crime and create better Jews. When Bingham made his first statement, Peters had advocated for his forced resignation. In his 1908 book *Justice to the Jew*, Peters wrote, "Today you will find Jews guilty of almost every crime in the Decalogue, from theft to murder, though it is but seldom the latter crime is perpetrated."[52] After noting the popularity of forgery, larceny, and some gambling games among Jews, Peters blamed Jewish crime on external urban influences. Like Herz, who had lamented, "When it has been for so many centuries the boast of the race that it produced neither criminals nor paupers in numbers worth serious attention, it is naturally distasteful to face the unfortunate facts of today,"[53] Peters placed the blame on city living. Echoing much of the same rhetoric that acculturated Jewish philanthropists used about immigrants, Peters explained that it was "coming to cities that made the Jews criminals."[54] Criminality was not a historical or essential Jewish problem, but rather an unfortunate effect of their modern living environments.

Mayer, Herz, Huntington, de Sola Pool, and Peters—a male Jewish judge, a female non-Jewish journalist, a male Episcopal priest, a male rabbi, and a male

Protestant minister—all saw city living and lack of religion as the cause of Jewish crime. They all thought that when Jewish men and boys went wrong, religion could and should right them. And furthermore, they all had similar gendered pictures of Jewish crime. Juvenile delinquency, pickpocketing, fraud, and other "gentle" property-based crimes could be Jewish, but violence, assault, and murder were not. These Americans assumed that Jewish men had a particular repertoire of ways that they could go bad. The American Jewish masculinity shaped in the beginning of the twentieth century had negative traits, but they were particularly Jewish traits. Jews and non-Jews tended to agree on these darker parts—deceit but not fisticuffs, theft but not murder.

Conclusion

The relationship between proper masculinity and law-abiding behavior looked the same across religious groups. Good masculinity and good religion meant law-abiding "good citizens," as the Catholic efforts to combat juvenile delinquency, the Episcopal priest's claims that Jewish criminals needed theism, and Jewish efforts to measure and alleviate Jewish crime all attest. But in the absence of religion, the men in these groups could become criminals, and then they were associated with different behaviors. When Jewish men broke the law, Jews and non-Jews imagined, they tended to do it in patterns different from those of their Christian neighbors. The negative qualities of Jewish masculinity, then, differed from some of the negative qualities of other American masculinities. When both Jews and non-Jews thought about Jewish men, they assumed that they did not partake of the male aggression and violence assumed of African Americans, nor did they reflect the uncivilized bellicosity associated with Native Americans. They were even unlike their Italian neighbors in New York. Where Italians were pugnacious and antagonistic, Jews were subtle and crafty.

The Bingham affair shows how Americans—Jews and non-Jews alike—saw Jewish crime. Bingham maligned Jews, and Jewish newspapers and communal leaders struck back in defense, but they all agreed about the nature of Jewish crime. They might disagree about how many Jews were criminals, how likely Jews were to commit crimes, or whether Jews were helping or hurting the city, but they all saw Jewish crimes as deceitful rather than violent, focused on property rather than persons. Even when Jewish communities objected vociferously to Bingham's initial off-the-cuff percentages, they granted his characterizations of Jewish crime: violent, interpersonal crime was un-Jewish. Some, like Bingham, saw this as a result of cowardliness or weakness, while others, like the Kehilla and Mark Twain, saw it as stemming from religious and ethical inclinations. But everyone agreed that when Jewish men transgressed the law, they tended to do it in predictable ways. Jewish masculinity, even at its criminal moments, was not an aggressive, physically dominating masculinity. The next two chapters focus on trials where Jewish men stood accused of crimes that seemed to violate these assumptions.

Notes

1. Theodore Bingham, "Foreign Criminals in New York," *North American Review* 188 (Sept. 1908): 383.

2. Ibid., 384.

3. Ibid., 348.

4. Albert Fried, *The Jewish Gangster in America* (New York: Columbia University Press, 1993), 29–30.

5. Christian Wilhelm von Dohm, *Uber die Burgerliche Verbesserung der Juden* (Berlin: Friedrich Nicholai, 1781)

6. Ibid., 383.

7. Frederick Bushee, "Ethnic Factors in the Population of Boston," *Publication of the American Economic Association* 4, no. 2 (May 1903): 106

8. Ibid., 101.

9. Ibid., 103. For a contextualized discussion of Bushee's depiction of black criminality, see Khalil Muhammad, *The Condemnation of Blackness: Race, Crime, and the Making of Modern Urban America* (Cambridge, MA: Harvard University Press, 2010), 100–103.

10. Ibid., 112.

11. "Work That's Unpopular," *Life* 52 (Oct. 1, 1908): 346.

12. "Give General Bingham What He Wants," *Life* 52 (Oct. 8, 1908): 385.

13. Gil Ribak, "The Jew Usually Left Those Crimes to Esau," *AJS Review* 38 (Apr. 2014): 6.

14. For an accessible and compelling exploration of the stereotype of the sexually aggressive black man, see Angela Davis, *Women, Race, and Class* (New York: Vintage, 1983).

15. Edward Bristow, *Prostitution and Prejudice: The Jewish Fight against White Slavery, 1870–1939* (Oxford: Clarendon Press, 1982).

16. David Biale, *Eros and the Jews: From Biblical Israel to Contemporary America* (Berkeley: University of California Press, 1997), 205.

17. "Criminality among the Jews," *Christian Observer* 97 (Jan. 20, 1909): 3.

18. See Jenna Weissman Joselit, *Our Gang: Jewish Crime and the New York Jewish Community, 1900–1940* (Bloomington: Indiana University Press, 1983), 56–58.

19. Jenna Weissman Joselit, "An Answer to Commissioner Bingham: A Case Study of New York Jews and Crime," *YIVO Annual of Jewish Social Science* 18 (1982).

20. Ribak, "The Jew Usually Left Those Crimes to Esau," 13.

21. Francis Oppenheimer, "Jewish Criminality," *Independent* 65 (Sept. 17, 1908): 640–642.

22. William McAdoo, *Guarding a Great City* (New York: Harper, 1906), 155.

23. Edwin Kuh, "The Social Disability of the Jew," *Atlantic Monthly*, Apr. 1908, 437.

24. Mark Twain, "Concerning the Jews" *Harper's Magazine* 99, Sept. 1899, 528–529.

25. *American Hebrew*, Nov. 29, 1912, quoted in Joselit, *Our Gang*, 43. Julia Richman's *Methods of Teaching Jewish Ethics*, likewise posed a question that unveiled similar assumptions: "Suppose a child's father has committed a crime, exploited in the newspapers, or spread through gossip; embezzlement, forgery, perjury, arson, any form of law-breaking" (33). All her hypothetical crimes for a Jewish father were nonviolent crimes.

26. Bushee, "Ethnic Factors in the Population of Boston," 112. Charles Bernheimer, *The Russian Jew in the United States* (Philadelphia: John Winston, 1905), 310–312.

27. Madison Peters, *Justice to the Jew* (New York: McClure Company, 1908), 210.

28. Joseph Gusfield, *The Symbolic Crusade: Status Politics and the American Temperance Movement* (Champaign: University of Illinois Press, 1986), 55–57.

29. Especially relevant here is Part II of Davis's work, "Alcohol and Anti-Semitism." Marni Davis, *Jews and Booze: Becoming American in the Age of Prohibition* (New York: NYU Press, 2012). For research on Jews and alcoholism in German-speaking lands, see Sander Gilman, "Alcohol and the Jews," *Patterns of Prejudice* 40 (Sept. 2006): 335–352.

30. Ribak, "The Jew Usually Left Those Crimes to Esau," 7–10.

31. *New York Times*, Sept. 17, 1908.

32. "Wrong about Jews, Bingham Admits," *New York Times*, Sept. 17, 1908, 16. For additional newspaper coverage of the apology, see Ehud Manor, *Louis Miller and Di Warheit ("The Truth"): Yiddishism, Zionism, and Socialism in New York, 1905–1915* (Sussex, UK: Sussex University Press, 2012), 38–40.

33. "Wrong about Jews," 16.

34. Quoted in Joselit, *Our Gang*, 57.

35. Bernheimer, *Russian Jew in the United States*, 55, 73.

36. Ibid., 40.

37. Ibid., 156.

38. Minutes of JCC, Feb. 1909, quoted in Goren, *New York Jews and the Quest for Community*, 45.

39. *American Hebrew*, Oct. 9, 1908, 560, quoted in quoted in Goren, *New York Jews and the Quest for Community*, 47.

40. Minutes of JCC, Feb. 18, 1909 and Dec. 1, 1908, quoted in quoted in Goren, *New York Jews and the Quest for Community*, 47.

41. Quoted in Joselit, *Our Gang*, 55.

42. Ibid., 221–222.

43. Ibid., 218.

44. "Jewish Chautauqua Summer Assembly," *Menorah* 2 (1903): 163.

45. Judith Herz, "Saving Citizens: The Children's Court is Doing—A Jewish Protectory in Sight," *New Era Illustrated Magazine* 4, no. 2 (Jan. 1904): 44–50. "Judith Herz" is actually a pseudonym for Mary Dunlop McLean, a non-Jewish woman who was fascinated with the Lower East Side and wrote with some frequency for the *New Era*. See Beth Kaplan, *Finding the Jewish Shakespeare: The Life and Legacy of Jacob Gordin* (Syracuse, NY: Syracuse University Press, 2007), 133.

46. Herz, "Saving Citizens," 45.

47. Bernheimer, *Russian Jew in the United States*, 349.

48. "Jewish Protectory," *Architecture* 20, no. 1 (July 15, 1909): 98.

49. Bernheimer, *Russian Jew in the United States*, 349.

50. "Missionary Work in New York: Episcopalians to Do Religious Work among the Jewish People," *Menorah* 5 (Nov. 1906): 249.

51. Ibid., 250.

52. Arthur Street, ed., *Street's Pandex of the News* (Chicago: Pandex Co., 1909), 30; Peters, *Justice to the Jew*, 219.

53. Herz, "Saving Citizens," 44.

54. Peters, *Justice to the Jew*, 219.

8 Leo Frank and Jewish Sexuality

As POLICE COMMISSIONER Theodore Bingham might have pointed out before he was heartily chastised, hundreds of Jewish men went on trial every year for "soft" crimes. Three of the most famous Jewish defendants of the early twentieth century, however, stood accused not of theft or insurance fraud, but of murder. In 1913 Leo Frank stood trial for the murder of a thirteen-year-old girl in Atlanta, and eleven years later Nathan "Babe" Leopold and Richard "Dickie" Loeb confessed to the murder of a fourteen-year-old boy. American newspapers dedicated thousands of column inches to each case. History, too, remembers these crimes and hearings: each has a number of popular and scholarly books dedicated solely to the story of its crime and punishment, each inspired a film version, and the Leo Frank case was even adapted into a musical.

The facts of the Frank case amounted to a tabloid's dream: the murder of a white girl, capitalists versus the working class, a dollop of North versus South animosity, changing testimonies, charges of the corruption of evidence, and an undeniable racial element. The trial of Leo Frank, a Jewish factory superintendent in Atlanta, was one of the most sensational of the decade. Thirteen-year-old Mary Phagan was found murdered in his Atlanta pencil factory, and although both the police and Pinkertons investigated, the evidence was highly contested. After briefly considering the factory's black janitor Newt Lee for the murder because of a note found with the body, the police turned to Frank, who had been the last to see her alive when she came to pick up her paycheck that Saturday. Frank was arrested, given a highly publicized trial, and convicted of the crime. His conviction was based largely on the ever-shifting testimony of Jim Conley, a black employee of the factory, and the public's racist conviction that Conley was not smart enough to fabricate a story or answer questions falsely on the stand. After numerous unsuccessful appeals, Governor Slaton of Georgia commuted Frank's death sentence to life in prison. Not long after he survived an attack by a fellow inmate, a mob dragged Frank out of the jail and lynched him.[1]

Retrospective analyses, and even the documents of the time, make an almost undeniable case in favor of Frank's innocence, but the tide of public opinion in Atlanta was against him. Many historians have asked why and how he could have been convicted and then lynched, what roles antisemitism and racism played in those events, and how this case compared to other Jewish "affairs" of the fin-de-siècle such as the 1894 Dreyfus affair in France and the 1903 Beilis affair in Russia.[2]

The purpose of revisiting the Leo Frank case here is not to uncover a heretofore neglected event of history. Excellent scholarly work has analyzed the details of the Leo Frank case in its political context and as a significant moment in American Jewish history. But gender is not a key part of most of these analyses,[3] and so here the goal is to understand the intersections of gender, sexuality, and criminality in public discourse about Frank. Because it was such a high-profile trial and received an enormous amount of media coverage, and because the perception of Frank's gender and sexuality was so closely tied to the perception of his guilt or innocence, the public discourse about Frank and his trial provides an important window into understanding Jewish masculinity—for Frank's defenders, how it should be, but for his detractors, how it was abnormal.

The Frank trial, appeals, and subsequent lynching constituted a major public event. Jeffrey Melnick has called the case and the persecution of Frank "a sacred text of American Jewish history."[4] It was certainly the most widely discussed Jewish criminal event of the early twentieth century. As such, it is a crucial moment for the historian to hear Americans air their assumptions about Jewishness. Jewish communities across the country expressed concern that the Frank case would plant or nurture ideas about Jewish men's criminality and deviant sexuality. There was so much concern that B'nai B'rith, in response, established the Anti-Defamation League, the national organization that has since worked to condemn negative public images of Jews. In an entirely different segment of the American population, the case helped launch the second incarnation of the Ku Klux Klan, which included some of Frank's lynchers among its leaders.[5] For both the historical actors themselves and for historians, the Leo Frank case is therefore critical to thinking about public images of Jewish men in the era.

Part of what is so remarkable about the case is how much everyone involved agreed on certain basic assumptions. In the American justice system, where the two sides are set up as adversaries, we might expect fundamental disagreement between the prosecution and the defense. And when it came to the facts of the case, there was plenty of disagreement. But amidst profound contention about Frank's guilt, the two sides held remarkably similar assumptions about the relationship of guilt to errant sexuality. Prosecution and defense, accusers and defenders in the press, Jews and non-Jews—all assumed that guilt and perversion were two sides of the same coin. If Frank had touched the victim Mary Phagan or others in his office inappropriately, then he was both a pervert and a murderer. If he was instead a proper husband and son who never crossed the lines of sexual propriety, then he was not a murderer. The idea that errant sexuality and criminality went together went unquestioned. The case highlights the dense nexus of criminality, gender, and religion, showing us otherwise hidden parts of the construction of Jewish masculinity. In particular, understanding the Frank case in light of the Bingham affair and the Leopold and Loeb hearing reveals surprising consistencies in the picture of American Jewish criminality and its relation to masculinity.

Although the case is a historical anomaly in some respects,[6] placing the Leo Frank affair alongside other moments of Jewish criminality shows that it is also a window into more general and wide-reaching ideas about American Jewish masculinity. As the Bingham affair demonstrated, this masculinity had both positive and negative characteristics. When we focus on the Frank case and pay special attention to masculinity and religion, several of these characteristics come to light. The prevailing set of cultural assumptions about gender associated Jewish masculinity with physical restraint or meekness; downplayed Jewish sexual aggressiveness and virility; posited a relationship among Jewish abnormality, crime, and sexual and gender difference; and also claimed a particular kind of Judaism as a defense.

This chapter begins by examining the ways that the media portrayed Frank's gender. It then focuses on presentations of Frank's sexuality, the charge of "perversion," and supporters' refutation of that charge by claiming that Frank was a good husband and son. The chapter concludes by considering the ways that religion in general and Judaism in particular interwove with these portrayals of Frank's gender, sexuality, and guilt or innocence.

"Aint Built like Other Men"? Evoking Gender in the Media

During the trial of Leo Frank, onlookers packed the courthouse each day, and others who could not fit inside would stand outside below open windows to hear the proceedings and, on occasion, audibly cheer on the prosecution. "The courtroom and streets were filled with an angry, determined crowd, ready to seize the defendant if the jury had found him guilty. Cheers for the prosecuting counsel were irrepressible in the courtroom throughout the trial," the *Atlanta Journal* reported.[7] Antipathy because of Frank's "Yankee" background[8] was present from the outset, but the location of the trial was not enough to explain why some non-Jews were so ready to believe ill of Frank. A prominent alternative theory, after all, was that Jim Conley, Frank's African American employee, had murdered Mary Phagan. Anti-black racism with its assumptions about black criminality and aggressive sexuality could have been more than enough reason for the public to assume that Conley was guilty. But public sentiment tended strongly against Frank. His position as the factory's superintendent and part owner stirred class conflict, as some Populist rhetoric demonstrated. In addition to calling Frank the "young libertine Jew . . . who has an utter contempt for the law" and referring to him as a "pervert," the Populist politician Tom Watson published screeds about Frank as a "capitalist" and "rich criminal." Frank's Jewishness, too, provided fodder for some accusers, even though Atlanta had a well-established acculturated Jewish community in addition to Eastern European immigrants. The combination of Frank's comparative wealth, education, quiet demeanor, and even smallness of stature allowed him to fit the image of the acculturated Jew and provide a contrast to the image of a rugged, physical American laboring man.

More than just reporting the case, the media shaped public opinion and perhaps even the outcome of the trial itself. Both pro-Frank and anti-Frank advocates saw newspapers as the major venue for making their cases. In response to dozens of letters from Jews throughout the country who were concerned that Frank was becoming the "American Dreyfus,"[9] the American Jewish Committee (AJC) ultimately decided that the best course of action was to influence media representations: "There is only one way of dealing with this matter," AJC founding member Louis Marshall wrote, "and that is, in a quiet unobtrusive manner to bring influence to bear on the Southern press."[10] The AJC chose to aid Frank in a way that it thought would avoid stoking antisemitism, but would also be effective. Marshall imputed immense power to the media to shape and reflect public opinion, and it seems he was correct. Georgians complained about "outside influence" on the case, by which they often meant northern media coverage and the appeals it generated on Frank's behalf.[11] Newspaper sales, especially of "extra" editions, rose and fell by the coverage of the events. The overwhelming majority of Jewish publications defended Frank, but some, such as the *American Israelite*, the Cincinnati Reform publication, withheld judgment—though it did issue calls for a fair trial free of "race prejudice." Non-Jewish publications were divided in their judgments about Frank, although Northern publications were more likely to defend Frank and Southern publications to condemn him.

Even before Frank went on trial the media began to emphasize how he was different from normative Southern men in bodily and psychological terms. The *Atlanta Constitution* described him as a "small, wiry man, wearing eyeglasses of high lens power. He is nervous and apparently high-strung. . . . His dress is neat, and he is a fluent talker, polite and suave."[12] The discourse of nerves and nervousness, suave talking, and intellect may have suggested both Jewishness and a deviation from manliness. Even a sympathetic reporter described Frank by saying "his was the nervous, bilious temperament."[13] The defense likewise relied on an explanation of his general nervousness, likening it to a physical ailment: "He is nervous almost to the point of St. Vitus dance. The finger of a detective pointed at him made him tremble."[14] Observers often remarked that Leo Frank's natural constitution seemed to be weak and nervous.

In the courtroom, Frank's gender was also on trial. When pencil factory worker Jim Conley took the stand, he claimed that at the factory Frank had once said to him, "Of course you know I ain't built like other men," which Conley explained was a reference to Frank's sexual habits and anatomy.[15] What did Conley mean? It may have been a veiled reference to circumcision, a practice and bodily marker that had accrued a host of sexual interpretations throughout history. Or

Conley may have hinted at some other abnormality of Frank's sexual organs. In the end, it does not matter precisely what Conley meant: what mattered was that he cast Frank as abnormally sexed and gendered. Claiming Frank had abnormal gender and sexuality, as Conley's testimony suggested, was key to casting him as a criminal.

Many supporters also characterized Frank's gender, but they framed it as genteel masculinity. "Small in stature; big in mind," the *Washington Post* wrote. "Frank is a man small of stature, but gives the instant impression of high culture and intellectual virility. His eyes are sharp and clear, even behind the glasses he always wears. His voice has a velvet softness, yet strong and manly in tone."[16] He was not strong or aggressive, but a different sort of manly.

The particular gendered and sexualized portrait of Frank contrasts with the more common images of murderers in the South. The nonaggressive, manipulative, and wily capitalist was hardly a typical image of a Southern murderer. Exploiter of workers, yes; murderer, no. In fact, we might have expected the prosecution and anti-Frank media to mobilize the most common ethnic or racial stereotype of those accused of violent crime: "brutish," "crude," "uncivilized" black men who raped white women. But Frank was none of these things, even according to his most outspoken detractors. He did not overpower an adult white woman; he did not even seduce a white girl with exotic appeal, as some whites anxiously worried black men would do to white women. "The psychology of the murderer, as surely proven by his crime, was that of a brute, crude, undeveloped. Frank is highly developed, a gentleman, a scholar," explained the former Second Deputy Police Commissioner George Dougherty to the *New York Times*. Dougherty implicitly— and elsewhere explicitly—relied on racial characteristics to support this gendered characterization. Frank was white, in most people's estimation, though at that time most people thought there were several white races, and Jews were not necessarily at the top of the racial hierarchy. Nevertheless, Conley was black, and that was enough to ensure that Frank's racial status marked him as more likely to be civilized and trustworthy, as Dougherty suggested. Furthermore, Frank "was of retiring disposition" and "deeply interested in charitable work," both characteristics not of a strong, brave, or assertive manliness, but rather of a more gentle and genteel masculinity. Frank was not effeminate, claimed his supporters, but neither was he a physically strong specimen.[17]

Perhaps Frank's trial attracted so much attention precisely because Jews did not seem *entirely* other. Unlike accused African Americans, Jews were not the primary racial other in the American landscape.[18] And unlike the stereotype of aggressive black men raping white women, Jewish stereotypes did not tend toward the strong, impulse-driven brute. Unraveling the mystery of Jewish otherness, especially when it came to sexuality, may have titillated non-Jewish audiences. Describing and diagnosing the particular qualities of this Jewish otherness might also seem to assuage nativist or racist fears of mysterious otherness by rendering it a known quantity with particular characteristics. In this view, "knowing" the Jewish criminal would be the most effective first step to combating the Jewish criminal.

In this way, American discussions about Leo Frank existed at the intersection of constructions of gender, ethnicity, and religion. Scholarly research about "intersectionality"—the idea that cultural concepts such as gender and race are not fully independent, but rather that these identity markers interact to create distinct experiences—reminds us that Frank's perceived guilt or innocence is not reducible to a single aspect of his identity.[19] To understand the Frank case, we need to look at a cluster of social constructions, including gender, sexuality, race, and religion. But the idea of intersectionality also reminds us that observers could focus on various aspects of Frank's identity, such as his gender or his religion, and those aspects could trump the others, such as his racial whiteness, in their imagination of Frank.

Frank's Sexuality, Family, and the Charge of Perversion

The combination of Frank's gender (quiet demeanor, small and weak body) and his Jewishness may have made it easier to believe that he also deviated from sexual norms. In addition to insinuating Frank's deviance from normative American masculinity, some newspapers—particularly those convinced of Frank's guilt—suggested he was sexually abnormal. Although in retrospect there is no evidence to support their claims, during and after the trial people accused Frank of everything from engaging in oral sex and homosexual acts to philandering and rape. The *Atlanta Constitution* reported that an unnamed employee said that Frank had "indulged in familiarities" with his young women employees.[20] Three days later, the *Constitution* reported that a policeman announced that he had seen Frank take a "young girl" to a "desolate spot in the woods . . . for immoral purposes."[21] Later he recanted, explaining that the man he saw could not have been Frank. A *Life* journalist claimed, "The prevalent opinion in Georgia was that Frank had had fair trials; that he was an habitual seducer of girls in his employ; [and] that he undoubtedly murdered Mary Phagan."[22] Somehow Frank's (imagined) status as a "habitual seducer" was not only a widely held opinion but was also relevant to the murder of the young woman. At first blush, one might think that the prosecutor's continuing insistence on discussing Frank's numerous sexual encounters and habit would paint an image of virility, the very stereotype of the masculine. But because his hypersexuality was oriented toward the young, it was cast as a misdirected and criminal sexual impulse.

Of all of the accusations, the charges of "perversion" were the most damning. A sympathetic observer from Atlanta told the *Washington Post*, "Once persuade a jury that a man is a pervert, and it doesn't matter about the other charges."[23]

The *New York Times* suggested that even if the jury had not been persuaded, the mere accusations would adhere to Frank: "It is a peculiarity—a most dreadful peculiarity—of such charges that, once made, they stick in spite of innocence."[24] These newspapers, in their defense of Frank, suggested the intimate links between sexual abnormality and criminality in the American imaginary.[25] If Frank were not a "real" man who had a "normal" sexuality, then criminal behavior was plausible, even likely. The case was tried not only on forensic evidence but also on Frank's ability to measure up to American norms of gender and sexuality: those who supported Frank argued for his status as a good husband, while those who accused him painted him as a pervert.

During the trial itself, the prosecution also attempted to discover—or at least plant in the imagination of the jurors—Frank's abnormal sexual practices. The Fulton County Court's solicitor-general and prosecuting attorney Hugh Dorsey suggested that Frank had made multiple, unwanted advances toward an office boy.[26] The boy flatly denied it. At another point, apropos of nothing, Dorsey asked an employee if he had heard of Frank "kissing girls and playing with their nipples on their breasts."[27] He asked witnesses if Frank "took girls in his lap at the factory," walked unannounced into the women's dressing room, or tried to take a girl with him when the factory closed.[28] They said they had not seen any such activity, but Dorsey continued to ask specific questions of each factory-employed witness about Frank's sexual practices. If Dorsey could prove that Frank approached many different boys and girls in the workplace, that would mean that Frank could neither properly direct nor contain his sexuality and that he pursued sexual activity in inappropriate settings and toward inappropriate persons—his young and subordinate non-Jewish employees. According to the picture Dorsey sought to paint, Frank's sexuality was excessive, misguided, and degenerate.

When it discussed the supposed objects of Frank's attention, the press consistently described them as "boys" and "girls," which subtly suggested that Frank had a sexual desire for immature people or even children. The word "girls" was common Southern parlance for young unmarried women as well as female children, but the word "boys" was generally reserved for male children. When the press used the two together—rather than referring to "girls" alone—the word choice strengthened the impression that Frank chose non-adults for his sexual exploits. The attraction to children also reinforces a defective or even deficient sexuality: Frank, a Jewish man, was unable to express sexuality toward an appropriate person, that is, an adult Jewish woman. The fact that he had not fathered children could serve as further evidence of his failure to achieve proper manliness.

Although newspapers often merely implied the connection between Jewishness and sexually deviancy, the inflammatory but influential politician Tom Watson trumpeted the evils of the "sodomite" Frank and his Jewishness. If the increased sales of his *Jeffersonian* are any indication, his opinion resonated with at least a segment of the public.[29] Many other rumors flew: the girl had been drugged, she had lacerations from a knife, her breasts were bitten and gnawed, Frank was a "pervert," he had two wives, and he had killed his first wife.[30] Watson's vitriolic pronouncements did not go unopposed—the *New York Times*, for example, ran an article titled "How the Jeffersonian Fanned Race Hatred"—but his violent rhetoric "fell on fertile soil."[31]

Whereas those who believed Frank to be guilty often connected "perversion" to the crime, Frank's defenders conversely recognized the importance of linking normative sexuality with innocence. The famous detective William Burns, when asked why he was certain of Frank's innocence, explained that Frank exhibited no perversions, and he ordered a battery of medical tests to "prove" that Frank was "normal."[32] Medical-legal discourse linked abnormality—in sexual, physical, and psychological terms—to criminality; the "normal" was associated with following norms of law, whereas the "abnormal" indicated a whole constellation of transgression of social norms.[33] Therefore, in seeking to portray Frank as "normal," Burns sought ipso facto to demonstrate his innocence. In a telegram to the *New York Times* Burns explicitly linked the possibility of perversion with the possibility of murder: "I insist that the charge of perversion was the very foundation of his conviction."[34] The *Chicago Daily Tribune* quoted a detectives' report that the crime had been committed by a "pervert of homicidal tendencies of the most pronounced type," and that Frank "is not a pervert and is innocent of the murder for which he was convicted."[35] Despite the fact that there was no indication of sexual assault, both those who supported Frank and those who thought him guilty believed that his guilt or innocence hinged on whether or not he was a "pervert."

Newspapers that supported Frank emphasized his position as a good husband and his wife's dedication not only to humanize him but also to argue for his gendered and sexual normality. Frank was married to Lucille Frank (nee Selig), a Jewish woman who supported him throughout the ordeal, but press coverage of her depended on the newspaper's opinion of Frank: papers that supported Frank dwelled on her, while those convinced of Frank's guilt rarely mentioned her. The largely sympathetic *New York Times*,[36] for instance, printed many stories referring to Frank's mother and wife. When it covered his last appeal, it reported his wife's reaction before mentioning any of Frank: "Mrs. Frank, wife of the young factory superintendent, who had wept silently as she sat only a few steps from where her husband stood, screamed, collapsed, and sank limp in her chair. It was several minutes before she could be removed from the courtroom," it began. The article went on to portray her as a dutiful, dedicated wife: "She was taken to Judge Hill's chambers, adjoining the courtroom where she could be revived. Shortly afterwards, at the persistent request of the young wife, she was driven in an automobile to the Tower to be with her husband."[37] By presenting Frank as a husband and his wife as an appropriately devoted and distraught woman, the *Times* depicted Frank as a man with a normal sexual arrangement: a devoted heterosexual marriage.

When Leo Frank won his court appeal, the *Chicago Daily Tribune* printed pictures of Frank, his wife, and Mary Phagan together in a cluster, with the two adults paired above and the child below, as if they were a nuclear family.[38] This family-like arrangement is particularly notable because the Franks did not have any children. The *Tribune* could not print a picture of him, his wife, and children and thereby provide evidence of his proper masculinity and sexuality. "Leo Frank, Who Wins Appeal, His Wife, and Girl Who Was Slain," read the article's title. When Frank was kidnapped from his jail cell, the *Tribune* again clustered sketches of Frank, his wife, and Mary Phagan under its front-page banner, "Leo Frank Kidnapped: May be Lynched."[39] Both articles were strongly supportive of Frank.

To emphasize his proper relationship with the women in his life, newspapers that supported Frank frequently reported on the support of his wife and mother, along with their coverage of newsworthy events. When a fellow prisoner attacked Frank with a knife, a *Los Angeles Times* headline called it a "tragedy" that occurred "as wife arrives to visit with her husband." The article about the stabbing concluded somewhat oddly, given its topic, with this sentence: "Mrs. Frank is in Milledgeville, where she had come to visit her husband."[40] As he recovered from the attack, Frank wrote a letter to a detective agency he had once employed. The *Washington Post* printed the letter in an article titled "Wife His 'Ministering Angel'" because Frank had written, "Surely God has let me live and aided me in this dark hour for a brighter day which must be near at hand. Mrs. Frank has been in this painful ordeal my ministering angel."[41] The *New York Times*, *Chicago Daily Tribune*, and *Washington Post* printed dozens of stories about Frank and his wife's support throughout the trial and appeals process: she "collapsed" in the courtroom at his sentencing, she "pled for simple justice" of the people of Georgia, and she was serving as "his stenographer" while he was in jail.[42]

A 1915 *New York Times* article about one of Frank's appeals argued that the false charges of perversion had caused Frank's conviction, suggesting that Mrs. Frank and her conduct were evidence of the falseness of both the perversion and the murder charges:

A number of the foremost physicians at Atlanta testified, by affidavit, that Frank had no taint of physical or mental degeneracy. Belief to the contrary, founded on falsehood and misunderstanding, had been largely instrumental in fastening the presumption of crime upon him. The statement of Frank's patient, affectionate wife, whose testimony had been excluded at his trial, of their mutual relations, of her unbroken faith in him, conclusively denying the assertion that there had been an estrangement after the arrest of Frank, was straightforward, and its unaffected pathos must have had its due effect on the prison commission.[43]

Although Frank had initially refused to let his wife see him in prison—"I could not bring myself to allow her to see me behind the bars of a jail," he explained—when he realized that he would be detained indefinitely and could not "spare her the pain and distress" by only talking to her on the phone, they had daily visits.[44] A "patient, affectionate wife" who supported Frank without reservation was evidence not only of Frank's lack of degeneracy but also of his innocence, supporters argued. Frank was neither a pervert nor guilty, as shown by the presence of a devoted wife, his love for her, and her love for him.

Frank's sympathizers also played up his close relationship with his mother. The *Washington Post* printed a letter from his mother thanking the paper for its support of Frank and describing the antisemitism in the courtroom.[45] The *New York Times* printed Leo Frank's statement in his last moments: "I think more of my wife and mother than my life."[46] After the mob dragged Frank from the jail, the *New York Times* reported, "Frank's statement just prior to his death that he loved his wife and mother better than he did his life came unexpectedly and without questioning."[47] The *Times* article explained that, even in his last moment, Frank pronounced his commitment to his heterosexual marriage and his mother. He was a good man, even in death. The *Times*, *Tribune*, and *Post* all painted Frank as a devoted husband and son, thereby emphasizing his gendered and sexual normality.

Frank's Judaism and Jewishness

Supportive newspapers also used Frank's synagogue membership as a way to project his innocence. As an active member of a Reform synagogue known in Atlanta as "The Temple," Frank practiced a rational, decorous religion. His rabbi, David Marx, vocally supported him from the outset and spoke to sympathetic journalists on his behalf. When the Georgia court denied Frank a retrial, Rabbi Marx was in the courtroom with Frank, his wife Lucille, her father Emil Selig, and Frank's attorney. The *New York Times* wrote, "Frank heard the news with calmness, and comforted his wife, who was greatly distressed. Rabbi Marx also showed deep emotion."[48] As a well-respected Atlantan who expressed his loyalty to America, Marx could only help Frank's quest to present himself to the public as an innocent man.

Even beyond the Jewish community, groups of petitioning citizens from New York to Texas, numerous Christian clergy, and writers of letters to newspapers spoke up for Leo Frank's innocence—or at least complained about the unfairness of his trial.[49] Convinced that the innocent Frank had already suffered too much, Alonzo Mills, a Presbyterian minister from Oakland, publicly offered to be executed in Frank's place.[50] Like much of the Jewish community, Frank's non-Jewish supporters often denied any link between Jewishness and criminality. Rev. Julian Rogers, an Atlanta Baptist, declared, "If Leo Frank is a criminal, it is not because he is a Jew, but in spite of it."[51] Rogers suggested that Jewishness would disincline one toward criminality or murder.

On the other side, the prosecution and anti-Frank media often painted Frank's Jewishness as related to his guilt. Reports frequently included the words "Jew" and "Jewish," and even the accounts that did not could still trade on other stereotypes and key words to reinforce his Jewishness. In his comparative study *The Jew Accused*, historian Albert Lindemann argues that antisemitism was not a major factor in the Leo Frank case, but this is because he tracked only the use of explicit terms: Jew, Jewish, Judaism.[52] He therefore neglects the work of cultural code words such as "intellectual," "nervous," and "rich," which could allude to Frank's Jewishness without explicitly naming it.

In fact, the prosecution intentionally avoided using the words "Jew" and "Jewish," in an effort to avoid seeming antisemitic. In his summation, Solicitor Dorsey reminded the jury that "the word Jew never escaped our lips," a strangely self-congratulatory and self-negating statement. Dorsey then went on to talk about other Jewish criminals, such as a New York lawyer named Schwartz and Judas Iscariot, explaining that "they rise to heights sublime, but they also sink to the lowest depths of degradation."[53] He linked Frank to perversion by relying on a more generalized discourse that indicated Jewishness without using the word "Jew."

Even at the time of the trial, journalists noticed the presence and influence of unsubstantiated rumors and code words. One Georgia journalist who wrote anonymously blamed Frank's conviction on a kind of whisper campaign: "The yellow-journal methods employed in reporting the pre-trial developments and the trial, together with endless word-of-mouth gossip concerning Frank and revolving around imaginary things which idle scandal said the 'papers couldn't print' caused the multitude in Atlanta and most of Georgia to become indelibly of the opinion that the young Jew was guilty." The author suggested that the images, not fully painted by the press, were filled in by the readers, who created their own ideas of these "unprintable" images of what Frank had done.[54] These "imaginary things" served to reinforce stereotypes, especially sexual, that already circulated in the American readers' cultural imaginary. The journalist's desire to remain anonymous also indicates how pervasive he or she felt these stereotypes were and how unpopular a defense of Frank on these grounds could be.

The anonymous writer also suggested that the public was more than willing to believe that a Jewish man was sexually deviant. The decision by Georgia's governor Slaton to commute Frank's death sentence to life in prison was followed by public outrage, which Tom Watson had instigated, the anonymous writer explained. Watson had provoked the public in his *Jeffersonian* by repeatedly de-picting Frank as a depraved murdering Jewish rapist who had taken the life of an innocent girl, such as when he focused on the physical aspects of Phagan's body and her underwear. The writer noted how Watson repeatedly used details, regard-less of their accuracy, to stoke the public's ire:

> Watson produced all the vague "rumors" as evidence and warped the testi-mony of the trial to suit his purpose. Weekly he described the poor dead girl's body and even paraded descriptions of her soiled underclothing before the public and played on the medical phases of the case, employing every avail-able emphasis to make report and suspicion appear as facts—which was like waving a red flag before a bull.[55]

The bull charged. Twenty-five armed men came to the jail, kidnapped Frank, drove him to Mary Phagan's hometown, and lynched him. A crowd quickly gathered, shot photographs, and took bits of rope and Frank's clothing as souve-nirs. Much of the Georgia public, angry over a white girl's murder—a particularly egregious violation of Southern genteel culture—saw the girl's death as related to a Jewish man's errant sexuality. Even in the absence of evidence of rape or sexual touching, the prosecution, the jury, and some of the non-Jewish media painted a picture of a Jewish man with abnormal sexuality and gender. If Leo Frank had committed the murder, he had a deviant sexual motive; and if Frank were sexu-ally deviant, then Frank must have committed the murder, went the circular and self-justifying logic.

After the twenty-five "Knights of Mary Phagan," as the men had called them-selves, lynched Frank, *The Jeffersonian*, announced, "A vigilance committee re-deems Georgia and carries out the sentence of the law on the Jew who raped and murdered the little Gentile girl Mary Phagan." Watson used the language of re-demption to explain the violent mob and extreme rhetoric to paint the Jewish Frank as a sexual deviant and a criminal. Never mind that neither the police nor the private detectives had found evidence of rape; for the *Jeffersonian*, sexual de-viance and crime were tautological. "In putting the Sodomite murderer to death," Watson continued, again twinning "Sodomite" with "murderer," "the Vigilance Committee has done what the Sheriff would have done if Slaton was not of the same mould as Benedict Arnold. Let Jew libertines take notice. Georgia is not for sale to rich criminals."[56] Watson knitted together the discourses of nationalism, race, class, and sexuality into a composite representation of Jewish otherness.[57] Taking the antisemitic stereotype of gentile-chasing Jewish men to a new level, Watson suggested that Frank chose a girl, perhaps for her innocence, but also for the physical reason that he was too weak or underdeveloped to seek a grown woman.

Frank was not always the sole target of sexual scrutiny: sometimes Jews as a group were targeted with him. Because Jewish communities and individuals from throughout the country donated money on Frank's behalf and called for political support for him, many non-Jews who thought he was guilty lashed out against all American Jews. *Life* indicted Jews in general along with Frank in particular when it stated, "Jews from everywhere . . . swore his character was good, whereas on his sexual side it seems to have been rotten."[58] This logic insisted that either Jews are liars, or they are unable to discern "rotten" sexual behavior from correct sexual behavior. More insidiously, it might even suggest that Jews secretly condone rotten sexual character and accept or cover for those who have it. This connection between Frank and "the Jews" as a whole allowed the public to tie not only Frank's money and defense to his Jewishness but also his "perversion."

The Boston Globe worried that the publicity of Frank's trial had fanned the flames of antisemitism. Myths circulated, claiming Judaism's tacit approval of men raping non-Jewish women. In these myths, Frank became the example of the lascivious Jewish man, out for sex with non-Jews regardless of their unwillingness. "No story was too wild or too salacious to be told of Frank in Atlanta during the progress of the trial. One, which was typical, was that the Jewish faith condoned the violation a Gentile women by the Jew," the *Globe* explained. The article showed how detractors could simultaneously present Judaism as an inferior religion and Jews as an inferior "race" without ever distinguishing between the two. The myths extended beyond claiming a male Jewish fetishization of non-Jewish women. The newspaper reported on rumors of other salacious sexual practices, such as those described in European sexual literature, imagined by an American audience to be lascivious and strange: "The narratives of Frank's supposed practices were like pages from the vilest European erotica. The public wallowed in the filth with which the accused man was pelted."[59] Frank's trial served as an occasion to reinforce Jewishness as otherness for those who were already inclined to link Jewishness to sexual deviance.

It also served as the occasion for Jews to organize a defense against social prejudice. If those who thought Frank was guilty sometimes grouped Jews together, Frank's defenders did so even more. Many (accurately) perceived the presence of antisemitism, and some saw the case as evidence for need for an organization that would defend both individual Jews and the Jewish community against instances of prejudice. The fraternal organization B'nai B'rith, of which Frank was a member, created the Anti-Defamation League "to preserve the good repute of the Jew and Judaism."[60] Alerting newspapers to the prejudicial reporting of Jewish criminality was one of the ADL's first projects. Why was a criminal's religion mentioned only when he was Jewish, the ADL asked? This practice needed to stop. Newspapers largely complied, quickly and quietly.

Even Frank's end at the hands of the lynch mob served as an occasion to discuss Jewishness and masculinity. One *Washington Post* letter to the editor, written by a John Phillips Meekin, claimed that Frank's comportment at the time of his death was both manly and worthy of emulation: it should be "worthy of notice when we find a man, criminal or non-criminal, guilty or not guilty, who goes quietly to his death and thus gives a manly lesson to quaking humanity in how to die." Frank, because he quietly dressed himself, did not "murmur," cry, or plead as the mob took him and hanged him, and spoke only the last, short tender words of love for his wife and mother, had a true manly end. The letter was published a week after the *Post*'s front-page coverage of Frank's death, which included the lynchers' "inside story" of Frank's composure on the seven-hour ride to Marietta, where he was hanged.[61] Meekin claimed that Frank's manly end connected him to his Jewish heritage: "Prejudice has always followed the Jewish race, but, all across the ages, the Jew has given the world a lesson worthy of emulation in how to die!"[62] Meekin's adulation of the honor of Jewish deaths suggested Jesus dying on the cross. (One reported also called the scene "like some religious rite," with observers behaving in a "curiously reverent manner."[63]) It also echoed the Hebrew-Christian missionary rhetoric that, as shown in chapter 2, championed a quiet and nonretributive Jewish masculinity.

Both Frank's supporters and detractors imagined that his gender and sexuality were closely related to his guilt or innocence. To his supporters, he was a gentle, small, well-educated, and quiet man with a devoted wife; for the others, he was a nervous, small, weak pervert given to the sexual pursuit of non-Jewish girls and boys. But for everyone, Frank served as an example of the intimate links between masculinity, crime, and Jewishness.

Conclusion

Jews do not get into bar brawls. They do not beat their wives. Jewish men are not physically aggressive or violent. Jews might embezzle money or commit fraud, but not assault and certainly not murder. These images of Jewish crime—some of which still resonate today—suggest the borders of Jewish masculinity: Jews and non-Jews agreed, despite evidence to the contrary, that aggression and violence were beyond the bounds of Jewishness. In these conversations about crime and criminality, everyone, including the Jews, granted these conceptions of Jewish masculinity.

Judaism, the Jewish community suggested in its responses to the Bingham affair and to the Leo Frank case, was incompatible with crime. During and after the Bingham affair, efforts to establish a Kehilla were motivated by the belief that that Judaism could serve as a moral compass and therefore deter crime. In one sense, this is no surprise. People often assume that religion—theirs or others—develops and supports a law-abiding morality. But in another sense, the connection of Judaism with innocence before the law took on a perhaps unexpected gendered component. Judaism could imply gendered and sexual normality, which would counterindicate criminal guilt. In the Leo Frank case, those who drew attention to Frank's Judaism also drew attention to his proper masculinity and sexuality. They emphasized his relationship to his wife and mother, as well as his connection with his rabbi. Identification of Frank's Judaism went hand in hand with depictions of his role as a gentle husband and son, while those who insisted he was guilty and a pervert never mentioned his Judaism.

Although these conversations about Jewish crime and criminality focused on a very small element of the Jewish population, they tell a much bigger story. Good Jewish men, of course, were not criminals. But when Jewish men committed crimes, people imagined that they did so in ways that fit with popular conceptions of Jewish masculinity in general. The cultural assumptions about Jewish men as not physically overpowering or violent were so strong that even when ideas about Jewish manhood and the facts of the crimes collided, the images of Jewish criminals as nonaggressive held fast.

The next chapter considers another instance of Jews and murder. Leopold and Loeb, unlike Frank, were unquestionably guilty. They confessed to the crime. Although the details of the cases and the reactions to them differed dramatically, the media representations nevertheless shared a number of characteristics. Despite the geographic and cultural differences between Chicago and Atlanta, the public conversation surrounding each case painted a similar portrait of the gender and sexuality of a Jewish male criminal. Detectives never presented evidence of rape or sexual contact for either victim,[64] yet all three Jewish men were publicly and repeatedly questioned about their own sexuality, and the media frequently discussed deviant sexual practices in both cases. All three were painted as brainy, intellect-, or commerce-driven men with little taste for violence itself.

Although at first, committing murder might seem incongruous with the image of a gentle, cowardly male Jewish criminal, the images and rhetoric of both Jews and non-Jews nevertheless might have sounded familiar to anyone who had paid attention to the Bingham affair. Frank's defenders portrayed him as a gentle family-focused man who was an active member of his Reform synagogue and on excellent terms with his rabbi. Those insisting on the guilt and punishment of the accused used images of cunning, calculating men who were small and weak, displayed abnormal male sexuality, and merely used violence as a means to an end. Later, for Leopold and Loeb, this would take a particularly interesting twist: because they had confessed to the crime, their defense counsel Clarence Darrow used the idea of abnormality to argue for their decreased culpability. Precisely because they were *unlike* other people and other Jews, as the evidence of their sexual desires and practices would attest, they could not be held to the same standards of culpability, Darrow argued.

Though the formal verdicts in the courtroom and the less formal verdicts in the press circulated similar images, the outcomes for the accused men were quite different. In one case, portrayals of abnormal gender and sexuality helped the jury and a segment of the American press convict Frank of a murder he did not commit. In the other case, similar portrayals worked toward a very different judicial end: the defense successfully argued that the very fact of inborn weak, overly intellectualized, and misguided sexual natures counted as a reason to exercise judicial leniency for the admitted murderers Leopold and Loeb. The same constructions supported the condemnation of one man who refused to admit his alleged gendered and sexual abnormality while also sparing the lives of two other men who admitted theirs. In this way, gendered constructions of Jewish men in American society could be marshaled in favor of either condemnation (in the case of those accusing Frank) or patronizing and medicalizing sympathy (in the case of those defending Leopold and Loeb from the death penalty). The two cases together show not only the very real cultural power of the construction of masculinity but also show how that construction could be mobilized to very different ends.

Notes

1. I limit my discussion of the case and its details because of the number of works already dedicated to it. For broader coverage of the case and its aftermath, see Matthew H. Bernstein, *Screening a Lynching: The Leo Frank Case on Film and Television* (Athens: University of Georgia Press, 2009); W. Fitzhugh Brundage, *Lynching in the New South: Georgia and Virginia, 1880–1930* (Urbana: University of Illinois Press, 1993); Leonard Dinnerstein, *The Leo Frank Case* (Athens: University of Georgia Press, 1999); Harry Golden, *A Little Girl Is Dead* (Cleveland, OH: World, 1965); Nancy MacLean, "The Leo Frank Case Reconsidered: Gender and Sexual Politics in the Making of Reactionary Populism," *Journal of American History* 78 (Dec. 1991); David Mamet, *The Old Religion* (New York: Free Press, 1997); and Steve Oney, *And the Dead Shall Rise: The Murder of Mary Phagan and the Lynching of Leo Frank* (New York: Pantheon, 2003).

2. Dinnerstein, *Leo Frank Case*; Jeffrey Melnick, *Black-Jewish Relations on Trial: Leo Frank and Jim Conley in the New South* (Jackson: University of Mississippi Press, 2000).

3. There are two notable exceptions: Nancy MacLean's analysis of the case as a window into the changed mores about women in the American South, and their relation to labor and politics, and Daniel Itzkovitz's literary reading of the trial and its implications for imagining Jewish sexuality.

4. Melnick, *Black-Jewish Relations on Trial*, 11.

5. MacLean, "Leo Frank Case Reconsidered," 920.

6. For instance, lynching Jews was extremely rare, and Frank was the only Jew murdered extrajudicially by hanging from a tree in the United States.

7. *Atlanta Journal*, Mar. 10, 1914, 8, quoted in Dinnerstein, *Leo Frank Case*, 94.

8. Frank was born in Texas, but Watson and many others frequently referred to him as a Yankee. This reference could help mobilize public opinion against him in a time when Georgians resented Northerners, especially industrialists and carpetbaggers.

9. Leo Frank's case never became a metonym for questions about nationalism, citizenship, and loyalty of Jews to their country the way the discourse surrounding Alfred Dreyfus's accusation and defense did. Moreover, France was not Atlanta, and the element of race in the United States complicated the story. Yes, Frank was a Jew, but some of the other characters in the case were black, and so in some cases, racism worked to *create* supporters of Frank. In France, in contrast, the Jewish Dreyfus represented the paradigmatic social other. Although it is difficult to measure relative degrees of antisemitism, a comparison indicates that French anti-Jewish discourse outweighed its American counterpart in both volume and vitriol. When it came to gendered representations, Dreyfus was accused of the nonviolent crime of treason (more characteristic of the imagined perfidious Jew out for profit), whereas Frank was accused of the violent murder of a girl (a seeming departure from the acts of a cunning but weak Jewish criminal).

10. Quoted in Dinnerstein, *Leo Frank Case*, 65. Also see the correspondence between Louis Marshall and Frank's rabbi, David Marx. Correspondence of Rabbi David Marx to Louis Marshall, Frank, Leo M. Correspondence of Rabbi David Marx with Louis Marshall and Anna Carroll Moore re: Frank case and his death. Small Collections. *AJA.*

11. For instance, the wording of a resolution condemning the commutation of Frank's sentence blamed "outside influence" for the decision. "Frank Plea Opposed at Atlanta Meeting," *New York Times*, June 6, 1915, 4.

12. *Atlanta Constitution*, Apr. 30, 1914.

13. Elmer Murphy, "A Visit with Leo Frank in the Death Cell at Atlanta." *Rhodes' Colossus*, Mar. 1915, 10.

14. "Frank's Fate Now in Slaton's Hands," *New York Times*, June 17, 1915, 1.

15. *Frank v. State, brief of evidence*, at 55. Also quoted in Dinnerstein, *Leo Frank Case*, 41.

16. "His Life to Vent Public Prejudice," *Washington Post*, Mar. 9, 1914, 4.

17. George S. Dougherty, "Frank Is Innocent, Says George S. Dougherty," *New York Times*, Jan. 10, 1915, 48.

18. On the construction of the relationship of criminality and blackness in this period, see Muhammad, *Condemnation of Blackness*.

19. Religion is rarely included in literature on intersectionality, but this may be a fruitful mode of future inquiry. For a classic description of intersectionality, see Kimberle Crenshaw, "Mapping the Margins: Intersectionality, Identity Politics, and Violence against Women of Color," *Stanford Law Review* 43 (1991): 1241–1299.

20. *Atlanta Constitution*, May 8, 1913.

21. *Atlanta Constitution*, May 11, 1913.

22. *Life* 66 (Sept. 2, 1915): 421.

23. "Frank's Life Now a Partisan Issue," special to the *Washington Post*, Mar. 11, 1914.

24. "Topics of the Times," *New York Times*, June 23, 1915.

25. Regina Kunzel's work on sexuality and prisons places this identification of perverts and crime as a relatively new and yet powerful development of the time: "If, in the preceding century, prison observers worried that prisons were places in which sexual *perversion* was regrettably rampant, in the twentieth century, prisons began to be perceived as sites in which *perverts* could be found in abundance." The focus had moved from the sexual *acts* to the abnormally sexual *persons*. Kunzel, *Criminal Intimacies*, 48.

26. Dinnerstein, *Leo Frank Case*, 51.

27. Ibid., 51. Demonstrating restraint, the employee did not reply by asking where else nipples might be located.

28. "Frank's Life Now a Partisan Issue."

29. John Higham, *Strangers in the Land: Patterns of American Nativism, 1860–1925* (New Brunswick, NJ: Rutgers University Press, 1983), 185.

30. "Move Resentence of Frank Today," special to the *New York Times*, Mar. 4, 1914; Dinnerstein, *Leo Frank Case*, 18–19.

31. "How the *Jeffersonian* Fanned Race Hatred," *New York Times*, Aug. 18, 1915, 3.

32. "Frank Is Normal, Physicians Report," special to the *New York Times*, Apr. 26, 1914, 11.

33. Foucault, *Abnormal*. See especially 1–54.

34. "Absolve Frank on Immorality Charge," *New York Times*, Apr. 25, 1914, 8.

35. "Burns Says Frank Will Not Hang," *New York Times*, April 4, 1914, 8; "Leo Frank's Case," *Washington Post*, Mar. 27, 1914; "Detectives Hold Frank Innocent," *Chicago Tribune*, Apr. 23, 1914, 7.

36. Louis Marshall had appealed directly to Adolph Ochs, the publisher of the *New York Times*, to advocate for a new trial for Frank. Marshall and Ochs knew one another from their work with the American Jewish Committee.

37. "Frank Death Day Set for June 22, His Wife Screams and Collapses as He Is Sentenced for the Fourth Time," *New York Times*, May 11, 1915, 24.

38. "Leo Frank, Who Wins Appeal, His Wife, and Girl Who Was Slain," *Chicago Daily Tribune*, Dec. 29, 1914.

39. "Leo Frank Kidnaped," *Chicago Daily Tribune*, Aug. 17, 1915.

40. "Leo Frank Attacked," *Los Angeles Times*, July 18, 1915.

41. "Wife His 'Ministering Angel,'" *Washington Post*, Aug. 18, 1915.

42. "Frank's Death Day Fixed for June 22," *New York Times*, May 11, 1915, 24; "Mrs. Frank Pleads for Simple Justice," *New York Times*, Mar. 1, 1914, 1, 3; "Mrs. Leo M. Frank, Stenographer for Her Condemned Husband," *Chicago Daily Tribune*, May 4, 1915, 8.

43. "The Appeal for Frank," *New York Times*, June 2, 1915.

44. "Frank Answers Questions: Came from Unfriendly Sources, and His Defenders are Elated," *New York Times*, Mar. 16, 1914.

45. "Frank's Mother Tells of Prejudice at His Trial," *Washington Post*, Mar. 17, 1914.

46. "Grim Tragedy in Woods," *New York Times*, Aug. 19, 1915, 1.

47. "New Inside Story of Frank Lynching" *New York Times*, Aug. 23, 1915, 5.

48. "Split Court Denies Frank New Trial," *New York Times*, Feb. 18, 1914, 3. The two justices who ruled in Frank's favor pointed to the inadmissibility (and flimsiness) of Conley's testimony on Frank's "lasciviousness."

49. The *Chicago Tribune*, for example, was "besieged with letters" decrying the "travesty of justice." Burton Rascoe, "Will The State of Georgia Hang an Innocent Man?," *Chicago Daily Tribune*, Dec. 27, 1914. Eugene Debs spoke out for Frank too. "Frank Railroad, E. V. Debs Asserts: Declares Race Prejudice Made Trial a Farce and He Had No Chance," *New York Times*, Dec. 28, 1914.

50. "Offers to Die for Leo Frank: Oakland Minister Will Take Place of the Condemned Man," *Los Angeles Times*, May 26, 1915.

51. "Pastors Demand Retrial for Frank," *New York Times*, Mar. 16, 1914, 1.

52. Albert S. Lindemann, *The Jew Accused: Three Anti-Semitic Affairs (Dreyfus, Beilis, Frank)* (Cambridge: Cambridge University Press, 1992).

53. *Atlanta Constitution*, Aug. 24, 1913; *Atlanta Georgian*, Aug. 23, 1913, quoted in Dinnerstein, *Leo Frank Case*, 52–53.

54. "A Public Man of Georgia, Why Frank Was Lynched: Was it Race Hatred, Dirty Politics, Yellow Journalism?," *Forum*, Dec. 1916, 686.

55. Ibid., 687.

56. Tom Watson, *Jeffersonian*, quoted in Daniel Itzkovitz, "Secret Temples," in *Jews and Other Differences*, eds. Jonathan Boyarin and Daniel Boyarin, eds. (Minneapolis: University of Minnesota Press, 1997), 179.

57. Itzkovitz, "Secret Temples," 179. This also recalls a more general relationship among whiteness, manliness, and the discourse of lynching in the South. As Jackson Lears claims, "Imbibing the potent brew of race and sex, Southern white men merged manliness and whiteness, redefining manhood in racial rather than occupational terms. And whether work or sex created the conflict that led to the lynch mob, its main mission was the reassertion of white manhood." Jackson Lears, *Rebirth of a Nation: The Making of Modern America, 1877–1920* (New York: HarperCollins, 2009), 107.

58. "The Jews of America and the Frank Case," *Life* 66 (Sept. 23, 1915): 577.

59. "Is Frank Another Dreyfus?," *Boston Daily Globe*, June 6, 1915.

60. Quoted in Deborah Dash Moore, *B'nai B'rith and the Challenge of Ethnic Leadership* (Albany: SUNY Press, 1981), 106.

61. "Lynchers Describe Frank's Death Ride," *Washington Post*, Aug. 23, 1915.

62. Letter to the editor: "Finds Notable Lesson in Quiet Shown by Leo Frank," *Washington Post*, Aug. 30, 1915.

63. Quoted in MacLean, "The Leo Frank Case Reconsidered," 940.

64. Melnick, *Black-Jewish Relations on Trial*, 15; MacLean, "The Leo Frank Case Reconsidered," 918, 936–937.

9 Bad Jews

The Leopold and Loeb Hearing

O<small>N</small> M<small>AY</small> 21, 1924, Chicago teenagers Nathan "Babe" Leopold and Richard "Dickie" Loeb kidnapped and murdered fourteen-year-old Bobby Franks. They took Franks from their South Side neighborhood, killed him, poured acid onto his face and circumcised penis to hinder identification, placed his body in a culvert, and began to write a ransom note to the boy's parents. Although they had planned to commit the perfect crime, a man had already discovered the body before the ransom note reached Mr. Franks, the water in the culvert washed away the acid so that the boy was identifiable, and Loeb dropped his custom-made glasses on the ground nearby. The police brought the two in for questioning, and eventually they confessed to the crime. Their families hired the famed, charismatic attorney Clarence Darrow, who had the young men change their pleas to guilty. Though much of the literature still calls the procedure a "trial," because they had already pleaded guilty, Leopold and Loeb had a sentencing hearing with a single judge. Unlike the procedure at a trial, the judge would not have to consider the jury's sentencing recommendation. Instead of jurors, reporters often sat in the empty jury box.[1] The judge imposed life sentences instead of the death penalty, marking a significant victory for Darrow and the defendants.

No one argued that Leopold and Loeb were typical Jewish men, given that they had planned and executed a kidnapping, a ransom demand, and a murder and had shown little remorse throughout the process. Unlike in the Bingham affair and the Leo Frank case, everyone agreed that the young men had committed the crime and that there was something profoundly wrong with them. Jews and non-Jews alike condemned the crime and its perpetrators. Even though Leopold and Loeb present a very unusual case, the hearing and the media reactions show us something much broader. The facts of the Leopold and Loeb case seemingly should have challenged the image of a gentle and nonviolent American Jewish masculinity, and yet the cultural assumptions about Jewish masculinity held fast.

How could Americans make sense of these young Jewish men? Leopold and Loeb should have presented a major challenge to the picture of American Jewish masculinity as nonviolent and gentle. The media could have portrayed a new version of Jewish male criminals. They could have adapted their portrayals to include interpersonal violence. They could have concentrated their rhetoric on the physical aggression of the crime or made connections between Jewishness and violence. But these moves were very rare. Explicit invocations of Leopold and Loeb's Jewishness appeared relatively infrequently, and the attorneys and witnesses in the hearing avoided mention of their Jewishness almost completely. On the occasions when the media mentioned it, they rarely discussed it at length. The hearing and the media, then, made sense of these young Jews who confounded their impression of Jewish masculinity by not explicitly calling attention to their Jewishness.

This does not mean that Jewishness was utterly marginal in the case, however. Although few parties engaged in explicit and lengthy discussion of Jewishness, the construction of American Jewish masculinity was both strong enough and distinctive enough that it could play a significant role even when it was only alluded to. As we have seen, ideas about American Jewish masculinity were strong in the sense that they were shared among both Jews and non-Jews and across many aspects of social life, and they were distinctive in the sense that norms of Jewish masculinity were not merely a replication of wider American norms. In this case, for instance, Jewishness, gender, and sexuality played roles in the arguments for and against giving Leopold and Loeb the death penalty, even without explicit discussion of their Jewishness. Both sides—pro-death penalty and against—linked the crime to improper masculinity and sexuality. For some observers, the Jewish criminals embodied these abnormal traits, but for others, Jews' different masculinity constituted an argument for their innocence.

Why would newspapers have spent so little time and space noting Leopold and Loeb's Jewishness? A universal embrace of Jews was certainly not the answer. Xenophobia and antisemitism were on the rise: In 1924, Congress voted in favor of the Johnson-Reed Act, which effectively closed the doors of Eastern European immigration, leaving them open but a narrow crack. Henry Ford had published his "International Jew: The World's Foremost Problem" just a few years earlier, in 1921, and was considering a run for the president. But a story about Jews committing violent murder, such as Leopold and Loeb had done, did not fit well even with this kind of antisemitic rhetoric. The violence and the murder did not accord with cultural ideas about Jewishness. Cultural ideas about Jewish masculinity ran deep, and even Jews' detractors shared assumptions about the aversion to violence and the gentleness of Jewish men.

The relative lack of discussion of Leopold and Loeb's Jewishness shows the power of the construction of American Jewish masculinity in another way: the press coverage did not often explicitly cite their Jewishness because it did not need to. Journalists and commentators were able to convey Jewishness without stating it directly. Certain characteristics—intellectual, physically weak, not fit for manual labor, perverted, and prone to illness and psychiatric imbalance—painted a gendered portrait of a Jewish man even without reference to race or religion. In his study, Paul Franklin argues for the persistent deployment and diffusion of such images even in the absence of direct accusation: "While references to homosexuality and Jewishness in the press and in the courtroom were often whispered or shrouded in innuendo, homophobia and antisemitism were nevertheless writ large in the public reception of the crime and the trial [sic]. What went unsaid in the course of the investigation and prosecution of Leopold and Loeb did so precisely because it went without saying."[2] Although the young men certainly interacted with young women, and both attorneys explored those episodes during the hearing, the experts at the hearing and the American media all indicated that Leopold and Loeb were not pursuing what were seen as proper relationships with women. Franklin demonstrates that an exploration of the representation of the young men's "homosexualist" and other "perverse" tendencies is essential to understanding the hearing.

The arguments in the hearing itself and the press coverage of that hearing emphasized four salient themes: Leopold and Loeb were abnormally gendered, they had abnormal sexuality, they were (or were not) mentally diseased, and they were also religiously deviant. In short, they were perverts with abnormal gender and mental functions. (As we see later, "pervert" connoted both sexual aberration and religious deviance.) But to what extent were these perverts responsible for their crime? That was the question. The state insisted that they were fully responsible because they were not mentally diseased, and they had therefore chosen their religious and sexual deviation. For the defense, mental disease was the cause of their sexual and religious deviation, which meant they were not fully responsible for the crime.

The cultural assumptions about the abnormal gender of Jewish crime opened the door to thinking about abnormal sexuality as a motivation for Jewish crime. If Jewish men were not sexually aggressive toward the appropriate people—adult Jewish women—then they might direct their sexual desires toward inappropriate people, such as boys or girls. Leopold and Loeb committed a violent crime related to their abnormal sexuality, which appeared in their own relationship and also possibly with the young victim.

The Leopold and Loeb case illuminates the complex relationship among Jewishness, gender, sexuality, and crime. This relationship was more associative than causal. No one argued that Jewishness caused criminal behavior or that "unmanly" men all became criminals. But when Jews did commit crimes, people imagined, the crimes were not those associated with the masculine faults of violence, aggression, or overpowering adult women sexually. This abnormal gendering of Jewish men's criminality allowed people to imagine abnormal sexuality as a motivation or criminal act. Jewish men's crimes were crimes of intellect, not passion; manipulation, not aggression; outsmarting, not overpowering. Jewish men did not commit crimes of violence—remarkably, even in the Leopold and

Loeb case, the hearing and the media classified the crime as part of Leopold's insistence on "experiment," rather than a gruesome act of murder—perhaps because Americans imagined that Jewish men had more intellect than physical prowess. When Jewish men did commit violent crimes, then, the culture needed an explanation.

This chapter tells the story of how a culture tried to make sense of a case that seemed to defy its ideas about Jewish gender. The facts of the case did not fit well with the construction of Jewish masculinity, so would observers adjust that construction, or would they find reasons to classify Leopold and Loeb as exceptions lying outside those norms but not challenging them? In the end, something like a consensus emerged: the two young men had some of the gendered characteristics of Jews, but they had strayed so far from Judaism that they should no longer be considered real Jews.

The chapter begins by showing the ways that Leopold and Loeb's gender were depicted in the hearing and the media. They were men, yes. But as soon as they confessed to the murder, the media painted them as abnormally gendered men. The next section shows how depictions of their sexuality worked in conjunction with their gender to paint them as abnormal. Then it explores how this gendered and sexual abnormality intersected with ideas of disease. Leopold and Loeb were abnormal men, everyone agreed. But were they diseased? Observers were split: those who wanted them to be spared the death penalty claimed they were; those in favor of the death penalty argued they were not. Finally, the chapter shows the critical role of religion in this discourse. By using the category of the "pervert," a word connoting both sexual deviance and religious deviance in the early twentieth century, the last section shows how religious abnormality and sexual abnormality mutually reinforced one another. Assuming that Leopold and Loeb had improper ideas about religion and God became the way that both Jews and non-Jews could make sense of these young Jewish criminals.

Abnormal Gender

From the moment the body was discovered, the crime became a media sensation.[3] As with the Bingham affair and Leo Frank case, American print media played a significant role in both shaping and reflecting public opinion. In addition, the transcript of the entire Leopold and Loeb sentencing hearing, with the exception of one portion of the proceedings borrowed by Darrow but never returned, is still extant. The investigation and hearing, like Leo Frank's trial, often focused on the defendants' departure from normative manhood in terms of gender. In the case of Leopold and Loeb, however, there was little debate about whether or not they were differently gendered. Rather, the debate was about how, how much, and whether or not their gendered abnormality connected to their culpability.

That masculinity would play a crucial role was apparent right from the start. Observers equated "manly" appearance and conduct with evidence for innocence: manly men would not have committed this crime. During the earliest stages of the investigation, a reporter interviewed Leopold and Loeb and became convinced of their innocence. He announced, "Their manly appearance and evident fearlessness were heavily in their favor."[4] The people who committed this crime would not appear manly, in the reporter's view, because such criminals are not properly masculine. If Leopold and Loeb were "manly," they could not be the perpetrators. But as law enforcement and journalists found more evidence to implicate Leopold and Loeb, descriptions of their normal masculinity marked by "manly appearance" quickly evaporated and were replaced by seemingly endless discourse about their abnormal appearance and sexuality. With this move, descriptions of them also shifted from "manly," which suggested adults, to "boys" or "young men." As they seemed more likely to be culpable of the crime, so too did they seem less manly to reporters.

Even before Leopold and Loeb were brought in for questioning, the newspapers fixated on the most telling clue: the eyeglasses found at the scene. These were no ordinary glasses, and they indicated what kind of person committed the crime. The *Chicago Daily Tribune* offered the headline, "Glasses Near Body Not Such as Man Wears." The speculation about the gender of the perpetrator continued: "A woman probably owned the pair of horn-rimmed spectacles picked up in the south side swamp. . . . 'It would be a strange man, a little bit of a wizened faced fellow, who could wear these,' said one of the opticians. . . . Not only are the circumferences of the lenses extraordinarily small for men's glasses, but the ear supports are far too short for the average masculine head, it was pointed out."[5] According to the optician, a normal man could not have worn these glasses. Chief of Detectives Michael Hughes explained how one could know other physical characteristics of the wearer from these glasses: "We know this: they were not purchased by a laboring man or a man who is employed with his hands. . . . Those who labor physically do not need such spectacles. . . . I am told it must have been a highly intelligent person who wore these glasses. A high-strung, nervous temperament."[6] Hughes's statement to the public clearly signaled the non-normative gender of the perpetrator: he would be nervous and weak, would not be a laborer, and would have a small, feminine face. These characteristics might also have suggested Jewishness. The reading glasses also gave away something else: they had a highly unusual patented hinge that the police identified and traced back to Leopold.

Ten days after the murder Leopold and Loeb were arrested. They were quickly brought in for questioning, and from then on, the press, the lawyers, and the expert witnesses no longer needed to speculate on the identity of the perpetrators; they could concentrate their speculations on the bodies and temperaments of these specific men. As the musing on the glasses suggested, one of the most obvious ways that both the medical experts who testified during the hearing and the press explored the young men's gender, sexuality, and criminality was through their bodies. The medical and the legal came together in the bodies of Leopold and Loeb. As Foucault has suggested, medical-legal discourse concerns itself primarily with "neither the medical nor the judicial"; rather "it addresses itself . . . to the category of 'abnormal individuals.'"[7] And in the Leopold and Loeb case, medical-legal testimony flooded the hearing and the papers. The discourse of this testimony constituted both Leopold and Loeb as possessing abnormal traits in a constellation of areas: physiology, sexuality, behavior, and thought. These traits served to reinforce one another, relying on and reiterating the links among criminality, abnormality, and sexuality.[8]

As the case gained publicity, famous phrenologists of the time offered their expert opinions in the press. These diagnoses often accompanied diagrammed sketches of Leopold and Loeb's faces. These diagrams combined medical information, such as the location of the pituitary gland (above the ear), with psychosexual and moral traits, such as "lacks reason, moral, and benevolent power" (on the forehead). According to one highly publicized diagram, Leopold had "sensuous lips," but the shape of his nose indicated "aggressiveness," while a spot behind his ear (circled as if by a football broadcaster) showed his "destructive instinct." His "sensuality"—a trait associated with womanhood—coexisted alongside his aggression and desire for destruction, which would have been associated with male vices. Thus Leopold was an odd mixture of masculine and feminine phenotypes, a strangely gendered character.

In addition to his "sensuous lips," Loeb also had "excessive vanity," and as one *Chicago Daily Tribune* phrenological sketch (and a similar one in the *New York Daily News*) indicated, his "feminine nature shows in the nose." The *Tribune* sketch's caption read: "A phrenologist pronounces this boy of a feminine type of mind, eager for applause and easily led,"[9] while another article discussed his "delicate hands."[10] Still another article quoted a phrenologist, who averred, "Leopold is the male, Loeb is the female, when it comes to a comparison of the temperaments of these two."[11] A psychoanalyst explained that Loeb's head showed "balance between a feminine and masculine type."[12] These articles painted both Leopold and Loeb with both masculine and feminine characteristics, noting that their differently gendered qualities were evident through their faces and bodily structure.

The press did not seem particularly concerned with differentiating Leopold and Loeb from one another, and so both were branded with abnormal sexuality and gender simultaneously. While one article cried, "Loeb Followed Leopold Whims, Expert Asserts," another announced, "Loeb 'Master' of Leopold under Solemn Made Pact; Sex Inferiority Is Factor."[13] Though the first article insisted that Leopold was dominant and the more masculine of the two men, the second article focused on his lack of masculine traits such as "his lack of physical prowess in athletics" and how he "felt inferior, physically, to others, and could not mingle on equal terms with them physically." The second article later quoted the phrenologist as saying, "The patient has always been something of a physical coward."

The *Chicago Daily Tribune* did not note any discrepancy between the two descriptions. The caption of the sketch of Leopold in the first article read, "This youth is declared by a phrenologist to be an intense believer in his own superiority over everybody." The caption of the picture (with the same notations, plus several labeled glands) in the second article claimed, "Nathan Leopold, alienists say, is mentally inferior to Loeb, and in the kidnapping and murder was acting under the latter's leadership. The phrenologist's study bears out the alienists' report." The press did not consistently describe Leopold and Loeb differently from each other, but they did assign a consistent constellation of traits to the two together. These traits, such as physical weakness, "sensuality," and other gendered characteristics, demonstrated that both Leopold and Loeb had abnormal physical and social traits.

Abnormal Sexuality

During the hearing, the prosecution often referred to the men's failed exploits with women; the point was that these men could not properly direct their sexuality. Moreover, although they were fixated on sex, they did not fruitfully experience it. The attorneys discussed how the men "picked up a couple of girls"[14] and, in reference to another event, "picking up a couple of 'Janes'" who ultimately "didn't come across."[15] Although the young men attempted, in these situations, to pursue sexual activities with women, the prosecution emphasized that Leopold and Loeb were unsuccessful. Their lack of success with "Janes" (prostitutes) indicated that even their inappropriate attempts at sex with women who purportedly have sex with any man did not culminate in success.

The most pervasive discussion of sexuality, however, focused on the men's fantasies, which were sometimes coded homosexual. The prosecution referred to their "vile and unnatural practices."[16] Robert Crowe, the state's attorney and lead prosecutor, insisted that what seemed like fainting spells or epilepsy were actually episodes of drunkenness and resulting debauchery. When Loeb was drunk one night, what looked like "frothing at the mouth" was actually his own vomit on his face. During this incident, Crowe insinuated, Loeb demonstrated his perversion: "He wanted to lick a couple of waiters."[17]

The prosecution even suggested that homosexuality might have been a motive for the crime. They sought to establish a fraught sexual relationship between the two perpetrators and then suggested that these abnormal inclinations led them to sexually assault Bobby Franks. The prosecutors dwelled extensively on a note from Leopold to Loeb suggesting that they not quarrel because people would see the argument as a "falling out of cock suckers."[18] One prosecutor asked Leopold several times if he had "commit[ed] any acts of perversion" on Loeb or another Jewish friend.[19] The attorneys read into evidence, at length, the medical examiner's report that suggested the victim's "rectum was dilated and would easily admit one middle finger," even though that same report indicated that there was no evidence of a "recent forcible dilation."[20] This detail of the particular finger seems to have been a case of an active imagination on the examiner's part, not least because an individual's fingers tend to be of similar diameter to one another. The court clearly considered this line of inquiry lurid: during a recess conversation about the "distended rectum," the court asked the women present to leave the courtroom.[21]

In addition to asking Leopold and Loeb directly about their sexual practices, both the defense and prosecution attorneys paraded a series of medical witnesses to discuss the young men's physiology and its relation to their deviant sexual behaviors and identities. The defense called the president of the American Psychiatric Association to explain how their overdeveloped intellect and underdeveloped bodies were consonant with their "manifestations of a more or less homo-sexual character," all of which suggested that they were diseased and therefore should not be held responsible to the same degree as healthy people.[22] The prosecution brought in Dr. Harold Douglas Singer, director of the Illinois State Psychopathic Institution and expert on "mental hygiene," who had read the medical reports in detail. "In that king-slave phantasy," Singer testified, "my experience with such phantasies would indicate that it has a homo-sexual significance."[23] Singer provided evidence for this interpretation of a "king-slave" fantasy as a homosexual one by citing sexual activity between Leopold and Loeb themselves: "In exchange for doing what Loeb wanted done, Loeb would submit to certain homo-sexual practices. That is a further indication of fact which would tend to support my general understanding of what such a phantasy would represent—that is, homo-sexual longing."[24] Both sides agreed that the defendants had homosexual desires and experiences and that those were relevant to the crime.

The papers found their own experts to comment on the defendants' bodies and minds, and these experts also described links between mental and sexual abnormality. They explored Leopold's supposed sadomasochistic fantasy, such as the *Chicago Daily Tribune*'s front-page banner headline, "Slayers 'King' and 'Slave,'"[25] and dozens more like it in the following weeks. Journalists marshaled phrenological diagrams to show that Loeb had a "great love of sex," but that Leopold's "sex feelings dominate his social ideals." The papers had fits of modesty, however, such as when they obliquely mentioned the men's pact dealing with "abnormal sex matters," which the *Tribune* deemed not fit to print.[26] These articles also conflated sexual practices, preference for sexual partners, physiology, and intellect. This conception of the intimate relationship between sexual and mental abnormality existed well beyond the case. For instance, in his 1917 address to the National Association of Jewish Social Workers on how to understand and pursue social work (or "relief work"), Samuel Rabinowich joined together "the mental defective, sexual degenerate, moral pervert, and the insane" into one category.[27] On a much larger stage, Sigmund Freud, Havelock Ellis, and other psychoanalysts argued for clear links between mental and sexual abnormality. Both the hearings and the media echoed this sense of the connection between Leopold and Loeb's abnormality and their crime.

Like Leo Frank, Leopold and Loeb faced speculation about their sexuality and sexual practices, and like Frank the newspapers connected any non-normative sexuality to the crime, even in the absence of evidence of sexual contact with the victim. Unlike Frank, though, there is significant evidence that Leopold and Loeb had a sexual history with one another, and although the press and the prosecution sometimes discussed their sexual interest in women, they fixated on the defendants' sexual desires for and experiences with men. In this, the press depicted the heterosexual, married Leo Frank and the former lovers Leopold and Loeb as having very similar excessive (and yet also failed) sexualities: all three could not properly direct their urges toward the "proper" people—adult Jewish women—but instead their sexuality came out in all sorts of wrong places toward the wrong people.

Whereas the prosecution referred to Leopold and Loeb as "men," the defense consistently used the word "boys." Darrow's closing remarks emphasized the issue of the defendants' age, insisting that "children" should never be put to death by the state: "I told your honor in the beginning that never had there been a case in Chicago, where on a plea of guilty a boy under 21 had been sentenced to death." He cited cases in which thirteen- and fourteen-year olds had been put to death—in the eighteenth century! Darrow chastised the prosecution for its backward-looking arguments, which "would be a disgrace to a race of savages." The prosecuting lawyers "stand here and read cases from the dark ages, where judges have said that if a man had a grain of sense left, it he was barely out of his cradle, he could be hanged because he knew the difference between right and wrong."[28] Darrow complained of the state: "Let me tell you something that I think is cowardly, whether [Leopold and Loeb's] acts were or not. Here is Dickie Loeb and Nathan Leopold, and the State objects to anybody calling one 'Dickie' and the other 'Babe' although everybody does, but they think they can hang them easier if their names are Richard and Nathan."[29] Darrow and the defense called them "boys" and used their nicknames, whereas the prosecution insisted on their full first names. The language of each side indicated each one's argument about life stage and criminal responsibility: perverted criminal "men" should be punished to the fullest extent, whereas perverted "boys" might not be sufficiently blameworthy to call for the death penalty.

Mental Disease

Both the prosecution and the defense agreed that Leopold and Loeb were mentally abnormal. But was this abnormality a disease? The prosecution argued that it was not. Sexual and criminal forms of deviance were related to their mental abnormality, according to the prosecution, providing evidence of their moral deficiency, but not of actual disease. The defense, in contrast, claimed that the "boys" suffered from mental disease and were therefore less culpable and should not receive the death penalty. The defendants' failure to live up to the norms of gender and sexuality would be the essential quality that helped convince the judge that their minds were guilty. However, the defense did not argue for their insanity because Leopold and Loeb had already entered a plea of "guilty" rather than "not guilty by reasons of insanity." Therefore, during the hearing, Darrow claimed that the salient categories were not sane and insane, but rather healthy and diseased.

One expert witness for the defense testified:

Q: You think he is insane then?

A: I don't think anything about it.

Q: He is sane?

A: I didn't use the words "sane" or "insane." . . . To my mind, this crime is the result of a diseased motivation.[30]

Leopold's and Loeb's abnormal minds were "diseased minds," the defense argued, and therefore they could not be held culpable to the same degree as someone with a healthy mind. Darrow posed this hypothetical argument: if the defense had chosen to make the case about Leopold and Loeb's sanity, the prosecution might say, "They may be mentally diseased, they may be abnormal, they may be everything you say but they know the difference between right and wrong and therefore they should be found guilty." It was for precisely this reason that Darrow deftly moved the grounds of the argument to the categories of health and disease as the basis for the sentence. Mental disease did not constitute "an adequate defense to the charge of murder," but the judge should consider it a factor in the "mitigation of the punishment," he claimed.[31]

Discussions of the relationship among sanity, insanity, and mental disease recurred throughout the sentencing hearing. The transcript indicates that the attorneys and judge spent at least three hours on the discussion of the difference between "mental disease" and "insanity" alone. Therefore it seems likely that the prosecution and the defense, along with the countless alienists and phrenologists, thought that the young men were in fact somehow defective. Some scholars argue that this defectiveness was all the more convincing because of its link to Jewishness: they were sexually deviant, raised in a rich and therefore infinitely permissive environment, and physically small and weak.[32]

The prosecution also brought experts to argue against any evidence of mental disease. Alienist William Krohn testified for the prosecution that his examination of the defendants revealed that they were mentally, if not morally, sound. Singer, despite his interpretation of their homosexual fantasies, insisted that both Loeb and Leopold had "healthy minds." He noted that they were not normal, but this was no reason to think of them as medically unwell: "In the first place, a paranoid personality is not a disease."[33] He explained that both paranoid personality and split personality, which affected both defendants in his estimation, were "entirely compatible with normal mental health."[34] He referred to x-rays and his analysis of the size of Loeb's sella turcica bone and the skull overall, as well the size of his pineal gland, to show visually how they were smaller than normal but should not be considered a sign of illness.

On the other side, in order to argue for a judicial diagnosis of disease, defense attorney Walter Bacharach read extensively from *Insanity and the Law.* The defense brought in experts who testified that Leopold and Loeb were most certainly abnormal and that their actions and perversions were the results of their diseased minds. Darrow, spunky as always, summed up the judge's choices: "There are only two theories; one is that their diseased brains drove them to it; the other is the old theory of possession by devils, and my friend Marshall could have read you books on that, too, but that has been pretty well given up in Illinois."[35]

Judge Caverly ultimately agreed that the young men were in fact abnormal and therefore exercised leniency in his sentencing: they would be imprisoned for life instead of executed. The decision was rendered in large part because of the expert witnesses' testimony. Caverly noted "the mass of data produced as to the physical, mental, and moral condition of the two defendants. They have been shown in essential respects to be abnormal," he explained.[36] Here Foucault's claims about courtroom testimony suggest the links between medical and legal modes of knowledge: "Expert opinion allows the offense, as defined by the law, to be doubled with a whole series of other things that are not the offense itself but a series of forms of conduct, of ways of being that are, of course, presented in the discourse of the psychiatric expert as the cause, origin, motivation, and starting point of the offense. In fact, in the reality of judicial practice, they constitute the substance, the very material to be punished."[37] In this way, Leopold and Loeb's "abnormality"—as demonstrated by interpretations of their sexualities—were both the cause and content of the crime. Their sexual and gendered abnormalities, complete with physiological and biographical "evidence" to confirm them, became consolidated with the crime.

Given that this "evidence" emphasized their Jewish traits, the media's construction of Leopold and Loeb further confirmed the figure of the abnormally sexualized Jew in the cultural imaginary. Unlike the coverage of the Leo Frank case, most articles did not explicitly state that Leopold and Loeb were Jewish, but this did not mean that their Jewishness escaped the public's notice. The *Chicago Defender*, a widely circulated newspaper written primarily by and for African Americans, summed up the crime: "Two rich young men, Nathan Leopold and Richard Loeb, suffering from some curious disease of the brain, kill a 14-year-old boy, hide his body, burn up his clothing, then, cornered by a pair of strangely-made spectacles, confess." However, the *Defender* continued, there was one "point you must not overlook: the two rich young men and their victim, Robert Franks, are all members of the Jewish race. . . . But you have not read in the papers that 'Nathan Leopold and Richard Loeb, members of rich Jew families have confessed to the murder."[38] The *Defender* implicitly compared the media coverage of these Jewish criminals to that of black criminals. Newspapers rarely failed to point out when a perpetrator was "a Negro," but in this case, Leopold and Loeb's Jewishness often went without remark. The *Defender* was on to something when it observed this trend. But the *Defender* implied that it occurred because Jews consistently got a cultural pass where blacks did not. However, as the Bingham affair and Frank case showed, sometimes Americans did call attention to Jewishness and insist on its relationship to certain kinds of crime; though not to the extent that blacks had, Jews had been maligned as a distinctive criminal element in a racialized way in earlier court cases and in the media. But that was not so in this case.

Religion

Leopold and Loeb were atheists. Anyone who read the papers knew it. "At the university on the admission card he preferred to register 'Atheist,'" H. S. Hulbert, one of the alienists who testified for the defense, reminded the judge during his testimony. "He believes there is no God, therefore, no right and wrong," declared the *Washington Post* on the front page of its Sunday, August 10, 1924, edition.[39] In another front-page story, the *Los Angeles Times* printed one of Crowe's question-and-answer sessions with Leopold:

Q: What, if any, religious belief do you entertain?

A: None.

Q: What is your idea of the existence of God?

A: I don't believe there is a God.

Q: What do you believe becomes of you when you die?

A: Your ashes return to ashes and your dust to dust. . . .

Q: You are what is popularly known as an atheist?

A: Yes.[40]

Religion became important during the hearing not as an isolated category, but as one inextricably tied to gender, sexuality, and normality. Religious deviance and sexual deviance each provided evidence for the other. Lawyers on both sides agreed that the defendants' denial of "religion," like their abnormal sexualities, was a bad thing. But while the defense argued that these two were evidence of disease, the prosecution claimed both were yet more evidence of moral failure and "bad judgment." Whether the simultaneous religious and sexual abnormality joined their criminality as yet another effect of their disease, or their choice to stray from religion was a cause of their sexual and criminal behaviors remained in debate. What was not up for debate, however, was the fact that these three were intimately related.

Media coverage of the Leopold and Loeb case provides a fascinating view into the ways in which the religious pervert and the sexual pervert were linked in the cultural imaginary. It shows how the category of religion, generically deployed, could construct criminality and sexuality. Scholars who have studied the case have noted Leopold and Loeb's atheism and interest in Nietzsche, but the role of religion has largely been mentioned only in passing. Throughout the hearing and often in the press, lawyers and writers used the generic term "religion," which masked the slippage between general concepts of theism and the particulars of Christianity. As both Jews and atheists, of course, Leopold and Loeb departed from both, which facilitated this slippage. (In fact, Loeb's mother was Catholic, but he was not raised Catholic, and the fact almost never came up in media discussions of the case.) Although neither scripture nor practice became a focal point, religious imagery, allusions, and, most of all, Leopold and Loeb's beliefs recurred throughout the hearing; thus the Leopold and Loeb case shows how the idea of religion contributed to the construction of sexuality.

When the press called Leopold and Loeb "perverts," it participated in a broader, early twentieth-century discourse about sexual desires and practices that differed from normative heterosexuality. Sexologists, in particular Havelock Ellis, Richard von Krafft-Ebing, and Sigmund Freud, had popularized the term "perversion" as an umbrella term including homosexuality, fetishes, and other nonprocreative sexual desires and behaviors. Despite Ellis's contention that perversion was a widespread and neutral fact of human sexuality, the term had entered popular discourse with a negative connotation. Average newspaper subscribers who had never read Ellis or Freud knew a "pervert" to be a sexual deviant.

But the term "perversion" had a longer history. Etymologically, it refers to a "turning from," and its earliest connotations were not about sexuality, but about moral or religious rightness. In his *Consolation of Philosophy*, the sixth-century Christian philosopher Boethius uses it in this sense. "[B]y their perversion to badness," he wrote of wicked men, "they have lost their true nature."[41] For Boethius and his medieval popularizers and interpreters, perversion meant turning away from what is right. "Pervert" came to apply to an apostate who had turned away from God and church, as in nineteenth-century descriptions of a person as a "pervert from the church."[42] This pervert could be either one who converted away from a religion or one who had left while expressing dissent and critique, but both implied deviation from religious norms and community.

In the closing statement of Cook County state's attorney Robert Crowe, these two perversions—religious and sexual—met in the persons of Leopold and Loeb, where they constituted evidence for their criminality and culpability. Crowe began by establishing his own religious stance, from which he would critique the perverted defendants—as well as take a shot at Darrow: "I believe in God, and that is a fault in this case, a fault not only to the two murderers, but a fault to the master pleader whose profession it is to protect murder in this county."[43] Moments later, alluding to the Lord's Prayer, he contrasted his explicitly Christian creed with the confused and wayward atheism of Leopold: "I have a right to forgive those who trespass against me in the hopes that I will in the hereafter be forgiven my trespasses. . . . I live that religion."[44]

But where Crowe claimed to emulate Jesus in forgiveness, he also claimed another version—a *per*version—of the story of the life of Christ within the case. He used elements of the story of the nativity to parody three expert witnesses in Leopold's and Loeb's defense. The hearing took place in the summer, so Crowe's comparison to the nativity story was all the more remarkable and not something we can write off as a ubiquitous seasonal allusion. "The three wise men from the East, who came on to tell your honor about those little babes and being three wise men brought on from the East, they wanted to make the picture a little more perfect." These three medical doctors had testified for the defense, providing medical evidence for the abnormality of Leopold and Loeb. Capitalizing perhaps on the Midwestern suspicion of East Coast city dwellers or even associations between Jews and northeastern cities, Crowe cast these doctors as foreigners who had arrived to tell a tale about Leopold and Loeb. At the same time he parodied the idea that Leopold and Loeb—or Babe and Dickie, as the defense called them—were mere children or childlike in their development. Crowe often sneeringly repeated the alienist William White's testimony that Leopold still talked to his teddy bear. He mocked the idea that Leopold and Loeb were innocent babes, who were brought gifts in the form of testimony by wise doctors from afar.

These "wise men," Crowe went on, presented stories of Leopold and Loeb as religiously confused, and here Crowe used the language of "pervert" in both its senses. One of these "wise men . . . was sacrilegious enough to say this pervert, this murderer, this kidnaper thought that he was the Christ child and that he thought that his mother was the Madonna, without a syllable of evidence anyplace to support the blasphemous and sacrilegious statement. Who said that this young pervert over there thought he was the Christ child?" Here Crowe referred to H. S. Hulbert, who had told the story of Leopold seeing a church's stained-glass window that depicted the Madonna and Christ child and then identifying his own mother with Mary. In his retelling of the defense's testimony, Crowe narrated an inversion of the nativity: The wise men were "sacrilegious" and "blasphemous," and they misidentified Christ. Or worse, they identified a false Christ. Leopold himself had deviated in his religious beliefs, and the alienists had followed suit. When Crowe called Leopold "this pervert, this kidnaper, this murderer" and "this young pervert over there," his word choice could allude to both Leopold's religious straying and his sexual acts.[45] Moreover, Leopold had also perverted the Virgin Mary by replacing her with his mother.

Darrow's summary also slid between Leopold's sexual perversion and his religious perversion in a way that suggested they were part and parcel of the same problem. "They found out something about Leopold; his sex life, his early sex life. He had some trouble," he summarized the expert medical testimony. "There were endocrine disorders. There was a phantasy life. There was the king-slave phantasy. There was a prolongation of the same phantasy over a period of years." Darrow continued with the litany of abnormalities: "His interest in religion. Your Honor remembers the churches. The idea his mother was a Madonna, his aunt was a Madonna. He classified the churches. His Christ idea. His atheism. That was confirmed by his mother's death."[46] Thus Darrow began his summary with Leopold's sexual perversion and ended with his religious perversion. In Darrow's account, his errant sexuality and errant religion were both results of his medical abnormalities.

This discursive link among religious deviance, sexual deviance, and criminality functioned as what Foucault calls a "switch point." Despite a lack of empirical evidence for these links—perhaps even because of a lack of empirical evidence—the medical-legal discourse posited their relationship. Foucault shows how the idea of perversity allowed medical ideas to function in the judicial context.[47] Medical doctors could provide expert testimony about their interpretations of a defendant's sexuality and mental conditions, which served as evidence for their guilt or innocence. For Foucault—and Leopold and Loeb—what allowed the construction of simultaneously criminal and sexual abnormality was this medical-legal discourse.

The Leopold and Loeb hearing shows us the nexus of religious, sexual, and medical abnormality, and legal culpability. During the hearing, attorneys repeatedly asked witnesses to explain the sexual practices, sexual desires, mental health, and religious ideas of the defendants. Dr. Hulbert, witness for the defense, said of Loeb, "My opinion is that he is not normal physically or mentally, and there is a close relation between his physical abnormalities, largely of the endocrine system, and his mental condition." Of Leopold, "His endocrine disorder is responsible for the following mental findings: his precocious mental development . . . that he fatigues if he overexerts himself and is nonaggressive. . . . [The fact that he is] neurotic and unmoral, and at the same time keen and witty is of endocrine origin. The early development of his sex urge is obviously of endocrine origin."[48] He also explained, "I have come to the conclusion that his sex glands are over functioning because of his short, stocky build . . . and the strong sex urge." The medical doctors tied together physical descriptions (fatigue, short build, "coarse hair," "round shouldered"), assessments about sexuality (a "strong sex urge"), and criminality ("unmoral"). Despite its incoherencies, this web of connections functioned effectively in the production of the cultural imaginary. Leopold and Loeb were "nonaggressive," had "coarse hair," experienced "muscle fatigue," and were "neurotic," so even when no one said they were Jewish, these cultural code words still suggested Jewishness. In addition, the pseudo-scientific discourse of phrenological sketches allowed Americans to "see" how these two Jewish men did not embody appropriate norms of manliness.[49]

Yet Crowe, Darrow, Hulbert, and other witnesses for both sides also explicitly commented on the defendants' religion. Many of the medical doctors offered their expert testimony on Leopold and Loeb's religious lives. The fact that they would begin a description of Leopold with comments on his religion should be remarkable. And yet, it happened time and again during the hearing. Hulbert explained of Leopold: "In his religious studies he was intensely interested in classification, as he was in other things too, and he finally found fault with God and as far as he was concerned he abolished God because God makes mistakes. . . . He then became an atheist. . . . Leopold finally conceived life existing without any god and there being no God there is no right or wrong *per se*." When the state's witness Dr. Church was asked about Leopold's beliefs and conduct, he said he could not comment, "excepting as to his attitude on religion." Both doctors saw themselves—and were seen by both attorneys—as possessing expert knowledge about the defendants' religion because they had knowledge of their physiology and, they also assumed, their sexuality.

For both the prosecution and the defense, then, Leopold and Loeb fit both the religious and the sexual definitions of perversion. Like Crowe, Darrow assumed that the two were connected, but their interpretation of the meaning of these perversions differed. Crowe argued that they were both evidence of poor character and morality, whereas Darrow argued that they were symptoms of mental disease. Several days before the closing statements, the defense had explicitly claimed that religious perversion was in fact a symptom of disease. Bacharach argued, "One of the symptoms of a paranoiac, as your honor will soon see, is that he usually has delusions of grandeur. He has delusions of self-importance, he has delusions that he is greater than anybody else. He identifies himself with some great religious character, with some king, or with some potentate of some kind, or with Christ, or with God."[50] The defense suggested that being a "paranoiac" was, in this case, basically a delusion of religion.

This paranoia was not merely a mental delusion; it extended to actions. Therefore, "the fact that he does not formulate his delusions into so many words, and go around saying, 'I am God Almighty,' does not in any way militate against the proposition that he believes he is."[51] Even if Leopold never announced that he was God, his behavior nevertheless could provide evidence of his religious delusion. If he "has acted as if were God Almighty, or Jesus, or Emperor Napoleon, you have just as much evidence of a delusion as if he went around saying it."[52] Darrow explained that these religious beliefs were not merely odd. They were evidence of mental disease: "What we claim is, if the court please, that his belief shows he is mentally diseased; that his belief in the superman, or that he is a superman, shows that his mind is not functioning properly, and shows that he has the tendencies of what the books call paranoid personality."[53]

For Darrow and the defense, Leopold and Loeb were perverts in both religious and sexual senses, and both perversions constituted evidence of disease. Crowe and the prosecution agreed that the defendants' "bad judgment" in perverting themselves from God facilitated sexual perversion as well as the kidnapping and murder. However, they maintained that both perversions were evidence of their badness, but not of disease. It would then be up to Judge Caverly to decide which account of perversion and culpability he found convincing in the case of the two young Jews. During the hearing, however, Caverly was not the only audience who inclined his ear toward the story of the crime and its punishment. The press reflected the hearing's focus on Leopold and Loeb's religious beliefs and philosophy, which both prosecution and defense suggested were tied to their sexual practices.

In addition, the Jewish community expressed its own concern about Leopold and Loeb's religious identification. However, instead of linking Jewishness to the cause of their abnormality, some reporters and editors in the Jewish press explained that its cause was precisely too little Judaism. For instance, Samuel Melamed, the editor of the *Chicago Jewish Courier*, wrote an article accusing the boys of deserting the Jewish religion and people. The *Chicago Daily Tribune* picked up the article and reprinted it under the headline, "Jewish Spokesman Says Crime Is Due to Neglect of Judaism." Leopold and Loeb never would have committed such a crime if they felt the responsibility and morals that were instilled by Jewish learning and communal belonging, Melamed argued. "If the parents of these two boys had given the children a Jewish education," he explained, "if they both had borne on their shoulders individual responsibility, if they had interested themselves in Jewish problems, if their hearts had bled for their people, if they had been consciously Jewish with Jewish souls, they would certainly not have devoted their entire time to 'pleasure and good times,' and would not have had the possibilities of going wrong. But both boys knew nothing of Judaism."[54] Melamed suggested that Judaism and its themes of both individual responsibility and responsibility to a group would have been a preventive force for boys who otherwise pursued "pleasure."

Melamed, also an ardent Zionist, suggested that these unfortunate boys lacked a sense of group belonging, in addition to lacking religious principles. Because they were neither Zionists nor members of the Jewish community, they could stray from the paths of morality and proper masculinity: "You can't convince me that if these two capable Jewish boys had interested themselves in Jewish problems in the Diaspora and Palestine—if they carried on their shoulders Jewish responsibility—that they would have surrendered themselves to such wild and unnatural passions."[55] If they had become good Zionists, perhaps they would be properly manly Jews and not "examples of moral anarchy." Without any sense of Judaism and Jewish belonging, they went astray: "The truth is that these two Jewish boys were not under the influence of Judaism, and they were not Jewish products, and the Jewish people have no moral control over them." He declined to explain the details of these "unnatural passions," but his article, published in both Jewish and non-Jewish newspapers, linked Judaism and the Jewish community to morality and distance from them to moral error and sexual deviance.

Melamed also worried that, despite his efforts to distance Leopold and Loeb from the Jewish community, non-Jews would still equate their abnormality and immorality with Jewishness: "Nevertheless, the anti-Semites will not fail to remind us that they are Jews and they will hold us responsible for the crime of two individuals who had no moral, religious, or social connection with us."[56] Melamed was only partly correct. Although media coverage frequently alluded to Leopold and Loeb's Jewishness alongside their sexual deviance, it rarely blamed Judaism or called on the Jewish community to account for the two young criminals. The Leopold and Loeb hearing had no analog of Tom Watson and his ilk, who had called Frank "the Jew libertine" and assailed the Jewish community for producing and supporting sexual predators. Even antisemites did not suggest that Leopold and Loeb were representative of other Jews.

The *National Jewish Monthly*, published by B'nai B'rith, likewise tied the crime and Leopold and Loeb's sexuality to their abandonment of the God of Israel. They explained that the boys had come to "logical ending of those who . . . deny the fact of God. Leopold and Loeb glory in their atheism and to this it has brought them."[57] Their crime was "reprehensible to normal minds."

The community sought to shift the discourse from the level of generalized Jewish racial or ethnic traits to the specific beliefs and actions of Leopold and Loeb as individuals. By painting them as "abnormal" according to the standards of Judaism, the Jewish community could align itself with broader American ideals. Jews displaced sexual and criminal abnormality from Jewishness in general to the particular bodies of these "boys" as one part of a larger project to claim Americanness for Jews and to shore up the normative value of Judaism as a moral religion.

Jews were not the only ones concerned about the religious beliefs and identification of the two young criminals. Non-Jewish religious leaders worried whether the crime reflected broader social trends. In June the Methodist minister Bob Shuler preached a sermon asking whether Leopold and Loeb should be hanged. "Our young people are becoming morally insane," he railed, and he asked rhetorically whether "painted faces, modern dress, present-day dances and pictures, bobbed hair and petting parties, modern-day dances [are] signs of moral decay."[58] Shuler claimed that made-up faces and "petting parties" were clear instances of sexuality outside of the proper bounds. Bobbed hair on women was an example of gender bending: short hair was for men, and women had decided to shear their long locks in favor of such masculine looks. He linked these violations of sexual and gendered propriety to violations of moral standards. "Moral insanity" was a corollary of violating gendered norms, and Leopold and Loeb were the most recent example of this perversion. For Shuler, and for others, they represented the extreme outcome, the horrible end to which all this modern dress and painted faces would lead.

The famed baseball-player-turned-evangelist Billy Sunday also depicted the crime as an example of moral decay in an article in the *Chicago Herald and Examiner*: "I think this hideous crime can be traced to the moral miasma which contaminates some of our 'young intellectuals.' It is now considered fashionable for higher education to scoff at God. The world is headed for Hades so fast that no speed limit can stop it."[59] He saw the two godless intellectuals as a sign of the moral decay of the nation: "Precocious brains, salacious books, infidel minds—all these helped to produce this murder."[60] Sunday's diagnosis suggested Jewishness without explicitly, or perhaps even consciously, considering it.

The stereotype of the overly intellectual Jew had pervaded anti-Jewish discourse from Henry Ford to William McAdoo's Jews and their "wordy arguments." As "infidels," Leopold and Loeb's non-Christian identity came to the fore. Intellect, bookishness, and rejection of Christianity could easily add up to Jewishness. Yet later that fall, Chicago-based Lutheran minister W. B. Norton held up the Leopold and Loeb hearing as a concern for all Americans, not just Jews. It was, he said, "nationwide in its effect. Such a crime can only come from a lack of the cultivation of the moral and religious life."[61] The kidnapping of a boy and the sexual perversions of the two defendants were a direct result of their refusal of religion. The Pentecostal pastor S. P. Lang insisted that Leopold and Loeb's only chance for salvation was to be hanged. Their crime grew out of their childhood where, Lang claimed, "the environment of the boys was such as to preclude any religious training."[62] All agreed that the lack of proper religious training had facilitated the boys' perversions, religious and sexual. They also saw Leopold and Loeb's crime and apparent moral indifference as indicators of the religious state of the nation.

The idea of "proper religion" in the Leopold and Loeb case also spurred conversation in a hotbed of religious debate: the ongoing fundamentalist-modernist debates in American Protestantism. Modernist and Unitarian minister Charles Francis Potter and his fundamentalist rival John Roach Straton exchanged words on the subject from their respective New York City pulpits. The *New York Times* reported that Straton said, "These young men are simply Modernists who have let their Modernism go to the full and logical limit of utter unbelief in God and heartlessness toward man. They are simply believers in the brute struggle for existence and the survival of the fittest."[63] Leopold and Loeb were yet more signs of the times. They had abandoned religion. If modernists were honest with themselves, Straton suggested, they would know that their theological positions and openness to Darwinism led to atheism and an utter lack of empathy. Straton took the sentencing hearing as an opportunity to reissue his warning about the dangers of modernism and the current path of American religion as he saw it: "I will sound once more a note of warning from this pulpit that more and more we can expect such things as this unless Modernism is checked, and unless faith is reestablished in a living God, and unless the authority of God as revealed in the Bible is taught to our children in our homes and churches and schools."[64] For Straton, Leopold and Loeb symbolized the dangers of modernism. Their crime and wanton atheism were a harbinger of things to come if modernism was left unchecked. Although for Straton, Protestant fundamentalism was best, he did not take issue with Leopold and Loeb's Jewishness. He identified the cause of the criminality as Leopold's and Loeb's desertion of religion, God, and the Bible. At the same time, he emphasized two of the tenets of his own fundamentalism: a revealed Bible and an authoritative living God. If Americans did not believe in these tenets, "such things as this" terrible crime would proliferate across the country.

Potter countered with his own, very different analysis of the crime and punishment. "We have witnessed this last week the remarkable spectacle of a Christian judge in sentencing two Hebrew boys for murder refusing to abide by the ancient law of their own people, although it is the established and generally accepted law of Christian countries." Potter did not argue against the value of Christianity. Quite the opposite: he argued for the superiority of Christianity, but for quite different reasons—and for a Christianity that was quite different from Straton's. Potter's Christianity demonstrated its superiority in its mercy and its support of moral and scientific progress. Earlier in the hearing, Potter had preached a sermon that denounced a witch hunt for "Modernist professors" and called for "a balanced philosophy, a religion for today which will recognize science, for the truth which science seeks and the truth which religion seeks are ultimately the same thing."[65] Judge Caverly acted in a Christian manner precisely when he refused the "ancient law" of the "Hebrews" of an eye for an eye. Instead, he went against both "ancient law" and "generally accepted law" to bestow mercy. In doing so, Caverly showed the progress of Christianity and its crucial role in promoting civilization, in Potter's eyes.

In their dueling sermons, Potter and Straton latched onto the Leopold and Loeb case as an important event for understanding American Christianity and its path. The following week the *New York Times* printed another story about the Potter/Straton theological feud. It quoted Potter as saying, "I heard my worthy opponent say in his pulpit last Sunday evening that it was the devil that made Leopold and Loeb kill the Franks boy. 'This crime,' he said, 'has come from the true adversary of God and man; we ought to call men away from the traps of the devil.' Then he went on to blame the Modernists for it all; and showed that he believed Modernism a child of the devil."[66] Straton and Potter, two loud voices in the fundamentalist-modernist controversy and minor players in the following year's Scopes trial, claimed from their pulpits that the crime and punishment of Leopold and Loeb showed the trajectory of religion in America.

The announcement of the verdict would provoke another round of sermons. Judge Caverly pronounced the sentence of life imprisonment on September 10, 1924, saying that Leopold and Loeb "have been shown in essential respects to be abnormal."[67] They might not be insane, but they did suffer from mental disease. However, Caverly claimed that their mental disease did not figure into his decision, but rather cited their ages as the reason not to impose the death penalty. At eighteen and nineteen, they were not fully developed, he explained. Caverly's pronouncement notwithstanding, the attorneys, papers, and religious leaders thought the case was about the gender, sexual, and religious deviance of two young men.

The *Washington Post* reported that six sermons preached on the Sunday after the sentencing, on September 14, 1924, in and around Chicago all spoke out against Caverly's decision not to sentence Leopold and Loeb to death. The sermon by Rev. William McNamee of St. Patrick's in Joliet was emblematic of these messages. It accused Darrow of attempting "to undermine the philosophy on which our civilization is based."[68] McNamee insisted, "We have real Christianity and we're not groping around in the dark, as Mr. Darrow seems to be. . . . We must condemn the false philosophy which Judge Caverly's decision advocates. We must have real men on the bench, not weaklings. It is a sorry setback for our reputed democracy." McNamee suggested that, by defending Leopold and Loeb against the death penalty and arguing for their decreased culpability, Darrow was undermining "our civilization," which he connected with "real Christianity." Caverly had followed Darrow down this dark and un-Christian path, and therefore Caverly was weak and not a "real man." Furthermore, such unmanly actions undermined the nation. Darrow, Caverly, Leopold, and Loeb had all deviated from Christianity, manliness, civilization, and the true nation of America by their actions.

The *Chicago Sunday Tribune* summarized the one-of-a-kind crime: "The wealth and prominence of the families whose sons are involved; the high mental attainment of the youths, the suggestions of perversions; the strange quirks indicated in the confession that the child was slain for a ransom, for experience, for the satisfaction of a desire for deep plotting; combined to set the case in a class by itself."[69] Whether the crime was "in a class by itself" or it was a symptom and an indicator of the state of American morality and religion as many of the clergy had opined, both Jews and non-Jews paid attention. It showed how not to be a man, how not to be an American, how not to be a Jew. It was masculinity, abnormality, and crime at its worst.

Conclusion

This chapter analyzed the ways that the Leopold and Loeb hearing and its media coverage claimed that the two young criminals did not exhibit normative manhood. It then moved to show how depictions of their sexuality joined with depictions of gender to portray Leopold and Loeb as abnormal. Then it showed how the construction of abnormality intersected with the construction of disease. All observers agreed that Leopold and Loeb were abnormal, but the question of whether they were diseased generated disagreement. Those who wanted them to be spared the death penalty claimed they were ill and therefore were less culpable; those in favor of the death penalty argued they did not suffer from disease. Finally, the chapter explored the double valence of the category "pervert"—both religious and sexual—to show how religious abnormality and sexual abnormality mutually reinforced one another.

In the end, then, the Leopold and Loeb hearing could have seriously challenged some of the assumptions about American Jewish masculinity, but it did not. Instead of taking the case as evidence that Jewish men could be violent, aggressive, and dominating, the media and the public took it as evidence that Leopold and Loeb were not really Jewish.

In the early twentieth century, American discussions of Jewish criminality revealed more general assumptions about Jewish men: they were nonviolent, not physically strong or confrontational, and not sexually aggressive toward women. This discourse echoed widely in the Bingham affair. But how could people make sense of the confessed violent murderers, Leopold and Loeb? Leo Frank was dragged to the gallows because of his alleged deviation from gender and sexual norms, but Clarence Darrow used these same representations to medicalize the Jewish deviations from sexual and gender norms and save Leopold and Loeb from execution.

The mainstream press often insinuated links between the defendants' Jewishness and real or imagined deviations from norms of sexual practices and desires. In both cases, members of the Jewish community took the opportunity to distance Judaism and Jewish community from "perversion" and deviance from sexual norms. Jewish men might be less aggressive, gentler, or otherwise differ from American norms of manliness, these Jewish sources implied, but Judaism in no way sanctioned the kinds of sexual acts these men had been accused of committing.

Taken together with the Bingham affair, the Leo Frank and Leopold and Loeb cases display a tightly woven web of assumptions about Jewishness, gender, sexuality, and crime. Jewishness was not tautologically associated with crime, but when Jewish men did commit crimes, both Jews and non-Jews assumed they were of a certain sort: perhaps conniving or profit-driven, but without violence, confrontation, or aggression. Jewish crimes, then, were not manly crimes. So how could Americans make sense of Jews who did commit violent crimes? Either they could dismiss them as anomalous, as Jenna Weissman Joselit and Gil Ribak show they did in many of the cases of Jewish organized crime, or they could come up with another explanation. In the Leopold and Loeb case and for those who thought Leo Frank guilty, that other explanation was abnormal sexuality: they were perverts.

Jews and non-Jews, the accused and their defenders alike, the participants and the media—in these three cultural moments, each agreed that abnormal masculinity and sexuality were linked with criminality. Improper religion too was both a cause of and evidence for criminality and abnormal sexuality. The Jewish community defended itself against Bingham with statistics, but it assented to the characterization of Jewish crime as nonaggressive. Jewish crime *was* different from non-Jewish crime, Jews implicitly argued, and such nonviolent masculinity was a good thing. Those who thought Leo Frank was guilty called him a pervert and a "libertine Jew," while those who maintained his innocence called attention to his connections to his wife, mother, and rabbi. Everyone knew that Leopold and Loeb were murderers, and thus everyone agreed that they had strayed from Judaism and had abnormal sexual desires and practices. The only question up for debate was just how deep their abnormality went and what the implications for their moral culpability would be.

Despite their markedly different circumstances, then, each of these three cultural moments linked crime with different masculinity and improper sexuality;

for some observers, the Jewish criminals embodied these abnormal traits, but for others, Jews' different masculinity constituted an argument for their innocence. In each case too, the cultural conversation aligned proper religion with normative gender and sexuality and associated the lack of religion with abnormal gender and sexuality and crime.

Notes

1. "Evidence against Loeb and Leopold Finished by State," *Los Angeles Times*, July 30, 1924, 1–2.

2. Paul B. Franklin, "Jew Boys, Queer Boys," in *Queer Theory and the Jewish Question*, ed. Daniel Boyarin, Daniel Itzkovitz, and Ann Pellegrini. (New York: Columbia University Press, 2002), 122.

3. And as Paula Fass has shown in her study of the case and its recurring role in American literature and film, it has continued to captivate Americans ever since. Paula Fass, "Making and Remaking an Event: The Leopold and Loeb Trial in American Culture," *Journal of American History* 80, no. 3 (Dec. 1993): 919–951.

4. "Shake Leopold-Loeb Alibi," *Chicago Daily Tribune*, May 31, 1924.

5. *Chicago Daily Tribune*, May 24, 1924, quoted in Franklin, "Jew Boys, Queer Boys."

6. "Try to See Franks Slayer through His Spectacles," *Chicago Daily Tribune*, May 29, 1924.

7. Foucault, *Abnormal*, 41–42.

8. See, in particular, the Jan. 8, 1975, lecture in Foucault, *Abnormal*, 1–30.

9. Quoted in "Another Study of Slayers," *Chicago Daily Tribune*, June 5, 1924; "Loeb Followed Leopold Whims, Expert Asserts," *Chicago Daily Tribune*, June 5, 1924. Also quoted in Franklin, "Jew Boys, Queer Boys."

10. "Elite of the Jail Think Leopold Aint So Much," *Chicago Daily Tribune*, June 4, 1924.

11. John Herrick, "Loeb Followed Leopold Whims" *Chicago Daily Tribune*, June 5, 1924.

12. "Charles Bonniwell Analyzes Characteristics of Student Slayers and Reveals their Inner Characters," *Chicago Herald and Examiner*, June 1, 1924. Also quoted in Franklin, "Jew Boys, Queer Boys."

13. "Loeb Followed Leopold Whims"; "Slayers King and Slave: Loeb 'Master' of Leopold under Solemn Pact Made; Sex Inferiority Is Factor," *Chicago Daily Tribune*, July 28, 1924.

14. Leopold and Loeb hearing transcript (July–Sept. 1924), 391.

15. Ibid., 485.

16. Ibid., 4260.

17. Ibid., 4232.

18. Ibid., 831–832.

19. Ibid., 831.

20. Ibid., 95.

21. Ibid., 4215.

22. Dr. William Alanson White, "Report on Richard Loeb and Nathan Leopold, Leopold-Loeb Collection," Leopold-Loeb Collection MS85, box 21, p. 44 Special Collections, Northwestern University. Also cited in Franklin, "Jew Boys, Queer Boys."

23. Hearing transcript, 3074.

24. Ibid., 3075.

25. "Slayers 'King' and 'Slave.'"

26. "Alienist Healy Gives Analysis of Two Slayers," *Chicago Daily Tribune*, Aug. 5, 1924.

27. Samuel Rabinowich, "Relief Problems," *Jewish Charities* 8 (1917): 173.

28. *Attorney Clarence Darrow's Plea for Mercy in the Franks Case* (Chicago: Wilson Publishing Company, 1924), 6–7.

29. Alvin V. Sellers, ed., *The Loeb-Leopold Case* (Brunswick, GA: Classic Publishing Co., 1926), 123.

30. Ibid., 2.

31. Hearing transcript, 1211.

32. Franklin, "Jew Boys, Queer Boys."

33. Hearing transcript, 3076

34. Ibid., 3078, 3076–3081.

35. Ibid., 3928.

36. *Attorney Clarence Darrow's Plea for Mercy*, 150.

37. Foucault, *Abnormal*, 15.

38. Roscoe Simmons, "The Week," *Chicago Defender*, June 7, 1924.

39. "Asserts Leopold Hate Crime, but Yielded to Leopold," *Washington Post*, Aug. 10, 1924, 1.

40. "Evidence against Loeb and Leopold Finished by State," 1–2.

41. Boethius, *The Consolation of Philosophy*, trans. H. R. James (London: Elliot Stock, 1897), 180–181.

42. See, for a few examples, A. R. Fausett, "Untitled Comments," in *Christianity in the Modern State*, ed. C. Dunkley (London: Bembrose and Sons, 1882), 343; Anonymous, *The Irish Church: Her Assailers and Defenders* (London: Simpkin, Marshall, and Co., 1968), 49.

43. Hearing transcript, 4162, 4164

44. Ibid., 4166.

45. Sellers, ed., *The Loeb-Leopold Case*, 238.

46. Ibid., 231.

47. Foucault, *Abnormal*, 33.

48. Sellers, *Loeb-Leopold Case*, 32.

49. Ibid., 27–32.

50. Hearing transcript, 3812.

51. Ibid., 3812–3813.

52. Ibid., 3813.

53. Ibid., 3814.

54. S. M. Melamed, "Jewish Spokesman Says Crime Is Due to Neglect of Judaism," *Chicago Daily Tribune*, June 2, 1924, 3.

55. Ibid.

56. Ibid.

57. *National Jewish Monthly / B'nai B'rith News Supplement* (n.p.: n.p., Feb. 1924), 290.

58. "Coming of the Prophet Seen," *Los Angeles Times*, Aug. 2, 1924.

59. "Hang the Slayers, Billy Sunday Says," *Chicago Herald and Examiner*, June 5, 1924, 3.

60. Ibid.

61. "Lutherans Urge Moral Training as Modern Need," *Chicago Daily Tribune*, Oct, 21, 1924.

62. "Pastor Sees Noose as Only Salvation of Leopold and Loeb," *Chicago Daily Tribune*, June 9, 1924.

63. "Leopold and Loeb Called Modernists," *New York Times*, Sept. 15, 1924, 16.

64. Ibid.

65. "Tells of Finding Note to Franks Sr." *New York Times*, June 9, 1924, 7.

66. "Says Devil Concept Trips the Orthodox: The Rev. Mr. Potter Declares Fundamentalists Must Dodge Question of His Origin," *New York Times*, Sept. 22, 1924.

67. *Attorney Clarence Darrow's Plea*, 150.

68. "Ministers Attack Caverly for Franks Decision: Must Have Real Men, Not Weaklings on Bench, One Declares at Chicago—Five Others Condemn Sentence for Loeb and Leopold," *Washington Post*, Sept. 15, 1924.

69. *Chicago Sunday Tribune*, June 1, 1924, 1.

Conclusion

This is a story about the construction of Jewish masculinity in the past. And yet the members of the Jewish men's group that I mentioned at the outset of this book would likely recognize reflections of themselves in the stories I have told here. In today's world, like the early twentieth century, norms of American Jewish masculinity echo aspects of wider masculine norms in American culture. To take one example, Jews still hold up examples of healthy Jewish bodies as contemporary paradigms for manliness. Many of my Jewish students, especially the men, are happy to tell their peers all about the paragons of American Jewish athletics. (In the last few years, NBA player Omri Casspi ranks only behind Canadian hip-hop artist Drake as the most mentioned celebrity Jew in student presentations.) But also, today many American Jews—and non-Jews too—think of Jewish masculinity as something just a bit different from normative American masculinity. For instance, neither Jews nor non-Jews associate Jewish men with occupations requiring hard labor or physical strength. Jewish doctors and lawyers live in the forefront of the American cultural imagination, where Jewish longshoremen, nightclub bouncers, and MMA fighters are largely invisible unless they become curiosities because of their oddity.

Similarly, images of Jewish men's criminal vices tend away from violent interpersonal crime. People still assume that Jewish men are rarely alcoholics or perpetrators of domestic violence. The financial criminal Bernie Madoff is far more recognizably Jewish to both Jews and non-Jews than, say, David Berkowitz, better known as the "Son of Sam" serial killer. When someone points out that Berkowitz was Jewish, another person usually pipes up and says, "But he was adopted" or "he said he worshiped the devil" or "he converted to Christianity in prison," all of which suggest that he was not *really* Jewish. Violent murder seems incongruous with Jewish masculinity, whereas the manipulation and cunning of a Ponzi scheme seem despicable but within the realm of possibility.

And, like the Christian missionaries of the early twentieth century, today many non-Jews and Jews alike see Jewish men as gentler than non-Jewish men. Take, for example, the phenomenon of non-Jewish women going on the website JDate in the hopes of finding a Jewish mate. They say that Jewish men are "nicer" or good material to become family men, but never that they expect someone muscular, assertive, or courageous[1]—even though plenty of the men on the site also fit that profile. Thus, the idea that both Jews and non-Jews view American Jewish masculinity as distinctive still resonates today.

Nevertheless, times have changed. The norms of American masculinity more generally are not the same as they were a century ago, and the same can be said of American Jewish masculinity. For example, American Jews today, like Americans more generally, have largely abandoned nostalgia for back-to-the-land movements and the ways they allowed people to imagine manliness through agriculture. (Israeli kibbutzim—communal settlements—took up a similar ideology, and even they are fading quickly these days.) Few Jews speculate about Native American membership in the ten lost tribes, just as fraternal orders such as the Improved Order of Red Men have drastically waned in importance for American men imagining and enacting their visions of masculinity.

The founding of the state of Israel and the Six-Day War in 1967 also changed the landscape of Jewish masculinities. Images of tanned, muscular, fighting Jews—dubbed "new Jews" by proponents—were not the pale Talmud scholars of Eastern Europe, the weakened Holocaust survivors depicted in the newspaper coverage of the war, nor the gentle and nonviolent Jews imagined by many early-twentieth-century Americans. The image of the "new Jew" offered yet another version of the norms of Jewish masculinity. Although this version is still most closely associated with Israel, American culture reproduces and sometimes valorizes it. The 2008 comedy *You Don't Mess with the Zohan*, featuring Adam Sandler as "the greatest Israeli soldier the world has ever known," offered a stereotyped—but nevertheless quite recognizable—version of this manly new Jew. The reach of this image in American culture suggests new developments in the available norms of Jewish masculinity.

In another sense, however, these developments suggest some historical continuity. Although images of muscular Israeli male soldiers may seem to reinforce the dichotomy between the manly Zion and the effeminate diaspora, mainstream American Jewish culture does not suggest that American Jewish men are deficient and should move to Israel to become more manly. Instead, the "new Jew" image has become affixed to Israel, but has not taken hold as the dominant mode for American Jewish men. To take an extreme illustration, the American rabbi and radical Meir Kahane's late 1960s Jewish Defense League that promoted armed defense (with the rallying cry, "Every Jew a 22!") and other violent tactics on behalf of Jews never gained a demographically significant following. If one were to write a similar book about masculinity and American Judaism in the twenty-first century, it would need to consider the availability and dissemination of these images, as well as rejections of them.

Moreover, Judaism's place as a religion in the United States has changed. The Cold War solidified the sense that Judaism was an American religion. For reasons only tangentially related to gender, American Christians and Jews argued that the

United States was a religious nation, unlike its enemy, the godless USSR.[2] As part of this political development, the term "Judeo-Christian" gained popularity in civic discourse about the United States.[3] Today, Judaism is often marshaled on the side of good, American religion because it seems more homegrown, racially white, and less politically threatening than Islam. American celebrity icons such as Madonna, Britney Spears, and Ashton Kutcher have embraced a popularized version of kabbalah (a form of Jewish mysticism), demonstrating both the acceptability of Jewish practice and Judaism's potential for universalism. Judaism, then, ranks as a "good" American religion in today's United States.

But also, as the popular embrace of kabbalah by some non-Jews suggests, the idea that a religion must be rational has waned. Many Jews too have begun to incorporate more kabbalistic ideas and texts into their religious practice, some Christians have also turned toward mystical traditions, and even several prominent atheists have embraced a mystical reverence toward nature.[4] More generally, the rise of "spirituality" in American religion also serves as evidence that, although rationality may still be coded masculine, it no longer has quite the hold on "good" American religion that it once did. These developments in American religion and American Jewish masculinity suggest the importance of the past in our contemporary understanding of gender and Judaism. The study of the past demonstrates the ways in which neither masculinity nor religion is a transhistorical given. Both are contingent, change over time, and therefore demand close contextual analysis.

This book also has lessons for scholarship about gender beyond the confines of American Judaism. The stories here support contemporary gender studies scholarship about "multiple masculinities," which suggests that every culture is more complex than a binary of normative ("hegemonic") masculinity versus deviance from the norm. This scholarship emphasizes that every society has many sets of gender norms and that these norms may even conflict with one another. A culture does not have just one single, unified, normative masculinity, but rather masculinity has many valences, and norms of masculinity differ by context and community.

Most of the scholarship exploring multiple masculinities deals with contemporary communities, so we might be tempted to think of it as a contemporary phenomenon. Given the growing prevalence of political discussions about gays, lesbians, and transgender persons, today we see that gender and sexuality are complex and diverse. But what about in the past? Some people wax nostalgic about the days when "men were men" and "women were women" and each had their roles and life seemed simpler, while others rail against the strictures of the rigid structures of gender in the past. So it might seem as if the complexity of gender is distinctively postmodern. But these historical accounts show us that multiple masculinities are not just a byproduct of postmodernism or more liberal gender politics. Gender has always been messy, complex, and multifaceted.

In fact, taken together, these chapters suggest that there are multiple multiples of masculinity: the norms of Jewish masculinity differed from hegemonic American masculinity, but there were also differences among versions of Jewish masculinity. When acculturated Jews promoted an American Jewish masculinity that was connected to the healthy body, the land, and productivity, they echoed larger norms of American masculinity. But when they agreed that Jewish masculinity was nonviolent, nonaggressive, and even gentle, they did not directly mirror other American norms about men as the controllers of their environment. And even among depictions of American Jewish masculinity, we saw differences. The Zionist state-builder did not embody the exact same kind of Jewish manhood as the agriculturalist. Not every Jew wanted to move out West, identify with Indians, learn scientific techniques of agriculture, and promote a rational, universal Judaism. Acculturated Jews thought that immigrant Jews should become healthier by moving out of the cities, working the land, or settling the West; yet, even from their own urban homes and offices, these acculturated Jews saw themselves as manly. Although these multiple and contradictory modes of embodying Jewish masculinity might seem to challenge the idea that there were strict norms associated with masculinity, it actually conforms to what we know about gender: No one person can ever be (or do) everything. One can never conform to all the norms simultaneously. And as recent sociological studies show, even the people who seem to do hegemonic masculinity best still cannot do it all.[5]

Because American masculinity is multiple—and even American *Jewish* masculinity was multiple—scholars are challenged to see its many manifestations. How can we ever be sure we have seen them all? This question is an easy one to answer: we cannot. We can never be certain that we have accounted for all the manifestations of gender norms. They do far too much work in far too many places and times for scholars to imagine they have offered a complete picture, no matter how many diaries they read, people they interview, and interactions they observe. Nevertheless, if one of our goals is to see these multiple sets of gender norms as they shape and are shaped by Americans, we may look to the margins. Here, I have argued, looking at the marginal and experimental moments in American Jewish life allows us to observe the multiplicity and complexity of gender. From these margins and experiments, we can more easily see what people are doing and thinking, especially when those behaviors and thoughts represent deviations from the norm. That is, in these places, social behavior, ideologies, and even self-representation are not as tightly organized or formally institutionalized. Even the more formal organizations represented here, such as the Galveston Movement, the National Farm School, and American Zionist publications, all demonstrated flexibility, negotiation, and change. Within these movements, the norms of masculinity and the practices associated with those norms were never set in stone: they differed according to circumstance and changed over time. This is not to say they were random, but rather that they defied uniformity. We know that no one really "does" gender completely and "properly" in the sense that they perfectly reflect all norms. No one performs hegemonic masculinity in all its aspects. So looking at the places where people's behaviors and ideas take place in slightly less institutionalized contexts—and therefore are more flexible and often do not conform precisely to gender norms—will actually tell us about how people "do" masculinity more generally. The margins can help highlight the multiplicity of gender norms that is characteristic of society as a whole.

But have we lost something by looking at the margins? This book is not, after all, primarily a story about how famous Jews such as philanthropist Jacob Schiff, Judge Louis Brandeis, or Rabbi Mordecai Kaplan imagined and performed masculinity. Perhaps in turning focus away from the elite and the mainstream, this story neglects to paint the picture of the true hegemonic Jewish masculinity. I do not think this is the case. As my discussion of the margins and experiments suggests, I have intentionally not taken the dominant and rather well-trodden pathway of looking for "core" practices of masculinity.[6] The reason I do not try to tell the story of a central normative Jewish masculinity is this: I do not think there was one. That is, most American Jewish men did not conform to—nor even attempt to conform to—a single, standardized set of practices. In their everyday lives, they did not form their thoughts or actions according to a fixed, coherent vision of masculinity. This is not to suggest that they never confronted ideological attempts to create or disseminate visions of a standard set of practices of masculinity or of hegemonic masculinity. Indeed the characters in this history confronted such norms. But the dominant experiences in these men's lives were of contingent and shifting modes of masculinity and adaptation to context, while unified or centralized versions of masculinity existed at the level of ideology and social projects. Put in the language of norms, the "normal" in the sense of the common experience was one of multiple and contingent practices of masculinity, whereas the "norm" in the sense of the ideal could be a unified or core set of practices.

Similarly, there was no unified American religion, no single core set of practices or beliefs that made one's religious life definitively count as American. I do not think we can understand the truth about American religion in the beginning of the twentieth century by looking at its center because there was no true center. The hegemony of Christianity, as I have called it here, was very real, but like hegemonic masculinity, it operated largely at the level of ideology and social project. Given this parallel, looking at American Judaism—itself a marginal and at times experimental religion—also allows us to see more clearly the norms of American religion at the time.

But though we have not lost out by looking at the margins, there are other possible costs to writing about masculinity. One danger in writing historical representations of masculinity is the erasure of women. There is an irony here: This study is indebted to women's historians and gender historians who earlier embarked on their quests of recovering women's stories and experiences. This study has taken many of these lessons about the constructed nature of gender and the importance of gender in historical processes and used them to talk about men and masculinity. But because cultural discourses about masculinity can often render women or femininity invisible, a focus on masculinity runs the risk of erasing women and thus repeating what feminist historians critiqued in the first place.

A countermove to this—though not a complete solution to women's erasure—is to look for women in these stories. Even though it should be obvious that women also participated in the construction of American Jewish masculinity, it was not always easy to find women's voices. This is no accident: many of the sources themselves render women invisible. When the Galveston Movement's David Bressler wrote about "persons," a category that excluded women, he obscured the presence of Jewish women as wives of men, as workers, as immigrants, and as pioneers in their own right. The conversations about immigrants' "poor physique" and "likely to become a public charge" spurred medical reports in Galveston that likewise did not comment on women, in spite of the fact that women too were inspected on arrival into the port. The National Farm School and Hirsch Agricultural School largely did not include discussions of women in their goals or publicity materials, despite the presence of women in their communities. Remaining silent on women's presence and femininity allowed these agricultural schools to emphasize the masculinity of producerism and the creation of healthy bodies through agricultural labor.

But the fact that the sources render women invisible is no excuse for the scholar to follow suit. Thus, even though femininity is often the hidden counterpart to masculinity, women's voices are not completely silent. Women's ideas and social practices contributed to the formation of masculinity. Settlement worker Lillian Wald worked with immigrants to instill "proper" gendered practices and tastes in both men and women. The women at NFS performed "feminine" labor so that the men could hone their own skills at masculine labor. And many other women weighed in at ideological levels: Boston reporter Mary Bronson Hartt brought the productive farmers of Woodbine to a wide and diverse audience; Mary Dunlop McLean under the penname "Judith Herz" offered observations and suggestions about young Jewish men and crime; in the pages of this book, Manya Gordon Strunsky, Zionist Helena Cohn, Julia Richman, and many others put their stamp on ideas about American Jewish masculinity. The story about American Jewish masculinity, then, is also a story about how women contributed to the shaping of the norms of masculinity, even when those cultural conversations often ignored women and femininity.

Men and women, immigrants and acculturated Americans, Jews and non-Jews—this is a story of a construction project with many hands. And masculinity touched on all areas of American Jewish life, from immigration projects to theology to crime. Here I have argued for the intertwined processes of shaping an American Jewish masculinity and claiming Judaism as a good, American religion. But there is much more to be said about the gender of Jewish men, and I hope that these pages have inspired others to take up questions about the relationships of masculinity and religion as social formations, both in the past and the present.

Notes

1. Sarah E. Richards, "You Don't Have to be Jewish to Love J-Date," *New York Times*, Dec. 5, 2005; Lisa Scherzer, "Looking for Mr. Goldstein: When Gentiles Seek Jewish Mates," Dec. 2002, http://www.interfaithfamily.com/relationships/interdating/Looking_for_Mr _Goodstein_When_Gentile_Singles_Seek_Jewish_Mates.shtml; "JDate: Not just for Tribe Members," Mar. 8, 2013, http://www.cosmopolitan.com/sex-love/news/a11976/non-jews-on -jdate/.

2. For the paradigmatic text of the time, see Will Herberg, *Protestant, Catholic, Jew* (Chicago: University of Chicago Press, 1955). See also Kevin Schultz, *Tri-Faith America: How Catholics and Jews Held Postwar America to Its Protestant Promise* (Oxford: Oxford University Press, 2011).

3. Mark Silk, "Notes on the Judeo-Christian Tradition in America," *American Quarterly* 36 (Spring 1984): 65–85.

4. Courtney Bender, "Things in Their Entanglements," in *The Post-Secular in Question: Religion in Contemporary Society*, ed. David Kyuman Kim, Philip Gorski, John Torpey, and Jonathan VanAntwerpen (New York: New York University Press, 2012), 43–76; Lisa Sideris "Science as Sacred Myth? Ecospirituality in the Anthropocene Age," *Journal for the Study of Religion, Nature & Culture* 9, no. 2 (2015): 136–153.

5. R. W. Connell and James Messerschmidt, "Hegemonic Masculinity: Rethinking the Concept," *Gender and Society* 19.6 (Dec. 2005): 838.

6. I owe a debt of gratitude to Judith Gerson, whose insightful reading sharpened my language to describe this concept.

Bibliography

Primary Sources

Archival Collections

American Jewish Archive (AJA), Cincinnati
    Felix Warburg Collection
    Henry Cohen Papers
    Jacob Schiff Papers
    Small Collections
American Jewish Historical Society Archive (AJHS), New York
    AJHS Monographs
    Baron de Hirsch Papers
    Galveston Immigration Plan Records
Briscoe Center for American History, University of Texas, Austin
    Henry Cohen Papers
    J. O. Dyer Papers
Central Zionist Archives (CZA), Jerusalem
    Jewish Territorial Organization (ITO) Papers
Northwestern University, Evanston, IL
    Leopold-Loeb Collection, Special Collections

Periodicals

American Hebrew
American Israelite
American Jewish Chronicle
Architecture
Atlanta Constitution
Atlanta Georgian
Atlanta Journal
Atlantic
Atlantic Monthly
Boston Daily
Boston Evening Transcript
Boston Globe
Charities and the Commons
Chicago Daily Tribune
Chicago Defender
Chicago Herald and Examiner
Chicago Tribune

Christian Century
Christian Observer
Christian Register
Emanu-el
Forum
Galveston News
Gleaner
Hebrew Union College Annual
Herald and Presbyter
Jeffersonian
Jewish Center
Jewish Charities
Jewish Era
Jewish Forum
Jewish Herald
Jewish Social Service Quarterly
Journal and Messenger
Life
Los Angeles Times
Lutheran Quarterly
Maccabaean
McClure's
Menorah Journal
Missionary Review of the World
Nation
National Jewish Monthly/ B'nai B'rith News Supplement
New Era Illustrated Magazine
New Outlook
New York Times
New-York Tribune
Our Hope
Popular Science Monthly
Proceedings of the American Jewish Historical Society
Reform Advocate
Southwestern Historical Quarterly
Sunday Oregonian
Washington Post
YHMA Bulletin

Printed Materials

American Jewish Year Book, 1900–1901. New York: American Jewish Committee, 1901.
Antin, Mary. *The Promised Land*. Boston: Houghton Mifflin, 1912.
Attorney Clarence Darrow's Plea for Mercy in the Franks Case. Chicago: Wilson Publishing Company, 1924.
Bacon, Alexander. *The Strange Story of Dr. Cohn and Mr. Joszovics (with apologies to Dr. Jekyl and Mr. Hyde)*. New York: n.p., 1918.

Barton, Bruce. *The Man Nobody Knows*. Indianapolis: Bobbs-Merrill Company, 1925.
Bernheimer, Charles. *The Russian Jew in the United States*. Philadelphia: John C. Winston Co., 1905.
Bingham, Theodore. "Foreign Criminals in New York." *North American Review* 188 (Sept. 1908): 383–394.
Blau, Joel. "The Modern Pharisee." *Atlantic* 129, no. 1 (Jan. 1922): 1–13.
Boethius. *The Consolation of Philosophy*. Translated by H. R. James. London: Elliot Stock, 1897.
Bressler, David. "Removal Work." In *Senate Documents*. Washington, DC: U.S. Government Printing Office, 1911.
———. "The Removal Work, Including Galveston." *Sixth Biennial Session of the National Council of Jewish Charities*. Baltimore: Kohn & Pollock, 1910.
———. *The Removal Work, Including Galveston*. N.p.: n.p., ca. 1910.
Bushee, Frederick. "Ethnic Factors in the Population of Boston." *Publication of the American Economic Association* 4, no. 2 (May 1903): 1–162.
Carr, John Foster. *Guide to the United States for the Jewish Immigrant: A Nearly Literal Translation*. Connecticut Daughters of the American Revolution, 1912.
Catalogue of the Baron de Hirsch Agricultural and Industrial School. New York: De Leeuw and Oppenheimer, 1898.
Catalogue of the National Farm School. Philadelphia: National Farm School, 1898.
Central Conference of American Rabbis Annual Report 45. Cincinnati: C. J. Krehbiel and Co., 1917.
A Century of Jewish Missions. Chicago: Fleming Revell Company, 1902.
Clark, Albert Irving. "The History of Galveston Island, 1518–1900." *Texas History Teachers' Bulletin* 7 (Nov. 1918): 53–59.
Cohen, Henry. "Settlement of Jews in Texas." *Publication of American Jewish Historical Society*. N.p.: n.p., 1894.
Cohn, Leopold. *The Story of a Modern Missionary to an Ancient People*. New York: American Board of Missions to the Jews, 1908.
Commencement Number of the HAS Record. Woodbine, NJ: Students of the Hirsch Agricultural School, ca. 1915–1917.
"Constitution." *Publication of American Jewish Historical Society*. N.p.: n.p., 1894.
Cotton, John. *The Powring Out of the Seven Vials, or An Exposition of the 16 Chapter of Revelation, with an Application of it to our Times*. London: n.p., 1642.
de Haas, Jacob. *Louis Dembitz Brandeis: A Biographical Sketch with Special Reference to His Contributions to Jewish and Zionist History*. New York: Bloch, 1929.
———. *Zionism: Why and Wherefore*. New York: Maccabaean Publishing Co., 1902.
Dyer, Joseph Osterman. *The Early History of Galveston*. Galveston: Oscar Springer Print, 1916.
———. "Historical Sketch: Comparisons of Customs of Wild Tribes near Galveston a Century ago with Ancient Semitic Customs." Galveston: Oscar Springer Print, 1916.
Eighteenth Annual Report of the National Farm School. N.p.: n.p., 1914.
Enelow, Hyman Gerson. *The Adequacy of Judaism*. New York: Bloch, 1920.
Fausett, A. R. "Untitled Comments." In *Christianity in the Modern State*, edited by C. Dunkley. London: Bembrose and Sons, 1882.

Fifteenth Annual Report of the National Farm School. N.p.: n.p., 1912.

Fifth Annual Report of the National Farm School. N.p.: n.p., 1902.

First Annual Report of the National Farm School. N.p.: n.p., 1901.

Fishberg, Maurice. *The Jews: A Study of Race and Environment.* New York: Walter Scott Publishing Co., 1911.

Forbush, William Byron. *The Boy Problem.* Boston: Pilgrim Press, 1907.

Fosdick, Harry Emerson. *The Manhood of the Master.* New York: Abingdon Press, 1913.

Fourteenth Annual Report of the National Farm School. N.p.: n.p., 1911.

Fourth Annual Report of the National Farm School. N.p.: n.p., 1901.

Franklin, Leo. "Message of the President." In *Central Conference of American Rabbis,* edited by Isaac Marcuson, 162–188. Cincinnati: C. J. Krehbiel and Co., 1920.

Friedman, Harry. "Gemara." In *Hebrew Union College Annual,* edited by Ephraim Frisch, 26–36. Cincinnati: Hebrew Union College, 1904.

Freuder, Samuel. *A Missionary's Return to Judaism: The Truth about the Christian Missions to the Jews.* New York: Sinai Publishing Co., 1915.

——. *My Return to Judaism.* New York: Zuckerman and Bros., 1922.

——. *My Return to Judaism,* 3rd ed. New York: Bloch, 1924.

Geiger, Abraham. *Judaism and Its History,* vol. 2. Translated by Maurice Mayer. New York: Thalmessinger, 1866.

Goldberg, David. "Woman's Part in Religious Decline." *Jewish Forum* 4, no. 4 (May 1921): 871–875.

Goldman, Joseph. *Judaism and Its Traditions.* Los Angeles: J. F. Rowny Press, 1919.

Gottheil, Richard, *Zionism.* Philadelphia: Jewish Publication Society, 1914.

Hall, G. Stanley. "The Efficiency of the Religious Work of the Young Men's Christian Association." *Pedagogical Seminary* 12, no. 4 (1905): 478–489.

——. "White Man's Burden versus Indigenous Development for the Lower Races." *National Education Association* 42 (1903): 1053–1056.

——. *Youth: Its Education, Regimen, and Hygiene.* New York: Appleton and Co., 1908.

Hall, Prescott Farnsworth. *Immigration and Its Effects upon the United States.* New York: Henry Holt and Co., 1906.

Hart, Lewis. *A Jewish Reply to Christian Evangelists.* New York: Bloch Publishing Co., 1902.

Herz, Judith. "Saving Citizens: The Children's Court is Doing—A Jewish Protectory in Sight." *New Era Illustrated Magazine* 4, no. 2 (Jan. 1904): 44–50.

Isaacs, Abram. *What Is Judaism?* New York: G. P. Putnam's Sons, 1912.

Jacobs, Joseph. *Jewish Contributions to Civilization: An Estimate.* Philadelphia: Jewish Publication Society, 1919.

James, William. *Varieties of Religious Experience.* New York: Modern Library, 1902.

Jastrow, Morris. *The Study of Religion.* New York: Charles Scribner's Sons, 1902.

The Jewish Communal Register of New York City. Kehilla: New York, 1918.

Johnson, Frank White. *A History of Texas and Texans.* New York: American Historical Society, 1916.

Kahn, William. "Jewish Agricultural and Industrial Aid Society, New York." In *Second Conference of Jewish Charities,* 83–96. Cincinnati: C. J. Krehbiel and Co., 1902.

Kant, Immanuel. *Critique of Practical Reason,* 3rd ed. Translated by Lewis White Beck. New York: Prentice-Hall, 1993.

Kohler, Kaufmann. "Christianity in its Relation to Judaism." In *Jewish Encyclopedia*, 49–59. Vol. 4. New York: Funk and Wagnalls, n.d.

——. "The Dangers, the Fallacies and the Falsehoods of Zionism III." *Reform Advocate* 33 (1907).

——. *Jewish Theology, Systematically and Historically Considered*. New York: Macmillan, 1918.

——. *Palestine and Israel's World Mission*. Pittsburgh: Rodef Shalom Congregation, 1918.

Kuh, Edwin. "The Social Disability of the Jew." *Atlantic Monthly*, Apr. 1908.

Leiser, Joseph. "Emil G. Hirsch." In *Famous Living Americans*, edited by Mary Griffin Webb and Edna Lenore Webb, 246–259. Greencastle, IN: Charles Webb and Co., 1915.

——. "Rabbi Benjamine's Experiment; or From Generation to Generation." *Menorah*, May 1902.

Lestschinsky, Von J. "Die Auswanderung der Juden nach Galveston." In *Zeitschrift fur Demographie und Statistik der Juden*, 177–184. Berlin: n.p., 1910.

Levin, Louis. "The Year, 5668." In *American Jewish Year Book*, 190–236. Philadelphia: Jewish Publication Society of America, 1908.

Levy, A. R. "Agriculture, a Most Effective Means to Aid Jewish Poor." In *Second Conference of Jewish Charities*, 97–107. Cincinnati: C. J. Krehbiel and Co., 1902.

Machen, J. Gresham. *Christianity and Liberalism*. Philadelphia: Presbyterian Guardian, 1923.

Macintosh, Douglas Clyde. "The New Christianity and World-Conversion." *American Journal of Theology* 18 (Oct. 1914): 553–570.

——. *Theology as an Empirical Science*. New York: Macmillan, 1919.

Mallery, Garrick. "Israelite and Indian: A Parallel in Planes of Culture." *Popular Science Monthly* 36 (Nov. 1889): 52–76.

Marcuson, Isaac, ed. *Central Conference of American Rabbis: Twenty-Sixth Annual Convention*. Cincinnati: Bacharach Press, 1915.

McAdoo, William. *Guarding a Great City*. New York: Harper, 1906.

Moses, Alfred. *Jewish Science: Divine Healing in Judaism, with Special Reference to the Jewish Scriptures and Prayer Book*. Mobile, AL: Temple, 1916.

Murphy, Elmer. "A Visit with Leo Frank in the Death Cell at Atlanta." *Rhodes' Colossus* (Mar. 1915): 3–12.

Nineteenth Annual Report of the National Farm School. N.p.: n.p., 1916.

Ninth Annual Report of the National Farm School. N.p.: n.p., 1906.

Nordau, Max. *Degeneration*. Berkeley: University of California Press, 1898.

——. "Muskeljudentum." In *Zionistische Schriften*. Cologne: Juedisher Verlag, 1909.

Obituary Records of Yale University. New Haven: Yale University, 1915.

Oppenheimer, Francis. "Jewish Criminality." *Independent* 65 (Sept. 17, 1908): 640–642.

Peters, Madison. *Justice to the Jew*. New York: McClure Company, 1908.

Philipson, David. "Are There Traces of the Ten Lost Tribes in Ohio?" *Publications of the American Jewish Historical Society* 13 (1905): 37–46.

Religious Bodies 1916: Separate Denominations. Washington, DC: Government Printing Office, 1919.

"Report of the Special Committee on Christian Missions to Jews." In *Central Conference of American Rabbis Annual Report,* 45. Cincinnati: C. J. Krehbiel and Co., 1917.

Richman, Julia. *Methods of Teaching Jewish Ethics.* Philadelphia: Jewish Chautauqua Society, 1914.

Rosen, Joseph A. "The HAS and the Jew in Agriculture." In *Commencement Number of the HAS Record.* Woodbine, NJ: Hirsch Agricultural School, 1915.

Ross, Edward Alsworth. "Racial Consequences of Immigration." *Century Magazine* 87 (Feb. 1914): 615–622.

Sellers, Alvin V., ed. *The Loeb-Leopold Case.* Brunswick, GA: Classic Publishing Co., 1926.

Seventh Annual Report of the National Farm School. N.p.: n.p., 1904.

Sixteenth Annual Report of the National Farm School. N.p.: n.p., 1913.

Sixth Annual Report of the National Farm School. N.p.: n.p., 1903.

Smither, Harriet, ed. "Diary of Adolphus Sterne." *Southwestern Historical Quarterly* 30 (Oct. 1926): 139–155.

Spinoza, Baruch. *Theological-Political Treatise.* Translated by Samuel Shirley. Indianapolis: Hackett, 2001.

Steiner, Edward. *Against the Current: Simple Chapters from a Complex Life.* New York: Fleming Revell, 1910.

———. *The Eternal Hunger: Vivid Moments in Personal Experience.* New York: Fleming Revell, 1925.

———. *From Alien to Citizen: The Story of My Life in America.* New York: Fleming Revell, 1914.

Street, Arthur, ed. *Street's Pandex of the News.* Chicago: Pandex Co., 1909.

Tenth Annual Report of the National Farm School. N.p.: n.p., 1907.

Thompson, Albert Edward. *A Century of Jewish Missions.* Chicago: Fleming Revell, 1902.

Twain, Mark. "Concerning the Jews." *Harper's Magazine* 99 (Sept. 1899): 528–529.

Twelfth Annual Report of the National Farm School. N.p.: n.p., 1909.

Twenty-Second Annual Report of the National Farm School. N.p.: n.p., 1919.

Twenty-Third Annual Report of the National Farm School. N.p.: n.p., 1920.

Wald, Lillian. *The House on Henry Street.* New York: Henry Holt, 1915.

Waldman, Morris. "The Galveston Movement." *Jewish Social Service Quarterly* (Mar. 1928).

Weinstock, Harris. *Jesus the Jew and Other Addresses.* New York: Funk and Wagnalls, 1902.

Wilhelm von Dohm, Christian. *Uber die Burgerliche Verbesserung der Juden.* Berlin: Friedrich Nicholai, 1781.

Wise, Isaac Mayer. *Reminiscences.* Translated and edited by David Philipson. Cincinnati: Leo Wise, 1901.

Yearbook of the Central Conference of American Rabbis. N.p.: n.p., 1901.

Secondary Sources

Albanese, Catherine. *America: Religions and Religion.* Boston: Wadsworth, 2013.

———. "Exchanging Souls, Exchanging Selves." In *Retelling US Religious History,* edited by Thomas Tweed, 200–226. Berkeley: University of California Press, 1997.

Alroey, Gur. "Galveston and Palestine: Immigration and Ideology in the Early Twentieth Century." *American Jewish Archives* 56 (2004): 129–150.

Anonymous. *The Irish Church: Her Assailers and Defenders*. London: Simpkin, Marshall, and Co., 1968.

Ariel, Yaakov. "The Evangelist at Our Door: The American Jewish Response to Christian
Missionaries." *American Jewish Archives Journal* 48 (Fall/Winter 1996): 139–160.

———. *Evangelizing the Chosen People: Missions to Jews in America, 1880–2000*. Chapel
Hill: University of North Carolina Press, 2000.

———. "A German Rabbi and Scholar in America." *European Judaism* 45 (Autumn 2012):
59–77.

———. "Kaufmann Kohler and His Attitude toward Zionism: A Reexamination."
American Jewish Archives Journal 43 (Fall/Winter 1991): 207–223.

Baader, Benjamin Maria, Sharon Gillerman, and Paul Lerner, eds. *Jewish Masculinities:
German Jews, Gender, and History*. Bloomington: Indiana University Press, 2012.

Bauer, Yehuda. "In Search of a Definition of Antisemitism." In *Approaches to Antisemitism: Context and Curriculum*, edited by Michael Brown. New York: American
Jewish Committee, 1994.

Bederman, Gail. *Manliness and Civilization: A Cultural History of Gender and Race in
the United States, 1880–1917*. Chicago: University of Chicago Press, 1995.

———. "The Women Have Had Charge of Church Work Long Enough: The Men and
Religion Forward Movement of 1911–1912 and the Masculinization of Middle Class
Protestantism." *American Quarterly* 41, no. 3 (Sept. 1989): 432–465.

Bender, Courtney. "Things in Their Entanglements." In *The Post-Secular in Question:
Religion in Contemporary Society*, edited by David Kyuman Kim, Philip Gorski,
John Torpey, and Jonathan VanAntwerpen, 43–76. New York: New York Univer-
sity Press, 2012.

Bercovitch, Sacvan "The Biblical Basis of the American Myth." In *The Bible in American Arts and Letters*, edited by Giles Gunn, 219–229. Philadelphia: Fortress Press,
1983.

Berkowitz, Michael. "'Mind, Muscle, and Men:' The Imagination of a Zionist National
Culture for the Jews of Central and Western Europe, 1897–1941." Ph.D. diss.,
University of Wisconsin, 1989.

———. *Zionist Culture and West European Jewry before the First World War*. Chapel Hill:
University of North Carolina Press, 1996.

Bernstein, Matthew H. *Screening a Lynching: The Leo Frank Case on Film and Television*.
Athens: University of Georgia Press, 2009.

Best, Gary. "Jacob Schiff's Galveston Movement." *American Jewish Archives Journal*
(Apr. 1978): 43–79.

Biale, David. *Eros and the Jews: From Biblical Israel to Contemporary America*. Berkeley:
University of California Press, 1997.

Boyarin, Daniel. *A Radical Jew: Paul and the Politics of Identity*. Berkeley: University of
California Press, 1994.

———. *Unheroic Conduct*. Berkeley: University of California Press, 1997.

Boyarin, Jonathan. *Thinking in Jewish*. Chicago: University of Chicago Press, 1996.

———. *Unconverted Self: Jews, Indians, and the Identity of Christian Europe*. Chicago:
University of Chicago Press, 2009.

Brandes, Joseph. *Immigrants to Freedom: Jews as Yankee Farmers! 1880's to 1960's.* Bloomington, IN: Xlibris, 2009.

Bristow, Edward. *Prostitution and Prejudice: The Jewish Fight against White Slavery, 1870–1939.* Oxford: Clarendon Press, 1982.

Brodie, Fawn M. *No Man Knows My History: The Life of Joseph Smith.* New York: Vintage, 1995.

Brown, Dona. *Back to the Land: The Enduring Dream of Self-Sufficiency in Modern America.* Madison: University of Wisconsin Press, 2011.

Brundage, W. Fitzhugh. *Lynching in the New South: Georgia and Virginia, 1880–1930.* Champaign: University of Illinois Press, 1993.

Carnes, Mark. *Secret Ritual and Manhood in Victorian America.* New Haven: Yale University Press, 1989.

Carter, Julian. *The Heart of Whiteness: Normal Sexuality and Race in America 1880–1940.* Durham, NC: Duke University Press, 2007.

Chiarella, Tom. "The 75 Things Every Man Should Do." *Esquire,* Apr. 22, 2015. http://www.esquire.com/lifestyle/g56/75-things-0808/.

Cohen, Naomi. *American Jews and the Zionist Idea.* New York: Ktav, 1975.

———. "The Maccabaean's Message: A Study in American Zionism until World War I." *Jewish Social Studies* 18 (July 1956): 163–178.

Connell, R. W., and James Messerschmidt. "Hegemonic Masculinity: Rethinking the Concept." *Gender and Society* 19 (Dec. 2005): 829–859.

Crenshaw, Kimberle. "Mapping the Margins: Intersectionality, Identity Politics, and Violence against Women of Color." *Stanford Law Review* 43 (1991): 1241–1299.

Davis, Angela. *Women, Race, and Class.* New York: Vintage, 1983.

Davis, Marni. *Jews and Booze: Becoming American in the Age of Prohibition.* New York: NYU Press, 2012.

Dekel, Mikhal. *The Universal Jew: Masculinity, Modernity, and the Zionist Movement.* Evanston, IL: Northwestern University Press, 2011.

Dekel-Chen, Jonathan. *Farming the Red Land.* New Haven: Yale University Press, 2005.

Deloria, Philip. *Playing Indian.* New Haven: Yale University Press, 1999.

Dembe, Allard E. *Occupation and Disease: How Social Factors Affect the Social Conception of Work-Related Disorders.* New Haven: Yale University Press, 1996.

de Zavala, Adina. *History and Legends of the Alamo and Other Missions in and around San Antonio,* edited by Richard Flores. Houston: Arte Publico Press, 1996 [1917].

Diner, Hasia. *The Jews of the United States, 1654 to 2000.* Berkeley: University of California Press, 2004.

———. *A Time for Gathering: The Second Migration, 1820–1880.* Baltimore: Johns Hopkins University Press, 1992.

Dinnerstein, Leonard. *The Leo Frank Case.* Athens: University of Georgia Press, 1999.

Eisenberg, Ellen. *Jewish Agricultural Communities in New Jersey.* Syracuse, NY: Syracuse University Press, 1995.

Fass, Paula. "Making and Remaking an Event: The Leopold and Loeb Trial in American Culture." *Journal of American History* 80 (Dec. 1993): 919–951.

Fessenden, Tracy. *Culture and Redemption: Religion, the Secular, and American Literature.* Princeton, NJ: Princeton University Press, 2006.

Flohr, Paul Mendes, and Jehuda Reinharz. *The Jew in the Modern World*. New York: Oxford University Press, 2010.

Foucault, Michel. *Abnormal: Lectures at the College de France 1974–1975*. Translated by Graham Burchell. New York: Picador, 1999.

Franklin, Paul B. "Jew Boys, Queer Boys." In *Queer Theory and the Jewish Question*, edited by Daniel Boyarin, Daniel Itzkovitz, and Ann Pellegrini, 121–148. New York: Columbia University Press, 2002.

Fried, Albert. *The Jewish Gangster in America*. New York: Columbia University Press, 1993.

Gal, Alon. "The Mission Motif in American Zionism, 1898–1948." *American Jewish History* 75 (June 1986): 363–385.

Gilman, Sander. "Alcohol and the Jews." *Patterns of Prejudice* 40 (Sept. 2006): 335–352.

———. *Freud, Race, and Gender*. Princeton, NJ: Princeton University Press, 1997.

———. *The Jew's Body*. New York: Routledge, 1991.

Ginzberg, Eli. *Keeper of the Law: Louis Ginsberg*. Philadelphia: Jewish Publication Society, 1966.

Glauz-Todrank, Annalise. "Race, Religion, or Ethnicity: Situating Jews on the American Scene." *Religion Compass* 8 (Oct. 2014): 303–316.

Glazier, Jack. *Dispersing the Ghetto: The Relocation of Jewish Immigrants across America*. Ithaca, NY: Cornell University Press, 1999.

Glenn, Susan. *Daughters of the Shtetl: Life and Labor in the Immigrant Generation*. Ithaca, NY: Cornell University Press, 1990.

Golden, Harry. *A Little Girl Is Dead*. Cleveland: World, 1965.

Goldman, Karla. *Beyond the Synagogue Gallery*. Cambridge, MA: Harvard University Press, 2001.

———. "The Limits of Imagination: White Christian Civilization and the Construction of American Jewish Womanhood in the 1890s." In *Imagining the American Jewish Community*, edited by Jack Wertheimer, 191–211. Waltham, MA: Brandeis University Press, 2007.

Goldstein, Eric. *Price of Whiteness: Jews, Race, and American Identity*. Princeton, NJ: Princeton University Press, 2006.

Goldy, Robert. *The Emergence of Jewish Theology in America*. Bloomington: Indiana University Press, 1990.

Gollaher, David. "From Ritual to Science: The Medical Transformation of Circumcision in America." *Journal of Social History* 28 (Fall 1994): 5–36.

Goren, Arthur. *New York Jews and the Quest for Community: The Kehilla Experiment, 1908–1922*. New York: Columbia University Press, 1979.

Greene, Daniel. *The Jewish Origins of Cultural Pluralism*. Bloomington: Indiana University Press, 2011.

Gurock, Jeffrey. "Jewish Communal Divisiveness in Response to Christian Influences on the Lower East Side, 1900–1910." In *Jewish Apostasy in the Modern World*, edited by Todd Endelman, 255–271. New York: Holmes and Meier, 1987.

———. *Judaism's Encounter with American Sports*. Bloomington: Indiana University Press, 2005.

Gusfield, Joseph. *Symbolic Crusade: Status Politics and the American Temperance Movement*. Champaign: University of Illinois Press, 1986.

Haas, Dennis. "The Conversion of Edward A. Steiner." June 15, 2004. https://www.grinnell.edu/news/conversion-edward-steiner

Hall, Stuart. "Cultural Identity and Diaspora." In *Identity, Community, and Cultural Difference*, edited by Jonathan Rutherford, 222–237. London: Lawrence & Wishart, 1990.

Hart, Mitchell. *The Healthy Jew: The Symbiosis of Judaism and Modern Medicine*. New York: Cambridge University Press, 2007.

———. *Social Science and the Politics of Modern Jewish Identity*. Stanford: Stanford University Press, 2000.

Herberg, Will. *Protestant, Catholic, Jew*. Chicago: University of Chicago, 1955.

Herman, Jessica. "JDate: Not Just for Tribe Members." *Cosmopolitan*, Mar. 8, 2013. http://www.cosmopolitan.com/sex-love/news/a11976/non-jews-on-jdate/.

Hertzberg, Arthur. *The Zionist Idea: A Historical Analysis and Reader*. Philadelphia: Jewish Publication Society, 1979.

Heschel, Susannah. *Abraham Geiger and the Jewish Jesus*. Chicago: University of Chicago Press, 1998.

———. "Gender and Agency in the Feminist Historiography of Jewish Identity." *Journal of Religion* 84 (Oct. 2004): 580–591.

Higham, John. *Strangers in the Land: Patterns of American Nativism, 1860–1925*. New Brunswick, NJ: Rutgers University Press, 1983.

Hirschman, Nancy J. "Intersectionality before Intersectionality Was Cool: The Importance of Class to Feminist Interpretations of John Locke." In *Feminist Interpretations of John Locke*, edited by Nancy Hirschman and Kirstie McClure, 155–186. University Park: Penn State Press, 2007.

Hoganson, Kristin. *Fighting for American Manhood: How Gender Politics Provoked the Spanish-American and Philippine-American Wars*. New Haven: Yale University Press, 1998.

Huhndorf, Shari. *Going Native: Indians in the American Cultural Imagination*. Ithaca, NY: Cornell University Press, 2001.

Imhoff, Sarah. "The Myth of American Jewish Feminization." *Jewish Social Studies* 21, no. 3 (2016).

Itzkovitz, Daniel. "Secret Temples." In *Jews and Other Differences*, edited by Jonathan Boyarin and Daniel Boyarin, 176–202. Minneapolis: University of Minnesota Press, 1997.

Jacobson, Matthew Frye. *Barbarian Virtues: The United States Encounter with Foreign Peoples at Home and Abroad*. New York: Hill and Wang, 2001.

———. *Whiteness of a Different Color: European Immigrants and the Alchemy of Race*. Cambridge, MA: Harvard University Press, 1998.

Jakobsen, Janet, and Ann Pelligrini. *Love the Sin: Sexual Regulations and the Limits of Religious Tolerance*. Boston: Beacon, 2004.

Joselit, Jenna Weissman. "An Answer to Commissioner Bingham: A Case Study of New York Jews and Crime." *YIVO Annual of Jewish Social Science* 18 (1982): 121–140.

———. *Our Gang: Jewish Crime and the New York Jewish Community, 1900–1940*. Bloomington: Indiana University Press, 1983.

Kaplan, Beth. *Finding the Jewish Shakespeare: The Life and Legacy of Jacob Gordin*. Syracuse: Syracuse University Press, 2007.

Kaplan, Dana Evan. "Rabbi Samuel Freuder as a Christian Missionary: American Protestant Premillennialism and an Apostate Returner, 1891–1924." *American Jewish Archives Journal* (1998): 41–74.

Kaplan, Marion, and Deborah Dash Moore, eds. *Gender and Jewish History*. Bloomington: Indiana University Press, 2010.

Kasson, John. *Houdini, Tarzan, and the Perfect Man: The White Male Body and the Challenge of Modernity in America*. New York: Hill and Wang, 2001.

Katz, Stephen. *Red, Black, and Jew: New Frontiers in Hebrew Literature*. Austin: University of Texas Press, 2010.

Kaufman, David. *Shul with a Pool: The "Synagogue-Center" in American Jewish History*. Hanover, NH: Brandeis University Press, 1999.

Kelly, Patrick. "The Sacramental Imagination, Culture, and Play." Licentiate's thesis, Weston Jesuit School of Theology, 1999.

Kimmel, Michael. *Manhood in America*. Oxford: Oxford University Press, 1998.

Klein, Christa. "The Jesuits and Catholic Boyhood in Nineteenth-Century New York City." PhD diss., University of Pennsylvania, 1976.

Koffmann, David. "The Jews' Indian: Native Americans in the Jewish Imagination and Experience 1850–1950." PhD diss., New York University, 2011.

Konner, Melvin. *The Jewish Body*. New York: Schocken, 2009.

Krasner, Jonathan. *Benderly Boys and American Jewish Education*. Waltham, MA: Brandeis University Press, 2011.

Kugelmass, Jack, ed. *Jews, Sports and the Rites of Citizenship*. Urbana: University of Illinois Press, 2007.

Kunzel, Regina. *Criminal Intimacies: Prison and the Uneven History of American Sexuality*. Chicago: University of Chicago Press, 2008.

Laqueur, Walter. *A History of Zionism: From the French Revolution to the Establishment of Israel*. New York: Schocken, 2003.

Lears, T. J. Jackson. "American Advertising and the Reconstruction of the Body." In *Fitness in American Culture: Images of Health, Sport, and the Body*, edited by Katherine Grover, 47–66. Amherst: University of Massachusetts Press, 1989.

———. *Rebirth of a Nation: The Making of Modern America, 1877–1920*. New York: HarperCollins, 2009.

Lederhendler, Eli. *Jewish Responses to Modernity*. New York: New York University Press, 1994.

Levitt, Laura. "Impossible Assimilations, American Liberalism, and Jewish Difference: Revisiting Jewish secularism." *American Quarterly* 59 (2007): 807–832.

Lindemann, Albert S. *The Jew Accused: Three Anti-Semitic Affairs (Dreyfus, Beilis, Frank)*. Cambridge: Cambridge University Press, 1992.

Lloyd, Genevieve. *The Man of Reason: "Male" and "Female" in Western Philosophy*. Minneapolis, MN: Univeresity of Minnesota Press, 1993.

Lopez, Donald. "Belief." In *Critical Terms for Religious Studies*, edited by Mark C. Taylor, 21–35. Chicago: University of Chicago Press, 1998.

Lott, Eric. *Love and Theft: Blackface Minstrelsy and the American Working Class*. Oxford: Oxford University Press, 1993.

MacLean, Nancy. "The Leo Frank Case Reconsidered: Gender and Sexual Politics in the Making of Reactionary Populism." *Journal of American History* 78 (Dec. 1991): 917–948.

Magid, Shaul. *American Post-Judaism.* Bloomington: Indiana University Press, 2013.

Malone, Michael P., and Richard W. Etulain. *The American West: A Twentieth Century History.* Lincoln: University of Nebraska Press, 1989.

Mamet, David. *The Old Religion.* New York: Free Press, 1997.

Manor, Ehud. *Louis Miller and Di Warheit ("The Truth"): Yiddishism, Zionism, and Socialism in New York: 1905–1915.* Sussex, UK: Sussex University Press, 2012.

Marcus, Jacob Rader. *United States Jewry 1776–1985.* Detroit: Wayne State University Press, 1989).

Marinbach, Bernard. *Galveston: Ellis Island of the West.* Albany, NY: SUNY Press, 1983.

Markel, H., and A. M. Stern. "Which Face? Whose Nation? Immigration, Public Health, and the Construction of Disease at America's Ports and Borders, 1891–1928." *American Behavioral Scientist,* 42 (1999): 1313–1330.

Masuzawa, Tomoko. *The Invention of World Religion: Or, How European Universalism Was Preserved in the Language of Pluralism.* Chicago: University of Chicago, 2005.

McCune, Mary. "Social Workers in the Muskeljudentum: 'Hadassah Ladies,' 'Manly Men,' and the Significance of Gender in the American Zionist Movement." *American Jewish History* 86 (June 1998): 135–165.

Melnick, Jeffrey. *Black-Jewish Relations on Trial: Leo Frank and Jim Conley in the New South.* Jackson: University of Mississippi Press, 2000.

Moore, Deborah Dash. *B'nai B'rith and the Challenge of Ethnic Leadership.* Albany, NY: SUNY Press, 1981.

Muhammad, Khalil. *The Condemnation of Blackness: Race, Crime, and the Making of Modern Urban America.* Cambridge, MA: Harvard University Press, 2010.

Newman, Louise. *White Women's Rights: The Racial Origin of Feminism in the United States.* New York: Oxford University Press, 1999.

Novak, David. "The Quest for the Jewish Jesus." *Modern Judaism* 8 (May 1988): 119–138.

Nugent, Walter. *Into the West: The Story of Its People.* New York: Alfred A. Knopf, 1999.

Oney, Steve. *And the Dead Shall Rise: The Murder of Mary Phagan and the Lynching of Leo Frank.* New York: Pantheon, 2003.

Orsi, Robert. *Between Heaven and Earth: The Religious Worlds People Make and the Scholars Who Study Them.* Princeton, NJ: Princeton University Press, 2005.

Ortner, Sherry. "Is Female to Male as Nature is to Culture?" In *Woman, Culture and Society,* edited by Sherry Rosaldo and L. Lamphere, 7–42. Stanford: Stanford University Press, 1974.

Paoletti, Jo and C. Kregloh. "The Children's Department." In *Men and Women: Dressing the Part,* edited by C. B. Kidwell and V. Steele, 22–41. Washington, DC: Smithsonian Institution Press, 1989.

Prell, Riv Ellen. "A New Key: Decorum and the Study of Jews and Judaism." *American Jewish History* 90 (Mar. 2002): 13–25.

Presner, Todd. *Muscular Judaism: The Jewish Body and the Politics of Regeneration.* New York: Routledge, 2007.

Prothero, Stephen. *American Jesus: How the Son of God Became a National Icon.* New York: Farrar, Straus, and Giroux, 2003.

Prucha, Francis Paul. *American Indian Policy in Crisis: Christian Reformers and the Indian, 1865–1900*. Norman: University of Oklahoma Press, 1976.

Putney, Clifford. *Muscular Christianity: Manhood and Sports in Protestant America, 1880–1920*. Cambridge, MA: Harvard University Press, 2009.

Ribak, Gil. "The Jew Usually Left Those Crimes to Esau." *American Jewish Studies Review* 38 (Apr. 2014): 1–28.

Richards, Sarah E. "You Don't Have to be Jewish to Love J-Date." *New York Times*, Dec. 5, 2005.

Riess, Steven, ed. *Sports and the American Jew*. Syracuse, NY: SUNY Press, 1998.

Ritterband, Paul, and Harold Wechsler. *Jewish Learning in American Universities*. Bloomington: Indiana University Press, 1994.

Rochelson, Meri-Jane. *A Jew in the Public Arena: The Career of Israel Zangwill*. Detroit: Wayne State University Press, 2008.

Rockoff, Stuart. "Galveston Project Symposium Keynote Address." Sept. 2009. http://www.utexas.edu/cola/depts/history/_files/downloads/news/fall09/galveston-project-talk.pdf.

Rogow, Faith. *Gone to Another Meeting*. Tuscaloosa: University of Alabama Press, 1993.

Rotundo, Anthony. *American Manhood*. New York: Basic Books, 1993.

Rubinstein, Rachel. *Members of the Tribe: Native Americans in the Jewish Imagination*. Detroit: Wayne State University Press, 2010.

Sanders, Ronald. *Lost Tribes and Promised Lands: The Origins of American Racism*. New York: HarperCollins, 1992.

Sanua, Marianne. *Going Greek: Jewish College Fraternities in the United States*. Detroit: Wayne State University Press, 2003.

Sarna, Jonathan. "The American Jewish Response to Nineteenth Century Christian Missions." *Journal of American History* 68 (June 1981): 35–51.

———. *American Judaism: A History*. New Haven: Yale University Press, 2004.

———. "Converts to Zionism in the American Reform Movement." In *Zionism and Religion*, edited by S. Almog, Jehuda Reinharz, and Anita Shapira, 188–203. Waltham, MA: University Press of New England, 1998.

———. *Jacksonian Jew: The Two Worlds of Mordecai Noah*. New York: Holmes & Meier, 1991.

Satter, Beryl. *Each Mind a Kingdom: American Women, Sexual Purity, and the New Thought Movement*. Berkeley: University of California, 1999.

Scherzer, Lisa. "Looking for Mr. Goldstein: When Gentiles Seek Jewish Mates." *Interfaith Family* (Dec. 2002). www.interfaithfamily.com.

Schmidt, Alvin J. *Fraternal Organizations*. Westport, CT: Greenwood Press, 1980.

Schultz, Kevin. *Tri-Faith America: How Catholics and Jews Held Postwar America to Its Protestant Promise*. Oxford: Oxford University Press, 2011.

Shapira, Anita. *Land and Power: The Zionist Resort to Force, 1881–1948*. Oxford: Oxford University Press, 1992.

Sideris, Lisa. "Science as Sacred Myth? Ecospirituality in the Anthropocene Age." *Journal for the Study of Religion, Nature & Culture* 9 (2015): 136–153.

Silberstein, Laurence ed. *Mapping Jewish Identities*. New York: New York University Press, 2000.

Silk, Mark. "Notes on the Judeo-Christian Tradition in America." *American Quarterly* 36 (Spring 1984): 65–85.

Slotkin, Richard. *Regeneration through Violence: The Mythology of the American Frontier, 1600–1860*. Norman: University of Oklahoma Press, 1973.

Smith, Jonathan Z. *Relating Religion: Essays in the Study of Religion*. Chicago: University of Chicago Press, 2004.

Stanislawski, Michael. *Zionism and Fin-de-Siecle: Cosmopolitanism and Nationalism from Nordau to Jabotinsky*. Los Angeles: University of California Press, 2001.

Stern, Josef. "Maimonides on the Covenant of Circumcision and the Unity of God." In *The Midrashic Imagination: Jewish Exegesis, Thought, and History*, edited by Michael Fishbane, 131–154. Albany, NY: SUNY Press, 1993.

Stone, Bryan Edward. *The Chosen Folks: Jews on the Frontiers of Texas*. Austin: University of Texas Press, 2011.

———. "Edgar Goldberg and the Texas Jewish Herald: Changing Coverage and Blended Identity." *Southern Jewish History* 7 (2004): 71–108.

———. "On the Frontier: Jews without Judaism." In *Lone Stars of David: The Jews of Texas*, edited by Hollace Ava Weiner and Kenneth Rosenbaum, 18–32. Waltham, MA: Brandeis University Press, 2007.

Stults, Taylor. "Roosevelt, Russian Persecution of Jews, and American Public Opinion" *Jewish Social Studies* 33 (Jan. 1971): 13–22.

Turner, Elizabeth Hayes. *Women, Culture, and Community: Religion and Reform in Galveston, 1880–1920*. Oxford: Oxford University Press, 1997.

Udelson, Joseph H. *Dreamer of the Ghetto: The Life and Works of Israel Zangwill*. Tuscaloosa: University of Alabama Press, 1990.

Umansky, Ellen. "Christian Science, Jewish Science, and Alfred Geiger Moses," *Southern Jewish History* 6 (2003): 1–35.

———. *From Christian Science to Jewish Science: Spiritual Healing and American Jews*. Oxford: Oxford University Press, 2004.

Urofsky, Melvin. *American Zionism from Herzl to the Holocaust*. New York: Bison, 1995.

Weiner, Hollace Ava. *Jewish Stars in Texas: Rabbis and Their Work*. College Station: Texas A&M University Press, 1999.

———. "Removal Approval: The Industrial Removal Office Experience in Fort Worth, Texas." *Southern Jewish History* 4 (2001): 1–44.

Wenger, Tisa. *We Have a Religion: The 1920s Pueblo Indian Dance Controversy and American Religious Freedom*. Chapel Hill: University of North Carolina Press, 2009.

Wertheimer, Jack. *Unwelcome Strangers: East European Jews in Imperial Germany*. New York: Oxford University Press, 1987.

Wyatt-Brown, Bertram. *Southern Honor: Ethics and Behavior in the Old South*. Oxford: Oxford University Press, 1982.

Index

Page numbers in italics refer to figures.

Abbott, C. H., 109
abnormality: and criminality, 26–27, 199–203. *See also* gender abnormality; sexual abnormality
Abraham, 35, *169*
acculturated Jews: on emotion in religion, 52; on "Jewish race," 22–23; philanthropy, 114, 119–121 (*see also* philanthropy); and rational American Reform Judaism, 13, 36, 38, 113, 119–122 (*see also* Reform Judaism); response to missionaries, 64, 68–69, 83–86; support for agricultural movement, 162–167, 171; use of term, 4–5; and Zionism, 182, 189 (*see also* Zionism)
Adler, Felix, 13, 53
African American men, 20, 209, 210, 227, 229, 255
aggressiveness, 19–20, 26–28, 81, 84–85, 202, 211, 214, 222, 238, 245, 265–266
agricultural movement, 2, *152*, 155–176; and the Bible, 168–169, 173–175; communal settlements, 155–157, 160, 165–166; farm schools, 26, 96, 155–160, 163, 165–167, 170, 175, 273; and Judaism, 167–175; press coverage, 166–167; and science, 170, 175; students, 163–164; support for, 162–167, 171; women in, 159–160, 164, 275
Albanese, Catherine, 11
alcoholism, 214
aliyah (immigration to Palestine), 186. *See also* Palestine; Zionism
American culture: construction of religion, 11–14; and difference, 201; exceptionalism, 185, 195; historical context, 1900–1924, 17–20; Protestant Christianity in, 15–17
American Hebrew, 212, 213
American Israelite, 82, 228
Americanization, 75–76, 82, 85, 102–103, 119, 121, 141, 219; and Christianity, 69–70; and American Jewish Committee (AJC), 228
American Psychiatric Association, 251
American religion, Judaism as, 2, 24, 28, 37–38, 58, 112, 129, 139, 182

Am Olam colonies, 171
Anti-Defamation League (ADL), 226, 237
anti-immigrant rhetoric, 97, 99–100, 108–109, 117, 214
Antin, Mary, 62
antisemitism, 97, 109, 133; and Jewish criminality, 205, 209–210, 225, 227–228, 235–237; Jews as effeminate, 63–64, 72, 74, 86, 186; rise in, 245; and urban conditions, 98, 103–104
apostates, 257
Architecture, 220
Ariel, Yaakov, 68
Aristotle, 39
arson, 205, 210
assault, 205, 208–214, 222, 238
assertiveness, 15, 20, 81–83, 192, 229, 270
assimilation, 11, 192, 206, 208; use of term, 4
atheism, 255–261
athleticism, 15, 22, 158–159, 166, 183
Atlanta Constitution, 228, 230
Atlanta Journal, 227
Atlantic Monthly, 212

Bacharach, Walter, 254, 259
back-to-the-land movements, 155–158, 161–162, 172, 175
"bad" religion: as emotional, particularistic, and ritualistic, 13–14 (*see also* emotion; particularism; rituals); and Indian-Israelite comparisons, 129; Judaism as, 97, 109–114
Balfour Declaration, 184
Baron de Hirsch Fund, 156, 166, 168
Barton, Bruce, 35, 39, 47, 50
Beard, George, 65
Bederman, Gail, 19, 69
beliefs: as central to religion, 38–39; use of term, 31–32
Bercovitch, Sacvan, 130
Berkowitz, David, 270
Bernheimer, Charles, 216, 220
Biale, David, 211
Bialik, Chaim Nachman, 187

Bible, 41, 54–55; Deuteronomy, 65–66; and Jewish agricultural past, 168–169, 173–175; New Testament, 84

Billikopf, Jacob, 106

Bingham, Theodore, 205–223; classification of Jewish criminals, 205–215; Jewish community response, 211–212, 215–222; on Jewish criminality, 26–27, 199–200, 202, 225, 227, 238, 255, 265

Blau, Joel, 84

Blaustein, David, 209–210

blindness, metaphors of, 64, 66

Blum, Ralph, 164

B'nai B'rith, 226, 237, 261

bodies, Jewish male: and Christian theology, 64–67; and connection to the land, 99–109; size of, 213. See also health; physical strength

body-centered piety, 62, 79–80, 82, 87, 107–114, 123, 170

Boethius, 256–257

Boston Globe, 237

Boyarin, Daniel, 23, 183

Brandeis, Louis, 4, 167, 176, 184, 274

bravery, 76, 129–130, 133–142, 146–147; physical, 194–195; and political work, 181–182, 190–192. See also courage

Bressler, David, 21, 103, 106–107, 109, 111, 114, 115, 117–119, 121, 275

Bryant, William, 74

Buddhism, 57

Bureau of Indian Affairs, 141, 143

Burnett bill, 193

Burns, William, 232

Burrough, Edgar Rice, 95

Bushee, Frederick, 209, 214

Butler, Judith, 8–9, 94

Carancahuas, 144–145

Catholicism, 13, 220, 222, 256

Caverly (judge), 254, 260, 264–265

Central Conference of American Rabbis (CCAR), 47, 68, 83, 163, 182

Chamberlain, Houston Stewart, 208

Charleston, 105

cheder, 107–108, 110, 170

Chicago, 101–102, 239. See also Leopold and Loeb hearing

Chicago Daily Tribune, 232, 248–251, 260, 265

Chicago Defender, 255

Chicago Herald and Examiner, 262

Chicago Jewish Courier, 260

chosen people, 55–56, 167–168

Christianity: as emotional, 49; fundamentalist-modernist debates, 43–44, 263–264; love as center of, 49–50; nativity story, use in Leopold and Loeb hearing, 257–258; as rational, 41, 43; sects, 55; as universal, 41, 43, 57. See also Catholicism; Christian theology; conversion to Christianity; Protestant Christianity

Christian Observer, 211

Christian theology, 84; and Jewish male body, 64–67

church, use of term, 31–32

circumcision, 73, 110, 228, 244

citizenship, 69–70, 184, 222

city life: acculturated Jews in, 99; as cause of criminality, 216, 219, 222; critiques of, 97–99, 101–106, 155, 163–167, 174, 176, 201. See also ghettos; New York City

civilization discourse, 85–86; and Judaism, 145–146; supersessionist theologies, 132–133

class conflict, 225, 227, 236

code words for Jewishness, 235, 245–246, 259

Cohen, Henry, 151; and Galveston Movement, 103, 106, 111, 113–115, 117–119, 121; and Indian-Israelite identification, 96, 128–130, 133–134, 136, 138–142, 146–147

Cohen, Naomi, 182

Cohn, Helena, 194, 275

Cohn, Leopold, 62, 64, 71, 74–75, 83, 85, 86

Cohon, Samuel, 37

Cold War, 271–272

Comanches, 144

communal agriculture. See agricultural movement

communal living, 144–145

Conference of Jewish Charities, 111

Congregationalism, 13, 24, 67, 78

Conley, Jim, 225, 227, 228–229

Conservative Judaism, 4

consumers, 155, 158, 208

conversion to Christianity, 24–25, 62–63, 86; and Jewish criminality, 220–221; as treatment for Jewish weakness, 66. See also Hebrew-Christian missionaries

conversion to Judaism, 78

Corput, Dr. (Galveston medical examiner), 117–118

Cotton, John, 143–144

courage: and criminality, 209–211, 213; intellectual, 215. See also bravery

Coushatta, 144–145

criminality: and "courage," 209–211, 213; and fundamentalist-modernist debates, 263–264; and gentleness, 200 (*see also* gentleness); and manliness, 248; and moral decay, 262; social construction of, 201–202

criminality, Jewish, 26–27, 199–203, 205–223; classification of, 205–223 (*see also* Bingham, Theodore); gangsters, 207–208, 218; and gender (*see* gender abnormality); and improper religion, 200–201, 246, 255–265; Judaism as antidote for, 215–222, 260–262; juvenile delinquency, 216–220, 222; as nonviolent, 200–203, 205–215, 218–219, 222, 238, 270; and sexuality (*see* sexual abnormality); violent, 207–208, 217–218, 238, 244–247, 265–267. *See also* Frank, Leo; Leopold and Loeb hearing

Crowe, Robert, 250, 255, 257–259

cultural pluralism, 38, 44, 52

Darrow, Clarence, 27, 239, 244, 252, 254, 257–260, 264–265

death penalty, 245, 247, 252–253, 264–265

decorum, 53, 82–83

de Haas, Jacob, 84, 186, 190

Dekel, Mikhal, 183

Deloria, Philip, 131, 141

democracy, 24–25, 28, 32, 52, 129–130

de Sola Pool, David, 193–194, 217, 221

Deuteronomy, 65–66

Deutsch, Gotthard, 68, 72, 79

deviants. *See* gender abnormality; perversion; sexual abnormality

diaspora, 180–196; as emasculating, 26, 65, 180, 186

Diner, Hasia, 10

divine covenant, 55–56

divine law, 171

divinity, 143

doctrine, 32

dogma, 37

Dohm, Wilhelm Frederick von, 208

domesticity, 159–160, 206, 213

domination, 28

Dorsey, Hugh, 231, 235

Dougherty, George, 229

Doylestown, Pennsylvania, 157

Dyer, Joseph Osterman, 128–130, 133–137, 140–145, 147

Dyer family, 137

Edwards, Jonathan, 134

effeminacy: antisemitic stereotype, 63–64, 72, 74, 86, 186; caused by "civilization," 131

Einhorn, David, 75

Eisenberg, Ellen, 156

elite Jews, 4, 53, 57

Ellis, Havelock, 252, 256

Ellis Island, 97, 98, 116, 121

emasculation, 35, 101–109, 146, 164, 173; and diaspora, 26, 65, 180, 186. *See also* feminization

embodiment, 49–50, 111. *See also* body-centered piety

emotion, 44, 48–52; gendered as feminine, 40–41, 82

end times, 67. *See also* premillennial Protestants

endurance, 15

Enelow, Hyman Gershon, 36, 38, 53–55, 58, 139, 146

enervation, 97, 163, 165, 176, 187

Enlightenment thought, 40–41, 208

Episcopalians, 67, 78

Ethical Culture, 13, 45, 53, 57

ethics, 50–51, 56–57, 113

ethnicity, 5, 8, 10, 14, 22–23, 72

Europe: Jewish farmers, 155; Jewish masculinity, 63; persecution of Jews, 120–121, 185–187; Western European Jews, 17

experiments, 27, 123, 273–274

faith: and reason, 45, 47; and theology, 37, 39; use of term, 31–32

family life, 1, 113, 115, 122, 201, 206, 230–234, 239, 270

farming. *See* agricultural movement; Galveston Movement

Federation of American Zionists (FAZ), 17, 163, 183, 185, 186, 188, 190

Federation of Jewish Organizations, 211–212

Federation Review, 212

feeling, 44. *See also* emotion

Felsenthal, Bernard, 182

femininity, social construction of, 6–7

feminization, 16, 35, 49–50, 63, 72–74, 86, 141, 146. *See also* emasculation

Fessenden, Tracy, 12, 43

Fishberg, Maurice, 107–108

Forbush, William, 19–20

Ford, Henry, 245, 262

Forverts, 212

Fosdick, Harry Emerson, 44

Foucault, Michel, 8–9, 201–202, 254, 258

Frank, Leo, 27, *153*, 199–200, 202, 211, 225–240; family, 230–234; gender abnormality, 227–230; intersections of gender, sexuality, and criminality, 226–227, 230, 239–240, 266; Judaism and Jewishness, 234–238, 255; lynching of, 225–226, 236, 238; press coverage and public opinion, 227–230, 247; racial status, 229; sexual abnormality, 226, 230–234, 236

Frank, Lucille (nee Selig), 232–234

Franklin, Leo, 69, 83

Franklin, Paul, 246

Franks, Bobby, 244, 251, 255

Freud, Sigmund, 252, 256

Freuder, Samuel, 63, 64, 78–83, 85, 86

frontier, 95, 97, 99–101, 140. *See also* Galveston Movement; Indian-Israelite identification

fundamentalism, 43–44, 263–264

Gaebelein, Arno, 64, 65–67, 69, 71, 86

Gal, Alon, 188

galut (exile), 181, 191–195. *See also* diaspora

Galveston, Texas, 106; Jewish community, 128–129; medical examiners, 117–118

Galveston Movement, 2, 25, 94, 96, 97–123, *151*, 273, 275; background, 99–101; connecting to the land, 101–109; piety and the male body, 109–114; productive labor, "poor physique," and evaluation of Jewish immigrant men, 109–114. *See also* Jewish Immigrants Information Bureau (JIIB)

Galveston News, 106, 142

Geiger, Abraham, 42, 135

gender: land, as female, 161–162, 164–165; in philosophical concepts, 36, 39–43, 82; social construction of, 6–11, 39–40, 94, 108, 181

gender abnormality: and criminality, 202–203; Leo Frank, 227–230; Leopold and Loeb hearing, 239–240, 245–250, 265–267

Gender and Jewish History, 20

gender norms, 7–9, 94, 100; and exercise, 102–103; at farm schools, 157; as "normal" and "ideal," 122; violation of, and moral decay, 262. *See also* gender abnormality

gender studies, 20–23, 272–273

gentleness, 20, 26–27, 33, 62–64, 67, 74, 75, 82–87, 200, 207, 209, 244–247, 270

German Jews, 192–193; use of term, 4

ghettos, 101–102, 104, 106, 113, 116, 164, 166, 176

Gilman, Sander, 63, 66

Ginsburg, Louis, 54

Glauz-Todrank, Annalise, 5

God: biblical covenant with chosen people, 55–56; embodied, 49–50

God's law, 171

Goldberg, David, 47–48

Goldberg, Israel, 192–195

Goldhaft, Tevye, 170

Goldman, Joseph, 62, 64, 71, 73–74, 76, 78, 81, 83, 85, 86

Goldman, Karla, 85

Goldy, Robert, 37

"good" religion: and agricultural life, 175–176; Judaism as, 38, 47, 51, 58, 130, 139, 168; as rational, emotionally controlled, and universal, 13–14, 38–43, 51 (*see also* rationality; universalism); and separation of church and state, 185; and Zionism, 182

Goren, Arthur, 216

Gottheil, Gustav, 182, 185

Gottheil, Richard, 185–186

Greek philosophy, 40–41

Greeks, 207

Grossman, Rudolph, 16–17, 84–85

Guide to the United States for the Jewish Immigrant, 171

gymnastics, 183

halakhah, 71, 110–111, 170, 175

Hall, G. Stanley, 18, 97, 131–132

Hanukkah, 190–192

Harper's, 213

Harris, Maurice, 173, 175

Hart, Lewis, 83–84

Hartt, Mary Bronson, 275

Hasidim, 168, 170; gender roles, 79, 80, 82, 99; physical strength and health, 119. *See also* body-centered piety

haskalah (Jewish Enlightenment), 32, 170

health, 15–16, 20, 22, 25, 245, 270; and Indian-Israelite comparisons, 133, 147; and the land, 93–123; "poor physique," 98–100, 104, 116–119, 275; and productive physical labor, 156–158, 161–163, 167, 172, 175. *See also* body-centered piety

Hebrew-Christian missionaries, 33, 62–87; and Christian theology, 64–67, 85; on Jewish masculinity, 64–67, 72–82; Jewish reactions to, 64, 68–69, 79, 83–86; missions to American Jews, 67–72; role of women in, 70, 72

Hebrew language, 192

Heller, Max, 79, 182

Hertzberg, Arthur, 183

Herz, Judith, 220, 221, 275
Herzl, Theodor, 78, 183, 184, 189–190
heterosexuality metaphors, 161–162
Hilfsverein der deutschen Juden (organization), 104, 105, 192
Hirsch, Emil, 15, 35, 36, 38
Hirsch Agricultural School (HAS), 155–160, 163, 165–167, 170, 175, 275
Hirschowitz, Louis, 163
historical progress, 85–86
homosexuality, 230, 246, 250–252
Hope of Israel mission, 71
Howe, Irving, 217
Hughes, Michael, 248
Hulbert, H. S., 255, 258–259
Huntington, W. R., 220–221
Hyman, Paula, 20
hysteria, 64–66

illness, metaphors of, 64, 66. *See also* health; weakness
immigrant Jews, Eastern European, 4–5, 17; and agriculture, 157, 170; and crime, 205; "likely to become public charges," 99, 117–118, 275; mission services for, 68; paternalistic attitudes toward, 189; persecution of, 120–121, 185–187, 193; physical strength and health, 93–99, 103–109, 114–121, 166, 186; "poor physique," 98–100, 104, 116–119, 275; religious practices, 33, 170; settlement in the West (*see* Galveston Movement); social programs for, 98, 102–103, 114; "uplifting," 102, 196; women and children, 115
immigration restriction, 38, 104, 166, 193. *See also* anti-immigrant rhetoric
Immigration Restrictionist League, 104
Improved Order of Red Men, 131, 141, 271
Independent, 212
Indian-Israelite identification, 25, 94, 96, 123, 128–147; closeness, 128–142, 146–147, 218; distance, 128–130, 134, 142–147; as historical relationship, 129, 134–135, 145
Indians, images of: as brave, resourceful, and attached to the land, 129–130, 134–142; Protestant attitudes, 130–134, 141; as violent, uncivilized savages, 129–130, 136, 143–146. *See also* Native American cultures
Industrial Removal Office (IRO), 104, 118–119
insanity, 253–255, 260
intersectionality, 5, 230
Irish immigrants, 209

Isaacs, Abram, 36, 38, 46, 51, 52, 55, 58
Islam, 52, 57
isolationism, 38
Israel, 271
Italians, 207, 209, 220, 222

Jacobsen, Matthew Frye, 69
Jakobsen, Janet, 11, 31
James, William, 44
Jastrow, Morris, 36, 38, 45–46, 51–52, 57–58
Jeffersonian, 232, 236
Jesus: gentleness of, 86; Jewishness of, 54; manly, 15, 35, 44, 47, 181; suffering of, 74–75
Jewish Agricultural and Industrial Aid Society (JAIAS), 17, 104, 114
Jewish Center, 94
Jewish Defense League, 271
Jewish educational pamphlets, 21–22
Jewish Encyclopedia, 17, 36, 49, 137
Jewish gangsters, 207–208, 218
Jewish Herald, 107
Jewish history, and gender studies, 20–23
Jewish Immigrants Information Bureau (JIIB), 99; officials, 106–121. *See also* Galveston Movement
Jewishness: as difference, 3–4, 10, 52–53; as race or ethnicity, 5, 8, 10, 22–23, 72; and racial otherness, 140, 229–230, 236–237; as religion, 5–6, 10
Jewish press, 211–212, 228. See also *individual publications*
Jewish religious practice, 31–32; and bodily health, 107–114; decorous, 53, 82–83; emotional and physical, 82; Sabbath observance, 110–111, 119, 170–171; *tefillin*, 139. *See also* body-centered piety; halakhah
Jewish Territorial Organization, 105
Jewish theology, 36–43
Jewish women: in agricultural movement, 159–160, 164, 275; mothers, 21; Orthodox, 79–80, 82; religious participation, 16, 35, 47–48, 50
JIIB. *See* Jewish Immigrants Information Bureau
Johnson-Reed Act (1924), 38, 245
Joselit, Jenna Weissman, 217, 266
Joszovics, Itsak Leib, 75
Judaism: as an American religion, 2, 24, 28, 37–38, 58, 112, 129, 139, 182; as antidote to crime, 215–222; as "bad" religion, 97, 109–114; beliefs, 38; compared to Christianity, 31, 37, 45–50; conversion to, 78; and democracy, 24–25, 28, 32, 52, 129–130;

Judaism: as an American religion (*cont.*)
emotion and sense perception, 41–42, 48–52,
110; ethics, 50–51, 56–57, 113; as "good"
religion, 38, 47, 51, 58, 130, 139, 168; as highly
developed religion, 46; justice as center of,
49; "legalistic" aspects, 54; legitimacy of,
68–69; as manly, 47; moral laws, 50–51, 56–57;
particularism, 11, 14, 42, 52–53, 56–58, 73, 111,
129; persecution of Jews, 120–121, 185–187, 192,
193; practice, 12, 32, 38; as rational, 8, 13–14,
25, 28, 32–33, 36, 39, 45–48, 101, 110–114,
120–122, 139, 168, 171; ten lost tribes of Israel
(*see* lost tribes theory); tribal nature of, 8, 25,
55, 69, 73, 129–130, 142–146, 184; as universal,
8, 13–14, 32–33, 36–39, 52–58, 129–130, 142, 168,
184; as unsectarian, 55. *See also* acculturated
Jews; conversion to Christianity; Hasidim;
Orthodox Jews; Reform Judaism
juvenile delinquency, 216–220, 222

kabbalah, 48, 52, 144, 272
Kahane, Meir, 271
Kahn, William, 111, 114, 120
Kallen, Horace, 37–38, 52–53
Kant, Immanuel, 14, 41, 42, 45–46, 48, 50, 51
Kaplan, Mordecai, 4, 274
Kasson, John, 19
Katz, Mark, 211–212
Kehilla, 211, 216–219, 222, 238
Kiev pogrom, 120
Kimmel, Michael, 19
Kishinev massacre, 120
Koffmann, David, 135
Kohler, Kaufmann, 36–46, 48–52, 54–56, 58;
Jewish Theology, 36, 49; on Zionism, 184–185
Kohler, Max, 118
Kohn, Joseph, 118
Krafft-Ebing, Richard von, 256
Krauskopf, Joseph, 155, 157–160, 163–168, 171,
175–176
Krohn, William, 254
Kuh, Edwin, 212
Ku Klux Klan, 226
Kunzel, Regina, 202
Kupferstein, Shya, 110–111, 119

Lafitte, Jean, 136
Lamarckism, 65, 108, 214
land: connection with, and healthy bodies, 25,
95, 99–109, 133; gendered as female, 161–162,
164–165; and Indian-Israelite comparisons,

129–130, 136–138, 146–147. *See also* agricultural
movement; back-to-the-land movements;
Galveston Movement
Lang, S. P., 262
Lears, T. J. Jackson, 95
Lederhendler, Eli, 70
Lee, Newt, 225
Leeser, Isaac, 135
Leiser, Joseph, 15, 54, 172
Leonard, Oscar, 107
Leopold, Nathan "Babe." *See* Leopold and Loeb
hearing
Leopold and Loeb hearing, 27, 199, 202, 211,
225, 244–267; age of defendants, 248, 252–253,
257; culpability, 239, 247–248, 253–255; death
penalty, 245, 247, 252–253, 264–265; gender
abnormality, 239–240, 245–250, 265–267;
homosexuality, 250–252; mental disease
and insanity, 253–255, 260; phrenological
sketches, *154*, 249–250, 259; public opinion,
247; religion, 255–265; sexual abnormality,
239–240, 245–247, 250–254, 256–260, 265–267
Levy, Abraham R., 112–113
Life, 209–211, 230, 237
Lilien, E. M., 180, 187, 190
Lindemann, Albert, 235
Lipsky, Louis, 182, 190–192
Lloyd, Genevieve, 33, 40–42
Locke, John, 41, 45
Lodge, Henry Cabot, 166
Loeb, Richard "Dickie," *154*. *See also* Leopold
and Loeb hearing
Los Angeles Times, 109, 233, 255
lost tribes theory, 133, 134–135, 140, 271
loyalty, 69–70
Lucas, Albert, 79
Lutheranism, 13, 24

Maccabaean (Zionist periodical), 163, 164, 183,
186, 188–195
Maccabaeus, Judas, 190–192
Machen, Gresham, 44
Macintosh, Douglas Clyde, 43
Madoff, Bernie, 270
Magid, Shaul, 54
Magnes, Judah, 70, 215, 217
Mallery, Garrick, 143
manly, use of term, 7
margins, 2–3, 9, 23, 24, 27, 70, 83, 94–95, 175,
180, 202, 273–274
Marshall, Louis, 215, 228

Marx, David, 234
masculine-feminine binary, 33; as hierarchy, 41
masculinity: cultural visibility of, 17–18; "in crisis," 18; multiple masculinities, 72, 272–273; normative American, 2–3, 17–20, 82–83, 270–276; and Christian manhood, 69–70; and criminality, 201; and Jewish masculinity, 3, 19, 63–64, 66, 97, 271; and medical knowledge, 118; overcivilization and effeminacy, 131; "savage" instincts and overcivilization, 19–20, 131–132, 146; shaped by religion, 2, 8–11; social construction of, 6–11, 276; as unmarked category, 21, 23, 181; use of term, 7
masculinity, Jewish: and the agricultural movement, 155–176; in Christian theological context, 64–72; and civic status, 69–70; compared to Christian masculinity, 15–17, 72–83; current attitudes, 1–2, 270–276; as gentle, 20, 26–27, 33, 62–64, 67, 74, 75, 82–87, 200, 207, 209, 244–247, 270; Hebrew-Christian missionaries on, 64–67, 72–82; as intelligent, 20, 245; Jewish and non-Jewish voices on, 3, 10, 100, 245; and Leo Frank case, 225–240; as nonviolent, 20, 26–27, 33, 62–64, 67, 85, 87, 200–203, 205–215, 218–219, 222, 238, 244–247, 265–267, 270; and normative American manhood, 3, 19, 63–64, 66, 97, 271; norms, 27–28, 93, 122 (*see also* Galveston Movement); and suffering, 62–64, 67, 74–75, 77, 84–87, 238; and Zionism, 180–196
Masuzawa, Tomoko, 11
Mather, Cotton, 134
Mayer, Julius, 219, 221
McAdoo, William, 212, 262
McCune, Mary, 180
McLaughlin, Allan, 103–104
McLean, Mary Dunlop, 275
McNamee, William, 264–265
media. *See* Jewish press; press coverage; *individual newspapers and periodicals*
medical discourse, 64–67; and legal knowledge, 254, 258–259
Meekin, John Phillips, 238
Melamed, Samuel, 260–261
Melnick, Jeffrey, 226
Men and Religion Forward Movement, 16
Mendelian genetics, 108
Mendes, Frederick de Sola, 221
Mendes, Henry Pereira, 79, 186–188
mental abnormality, 251–252

mental disease, 246, 253–255, 260
Merkel, Howard, 117
Methodism, 13, 24
methodology, 23. *See also* margins
Meyer, Martin, 79
Midrash, 168
milhemet hasafot ("the war of the languages"), 192
Mills, Alonzo, 234
missionaries, 62, 84–86; to Native Americans, 141; women as, 70, 72. *See also* Hebrew-Christian missionaries
The Missionary Review of the World, 76
modernism, 43–44, 263–264
modernization, 81
monotheism, 145
morals, 50–51, 56–57
Morgen Zhurnal, 212
Mormonism, 8, 24
Moses, 35, 36
murder, 199, 208, 225, 239, 244–245. *See also* Frank, Leo; Leopold and Loeb hearing
"muscle Jew," 74, 180, 208
muscular Christianity, 15–17, 33, 35, 39, 47, 58, 63, 80–81, 85, 86, 132
mysticism, 51–52; Jewish, 272

National Farm School (NFS), 155–160, 163, 166–167, 170, 175, 273, 275
National Immigration Conference, 104
National Jewish Monthly, 261
nationalism, 69, 85–86, 184; secular, 182, 187
Native American cultures: in early twentieth century, 141; religious customs, 8, 13–14, 24. *See also* Indian-Israelite identification; Indians, images of
nativism, 69, 214
natural law and nature, 171–172, 175, 176. *See also* land
nervous diseases, 64–67
neurasthenia, 64–67
New Era Illustrated Magazine, 219
Newman, Louise Michelle, 85
New Orleans, 105
New Outlook, 62
newspapers. *See* Jewish press; press coverage; *individual newspapers*
New York American, 215
New York City: Jewish community, 5, 102, 114, 199, 211–212, 215–222; Jewish crime, 26–27, 199–200, 205–222
New York Daily News, 249

New York Times, 200, 229, 230, 232–234, 263–264
New-York Tribune, 166
Nietzsche, Friedrich, 256
Noah, Mordecai Manual, 135
Nordau, Max, 74, 180, 183, 189–190, 208
norms: deviation from, 18–19, 273 (*see also* gender abnormality; perversion; sexual abnormality); unarticulated, 9 (*see also* margins). *See also* gender norms; masculinity, normative American
North American Review, 199
Norton, W. B., 262
Novak, David, 54

Odessa pogrom, 120
Optowski (immigrant), 118–119
Orsi, Robert, 13, 43
Orthodox Jews, 62, 170; gender roles, 79, 80, 82, 99
Osterman family, 137. *See also* Dyer, Joseph Osterman
Our Hope (journal), 64–66

Palestine, 26, 107, 109, 162, 171, 173, 176, 180–189, 192–195, 261. *See also* Zionism
Palitz, Bernard, 165–166
particularism, 11, 14, 38, 42, 52–53, 56–58, 73, 111, 129
passivity, 26, 39, 180
Patton, A. E., 97, 99, 100, 117, 121
Paul, 54, 74
Pellegrini, Ann, 11, 31
Penn, William, 134
periodicals. *See* Jewish press; press coverage; *individual periodicals*
Perla, David, 93–94
persecution of Jews, 120–121, 185–187, 192, 193
perversion: in Leo Frank case, 226, 230–234, 236; link between religious and sexual deviance, 246–247, 256–260, 265–267. *See also* sexual abnormality
Peters, Madison, 214, 218, 221
Phagan, Mary, 27, 225–227, 230, 233, 236
Philadelphia Sunday Dispatch, 68
philanthropy, 102–103, 114, 119–121, 157, 184
Philipson, David, 135
Philo of Alexandria, 41
phrenology, *154*, 199, 249–250, 259
physical labor, 26, 66, 146; by women, 160. *See also* productivity

physical strength, 15–16, 19, 28, 76–80, 82–83, 106, 191; and Zionism, 180–183. *See also* weakness
pickpocketing, 207, 220
piety. *See* body-centered piety
Pioggi, Louis "The Lump," 208
pioneers, 95, 97, 114, 119, 140; rugged and manly, 100–101, 119. *See also* Galveston Movement; Indian-Israelite identification
pogroms, 120–121
politics, and Jewish manliness, 181–182, 190–192
"poor physique," 98–100, 104, 116–119, 275
Popular Science Monthly, 103
postmillennial Protestants, 67
Potter, Charles Francis, 263–264
Prell, Riv Ellen, 20
premillennial Protestants, 67–68, 71–72, 85, 86
Presner, Todd, 63, 183
press coverage: of agricultural movement, 166–167; of black criminality, 255; code words for Jewishness, 235, 245–246, 259; Leo Frank case, 225, 227–238; Leopold and Loeb case, 225, 244–267; shaping public opinion, 247. *See also* Jewish press; *individual newspapers and periodicals*
producerism, 156–162, 165, 208
productivity, 101, 104, 111–112, 114–122, 141, 155, 161–167, 208, 209–210, 220; and criminality, 206
Progressive Era: masculinity, 17–20; social programs, 102–103, 121
prostitution, 115, 211, 250
Protestant Christianity: in American culture, 15–17; as feminized, 35, 47, 49; Indians, images of, 130–134, 141; masculinity, 15–17, 20, 33, 35, 39, 47, 58, 63, 66–67, 80–86, 132; missionaries, 84–86 (*see also* Hebrew-Christian missionaries); as model of religion, 10–14, 24, 31–32, 43–45, 58, 63; nonmillennial, 67, 85; postmillennial, 67; premillennial, 67–68, 71–72, 85, 86; "public Protestantism," 11–12; and religious constructions of gender, 32–33; "stealth Protestantism," 11–13, 31
Publications of the American Jewish Historical Society (PAJHS), 135, 137, 142
Pueblo Indian dances, 143
Puritans, 169
Putney, Clifford, 15

rabbinical training, 78
rabbinic literature, 54–55
Rabinowich, Samuel, 252

races, white, 22, 229
race science, 108–109, 117
racial otherness, of Jews, 140, 229–230, 236–237
racism, anti-black, 155, 225, 227
rape, 211, 229–230, 236, 239
rationality, 24; of Christianity, 41, 43; compared to emotionalism, 50–51; gendered as male, 36, 40–43; of Judaism, 8, 13–14, 25, 28, 32–33, 36, 39, 45–48, 101, 110–114, 120–122, 139, 168, 171; reason-affect binary, 33, 47–48; and universalism, 40–43 (*see also* universalism)
reason. *See* rationality
recapitulation theory, 131–132
Reform Judaism, 4–5, 36; response to Christian missionaries, 64; as superior, 42, 111–114, 121; support for agricultural movement, 163, 171; women's participation in, 16, 35, 47–48, 50; and Zionism, 173, 182. *See also* acculturated Jews
regeneration, 70, 72
religion: shaped by masculinity, 2, 8–11; sincerity of belief, 9–10; social construction of, 6–11, 274, 276. *See also* "bad" religion; Catholicism; Christianity; "good" religion; Jewish religious practice; Judaism; Orthodox Jews; Protestant Christianity; Reform Judaism
religious deviance. *See* perversion
religious progress, 48; and manliness, 20, 42; toward universalism, 57–58
religious schooling, 107–108, 187
resourcefulness, 129–130, 133, 139–142, 146–147
Reyman, Theodore, 116
Ribak, Gil, 266
Richman, Julia, 50–51, 56–58, 184, 275
Riis, Jacob, 166
rituals, 113; Jewish, 71, 139, 170–171 (*see also* Jewish religious practice); Native American, 139, 143; role in religion, 31–32
Rogers, Julian, 235
Roosevelt, Teddy, 18, 95, 97, 131, 133, 169, 181
Rosen, Joseph, 155–156, 160–162
Rosenau, William, 172–173, 175
Ross, Edward Alsworth, 116, 213
Rotundo, Anthony, 7
ruggedness, 15–16, 100–101, 119, 228
Russia, 155
Russian Jews, 205. *See also* immigrant Jews, Eastern European

Sabbath observance, 110–111, 119, 170–171
Sabsovich, H. L., 157

Sargent, Frank, 166
Sarna, Jonathan, 10
Schechter, Solomon, 187
Schiff, Jacob, 4, 104, 113, 117, 121, 217, 274
Schulman, Samuel, 5, 216–217
secular nationalism, 182, 187
self-sufficiency, 19, 114–121, 140, 161–162, 167, 172, 175, 195
sense perception, 41–42, 48–52
settlement houses, 102, 201, 217
settlement-style missions, 68
sexual abnormality, 26–27, 239; and crime, 200–203, 210–211; as Jewish stereotype, 210–211, 254–255; Leo Frank, 226, 230–234, 236; Leopold and Loeb hearing, 239–240, 245–247, 250–254, 256–260, 265–267; and mental abnormality, 251–252 (*see also* mental disease). *See also* perversion
sexual predators, 210–211. *See also* rape
shammos (attendant or sexton), 79–81
Shema, 56
Shuler, Bob, 262
Singer, Harold Douglas, 251, 254
sissies, 19–20, 35
Six-Day War, 271
Slaton (governor of Georgia), 225, 235
Slotkin, Richard, 131
Smith, J. Z., 8, 11
Smith, Joseph, 135
social distance, 130
Social Gospel, 67, 102
social margins. *See* margins
social programs, 102–103, 201. *See also* philanthropy
Society for the Promotion of Christianity, 68
soldiers, 194–195
"Son of Sam," 270
Spinoza, 58
spirit, 44
"Spiritual Zionism" (Mendes), 187
Spiritualism, 82
sports, 22
Steiner, Edward, 63, 64, 75–78, 83, 85, 86
Stern, A. M., 117
Sterne, Adolphus, 137–138, 142
Stolz, Joseph, 79
Straton, John Roach, 263–264
Strauss, Oscar, 168–169, 173–175
strength. *See* physical strength
Strong, Josiah, 97
Strunsky, Manya Gordon, 21–22, 275

Sufism, 52
Sukkot, 170
Sunday, Billy, 262
supersessionist theologies, 132–133
superstition, 110–111, 144, 170, 171
Supreme Court, 9–10
synagogue, 12, 16, 53–54
Szold, Henrietta, 176

Taft, William Howard, 155, 166
Tageblatt, 212
Talmud, 7, 54, 75, 108, 168, 187
Tarzan, 95, 181
Tashrak, 70
teffilin, 139
Teller, Sidney, 101–102
Temple Emanu-El, 220
theology, 39. *See also* Christian theology;
    Jewish theology
Thompson, Albert Edward, 70
Tietch, Samuel "Cyclone Louie," 208
tribal religion, 8, 14, 25, 55, 69, 73, 129–130,
    142–146, 184
Twain, Mark, 213, 222

Unitarianism, 13, 53, 57
universalism, 24, 52–58; of Christianity, 41, 43,
    57; gendered as male, 36, 40–43; of Judaism,
    8, 13–14, 32–33, 36–39, 52–58, 129–130, 142,
    168, 184; and Zionism, 187–188
urban life. *See* city life; ghettos
US Armed forces, 194–195
US Census Bureau, 12, 32, 39

vices, 214
violence, 26–28, 77; pogroms, 120–121. *See also*
    assault; criminality; murder

Wald, Lillian, 102, 275
Waldman, Morris, 113, 118, 119
Warheit, 212
Washington, George, 168
Washington Post, 229, 230, 233–234, 238, 255,
    264
Watchorn, Robert, 160, 166
Watson, Tom, 199, 200, 227, 231–232, 235–236, 261
weakness, 69, 97, 107, 157, 167, 180, 187, 245;
    and crime, 206–210, 222. *See also* physical
    strength
Weininger, Otto, 208

Weinstock, Harris, 62
Wenger, Beth, 20
Wenger, Tisa, 14
the West: Jewish settlement in, 19, 25, 94, 98,
    104–109, 122 (*See also* Galveston Movement).
    See also frontier; Indian-Israelite
    identification; pioneers
Western philosophy, 14; gendered concepts,
    39–43
White, William, 257
white races, 22, 229
"white slavery," 115, 211
"Wild Tribes" pamphlet (Dyer), 128–130,
    133–137, 140–145, 147
Williams, Roger, 134
Wilson, James, 169, 172, 175
Wise, Isaac Mayer, 37, 70
Wise, Stephen, 54, 78
Wister, Owen, 100
women: and civilization discourse, 85; erasure
    of, 275; immigrants, 115; as marked category,
    181; as missionaries, 70, 72; nervous diseases,
    64–66; sex trade in, 115, 211. *See also* Jewish
    women
women's history, 20–21
Woodbine Colony, 155–159, 165–167, 175
World War I, 167

xenophobia, 38, 97, 133, 245

Yiddish, 106, 189
Young Men's Hebrew Association (YMHA), 22,
    93–94
Young Women's Hebrew Association (YWHA),
    93–94

Zangwill, Israel, 105–106, 119
ZBT fraternity, 185
Zevin, Israel Joseph, 70
Zionism, 26, 63, 94, 96, 105, 107, 162, 173;
    European, 181, 183–190; and exile, 182, 185,
    193; and Galveston Movement, 109; and
    masculinity, 180–196, 261; overview, 183–188;
    publications, 273 (see also *Maccabaean*);
    and religion, 187–188; secular nationalism,
    182; support for Jewish farmers, 163; and
    universalism, 187–188. *See also* Federation
    of American Zionists
Zoroastrianism, 57
Zweifach, Max "Kid Twist," 208

SARAH IMHOFF is Assistant Professor in the Department of Religious Studies and the Borns Jewish Studies Program at Indiana University. Her research focuses on religion and the body, including work on gender and American Judaism both historically and in the present, the role of DNA and genetic discourse in constructions of Jewishness, and the history of the field of religious studies.

CPSIA information can be obtained
at www.ICGtesting.com
Printed in the USA
LVHW082036191119
637872LV00013B/1371/P

9 780253 026217